THE
COLLINS GARDEN
BIRDWATCHER'S
BIBLE

William Collins
An imprint of HarperCollins*Publishers*
1 London Bridge Street
London SE1 9GF
WilliamCollinsBooks.com

First published by William Collins in 2020

10 9 8 7 6 5 4 3 2 1

Written by Christopher Perrins, Sonya Patel Ellis, Paul Sterry and Dominic Couzens

A catalogue record for this book is available from the British Library.

ISBN 978-0-00-840559-5

Text by Sonya Patel Ellis except where otherwise specified
Original illustrations © Lynn Hatzius, see page 406–409 for details
Design by Eleanor Ridsdale
With design assistance from Gareth Butterworth
Picture research by Jo Carlill
Project management by Ruth Redford

Printed and bound in Slovenia

DISCLAIMER
The publishers urge readers to be responsible birdwatchers.
Please see pages 18–19 for details on safe and responsible birdwatching practise.
Additionally, please familiarize yourself with local and national restrictions and safety measures.

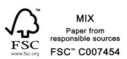

THE HISTORY OF BIRDS

PRACTICAL BIRDWATCHING & IDENTIFICATION

THE COLLINS GARDEN BIRDWATCHER'S BIBLE

A PRACTICAL GUIDE TO
IDENTIFYING AND UNDERSTANDING
GARDEN BIRDS

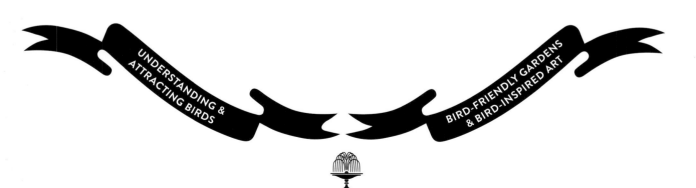

UNDERSTANDING & ATTRACTING BIRDS

BIRD-FRIENDLY GARDENS & BIRD-INSPIRED ART

WILLIAM
COLLINS

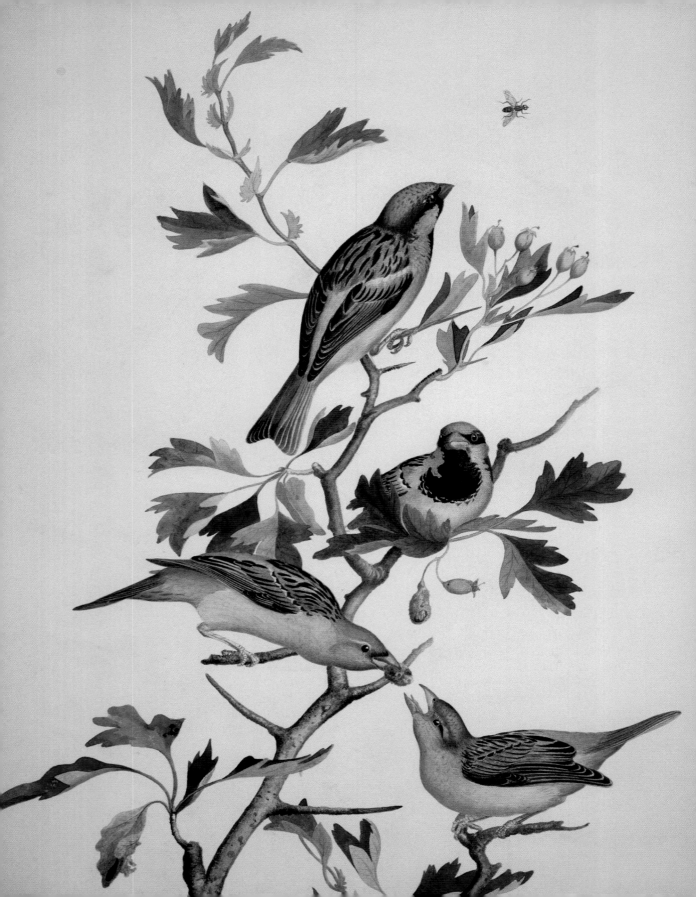

CONTENTS

Opposite *House Sparrows (Passer domesticus)* from
William MacGillivray's *British Animals* (1831-41)

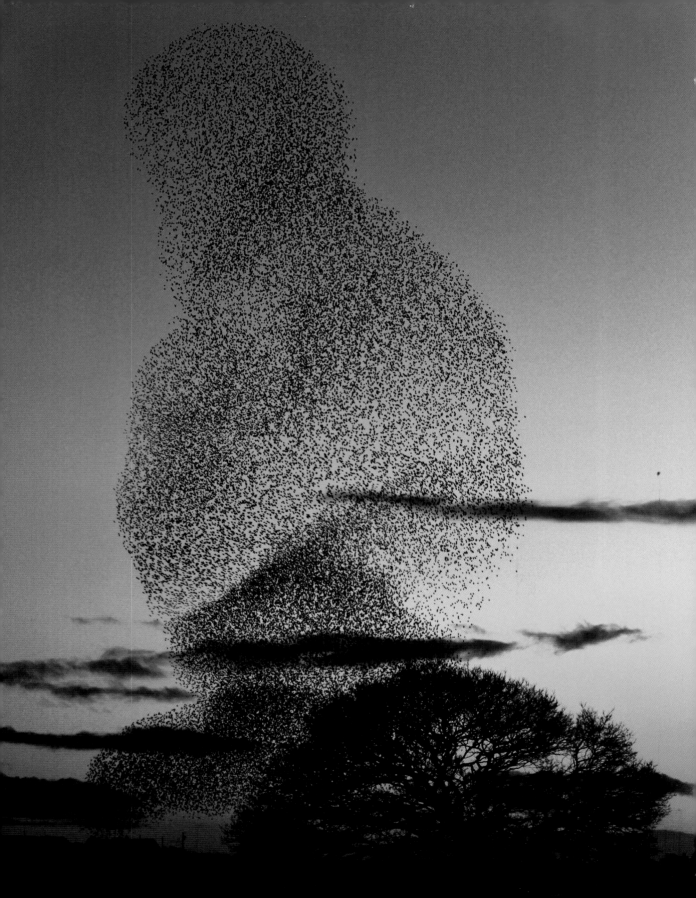

INTRODUCTION

Imagine there was a pastime that was fun, absorbing for all ages, easily accessible to anyone, proven to be good for your mental and physical health, remarkably inexpensive, ethically sound and a gateway to a richer life – a pastime good for both the anguished soul and the anguished world. Now imagine you could undertake this pastime with no preparation, anywhere you live and at any time of year, dipping in from time to time or immersing yourself completely.

Welcome to birdwatching, a hobby that is exploding worldwide. In the UK, more than a million people pay their subscription to the main bird conservation charity, the RSPB. The birdwatching community was once skewed towards the middle aged and retirees, but its appeal has broadened enormously in recent years, attracting huge numbers of younger participants. Birdwatching is now mainstream; but more than that, it is trendy, and a trend that is here to stay. It ticks the boxes for wellness of soul and environment.

For millennia, humans have looked at birds at a basic level. People still watch, but the possibilities have expanded. Now we can take part in citizen science, photograph birds through telescopes using smartphones, communicate sightings through internet forums, use identification apps; many of us can even travel abroad to enjoy seeing different species. Birdwatching is the perfect hobby for the twenty-first century.

This book is the ideal companion to this perfect pastime. It is largely aimed at those who might not have tried birding before, but it also provides a rich source of information for those further along the birdwatching journey. It is a handbook for the backyard and the backwoods, helping you identify the more familiar species, but also providing a mine of information about birds in general.

The handy At-a-glance section on pages 34–35 provides thumbnail illustrations of a selection of 65 familiar species, followed by a stunning profile of each one, with photographs, distribution map and a factfile

Opposite A murmuration of Starlings fill the evening sky

of details on characteristics, location, food sources and more. The species featured have been carefully chosen to be representative of those seen around houses and gardens across the country. 'Garden birds' are not a distinct classification, and within ornithological circles, debates as to inclusion abound. With so many possible species, we have decided to omit most waterbirds, since these will mainly be seen on field visits and away from gardens.

Birds are remarkable creatures, from their powers of flight to their remarkable sense and astounding transcontinental migrations. Their origin is a shock, too; we now know that birds are the only surviving dinosaurs! This book has the whole story of a bird, from egg to chick to fledged juvenile, to adult fighting for survival. It covers reproduction, territory, song, parental care and navigation, and presents amazing facts all along the way. It examines how the birds of Europe and North America came to be where they are, takes stock of their fortunes and discusses what might happen to them in the future. Part of that, of course, is down to us, and the last part describes how to start birdwatching so that you can best appreciate the birds around you. This includes information on societies to join and other ways to immerse yourself in this amazing hobby.

There is helpful information for the birdwatcher, providing fun and practical guidance about how you might help the birds of your backyard and beyond. Millions of people across the world, in many countries and in all climates, enjoy providing food and water to their garden visitors, from robins and starlings to owls and colourful finches. The sheer delight of attracting something new and different is a feeling few of us ever forget, and it is a special pleasure simply to revel in the hive of activity that we have caused. Birds benefit enormously from our provision, and some species have changed their habits and distribution as a result. In this section we provide tips of what food to provide and how to provide it, as well as practical craft tips about how to make your own bird feeders, bird boxes and baths. Another great way to benefit birds is to plant your garden or yard with suitable plants that will keep providing the insect life, seeds and fruits that they need, and this section provides advice and recommendations.

Birds have informed and instigated countless artforms over the centuries. It is therefore important to be able to present a celebration of birds in art, sculpture, photography, craft and style. This is illustrated with copious examples of the multitude of ways in which birds can be depicted, together with short profiles of a wide and eclectic range of contributors. There are examples from around the world, and across a range of media, from the illustrations of John James Audubon to the paintings of Frida Kahlo, and from Bird Photographer of the Year to the designs of Charley Harper.

Birdwatching, indeed, has a worldwide reach. No human being is ever far from a bird, and this is one of the many reasons why looking for birds is so satisfying; some of the greatest experiences are on everyone's doorstep, wherever that doorstep may be. It is also a hobby that brings people together, from birdwatching buddies who go out each weekend to their local patch, to people using local guides abroad to discover new species. Social media ensures that no birdwatcher ever need feel isolated.

The world we know is a troubled place. We are recovering from a worldwide epidemic, and people seem to be polarised as never before. But beyond the human sphere, nature remains. It is bruised and battered, but still awesome and wonderful; we have a responsibility to protect it. One key, both to help ourselves and the world, is to look outside ourselves and wonder at the extraordinary creatures with which we share the planet.

Opposite *Black and Yellow Warblers (Dendroica Magnolia)* from John James Audubon's *Birds of America* (1827-38)

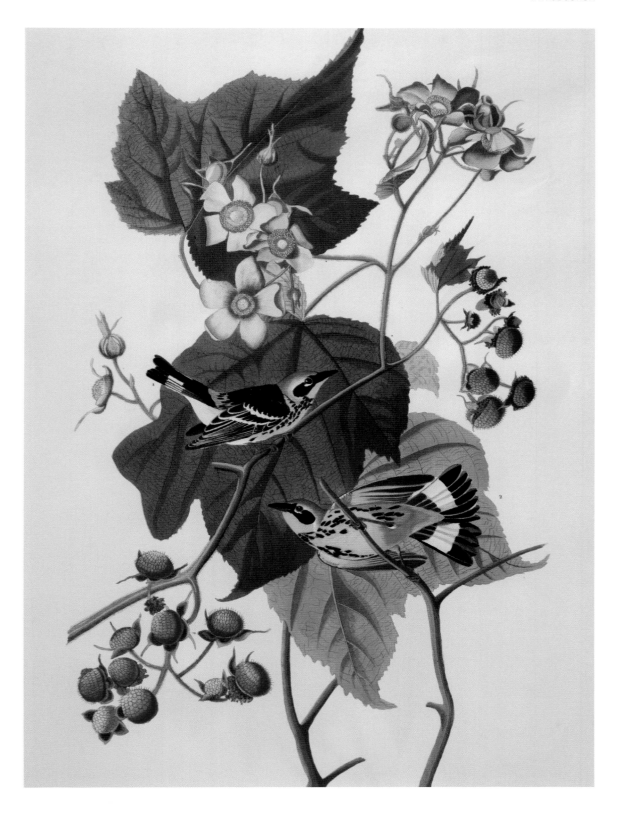

HOW TO USE THIS BOOK

The Collins Garden Birdwatcher's Bible is a collective and connective celebration of some of the Earth's most beautiful creatures, from how our feathered friends evolved, appear and function, to how to identify them and attract a range of common, garden or woodland species to visit us, to the story of birds in art.

Birds are endlessly fascinating creatures, particularly when you delve into their ancestry, their ability to fly, the science behind their coats of many colours or the symbolism attached to species such as eagles, doves or goldfinches in literature and art. There are also endless ways to appreciate them, whether that's through intellectual pursuit of what makes a bird, helping to conserve the myriad species still present on this Earth, providing food or nesting sites to help attract them to your backyard, or via the rewarding pastime or dedicated career of birdwatching or birding – or we may just stare in wonder at their beauty, quirks or characteristics, which are the focus of the ornithological art, illustration and photography found throughout this book.

To help navigate such flights of knowledge and fancy, *The Collins Garden Birdwatcher's Bible* is divided into four chapters that explore all of these elements. There is also a guide to Safe and Respectful Birdwatching Practice (see pages 18-19), a Glossary of Bird Terms (see page 20-23), and suggestions for Further Reading and Resources (see page 386–389).

The book opens with Chapter 1: Garden Bird Species – a narrative that traverses millions of years, from the first identifiable birds to the avian world of the present day. The story opens with a brief history of the Origin of Birds (see page 26), hurtling back in time some 140 million years to the reptilian yet feathered 'missing link' known as *Archaeopteryx lithographica*, to the flight-capable seabird-like creature known as *Ichthyornis*, the ancient forerunner of familiar species such as geese, partridges and flamingos. By the end of the Eocene era, birds had most definitely arrived and with them a flight-path of evolutionary adaptations concerning aerodynamic and postural skeletal and muscular aspects of Bird Anatomy (see page 28), the process of feeding (see page 30), the reproductive Life cycle (see page 33), and ultimately birds' ability to survive.

Segueing into an introductory guide to Garden Bird Species (see pages 34–35) *The Collins Garden Birdwatcher's Bible* lists over fifty of the most easily identifiable garden or woodland birds, from wrens, robins, starlings, waxwings, blackbirds, warblers and finches to doves, owls, woodpeckers, swallows, swifts and kingfishers. Each illustrated entry comes with a short description and fact file pertaining to the species' typical size, markings, habitat, food preference, voice, and distribution to help you spot the difference between families of birds such as the tits or to help you become familiar with brightly coloured national treasures such as bullfinches and siskins.

Each **species** is introduced by its most commonly used English name followed by its scientific name. In the main these names are those recommended and used by the British Ornithologists' Union.

Starling
Sturnus vulgaris

The main text for each species provides detailed information on appearance and plumage for all relevant ages and sexes. In addition, behavioural habits and background information are described where it helps the reader gain an insight into the bird in question.

The Starling is a common sight in rural and urban areas and an extremely vocal bird, uttering a range of sounds. The sexes are similar but usually separable with care during the summer. The summer adult has entirely dark plumage with an obvious oily sheen and an iridescence that includes green, bronze and blue tones when seen in good light. The bill is yellow and the legs are reddish. The bill of the male has a blue base to the lower mandible, and the female generally displays some spotting on the underside. The winter adult is beautifully adorned with strikingly contrasting pale feather tips. These take the form of white 'V'-shaped marks on the breast, bronze spots on the head and back and bronze edges to the wing feathers. The bill is dark. The juvenile has uniformly grey-brown plumage with a dark bill, acquiring adult plumage in the main by the autumn, but often retaining the grey-brown to the head and neck. By the first winter the plumage is indistinguishable from the adult. In flight, note the diagnostic short triangular-shaped wings seen in all birds.

The Starling typically forms large flocks outside the breeding season. Numbers in western Europe are boosted in autumn by birds that have migrated from further east and north to avoid harsh winter weather. Hundreds of thousands of birds congregate at popular roosting sites such as lowland marshes, the flying flocks forming huge clouds in the sky at dusk; this display can be spectacular. Its nest is a grass platform in a tree hole, nest box or building

Previous Page A spectacular murmuration of Starlings **Above** Although the species is still common and widespread, numbers of breeding and wintering birds have declined significantly in Britain in particular **Opposite** A solitary Starling is an unusual sight and most are found in sizeable flocks

FACTFILE
Length: 20–22cm (8–8¾in)
Wingspan: 37–42cm (14½–16½in)
Habitat: an adaptable species that occurs in a variety of habitats from lowland farmland, marshlands and open countryside to coastal regions and urban areas
Food: feeds on insects and other invertebrates, seeds and fruits
Status: widespread and abundant resident breeding species, present year-round in most of the region. Numbers are boosted in the winter months by birds migrating here from further east and north
Voice: an enthusiastic mimic and lively songster. Song includes mimicry of other bird song and man-made sounds. Also utters various clicks and descending whistles

The Factfile section provides an easy reference to important information about each species: Length; Wingspan; Habitat; Food; Status; and Voice.

The maps depict geographical ranges, a species' seasonal occurence being represented by different colours:

■ indicates a species' presence year-round

■ indicates a species' presence during spring and summer

■ indicates a species presence from late autumn and throughout winter

■ indicates a species' presence on migration

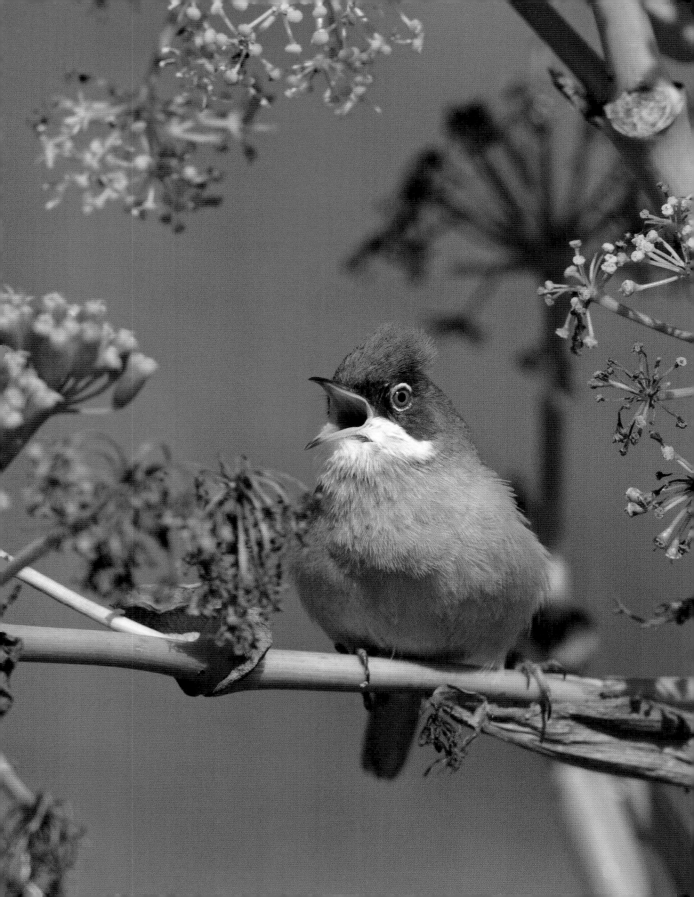

Written in the era of Coronavirus, with locked down streets free of cars and skies devoid of aeroplanes, birds are particularly symbolic of the daily freedoms that we may have taken for granted in our former lives. Watching birds go about their daily lives – foraging and feeding, making nests and mating, fluttering and flying – can also be incredibly uplifting, especially when accompanied by an amplified soundtrack of chirping, tweeting and birdsong. Delve into Chapter 2: Birdwatching for Beginners and you'll find an ideal introductory or refresher course on avian habits and habitats that make such observations even more poignant.

The Life of a Bird (see page 182) provides a fascinating insight into avian life followed by a foray into the differences between Birding and Birdwatching (see page 252) and some of the key figures and moments in the history of ornithology. While it's not necessary to own all the latest bird books, binoculars, high-tech camera attachments or specialist clothing to enjoy the company of birds, some basic Equipment and Outfitting (see page 256) can make even an everyday experience much more rewarding, and there are tips and advice on optional extras for if you want to turn a hobby into a dedicated something more serious.

Go behind the scenes of the life of a Hatchling (see page 184) – a bird's-eye view of what it takes to hatch, from an egg and survive those first few crucial hours or days. Explore the nature of Eggs (see page 202) – how they are formed, their size and shape, variations in colour and the contents that, after Incubation (see page 204), give life to a baby bird. In order to lay such eggs, birds must first make a home in the form of a Nest (see page 198) – high in the trees, deep within bushes, among reeds, in the eaves or houses or in burrows or caves. Young birds are very much reliant on Parental Care (see page 207) until finally able to fend for themselves as fully fledged juveniles, able to

Opposite A young male Spectacled Warbler (*Slyvia conspicillata orbitalis*) in song

practise skilled Foraging Behaviour (see page 186), Running, Hopping, Walking and Perching (see page 192), and Flight (see page 188).

Flight is one of the most enthralling lines of enquiry when it comes to birds, as they are the only vertebrates with this ability apart from bats. The anatomy and skill that enables the wonder of taking off, fluttering, soaring, gliding and turning has fascinated humans for tens of thousands of years. The endurance required to journey across wide oceans and land masses during Migration (see page 210) is truly awe-inspiring to behold. Bird communication is another marvel, most especially the world-enhancing gift of Bird Song (see page 194) and calls including the vast repertoire and mimicking abilities of birds such as the Marsh Warbler.

Flight and communication – through visual displays and voice – are also paramount when it comes to staking out territory. Territorial Behaviour on page 196 provides an enlightening guide to the lengths birds will go to in order to attract a mate and defend vital resources and their young, helping to reduce disease, predation, aggression and over-population at the same time. Chapter 2 explains the ecology of birds, how they fit into the environment in which they live and how they co-exist with other organisms, including humans. Find out about birds' strategies for survival and how they live, feed, and breed.

Birds account for over 11,000 of all known creatures on Earth – although some scientists estimate that there may be nearly twice as many due to the 'hidden' diversity of species that look to us to be similar to one another. However, over 150 birds are known to have become extinct over the past few hundred years and over 400 avian species are currently listed as endangered. With threats including manmade habitat loss and climate change, consider the effects on bird Population (see page 217). There are lots of things that we can do to turn the tide for birds with dwindling numbers through Protection and Conservation (see page 222) of natural habitats. For a list of national and international organizations that undertake and promote critical work in the wild, turn to Further Reading and Resources on page 389.

Addressing these issues at ground level, Chapter 3: Attracting Birds provides a hands-on introduction to the Bird-Friendly Garden (see page 266) starting with an overview of Foraging and Feeding habits (see page 268) according to species preference and season. Packed with planting tips and advice for all kinds of spaces, from large landscapes and gardens to small balconies or backyards, it's easier than you think to incorporate at least some of what birds need or love.

Trees and Hedges (see page 272) such as hawthorn, mountain ash, firethorn and holly provide fruits, nesting sites, shelter, refuge and perches, for example. While Flowers, Shrubs and Grasses (see page 276) such as sunflower, coneflower and panic grass attract bird-tempting insects and bugs, and provide nutritionally important seeds through autumn and winter. Pollinating birds such as hummingbirds are also attracted to certain blooms, to the delight of those lucky enough to share their territories with these beautiful creatures. It's also possible to put out supplementary food in the form of seeds, nuts, fat balls or grubs, especially welcome in breeding season or winter. Read all about Bird Tables, Feeders and Baths on page 282, including step-by-step guides on how to make a Bird Table (see page 284), a Fat Ball (see page 286) or a Bird Café (see page 288). Birds need water too, so there's also a guide to crafting a simple Bird Bath (see page 287) and advice on how to keep feeding and water stations clean.

Breeding and Shelter (see page 290) are also key factors in a bird-friendly garden. Climbers and Vines (see page 292), for example, often provide delicious and nutritious berries or seeds but also ideal foliage, branches or hidey-holes for nests,

roosts or shelter from predators. Plants such as ivy or clematis can also be grown in relatively small spaces, up a trellis, wall or fence. Less ornamental features such as Woodpiles and Compost Heaps (see page 296) harbour an abundance of food, shelter and nesting places for birds, with extra support from bird-friendly plants such as nettles, borage, cleavers, dandelions, elderberry and yarrow. Bolstering plant diversity, providing seasonal food and leaving corners of the garden to go wild is also part of Thinking Sustainably (see page 306), a crucial mind set in terms of bird protection and conservation but also one that can bring huge rewards in terms of bird watching and song.

Celebrating birds in all their glory and diversity is the main theme of Chapter 4: Birds in Art with The Art of Birds (see page 310) setting the scene with a soaring guide to over 40,000 years of bird-themed or inspired art. From the first fledgling impressions of birds in Palaeolithic cave art, through symbolic paintings, ornithological illustrations and decorative displays, to today's intimate high-tech photography of avian life, it's clear that birds have always held a huge power to intrigue, uplift and teach us much about the natural world and the role that we play in it.

Explore the world of Ornithological Art and Illustration (see page 320), celebrating the works of master bird artists and observers past and present from John and Elizabeth Gould and James Audubon to Roger Tory Peterson, David Sibley, Matt Sewell and Jane Kim. From beautiful paintings to painstakingly produced prints to huge murals expressing the evolution of birds, what flocks these works together is the scientific study of birds through time, place and classification as well as the exquisite portrayal of them.

The twentieth century not only saw advances in modern art but also major technological change including the invention of the first portable cameras. From early black-and-white snapshots of birdlife by Eric Hosking to high-resolution portraits or cinematic documentaries by Bence Máté or

Opposite A Barn Owl (*Tyto alba*) perches on a fence

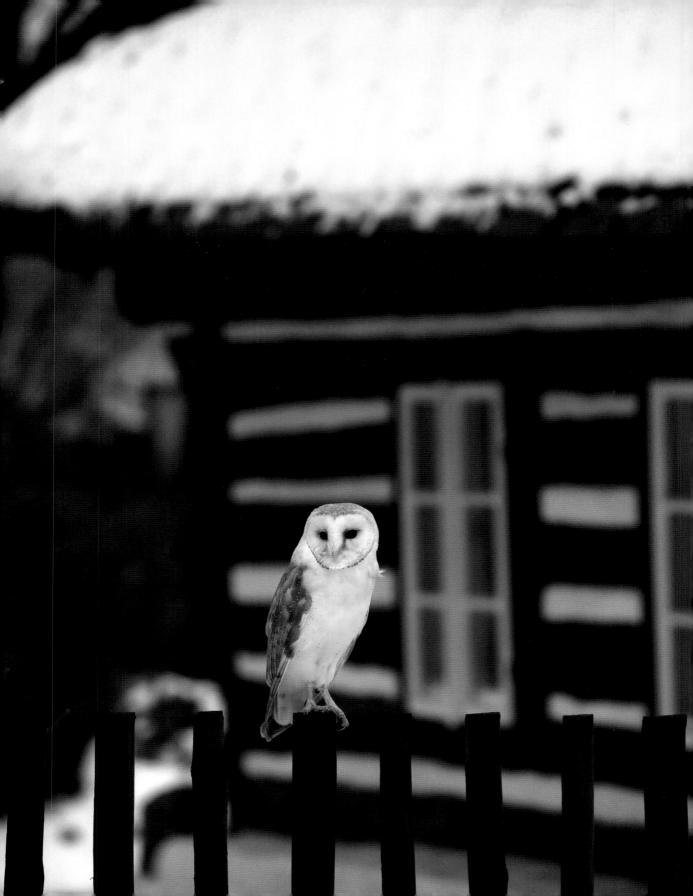

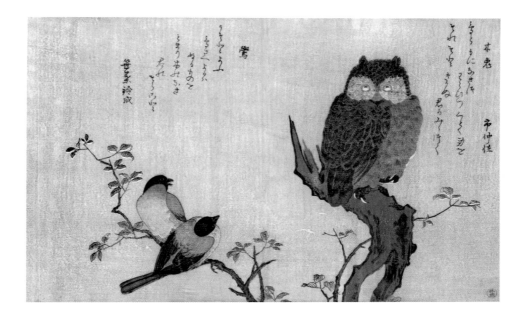

David Attenborough, Photography and Film of birds (see page 342) now allow us to get closer to avian life than ever before, including rare or typically shy species. Zoom, macro and studio photography also facilitate detailed portraits of birds' physical or habitual features by artists such as Thomas Lohr or Leila Jeffreys. There's also background on the internationally renowned Bird Photographer of the Year (BPOTY) competition for those interested in capturing birds on film (see page 343).

Our metaphysical relationship with birds is perhaps best expressed through the Painting and Sculpture they have inspired (see page 332). From spiritually invested bird-and-flower paintings exemplified via the Japanese art of *Kacho-e* and iconic dove drawings by Pablo Picasso, to Constantin Brancusi's soulful *Bird in Space* sculpture or Frida Kahlo's self portraits with her pet parrots, the bird as muse is a timeless theme. We seek to capture their richly coloured plumage or their soaring flight but we also see birds as symbols of peace, hope, power, familiarity and joy.

Some of the most memorable or charming images of birds, however, have been created in the disciplines of Design, Craft and Style (see page 358), from bird-inspired, ancient textiles and ceramics and the Arts and Crafts motifs of artists William Morris and C.F.A. Voysey to the beautiful stylized or illustrative prints of Charley Harper or Robert Gillmor. While some of these works are incredibly detailed or decorative, others such as Edward Lear's 'coloured birds' sum up the defining characteristics of our feathered friends in a few allegorical lines and words, the mark of an ornithological illustrator as well as a humorous artist and poet.

Last but not least, A Swan Song for the Birds (see page 374) pays homage to the birds that, although preserved for posterity in galleries and museums, sadly didn't make it to the present day: the dodos, passenger pigeons, Labrador ducks, Carolina parakeets and great auks. Art provides a vital visual reminder to celebrate the true wonder and diversity of today's avian world by observing and representing birds, but also by conserving them and their habitats for millennia to come.

Above An Owl and Two Eastern Bullfinches from Kitagawa Utamaro's Birds Compared in Humorous Songs (1791) **Opposite** Bullfinch and Weeping Cherry Tree (1834) by Katsushika Hokusai

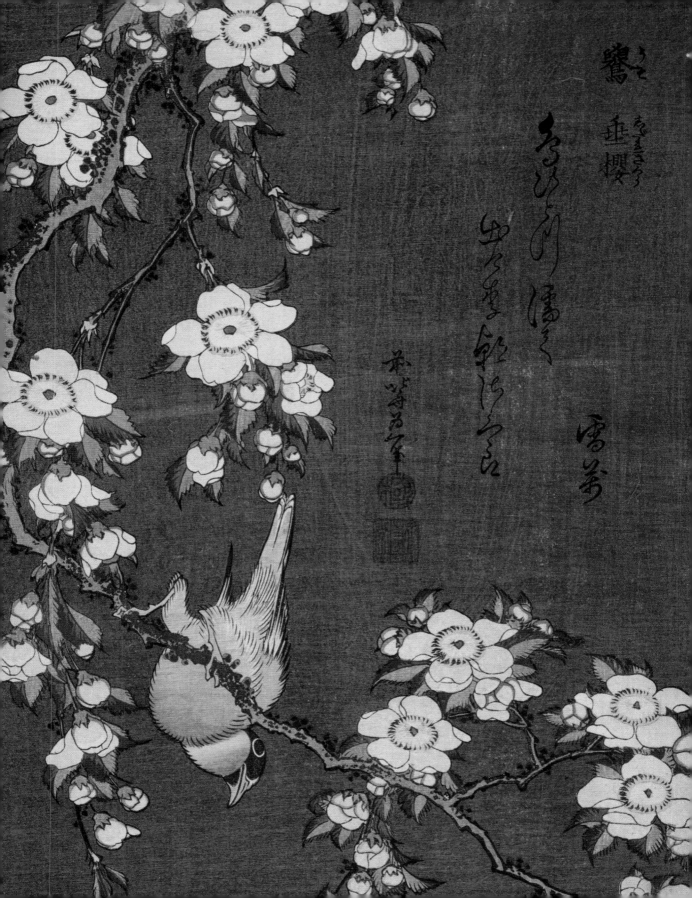

SAFE AND RESPECTFUL BIRDWATCHING PRACTICE

Whether you're new to birdwatching or a fully fledged birder, following a widely agreed birdwatchers' code of conduct helps protect birds while allowing everybody to enjoy the wonders of the avian world, now and for years to come.

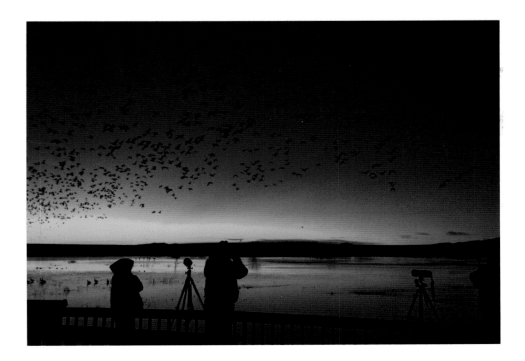

Millions of people take part in birdwatching or birding activities each year around the globe – three million in the UK – supported by ornithological societies such as the RSPB (Royal Society for the Protection of Birds), the BTO (British Trust for Ornithology) and the international partnership known as BirdLife. This is great news on two counts: one, you're part of a huge and growing community of like-minded souls and two, there's plenty of great official advice out there on how to observe birds respectfully and safely, including the widely adopted birdwatchers' code.

Gear up

Sport dark, easily camouflaged clothing to help keep a low profile and stop birds see you coming. Check the weather and bring appropriate gear for rain showers, wind or strong sunshine: invest in a good waterproof/windproof jacket, hiking shoes (and comfortable socks), sun cream and hats for winter and summer. Seasoned birdwatchers also never leave the house without a pair of binoculars, a pen and paper to record sightings, a bird guide, a map (if you're in unfamiliar territory) and some drinks and snacks. A smartphone can also be handy for taking snaps or notes as well as helping with navigation and communication including emergency calls.

Avoid disturbing birds

If birds are disturbed during the breeding season they may keep away from their nests, leaving chicks hungry or enabling predators to take their eggs or young. It is also illegal to ever remove or harbour wild bird eggs, or to disturb nests in the breeding season. In cold weather or just after migrants have made a long flight, repeatedly disturbing birds can significantly impact on vital energy needed for breeding or foraging in order to survive the winter. If a bird makes repeated alarm calls, flushes – flies or runs away – or appears to freeze, you're too close. Staying on roads and paths where they exist can help to avoid disturbing habitats used by birds, as can becoming more familiar with flock or species behaviour.

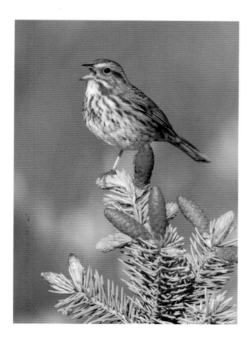

Use equipment wisely

Camera flashes should be turned off, or a filtered flash, at most, used for night photography. If you're serious about getting the ultimate photographic bird shot, consider using a telephoto lens or a bird hide where you can get a great view of birds without making your presence known – see Bence Máté's photography (see page 356) for inspiration. Making sound recordings of birds can be wonderfully rewarding but playing songs to attract birds is controversial so limit its use, obey local restrictions, keep quiet around rare birds, ask permission if you are in a group and take care to avoid invading a bird's territory or confusing birds during the breeding season.

Be an ambassador for birdwatching

This means being kind, considerate and friendly to birds, fellow birdwatchers and birders as well as those not interested in birds at all. Remember to follow the laws of the countryside at home and abroad including closing gates, never trespassing on private land and 'leaving no trace' of litter, trampled vegetation or disturbance to any wildlife. It's also helpful to report findings to bird conservation organizations but think twice about passing on information about rare species to fellow birders or birdwatchers too quickly. Consider the potential impact to the birds and their habitats, plus the people or communities who live nearby. Last but not least, enjoy yourself. There's no rule that says you can't inspire others to observe, conserve and protect birds via the example you set and the enthusiasm you bring.

Opposite Birdwatchers observing flocks of Snow Geese taking off in the Bosque del Apache National Wildlife Refuge, New Mexico, USA **Above** A Song Sparrow (*Melospiza melodia*) in song

BIRD TOPOGRAPHY AND GLOSSARY

Ornithologists give precise names to distinct parts of a bird's body, both to the bare parts (legs and bill, for example) and areas of feathering (wing coverts, primaries and the like). These terms have been used throughout the book to ensure precision and to avoid ambiguity about what is being described or discussed. As a reader, an understanding of this terminology helps with interpretation of the descriptive text in the book. It is also helps when talking about bird identification with other birdwatchers, and is useful in the process of identification in the field. On the following pages, a glossary of terms helps with the learning process, and annotated photographs show the important anatomical and topographical features for a range of common bird species.

Adult A fully mature bird.
Axillaries The area of feathers that cover the 'armpit' of the bird; this is only visible on stretched wings or in flight.
Bill The beak.
Carpal The 'wrist' of a bird, formed at the bend of the wing.
Coverts Areas of contour feathers found on the upperwing, underwing, uppertail and undertail.
Culmen The upper ridge of the bill.
Eye-ring A ring of feathers, often colourful, that surrounds the eye.
First-winter A bird's plumage in its first winter after hatching.
Forewing The leading edge of the upperwing.
Gorget A patch of colour on the throat of a bird - especially hummingbirds.
Immature A bird that is any age younger than an adult.
Juvenile A young bird with its first set of full feathers.
Lek A communal display.
Lores The area between the eye and the bill.
Malar A band or stripe of feathers on the side of the throat, in front of and below the submoustachial stripe.
Mandibles The two parts of a bird's bill: upper and lower.
Mantle Feathers covering the back.

Siskin

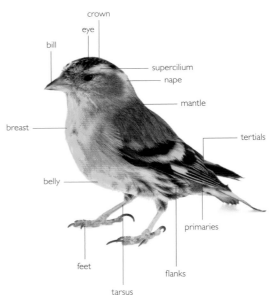

crown
eye
bill
supercilium
nape
mantle
breast
tertials
belly
primaries
feet
flanks
tarsus

Eastern Bluebird

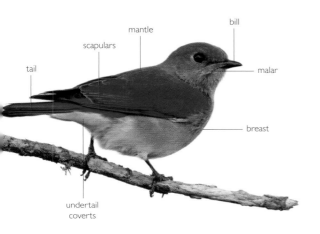

bill

mantle

scapulars

tail

malar

breast

undertail
coverts

Migrants Birds that have different geographically separate breeding grounds and winter quarters. Many birds of the region are breeding visitors, present here in spring and summer but wintering as far away as Africa. A few species use northwest Europe as their wintering grounds, and breed further north.

Moustachial stripe A stripe that runs from the bill to below the eye, fancifully resembling a moustache.

Nape The hind neck.

Nidifugous Born or hatched in an advanced state.

Nidicolous Born or hatched in an undeveloped state.

Orbital ring Ring of bare skin around the eye, often brightly coloured.

Pelagic Associated with or living in the open ocean.

Primaries The main flight feathers found on the outer half of the wing.

Primary projection The visible extent of the primary feathers beyond the tertials on the folded wing.

Rufous Reddish-brown in colour.

Scapulars A group of feathers that form the 'shoulder' of the bird between the back and folded wing.

House Sparrow

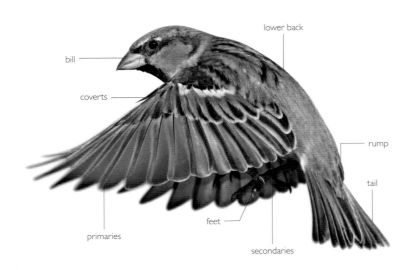

lower back

bill

coverts

rump

tail

primaries

feet

secondaries

Seabird A species that, outside the breeding season, spends its life at sea.

Second-winter A bird's plumage in its second calendar winter after hatching.

Secondaries A group of relatively large flight feathers that form the inner part of the wing.

Species A taxonomic description relating to a population, members of which breed with one another but not with others. A species' scientific name is binomial, comprising the genus name first followed by the specific name; taken together the name is unique.

Submoustachial stripe The contrasting line of feathers below the moustachial stripe.

Supercilium A stripe that runs above the eye.

Tarsus The obvious main section of a bird's leg, below the 'knee'.

Tertials The innermost flight feathers.

Third-winter A bird's plumage in its third calendar winter after hatching.

Tibia The area of the leg above the 'knee'.

Vent The area underneath the tail, covered by the undertail coverts.

Wingbar A bar or band on the wings, created by aligned pale feather tips, often those of the wing coverts.

Black-headed Gull

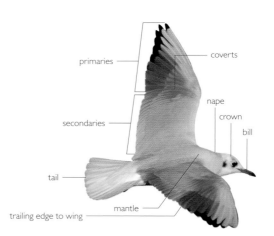

American Goldfinch

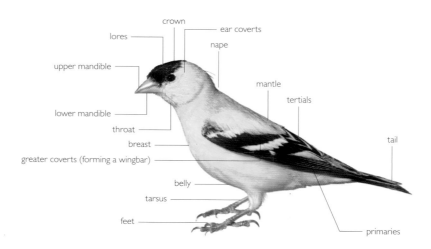

European Starling

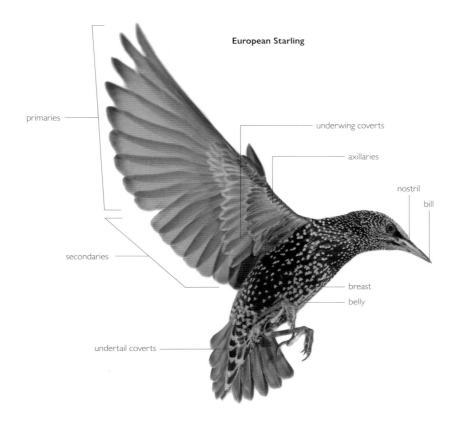

primaries

underwing coverts

axillaries

nostril

bill

secondaries

breast

belly

undertail coverts

Common Grackle

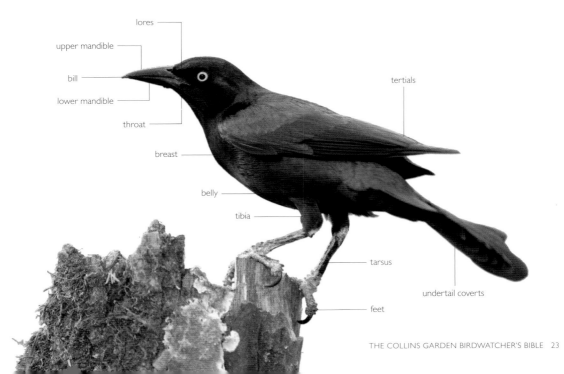

lores

upper mandible

bill

lower mandible

throat

breast

belly

tibia

tarsus

feet

tertials

undertail coverts

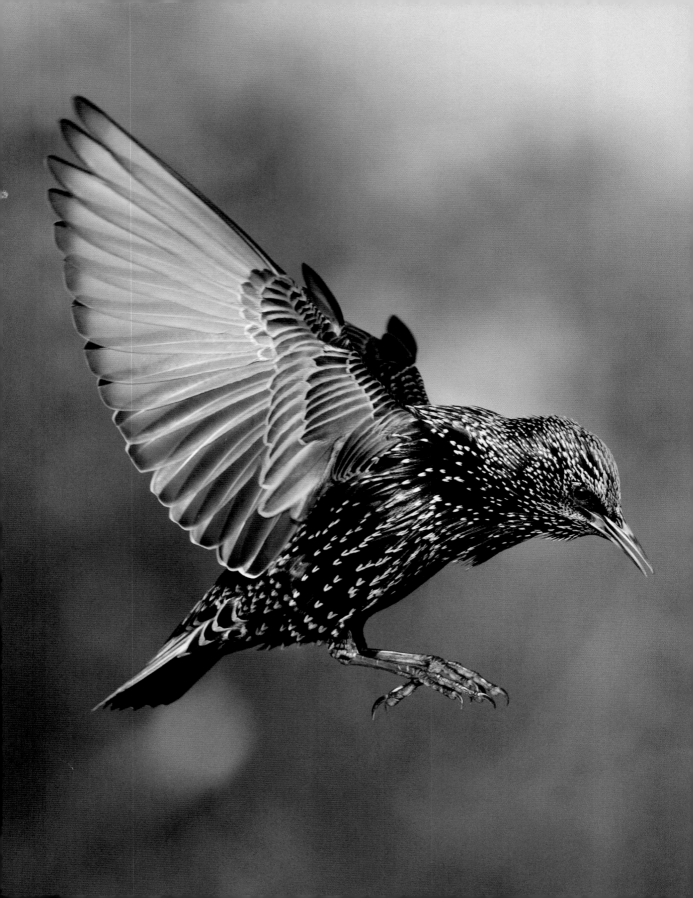

CHAPTER ONE

GARDEN BIRD SPECIES

The Place of Birds in the Animal Kingdom

THE ORIGINS OF BIRDS

Traces of animals and plants – fossils – exist in rocks that were formed many millions of years ago. Initially animals evolved in the sea; but later the early lung-fish and amphibians conquered the land to be followed by the reptiles. Two branches of reptiles played very important parts in the history of animals; these are the synapsids, which eventually gave rise to the mammals; and the sauropsids, which evolved into modern reptiles and birds. Between 240 and 65 million years ago, a branch of the sauropsids, the dinosaurs, became the dominant group of land animals; these included most of the largest that have ever existed, such as the famous *Tyrannosaurus rex*.

Living alongside these huge animals were many smaller sauropsids, which evolved into an extensive range of small, agile and fast-moving creatures, some of which ran on two feet and sometimes climbed using their forelimbs. Being smaller and more fragile than the larger dinosaurs there are fewer fossil remains and for a long time they were less well-known.

In 1861 workers in a slate quarry in Bavaria, Germany discovered what at first seemed to be just another one of these small sauropsid fossils. But, beautifully preserved in the fine slate were feathers on the wings and tail! *Archaeopteryx lithographica* (literally 'ancient-wing in picture stone') became one of the world's most famous fossils; it caused a sensation because it looked like a 'missing link' between reptiles and birds – among other features it had a long, bony tail and reptile-like teeth. Recent finds, especially from China, have unveiled a great radiation of forms from the beginning of the Cretaceous (145–65 million years ago). While *Archaeopteryx* is a striking fossil, there are many other small dinosaurs, some anatomically so similar to birds that they blur the traditional distinction between birds and reptiles. One widespread feature is some sort of feather-like structure covering the body. These could not have been used for flight, but may have been used for camouflage or display. Another likely function was for insulation and the probable reason for this was that these animals were warm–blooded and needed a coat in order to be able to maintain their body temperature.

By some 70 million years ago many lines of these smaller dinosaurs existed alongside their vastly larger cousins. Then, a little over 66 million years ago, came the single most important happening in the history of birds: a massive earthquake. The Chicxulub Eruption occurred in the Caribbean Sea off the coast of Honduras. Its immediate impacts – tsunamis across the whole of the Caribbean, forest-felling gales and the fall-out of volcanic debris across the whole of North America – were almost minor compared with the global effects. For several years clouds of dust, hanging in the atmosphere, cut out the light and killed off most of the vegetation and the animals dependent on it; some 70 per cent of the plant and animal species, including all of the big dinosaurs, both on land and in the sea, became extinct.

This episode is known as the Cretaceous-Paleogene (K–Pg) boundary and had important outcomes. With the stage lacking its major players, there was scope for a cast of smaller players. Some of those who had survived were able to move centre-stage and become the major players. And they did! Many groups of both mammals and birds first appear in the fossil record at this time.

The story that the dinosaurs became extinct at this time is not quite true; one small and insignificant group survived and flourished: birds *are* dinosaurs!

Previous Page A Starling landing **Opposite** *Archaeopteryx lithographica*, considered to be the earliest known bird

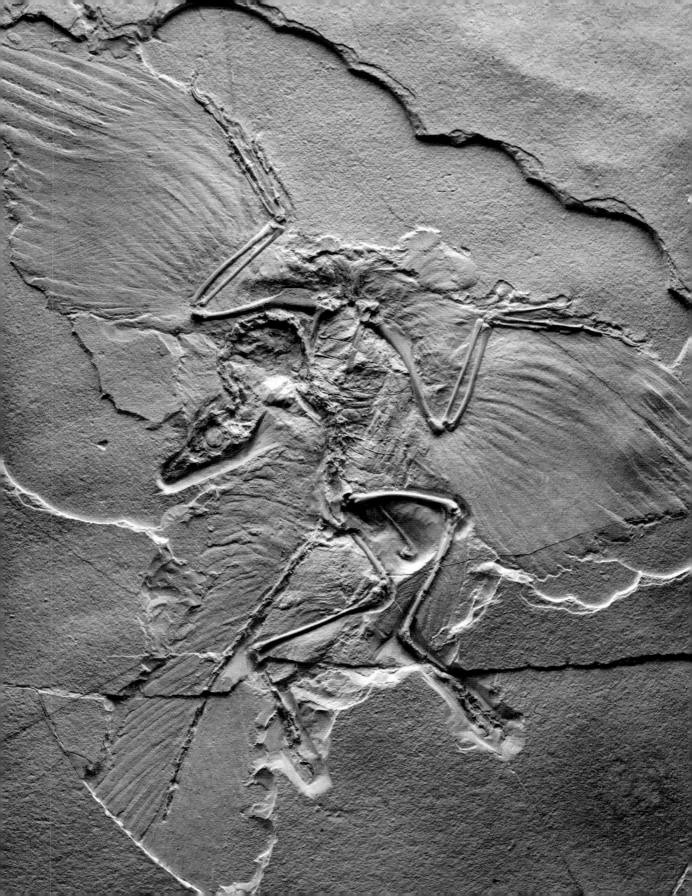

CHARACTERISTICS OF BIRDS

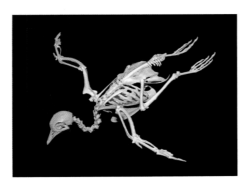

In general form all birds are very similar to one another. Birds have such a constant form because of the need to be able to fly efficiently. Flight is one of the most useful, and one of the most energy-demanding methods of locomotion. In order to make it as economical as possible – indeed in many species to make flight possible at all – birds cannot deviate from sound aerodynamic design. Only in a few species, such as the ostriches and the penguins, which have abandoned flight, has it been possible to alter greatly the basic size and shape.

It is possible to see adaptations for flight in virtually every aspect of a bird's anatomy; evolution has made birds as light as possible, and as maneuverable as possible. However, since there is also a great need of power for flight, some parts, such as the flight muscles, could not be greatly reduced.

The skeleton

The skeleton of a bird shows a number of marked adaptations for efficient flight, all of which can be looked on as helping to reduce weight or to make the bird as compact and maneuverable as possible.

The weight of the bird's skeleton has been reduced in a number of ways. Some parts have been greatly reduced and many of those bones that remain have been considerably lightened. In areas such as the spine and synsacrum, bones have fused together, reducing the need for muscles and other tissues to hold them together. The skeleton of a pigeon is only 4.5 per cent of the bird's total body weight. Many bird bones are hollow tubes instead of being almost solid like those of mammals; the outer surface of the bone remains big enough to provide adequate attachment for muscles, but its weight is much reduced.

The limbs and the muscles

All terrestrial animals use one or both pairs of limbs for locomotion. Most use both pairs of limbs simultaneously and these are positioned so that the animal's centre of gravity falls between the limbs. Birds, however, have two quite different modes of locomotion – flying and walking or swimming. In order to do both efficiently, they must have the centre of gravity close to the base of both sets of limbs, and this has led to certain modifications.

When in flight, a bird's body hangs from the shoulder joints and the centre of gravity lies just beneath the shoulders. However, this means that the centre of gravity is well forward of the hip joint; so a perched or standing bird balanced at its hips would be in danger of falling forwards when it walked. The bird's skeleton has adapted to deal with this problem. The top section of the leg, the femur, is tightly held along the sides of the body by muscles. The lower end of the femur then performs as if it were the hip joint; because this is nearer to the centre of gravity, the bird has less of a problem balancing when it is walking.

In order to power its wings, a bird needs a massive power source and this is provided by the great flight muscles. In most species the weight of the flight muscles is about 15 per cent of the bird's total weight, but in Hummingbirds this may be as high as 30 per cent.

Above Skeleton of a Pigeon **Opposite** A Ringneck Dove rises into the air

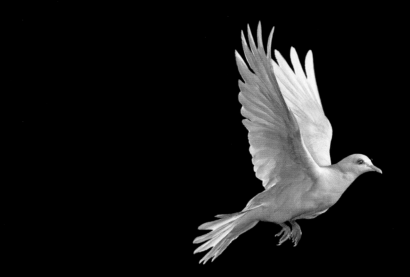
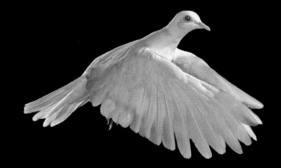
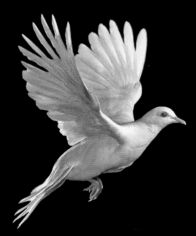

FEEDING

Although the weight of a bird's head has been reduced by the loss of the heavy jaws and teeth of its reptilian ancestors, food still has to be collected, caught or torn up, and birds need to use some sort of tool for this. Beaks vary in design in order to deal with a wide variety of food. A good clue to a bird's food can be found in the sort of beak it has.

Despite the wide range of forms, the basic design of the *beak is* similar in all birds. The upper mandible is firmly attached to the skull, though in many species there is a small amount of articulation between the mandible and the skull. The lower mandible, like the human one, is much freer, articulating at its base with and held to the skull only by muscles.

The horny outer surface of the bill is, like scales and fingernails, made of keratin. This wears away and is replaced.

Natural selection has resulted in a great diversity of bills, each enabling its owner to cope with a specific diet. The most generalized bill, such as those of warblers and thrushes, is a pointed one of medium length; this can be used for collecting a wide variety of foods from insects to fruits. Warblers do little more than stab their insect prey to kill it; Song Thrushes hold prey such as snails, which they beat on a rock; both swallow their prey whole, as do many other birds. Although the bill of the starling is similar, it has much more powerful muscles for opening the bill; it probes into soil and forces the bill open so as to enlarge the hole to enable it to withdraw any prey that it finds.

The master hammerers are, of course, the woodpeckers; the Great Spotted Woodpecker often makes a small hole in a tree branch in which to wedge nuts or seeds while it hammers them open. At other times a woodpecker uses its bill for opening up wood to get at burrowing insects. They may even take the young of hole-nesting birds such as tits. They have very long tongues with which to reach and grasp the prey, and special adaptations of the skull that reduce the shock of the hammering to the brain. The Green Woodpecker can extend its tongue four times the length of its bill, the Wryneck five times.

The bills of finches have evolved specializations for opening seeds. The upper mandible has a groove in which the seed can be held by the tongue while it is split by the cutting edge of the lower mandible. The extreme development of this type of bill is found in the Hawfinch, which has the largest beak of any European finch; the jaw musculature is also exceptionally large. The Hawfinch is able to split open the stones of cherries and olives, a feat requiring a crushing force of 4 kilograms (8¾ pounds) per square centimetre or more. The Crossbills have unusual beaks, which enable them to

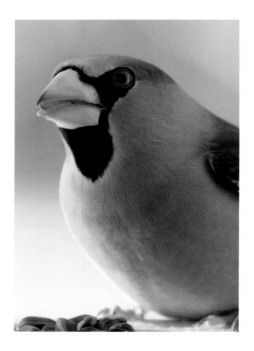

Left A Hawfinch **Opposite** The digestive system of a bird

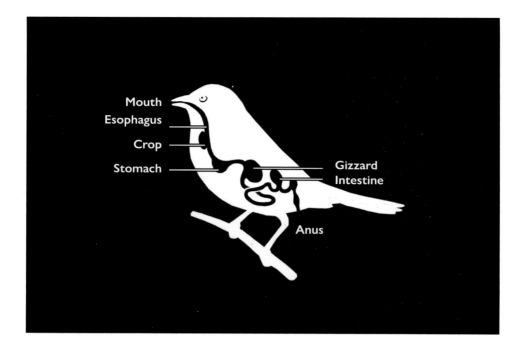

twist open the scales of conifer cones and scoop out the seeds with their tongues.

The jaw muscles of birds of prey are also powerful; many of these birds use their bill for tearing large prey into pieces small enough to swallow. They may also actually use the bill to kill their prey. The owls do not normally tear up their prey, but swallow it whole; their bill and jaw muscles are less powerful.

The weakest bills are found in many of the insectivores such as the Flycatchers, Swallows, Swifts and Nightjars. These species mostly catch flying insects and rely on a very wide gape to give them the best chance of doing this.

The crop

Many birds accumulate their food, initially, in a thin-walled extension of the esophagus – the crop. No digestion takes place here. It is simply a temporary storage place and allows a finch, for example, to alight, swallow a large number of small seeds in a short space of time and then retire to the safety of a bush to digest them. The bird can also take a large quantity of seeds to roost with it and digest them during the night, so shortening

the period over which it has to go without food. Many birds, such as some seabirds and pigeons, carry food long distances in their crops to their young. In pigeons and flamingos, the crop wall becomes thickened during the nesting period and the cells from these thickened areas are sloughed off to provide a milk-like substance for the chicks.

The gizzard

Because birds no longer have sets of teeth with which to grind up their food, this treatment has to be carried out elsewhere. Birds that eat insects, fish or meat do not have a great problem since their stomachs have strong juices and their food is easily digested. This is not so true of the birds, such as finches, that eat vegetable matter. They need to be able to grind up their food into fine particles to digest it properly. They do this in the gizzard, the muscular forepart of the stomach; hard material to serve as teeth are needed for the grinding process, so these birds take in grit and mix it with the food.

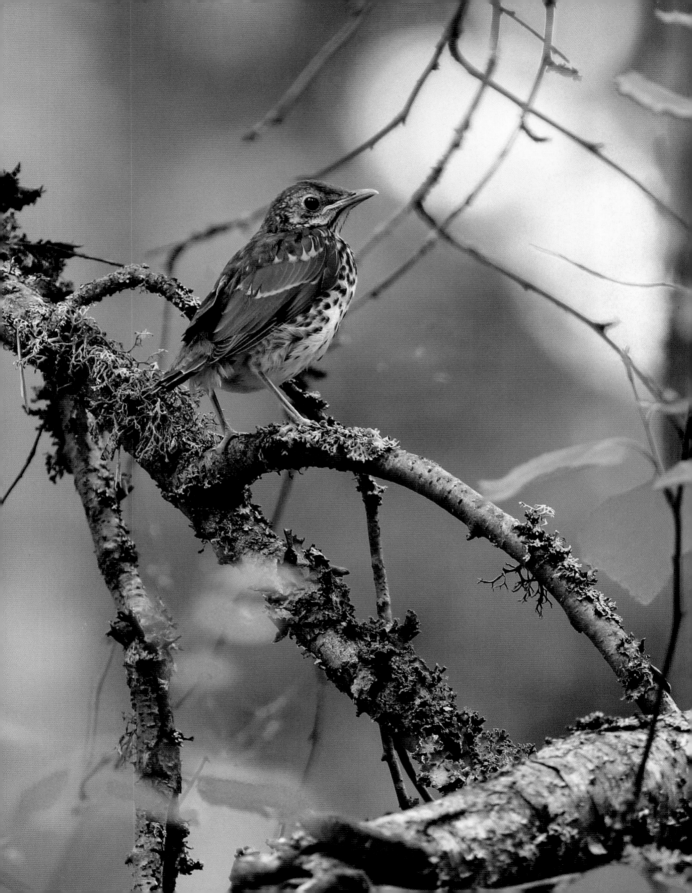

THE LIFE CYCLE OF A BIRD

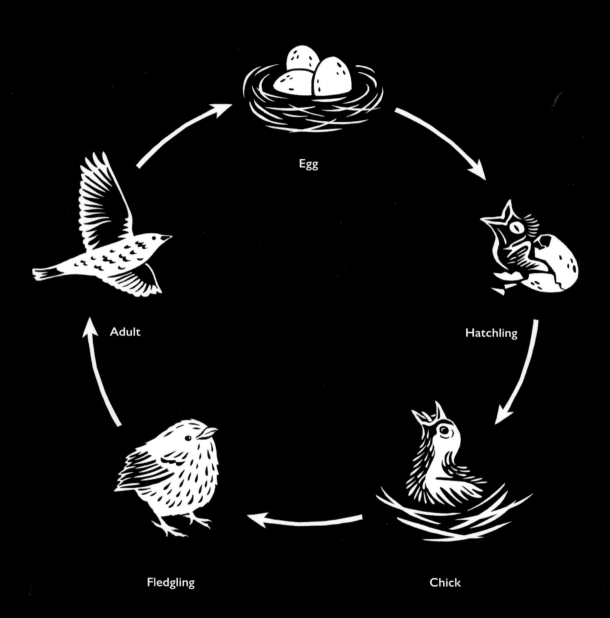

Egg

Hatchling

Chick

Fledgling

Adult

Opposite A Song Thrush chick perches on a branch
This page The life cycle of a bird

AT-A-GLANCE GARDEN BIRDS

Sparrowhawk
Accipiter nisus
page 36

Pheasant
Phasianus colchicus
page 38

Black-headed Gull
Chroicocephalus ridibundus
page 40

Rock Dove/Feral Pigeon
Columba livia
page 44

Woodpigeon
Columba palumbus
page 46

Collared Dove
Streptopelia decaocto
page 48

Tawny Owl
Strix aluco
page 52

Little Owl
Athene noctua
page 54

Kingfisher
Alcedo atthis
page 56

Swift
Apus apus
page 58

Ring-necked Parakeet
Psittacula krameria
page 62

Green Woodpecker
Picus viridis
page 64

Great Spotted Woodpecker
Dendrocopos major
page 66

Swallow
Hirundo rustica
page 70

House Martin
Delichon urbicum
page 72

Pied Wagtail/White Wagtail
Motacilla alba
page 76

Waxwing
Bombycilla garrulus
page 78

Wren
Troglodytes troglodytes
page 82

Robin
Erithacus rubecula
page 84

Blackbird
Turdus merula
page 88

Fieldfare
Turdus pilari
page 90

Redwing
Turdus iliacus
page 92

Song Thrush
Turdus philomelos
page 94

Mistle Thrush
Turdus viscivorus
page 96

Dunnock
Prunella modularis
page 100

Whitethroat
Sylvia communis
page 102

Blackcap
Sylvia atricapilla
page 106

Chiffchaff
Phylloscopus collybita
page 108

Willow Warbler
Phylloscopus trochilus
page 109

Goldcrest
Regulus regulus
page 110

Spotted Flycatcher
Muscicapa striata
page 112

Blue Tit
Cyanistes caeruleus
page 116

Great Tit
Parus major
page 118

Marsh Tit
Poecile palustris
page 120

Coal Tit
Periparus ater
page 122

Long-tailed Tit
Aegithalos caudatus and
Aegithalos rosaceous
page 124

Nuthatch
Sitta europaea
page 128

Treecreeper
Certhia familiaris
page 130

Jay
Garrulus glandarius
page 134

Magpie
Pica pica
page 136

Carrion Crow
Corvus corone
page 138

Hooded Crow
Corvus cornix
page 139

Jackdaw
Corvus monedula
page 141

Rook
Corvus frugilegus
page 142

Starling
Sturnus vulgaris
page 146

House Sparrow
Passer domesticus
page 148

Tree Sparrow
Passer montanus
page 150

Greenfinch
Chloris chloris
page 154

Goldfinch
Carduelis carduelis
page 156

Siskin
Spinus spinus
page 158

Chaffinch
Fringilla coelebs
page 160

Brambling
Fringilla Montifringilla
page 162

Bullfinch
Pyrrhula pyrrhula
page 166

Lesser Redpoll
Acanthis cabaret
page 168

Reed Bunting
Emberiza schoeniclus
page 172

Yellowhammer
Emberiza citrinella
page 174

Sparrowhawk

Accipiter nisus

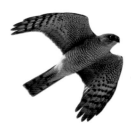

The Sparrowhawk is a common but unobtrusive raptor, most often seen only fleetingly. The sexes are separable. The adult male is considerably smaller than the female and has uniformly blue-grey upperparts and head. The underparts, including the underwing coverts, are a warm reddish-brown and strongly marked with a pattern of fine dark barring. The eye is orange-yellow and the heavily hook-tipped bill is dark. The larger adult female has grey-brown upperparts and head; the underparts are pale and display fine dark barring. The eye is yellow. The first-winter bird recalls the adult female, but has browner upperparts and paler underparts marked with strong brown barring. The legs in all birds are yellow, and note the long toes, designed to pluck prey from the air. In flight, the short rounded wings and barred square-cut tail are diagnostic.

Traditionally a bird of woodland habitats, the Sparrowhawk is an increasingly common sight in urban areas, particularly gardens, where it is usually glimpsed briefly. It feeds by catching small birds on the wing and is readily attracted to garden feeding stations owing to the concentration of suitable prey. Displaying males can be observed during the spring soaring overhead, but otherwise the flight is low and rapid. It nests in trees, constructing a platform of twigs.

FACTFILE

Length: 30–40cm (12–16in)
Wingspan: 60–75cm (23–29in)
Habitat: favours wooded habitats in both rural and (increasingly) urban areas
Food: feeds on small birds, which it catches on the wing
Status: common and widespread resident breeder present year-round throughout the region. Birds in the extreme north migrate south for winter
Voice: when alarmed, utters a shrill 'kew, kew, kew'

The map key is included in the *How to use this book* section on page 11

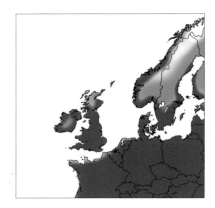

Above In flight, note the broad, rounded wings and long tail; immature birds tend to have heavily barred underparts **Opposite Top** Female in flight, when hunting, flight is typically low and level, with birds often flipping over a hedge or a wall for a surprise attack **Opposite Bottom** A male has proportionately longer toes than a female, useful because generally he specializes in catching smaller, more agile bird species

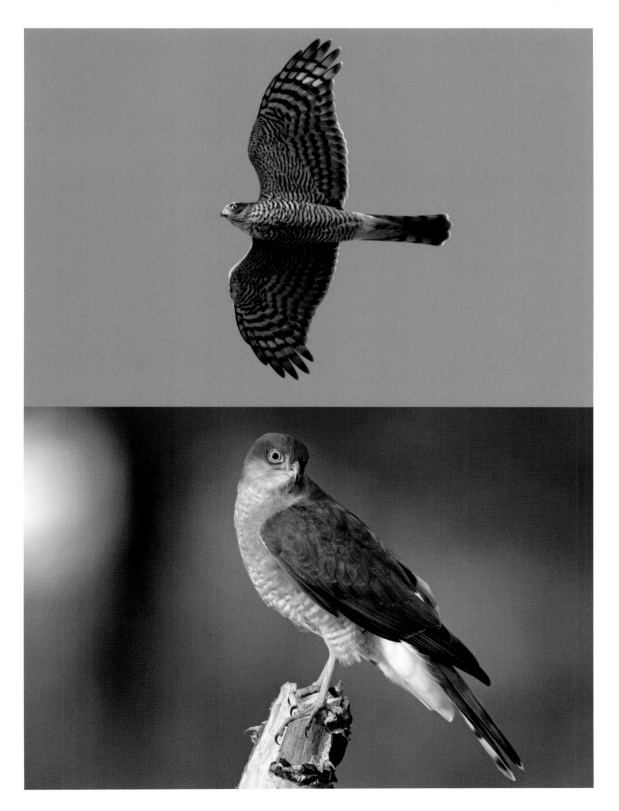

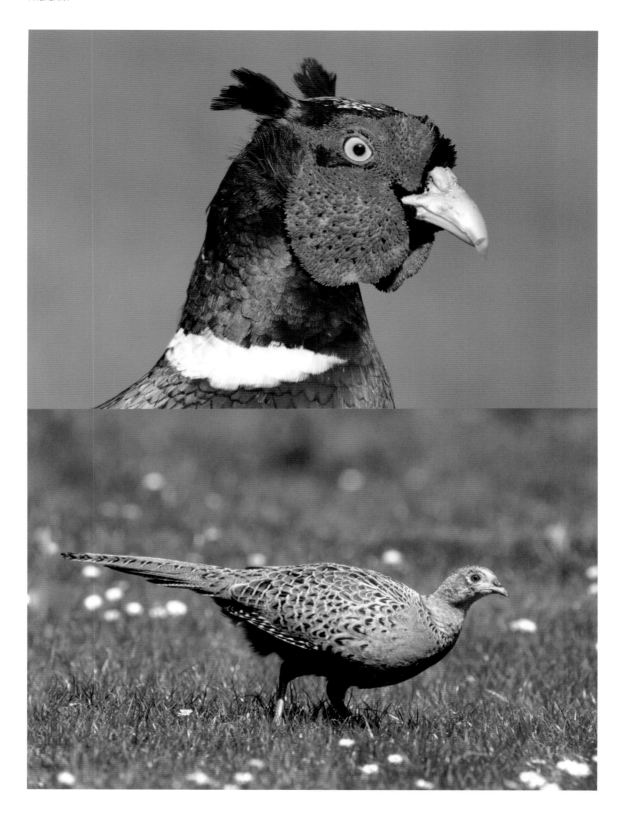

Pheasant

Phasianus colchicus

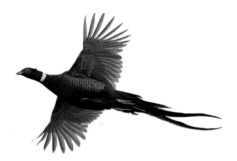

The Pheasant is a large and colourful gamebird. The sexes are strikingly dissimilar. The adult male has rich orange-brown plumage and a dark blue-green head that can display a metallic sheen in good light. The eye is surrounded by an obvious rounded, bright red wattle. The neck is commonly adorned with a white neck ring, although some birds lack this feature. The long, showy tail is orange-brown with dark barring. The adult female is modest in comparison, being smaller than the male with finely mottled, buffish-brown plumage overall and a shorter tail. The juvenile resembles a small adult female with a short tail. In flight, note the broad, rounded wings and long, finger-like primaries.

The Pheasant originates in Asia and has been introduced in the region over many centuries. Its breeding status is hard to determine owing to the millions of birds that are bred in captivity and released each year for shooting. It is a familiar sight in rural areas and commonly flushed from cover, taking flight with a series of rapid noisy wing-beats, accompanied by its distinctive alarm call. It roosts in trees and nests on the ground.

FACTFILE

Length: male 65–90cm (25–35in); female 55–70cm (21–27in)
Wingspan: 80–90cm (31–35in)
Habitat: occurs primarily in farmland and woodland habitats
Food: feeds on a variety of seeds and invertebrates
Status: introduced and now common and widespread. A very popular hunting quarry, numbers are boosted significantly by the release of captive-bred birds by the shooting industry
Voice: territorial males utter a loud and unmistakable 'coo-cukk' shrieking call, accompanied by vigorous wing beating. When alarmed or flushed a loud 'ke-tuk, ke-tuk, ke-tuk' is uttered, accompanied by conspicuous and rapid wing-beats as it flies away

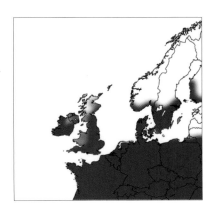

Above Male in flight, note the broad, rounded wings and very long tail, accompanied by loud calls **Opposite Top** Male life-size. At close range, note the male's bright red wattle, beady yellow eye and tufts of feathers at the back of the head; in good light a sheen can be seen on the neck feathers **Opposite Bottom** A female's plumage is overall brown with dark centres and white margins to the back feathers

Black-headed Gull

Chroicocephalus ridibundus

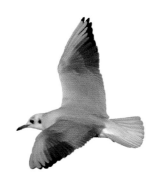

The Black-headed Gull is a commonly encountered medium-sized gull that occurs in a wide variety of habitats. The sexes are similar but summer and winter plumages differ. The summer adult has predominantly white plumage with a pale grey back and pale grey upperwings with black wingtips. The head is striking, being dark chocolate-brown, appearing almost black at distance or in poor light. Note the subtle and incomplete white eye-ring. In the winter adult, the dark head is replaced with white, marked with dark smudges above and behind the eye. In flight, all adults show a white leading edge to the outer wings. The juvenile has brown upperparts with an orange flush; the underparts are pale. By late autumn, it has usually acquired first-winter plumage and displays a dark carpal bar, tail tip and trailing edge to the wings. Adult plumage is acquired by the following spring.

This is the most abundant and commonly seen gull in the region owing to its numbers and the wide variety of habitats it is found in. It favours freshwater habitats for breeding, nesting on the ground in a shallow scrape lined with leaves and feathers. Its numbers are boosted during the winter months by birds that have migrated from harsher climates to the east and north.

FACTFILE
Length: 38–44cm (15–17in)
Wingspan: 94–105cm (37–41in)
Habitat: found in a wide range of habitats, from sheltered coastal areas and freshwater lakes, rivers and reservoirs to farmland and even urban locations
Food: an opportunist, feeding on a varied diet of invertebrates, plant material and household waste and scraps
Status: common and widespread, present year-round throughout the region
Voice: utters various raucous calls including a nasal 'kaurrr'

Above Adult winter. The otherwise clean, white head has a black patch on the ear coverts and is sullied by dark smudges around the eye. Typically seen in flocks at this time of year; birds are quick to take advantage of free hand-outs of food **Opposite** The wing pattern is distinctive and, once learned, provides a reasonably foolproof means of identifying even distant birds

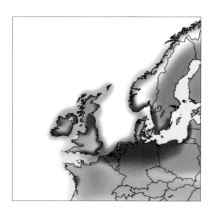

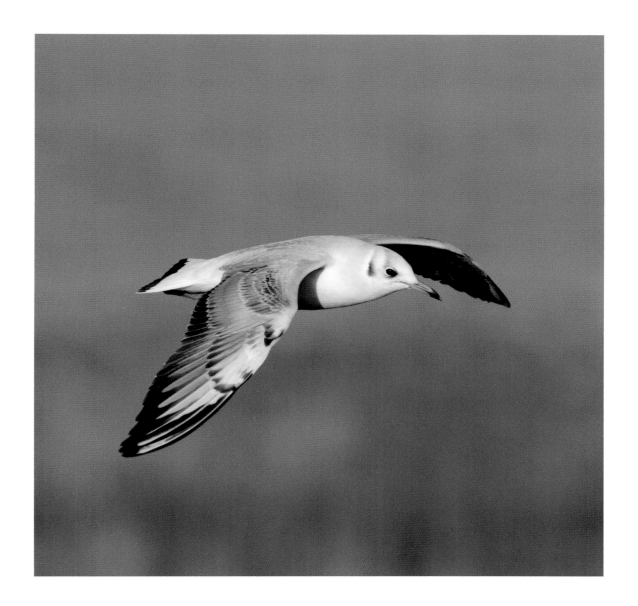

Pigeons and Doves
columbidae

Britain has five species of pigeon and dove, which is a paltry total considering that there are more than 300 kinds in the world, many of them brightly coloured. However, our birds make up for their modest colouration by being generally common, easy to see and noisy. Turtle doves were once abundant but have suffered an extraordinary crash in population, down 94 per cent since 1995 and in genuine danger of disappearing from the UK altogether. It is the only one of our species to be strongly migratory, arriving in April and departing for Africa in September. This migratory habit could be part of its downfall: turtle doves are often shot in large numbers on their way south.

There is no real difference between a pigeon and a dove. In fact, the famous white doves that are often symbolically released are the very same as our street pigeons, just ones that have been selectively bred in captivity.

Several pigeons and doves are remarkably well adapted to the human world. Feral Pigeons (see page 45) are descended from Rock Doves and breed on the ledges of buildings, often deep in the heart of cities, and come to be fed in parks. Woodpigeons (see page 46) are everywhere, from urban centres to deep forests and from gardens to farmland. They build a poorly constructed open, stick platform in trees and shrubs. Meanwhile, collared doves (see page 49) are the quintessence of suburbia, seemingly adorning every rooftop aerial as they sing a cooing dirge. The Stock Dove is something of an exception, preferring woodland and open country where it nests in cavities. It is easily overlooked and not familiar to many.

The pigeons are still more conspicuous in spring and summer as they exhibit some well-known and easily seen displays. Woodpigeons fly upwards, wing-claps and then glides down in a long, linear display. Collared and turtle doves fly up at a steeper angle and then usually spiral down. Meanwhile, Stock Doves fly in a wide circle and often hold up their wings in a 'v' as they glide; Feral Pigeons perform a similar but more subtle display.

Pigeons are famously productive, raising several broods a year, each of two chicks. Even the migratory turtle dove may raise two broods. Feral Pigeons and collared doves may nest continually throughout the year, with up to six successive broods. The squabs are fed not on grain, but a curd-like substance, 'pigeon milk', secreted from the crop.

People often think you never see baby pigeons but that is because the baby, once it has left the nest (usually after three to four weeks), is the same size as the adult, and with similar plumage.

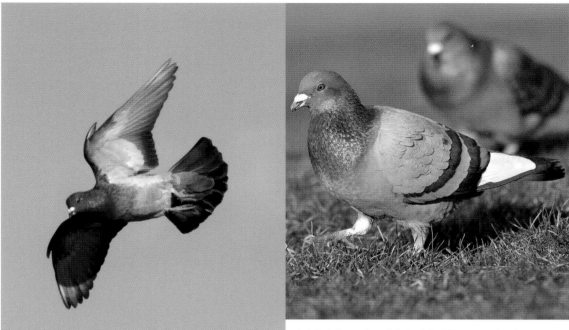

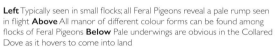

Left Typically seen in small flocks; all Feral Pigeons reveal a pale rump seen in flight **Above** All manor of different colour forms can be found among flocks of Feral Pigeons **Below** Pale underwings are obvious in the Collared Dove as it hovers to come into land

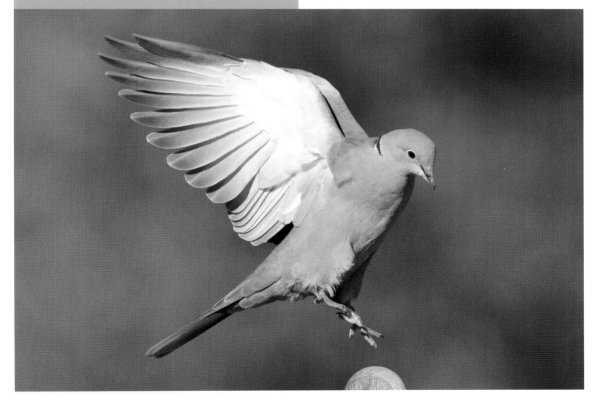

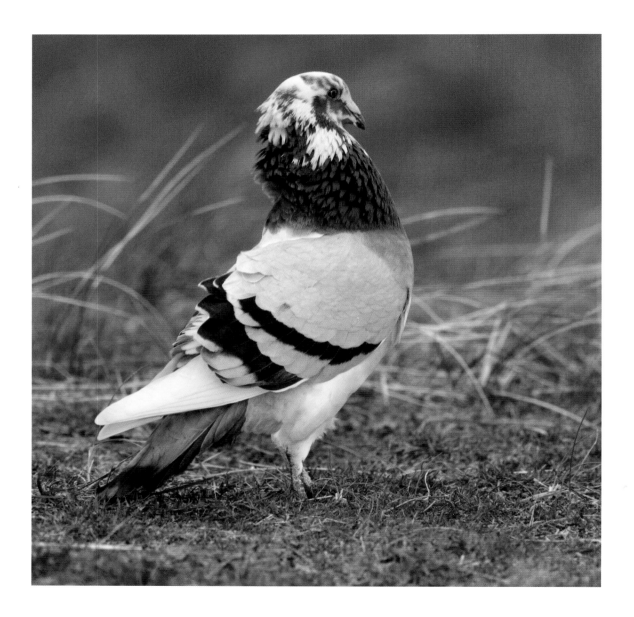

Rock Dove/Feral Pigeon

Columba livia

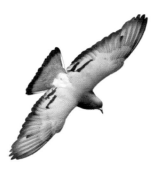

The wild Rock Dove is a shy bird of wild and inaccessible rocky coasts and cliffs. The sexes are similar. Much smaller than Woodpigeons, the adult Rock Dove has overall blue-grey plumage, palest on the upperwings and back, the breast flushed with pinkish-maroon. The upperwings are marked with two well-defined dark wingbars, obvious both in flight and in standing birds. In flight, note the small white rump patch, the dark trailing edge to the upperwings, dark terminal bar to the tail and white underwings. The juvenile is similar to the adult. The Feral Pigeon is the urbanized descendant of the Rock Dove. Its plumage is widely variable, from pure white to almost black, and many combinations between.

The species forms flocks and, in the case of Feral Pigeon, these can number many hundreds of birds. The Rock Dove is a fast-flying and rather timid bird, which nests on rocky ledges and can be tricky to observe. The Feral Pigeon has adapted well to urban areas and is now abundant in many towns and cities, generally being extremely tame.

FACTFILE
Length: 31–34cm (12¼–13¼in)
Wingspan: 63–70cm (24¾–27½in)
Habitat: rocky coastlines and coastal cliffs, open countryside, with feral populations in urban areas
Food: feeds on a variety of plant seeds, grains, other vegetation and invertebrates
Status: Rock Dove is a local resident breeding species, restricted to suitable habitat in coastal regions to the north and west of Britain and Northern Ireland. Its true status is hard to assess because of the large populations of Feral Pigeons throughout the region, some of which return to the wild
Voice: utters a variety of cooing calls

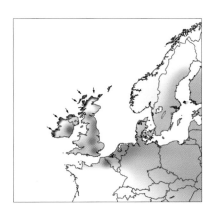

Above Flight is rapid when alarmed, but leisurely when relaxed and coming into land **Opposite** Many Feral Pigeons have identical plumage to their Rock Dove ancestors – as a rough guide, Rock Doves are shy so if you can get close to the bird in question it will almost certainly be one of their domesticated cousins

Woodpigeon
Columba palumbus

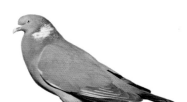

The Woodpigeon is a rather plump bird that is present in large numbers in many rural areas throughout the region. The sexes are similar. The adult has predominantly blue-grey upperparts and underparts, the breast flushed with pinkish-maroon. The side of the neck is marked with a diagnostic white patch. In flight, note the large white crescent-shaped marking traversing the upperwing (absent in Stock Dove). The wingtips are noticeably dark and there is a dark terminal band to the tail. The yellow-tipped, reddish bill has an off-white base. The eye is pale yellow and the legs are pinkish. The juvenile recalls the adult but has duller plumage overall and lacks the white neck-patch.

The Woodpigeon is a very successful species in many rural areas, and an increasingly common sight in urban locations. It has benefited directly from the increased production of oilseed rape. It nests in trees and tall bushes, constructing an untidy platform of twigs. A strong flier, it performs aerial displays during the spring, and the loud clattering of its wings as it takes flight is a familiar sound. Outside the breeding season it can form large flocks.

FACTFILE

Length: 40–42cm (15¾–16½in)

Wingspan: 75–80cm (29½–31½in)

Habitat: favours farmland and open grassland adjacent to hedgerows and woodlands. It is becoming increasingly common in urban areas

Food: feeds primarily on vegetation and invertebrates

Status: common and widespread resident breeding. Species throughout most of the region. Some southward migration occurs during the winter from Scandinavia

Voice: utters a series of soft, monotone 'oo-oo-oo-oo-oo' calls, the emphasis on the second of five syllables

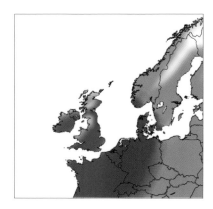

Above Although primarily a farmland species, Woodpigeons are often found in rural gardens; clover leaves in lawns are a favourite food
Opposite White markings on the neck and wings are certain identification features

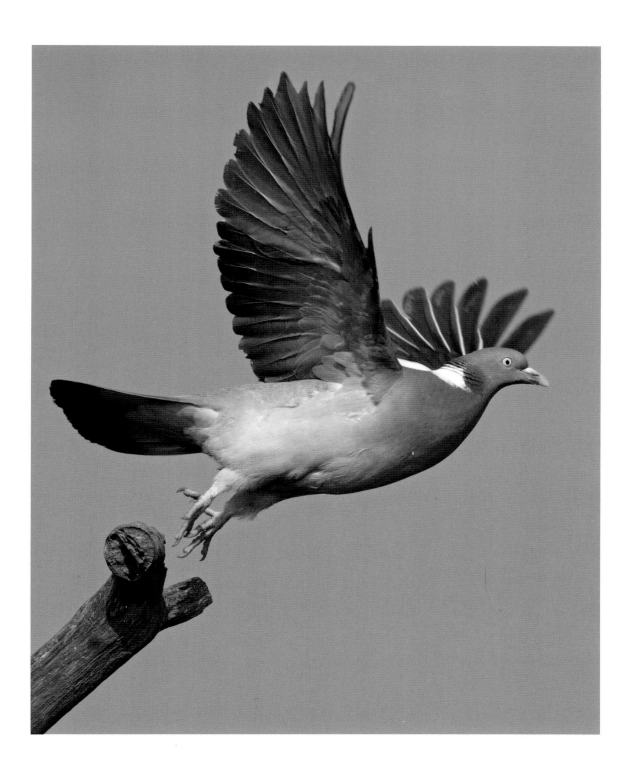

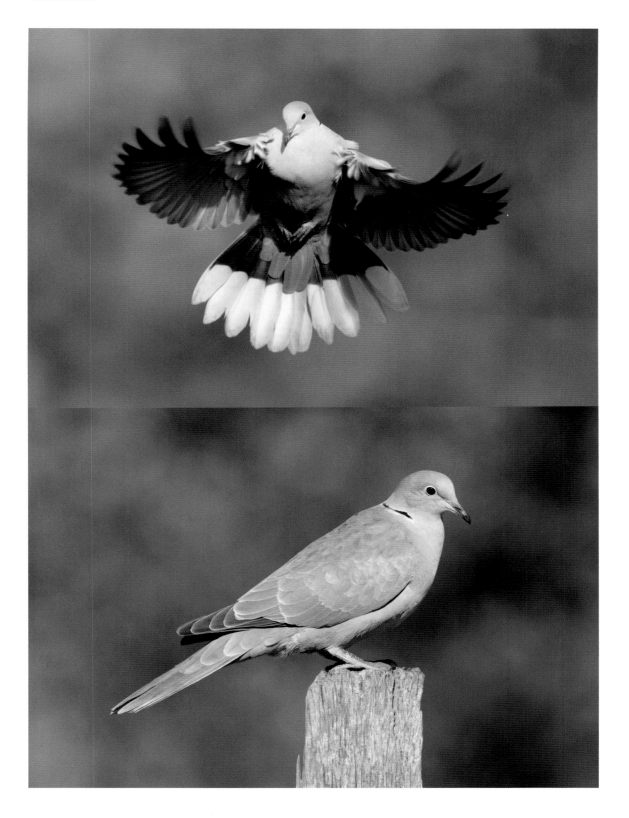

Collared Dove

Streptopelia decaocto

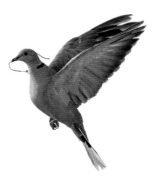

The Collared Dove is a familiar small pigeon. The sexes are similar. The adult has mainly uniform sandy-grey plumage; the head, neck and breast are flushed pinkish. A conspicuous dark half-collar marks the nape. In flight, note the black tips to the wings, the pale-coloured underwings and the broad white terminal band on the undertail. The slender, rather dainty bill is black, and the legs are reddish. The eye is dark red with a pale orbital ring. The juvenile is similar to the adult but duller overall, with pale fringes to the back feathers and lacking the half-collar marking.

The Collared Dove is a recent addition to the region's fauna: the species' range expanded across the region during the early twentieth century, linked directly to the expansion of arable farmland and cereal production. It nests in trees, constructing a rough platform of twigs. Flight is assured and swift on a series of fast, clipped wing-beats and dipping glides on bowed wings.

FACTFILE

Length: 31–33cm (12¼–13in)
Wingspan: 47–55cm (18½–19½in)
Habitat: found in a variety of habitats including gardens, orchards, farmyards and urban parks
Food: feeds primarily on seeds and cereal grains
Status: widespread resident breeding species found year-round throughout the region in suitable habitats
Voice: utters a repetitive trisyllabic 'oo-oo-oo' song, with the emphasis on the first two syllables

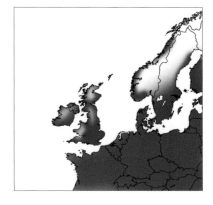

Above Pale underwings are obvious in birds that hover as they come into land **Opposite Above** Seen from below, the outer half of the tail is white and contrasts with the dark inner half **Opposite Below** In garden settings, often spends time just sitting on fence posts

Owls

Strigidae and Tytonidae

There are five species of Owl in Britain, plus a handful of rarities including the Snowy Owl, which bred in Shetland for a few years in the 1960s and 1970s and still turns up somewhere most years. The Tawny, Little, Long-eared and Short-eared Owls are all in the family Strigidae, which has about 230 species; while the Barn Owl, with its heart-shaped facial disc and peculiar ghostly pale plumage, is in the family Tytonidae, which has twenty species.

Owls are famous for being nocturnal birds of prey, coming out at night to hunt. In reality though, many use the twilight hours, dawn and dusk, for peak feeding, and Tawny Owls in urban and suburban areas are not beyond using the light cast by streetlamps to help them feed. Little and Short-eared Owls quite regularly forage in broad daylight. Although their eyes are strongly adapted for low light levels, they have no problem with sunlight; Tawny Owls have even been recorded sunbathing!

Although Owls see relatively well in the dark, it is their hearing that is truly extraordinary. The Barn Owl for example, is able to catch food in total darkness, using just its ears to detect the rustling made by a mouse or rat. The left ear opening is set slightly higher up the skull than the right ear opening, which means that sounds coming from above or below will be registered at each ear at fractionally different times. Combine this with sounds coming from the horizontal plane, which will arrive at the left or right ear at similarly minute differential time intervals, and you have the recipe for complete three-dimensional hearing capability. Many other Owls also have asymmetrical ear openings. Owls also have specially adapted soft plumage, which means that they can fly silently without impeding their hearing abilities as they hunt.

Owls are equally famous for their marvellously evocative advertising calls. The quavering hoots of the Tawny Owl are used in every TV soundtrack to evoke night-time chills. Long-eared and Short-eared Owls also make deep hooting calls, the Barn Owl squeals and the Little Owl (which eats many insects as well as rodents) has a yelping call.

Owls don't build their own nests, but instead simply lay eggs on a suitable platform such as in a tree hole, a Crow's old nest (especially Long-eared Owls) or on the ground (Short-eared Owls). The eggs are laid at intervals and incubation begins straight away, meaning that, in an Owl brood, which may number two to eight chicks, the young are all of different ages. When food is scarce, the oldest in the brood get the lion's share and their younger siblings starve to death. However, if food is abundant, Owls can be very productive. In the case of the Tawny Owl, the parents look after their surviving chicks for a couple of months, overseeing their early attempts at hunting.

Tawny Owls are remarkably sedentary, and a pair may live in the same neighbourhood for a decade or more, never leaving their territory and defending it with violence where necessary. By complete contrast, Long-eared and Short-eared Owls are often migratory. In some years, large numbers of both these species come to Britain in October for the winter, adding to our resident population.

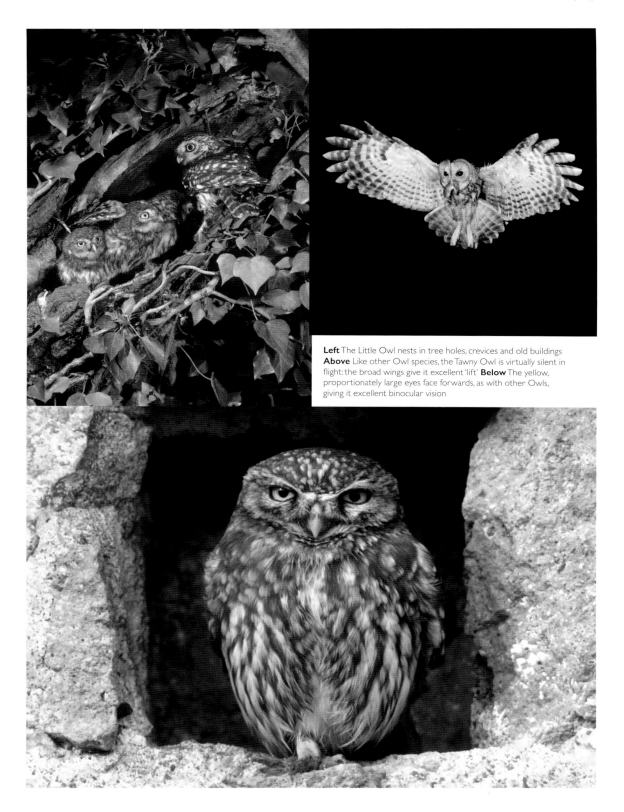

Left The Little Owl nests in tree holes, crevices and old buildings **Above** Like other Owl species, the Tawny Owl is virtually silent in flight: the broad wings give it excellent 'lift' **Below** The yellow, proportionately large eyes face forwards, as with other Owls, giving it excellent binocular vision

Tawny Owl
Strix aluco

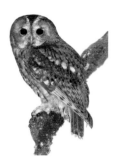

This is a medium-sized owl and the most commonly encountered of its kind throughout most of the region. The sexes are similar. The adult has beautifully marked variable plumage of chestnut-brown or grey-brown; the upperparts are darker, with dark streaks and pale spots. Its underparts can appear quite pale and are dark-streaked. Note the large rounded head and the dark eyes set in a well-defined facial disc. Grey patches mark the plumage surrounding the eyes. Note also the small yellowish bill and the lack of ear tufts. In flight, the broad, well-rounded wings appear quite pale on the underside and, on close inspection, are marked with brown barring on the primary feathers. The feathered legs and feet are buff. The juvenile is similar to the adult once the downy feathers have been lost.

More often heard than seen, the Tawny Owl is most vocal in the late winter and early spring when territorial boundaries are being disputed. It is a nocturnal owl that spends the day roosting in the trees, remaining well hidden with its superior camouflage; it is, however, regularly mobbed when discovered by small songbirds. The Tawny Owl nests in tree holes and cavities, and sometimes uses purpose-built nest boxes. Its flight is slow and leisurely. An adaptable species found in a variety of habitats, it is tolerant of close proximity to human habitation.

FACTFILE

Length: 38–40cm (15–15¾in)
Wingspan: 82–96cm (32–37¾in)
Habitat: favours deciduous or mixed woodlands, gardens and suburban parks
Food: feeds on a variety of small mammals, insects, birds, amphibians and earthworms
Status: a resident breeding species, present year-round and common and widespread in suitable habitats. Absent from the extreme north of the region
Voice: utters a sharp 'kew-wick', together with the classic owl hooting calls

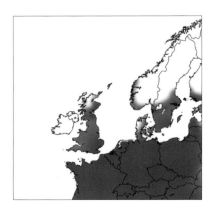

Above Typically, it moves its head rather than its body when alerted to the presence of prey by sound or movement **Opposite** The plumage is overall brown but subtly and beautifully patterned with dark streaks and white spots

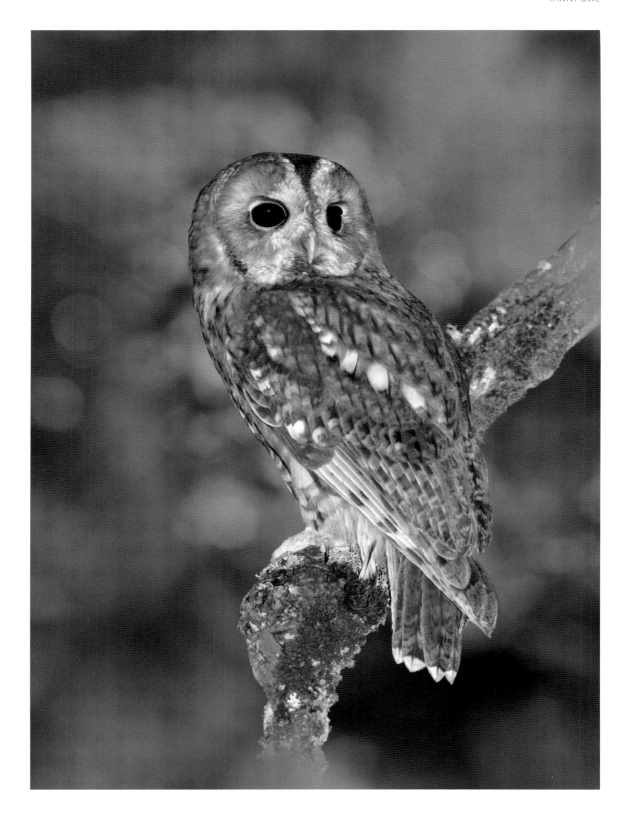

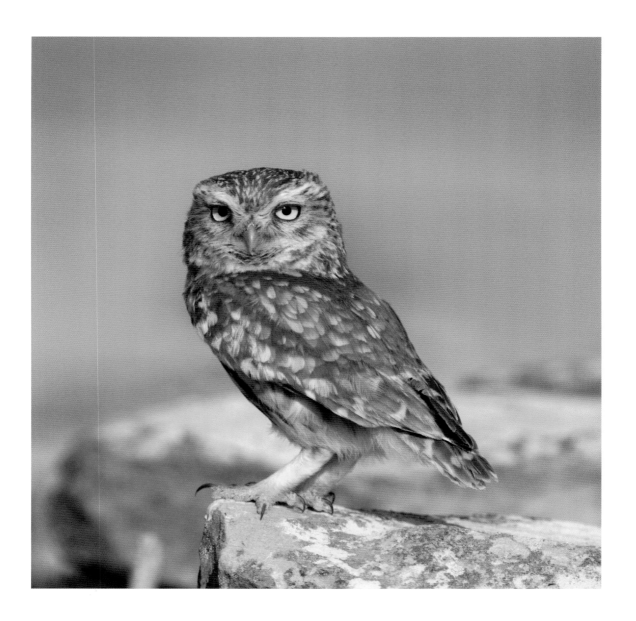

Little Owl
Athene noctua

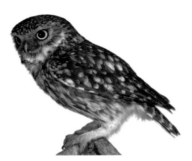

This is an easily recognized, rather small and dumpy owl with a short tail and relatively large head. The sexes are similar. The adult has rich brown upperparts adorned with whitish spots; the underparts are pale and heavily marked with dark streaking. Note the large staring yellow eyes and the rather rectangular buffish-grey facial disc. Its bill is grey-brown, the feathered legs are buff-white and the feet are brown. The juvenile is similar to the adult but with more subdued spotting and streaking, particularly on the head. The flight is diagnostically undulating, typically close to the ground.

Habitually perching out in the open and often active during the hours of daylight, the Little Owl is one of the easiest of the owls to see. It often stands erect, bobbing its head up and down and making hissing calls when alarmed. It nests in tree holes, crevices and old buildings.

FACTFILE
Length: 21–23cm (8¼–9in)
Wingspan: 50–58cm (19½–22¾in)
Habitat: favours open countryside, typically farmland with adjacent hedgerows and scattered woodland
Food: feeds primarily on insects, but also consumes small mammals, birds and earthworms
Status: an indigenous resident breeding species of mainland Europe and introduced to Britain during the nineteenth century. Absent from Scandinavia
Voice: utters a repetitive and agitated cat-like 'kiu' in the early evening

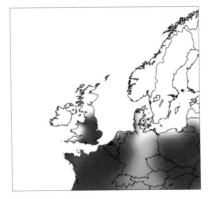

Above As with other owl species, a Little Owl is able to turn its head through almost 360 degrees, with the result that it misses very little of what goes on around it **Opposite** The body is rounded in outline and the head is proportionately large, even by owl standards

Kingfisher
Alcedo atthis

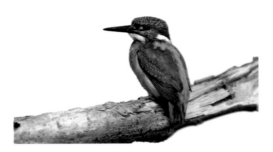

The Kingfisher is a strikingly colourful little bird with a dagger-like bill. The sexes are similar but separable with care. The adult male has bright electric-blue upperparts, the large head marked with an orange and white patch at the side of the neck, and a white patch on the chin. The underside is bright orange-red. The eyes and long bill are dark, and the legs and feet are red. The adult female is similar but the base of the lower mandible is flushed with orange. The juvenile recalls the adult but has muted colours and a pale tip to the bill.

The Kingfisher is one of the most colourful birds of the region. Sightings are often brief affairs, but its bright plumage is unmistakable, the bird commonly seen flying swiftly, close to the water's surface with rapid wing-beats. Flight is generally accompanied by its distinctive call. The Kingfisher requires clear water in which to feed, seeking perches directly above shallow water from which it plunge-dives for small fish. It nests in holes which it excavates in steep-sided waterside banks.

FACTFILE
Length: 16–17cm (6–6¾in)
Wingspan: 24–26cm (9½–10¼in)
Habitat: freshwater habitats such as streams, rivers, gravel pits, lakes and reservoirs. Occasionally seen on coasts in winter
Food: feeds primarily on small fish
Status: mainly a sedentary resident breeding species, present year-round throughout most of the region, with the exception of the extreme north
Voice: in flight, utters a diagnostic high-pitched 'tist-tseee'

Above Kingfishers are often easiest to see during the winter months, when the leaves are off the trees; the species' unmistakable outline and plumage colours make identification easy **Opposite** In flight, the bright sky-blue rump and centre to the back catch the eye; birds dive head-first into shallow water to catch small fish and large invertebrates such as dragonfly larvae

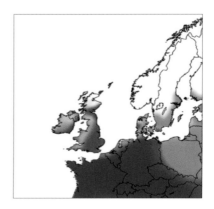

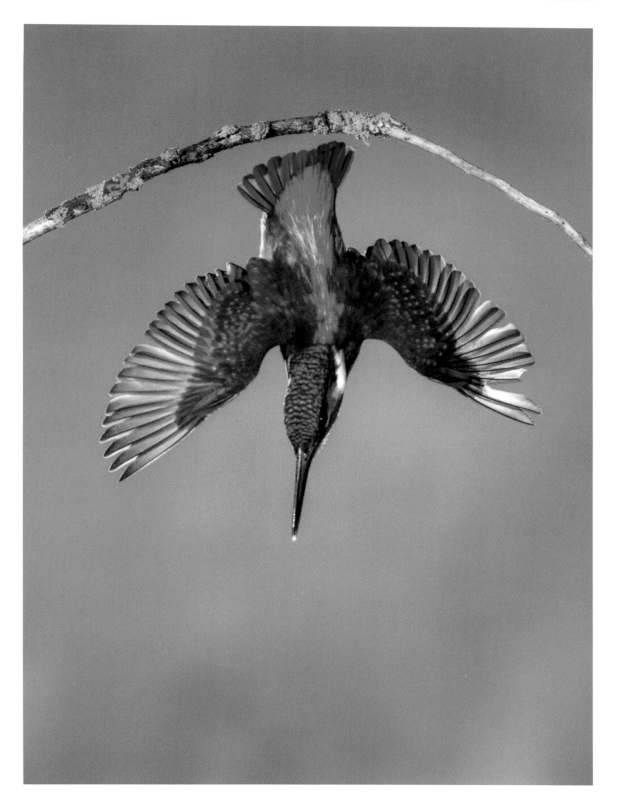

Swift

Apus apus

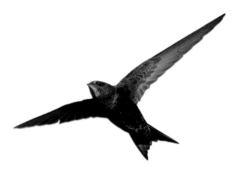

The Swift is a common summer visitor and entirely airborne when not at the nest, eating, sleeping and even mating on the wing. The sexes are similar. The adult has uniform blackish-brown plumage. In good light, and at close range, a pale patch can be seen on the throat. In flight, the Swift has an anchor-like profile, with a streamlined, bullet-shaped body and long and slender curved wings. The tail is forked, but often held closed in active flight. The eye and small bill are dark. The juvenile is similar to the adult but with darker plumage, a lighter throat patch and pale forehead.

The Swift is mostly seen in small groups gliding on stiffly held wings; when required the wing-beats are rapid and whirring. A fast and aerobatic flyer, its large gape helps it catch flying insects on the wing. It nests in buildings, usually in roofs and loft spaces, constructing a shallow cup of plant material and feathers. The young develop quickly and migrate to the African wintering grounds with the adults.

FACTFILE

Length: 16–17cm (6–6¾in)

Wingspan: 42–48cm (16½–18¾in)

Habitat: occurs around manmade structures, using loft spaces, church roofs and farm buildings in which to nest. Often congregates in areas with prolific insect life, and seen mainly in the air

Food: feeds on insects that it catches on the wing

Status: a summer breeding visitor, present mainly May to August. Widespread throughout much of the region. Overwinters in Africa

Voice: utters a loud screaming shrill call during the breeding season, typically within groups of birds in flight

Above The outline in flight is distinctive with narrow swept-back wings and a forked tail that is fanned when birds are turning or banking
Opposite Often seen in loose flocks near colonies and over areas where the feeding is good

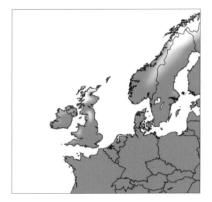

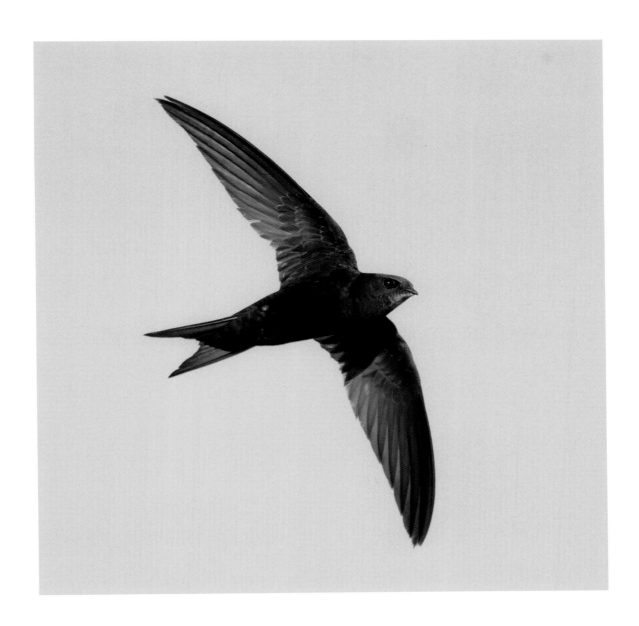

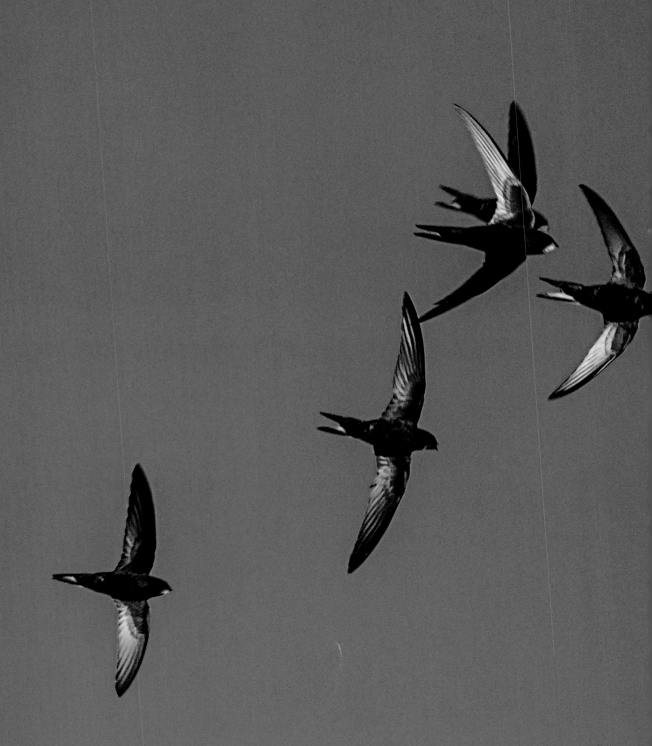

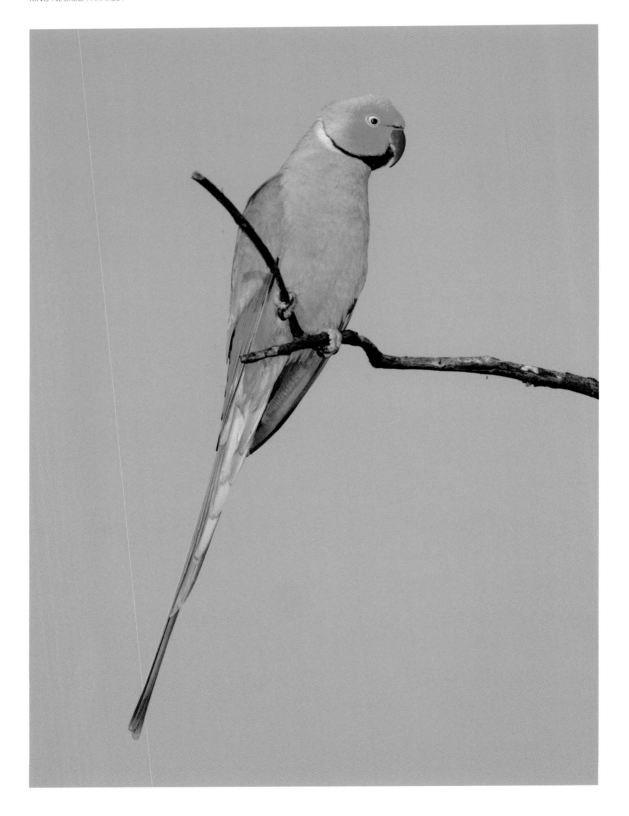

Ring-necked Parakeet
Psittacula krameria

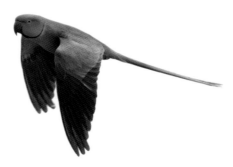

The Ring-necked Parakeet is an established alien species with colourful plumage and a distinctive long-tailed outline in flight. The sexes are similar but are separable with care. The adult male has primarily bright green plumage, but note the dark primary flight feathers, obvious both in flight and at rest. The tail is exceptionally long. The parrot-like red bill is powerful and heavily hook-tipped. The bird is also marked with a red eye-ring and a pinkish neck-ring, which is dark-bordered towards the lower half and merges with the black throat. The adult female is similar but lacks the throat and neck markings of the male. The juvenile recalls the adult female.

A rather bizarre addition to the European list, the Ring-necked Parakeet has established an extraordinarily successful feral population in localized areas. It nests in tree holes, often high above the ground. Outside the breeding season, it forms large flocks and is often seen roosting in trees. Its flight is strong and direct on rapid wing-beats.

FACTFILE
Length: 40–42cm (15¾–16½in)
Wingspan: 42–48cm (16½–18¾in)
Habitat: urban parks, city suburbs and open woodland
Food: varied diet consisting of fruits, flowers and seeds, and a regular visitor to bird tables in the areas it inhabits
Status: its natural range is Asia and Africa, but escapee captive birds have established large resident populations in certain areas. London and its suburbs are the stronghold, and large numbers are a regular sight in its parks
Voice: utters loud squawking calls, especially in flight

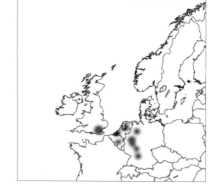

Previous Page Swifts are mostly seen in small groups gliding on stiffly held wings **Above** In flight, the long slender tail gives the bird a very distinctive outline **Opposite** Also known as a Rose-ringed Parakeet, the bright green plumage and unmistakable outline make for easy identification; only the male has the neck ring

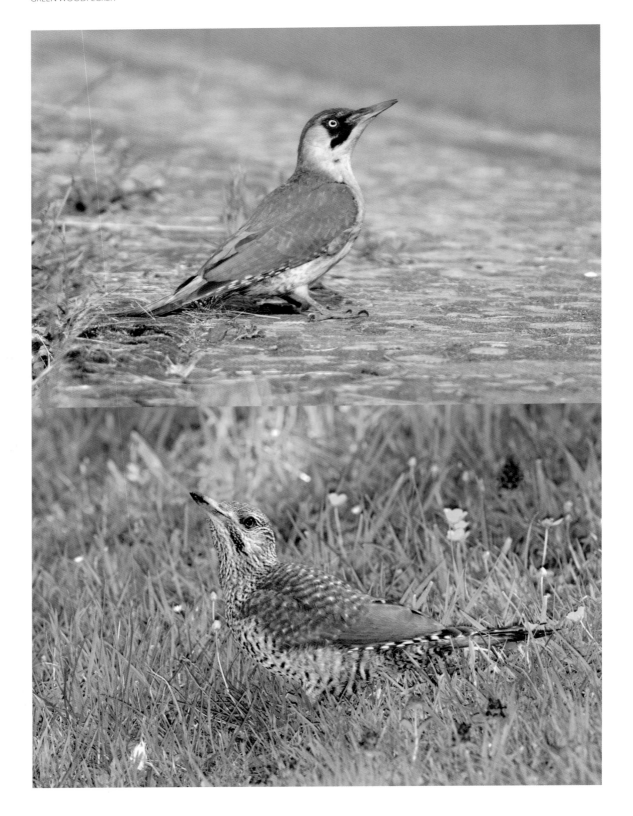

Green Woodpecker
Picus viridis

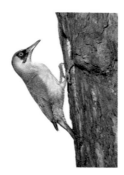

The Green Woodpecker is a rather timid and nervous bird that is often tricky to observe at close quarters. The sexes are similar but separation is possible with care. The adult male has bright olive-green upperparts, a bright yellow rump and dark primary feathers spotted with white (the latter two features are most obvious in flight); the underparts are whitish. The head is marked with a red crown, a bold black mask patch surrounding the eye and a red-centred black moustachial stripe. The large dagger-like bill is grey with a yellowish flush to the lower mandible. The adult female is similar but lacks the red centre to the moustachial stripe. The juvenile is similar to the adult but heavily marked with dark streaks on the head and underside, and white spots on the back.

This is a shy bird that takes to the wing at the slightest sign of danger. Its flight is low and distinctively undulating, often accompanied by its yaffling call. The Green Woodpecker feeds almost exclusively on the ground, using its long tongue to extract ants from their nests. It nests in holes that it excavates in trees and can often be observed climbing up trunks using its long tail for support.

FACTFILE

Length: 32–34cm (12½–13¼in)
Wingspan: 40–50cm (15¾–19½in)
Habitat: woodlands, parks, orchards and gardens
Food: feeds almost exclusively on ants and their larvae; some seeds and fruits
Status: widespread resident breeding species present year-round throughout the region, with the exception of northern Scandinavia and Ireland
Voice: utters a distinctive loud and yelping song, comprising a dozen or more sharp, rapid notes, often referred to as 'yaffling'

Above Actively furtive when nesting, birds are very reluctant to reveal the nest hole's location when there aren't any observers nearby; in poor light, the male's red centre to the 'moustache' is easily overlooked **Opposite Top** Female. Before it commits to feeding on the ground, where it is potentially vulnerable to predators, a bird will often scan around from a perch, looking out for danger **Opposite Bottom** Juvenile. The plumage is heavily streaked and spotted by comparison to an adult bird; all birds are extremely wary when feeding on the ground, lifting the head periodically to check for danger

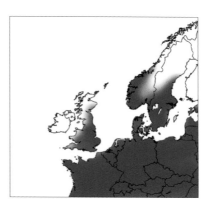

Great Spotted Woodpecker

Dendrocopos major

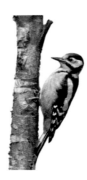

The archetypal common pied woodpecker. The sexes are similar but separable with care. The adult male has mainly black upperparts and grubby white underparts. It has elongated white shoulder patches and narrow white barring towards the black tail. The head displays white cheeks and a white throat; the black cap and nape are connected to a black stripe that runs from the base of the bill. Note the small red nape patch and the bright red vent. The dagger-like bill, legs and feet are grey. In flight, the white barring on the wings and white shoulder patches are obvious. The adult female is similar, but lacks the red nape patch. The juvenile recalls the adult male but has a conspicuous red crown and the vent colouration is duller.

A Great Spotted Woodpecker's flight is characteristically undulating, rising on rapid wing-beats, followed by a closed-wing glide and dip. It excavates holes in rotten tree trunks and wood, both for food and to create chambers in which to nest. The territorial 'song' is produced by the bird 'drumming', hammering the tip of its bill rapidly and loudly on a tree trunk. This is the most likely woodpecker to visit garden tables and feeders.

FACTFILE

Length: 23–24cm (9–9½in)
Wingspan: 34–39cm (13¼–15¼in)
Habitat: prefers mature deciduous woodland, but a versatile species that can be found in a variety of habitats with trees, including parks and gardens
Food: feeds primarily on insects but will also take eggs and nestlings of other birds and some seeds and fruits. A common visitor to garden tables and feeders
Status: widespread resident breeding species, present year-round. The commonest woodpecker species encountered throughout the region in suitable habitats. Occasional visitor to Ireland
Voice: utters a loud, high-pitched 'tchick' alarm call. Males frequently 'drum' during the spring when establishing breeding territories

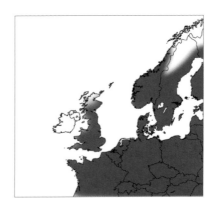

Above A female lacks the male's red nape but it can be surprisingly hard to determine the presence or absence of this feature, except at just the right angle **Opposite** The bold white shoulder patch and spots on the wings are striking in flight

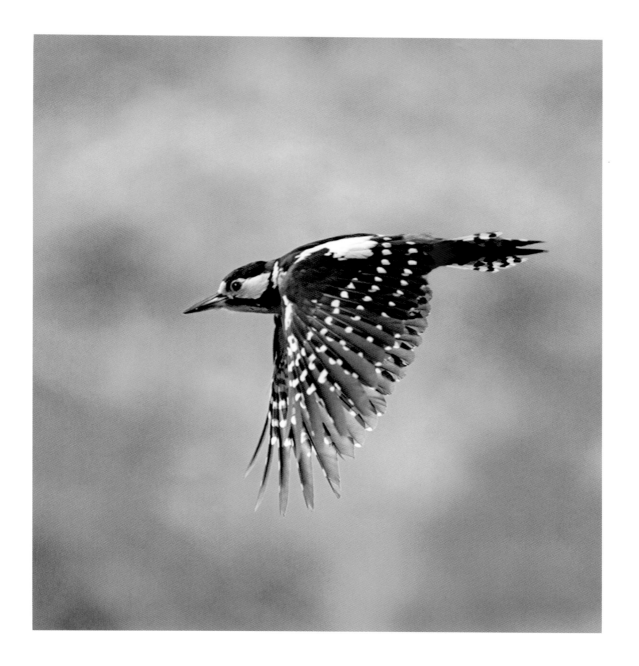

Passerines
Passeriformes

The passerines are a very large grouping of birds, the order *Passeriformes*, consisting of about 140 families and 6,500 species, which accounts for more than half the world's total. The name arises from the scientific name of the Sparrow, *Passer*, and indeed many passerines are small, land-loving and liable to perch and hop. Many of our most familiar birds, including Tits, Finches, Larks, Robins, Starlings and many others are passerines. The passerines are considered to be the most advanced or derived of birds, latest in the fossil record and responsible for much recent radiation into species.

Passerines are anatomically related in various ways, but most importantly in their foot anatomy and in their song-producing apparatus, the syrinx. Put simply, the passerines are good at perching and singing. The arrangement of the foot is known technically as 'anisodactyl': three toes pointing forward and one backwards, meeting at the same level. This enables the birds to perch easily by wrapping their toes around a

branch or other surface. There is also a tendon in the leg that causes it to stiffen when perching, allowing a tight grip even when the bird is asleep.

Passerines also have a particularly well-developed syrinx, located at the base of the windpipe (trachea), where the two bronchi branch into the lungs. This enables these songbirds to produce loud, varied and often tuneful songs. Even the crows, which are the world's biggest passerines, can produce a wide variety of sweet sounds.

Passerines abound in forests and shrubbery, but very few are associated with the sea. One family, the dippers (Cinclidae) is aquatic, feeding within fast-flowing freshwater streams. Others, such as wagtails and pipits, are often found by water and frequently get their feet wet, but on the whole passerines are land-birds. Swallows and Martins constitute one of the few aerial families. Almost all are small-bodied although Hummingbirds, which include the world's smallest birds, are not passerines.

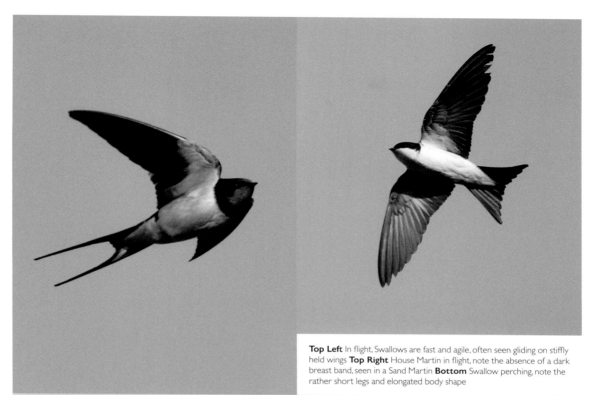

Top Left In flight, Swallows are fast and agile, often seen gliding on stiffly held wings **Top Right** House Martin in flight, note the absence of a dark breast band, seen in a Sand Martin **Bottom** Swallow perching, note the rather short legs and elongated body shape

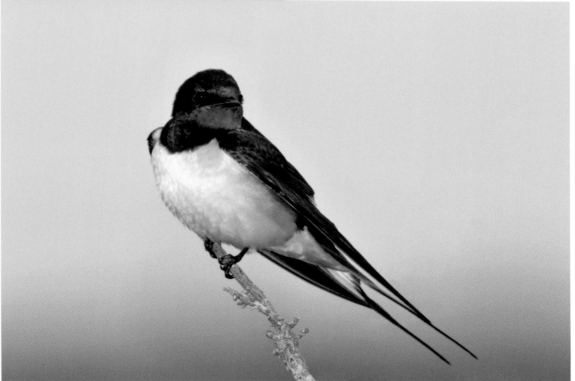

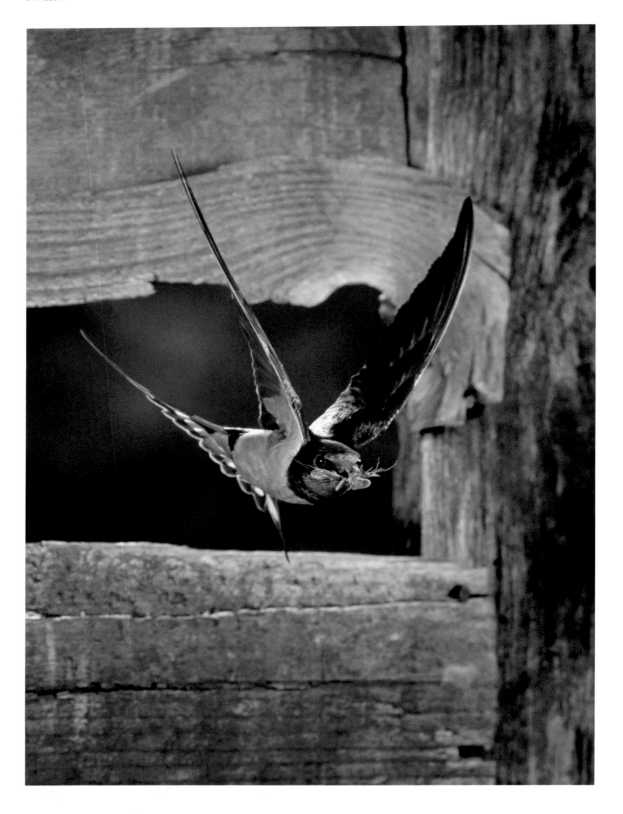

Swallow
Hirundo rustica

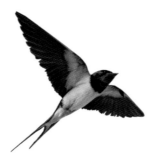

This iconic summer visitor is instantly recognizable by its pointed wings and long tail streamers. The sexes are similar, although the male generally has longer tail streamers than the female. The adult has a blue-black head and upperparts with a metallic sheen when seen in certain lights; the underparts are white, the dark breast forming a clear demarcation. The throat and forecrown are brick-red. The slender bill, legs and feet are black. In flight, and from below, note the dark primary flight feathers and the white subterminal band to the tail, made up of a series of adjacent white spots. The wings are slender and pointed, the tail deeply forked and the long tail streamers are diagnostic. The juvenile resembles the adult but the tail streamers are shorter, the plumage lacks the glossy sheen and the throat is buffish-red.

Swallows are classic summer visitors in rural areas, their arrival traditionally used as a seasonal barometer. It is a fast and agile flyer, often seen gliding on stiffly held wings catching insects on the wing. It collects mud for nest building from puddles and pools. The nest is cup-shaped, lined with feathers and built on top of a ledge or rafter, typically in a stable or rural outbuilding. The adults can often be observed feeding fledglings perched on overhead wires close to nesting sites.

FACTFILE
Length: 17–19cm (6¾–7½in)
Wingspan: 32–35cm (12½–13¾in)
Habitat: favours farmland and open countryside, often seeking farm buildings, stables and other rural buildings in which to nest
Food: feeds on insects and airborne spiders, which it catches on the wing
Status: widespread summer breeding visitor found throughout the region in suitable habitat; present mainly April to September. Overwinters in Africa
Voice: call is a sharp 'vit' uttered in flight. The male produces a warbling song, often delivered while sitting on overhead wires

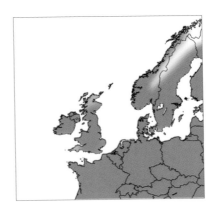

Above In flight, the wing shape and long tail streamers make identification straightforward **Opposite** Catching food on the wing

House Martin

Delichon urbicum

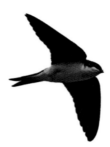

The House Martin is a rather compact and stubby-looking summer visitor, instantly recognizable in flight by its white rump. The sexes are similar. The adult has a dark blue-black head and upperparts, with a strikingly white rump that is most obvious in flight. The underparts, including the chin and breast, are white; seen in flight, the undersides of the wings are grey. The small bill is black, the legs are feathered white and the feet are pink. In flight, note not only the white rump but also the triangular-shaped wings and the short forked tail. The juvenile is similar to the adult but with grubby white underparts and slightly duller plumage overall.

The House Martin's flight is swift and agile, a mixture of lengthy glides on stiffly held wings and bouts of rapid wing-beats. It is a familiar summer visitor that favours towns and rural villages, nesting either singly or in small colonies. It collects mud for nest building from puddles and pools. The nest itself is a half-cup of mud lined with feathers, which it attaches to a vertical surface under the eaves of a house or farm building, or beneath another overhanging feature.

FACTFILE
Length: 13–15cm (5–6in)
Wingspan: 26–29cm (10¼–11½in)
Habitat: associated with areas of housing and farmyards, nesting in the eaves of houses and other buildings. Occasionally nests on cliffs and in cave entrances
Food: feeds on insects and airborne spiders, caught on the wing
Status: widespread summer visitor found throughout the region, present mainly April to September. Overwinters in southern Africa. Numbers have declined in recent years
Voice: call is a distinctive 'prrrt', uttered in flight

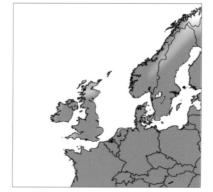

Above Seen from below in flight, note the absence of a dark breast band, seen in Sand Martins **Opposite Top** It takes several days for a House Martin to build its mud nest and repairs and additions are made throughout the breeding season **Opposite Bottom** Gathering mud for its nest

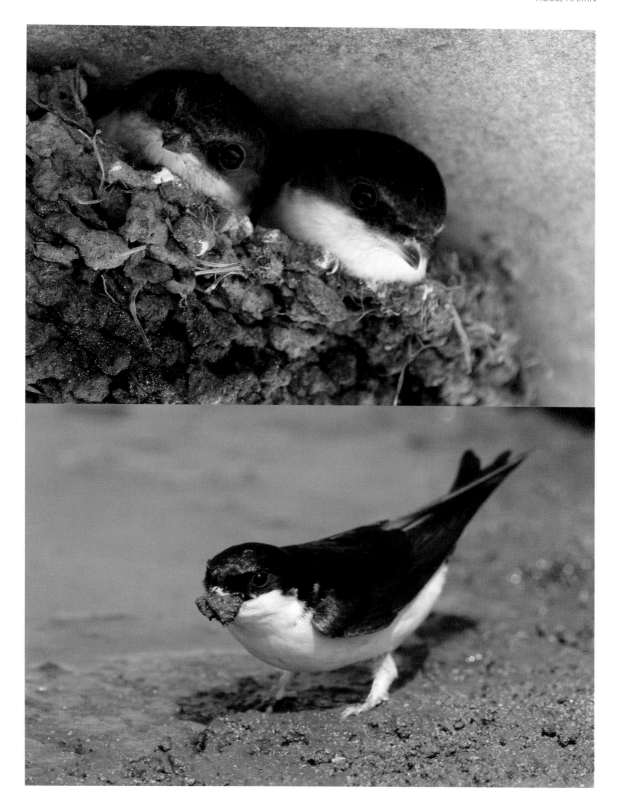

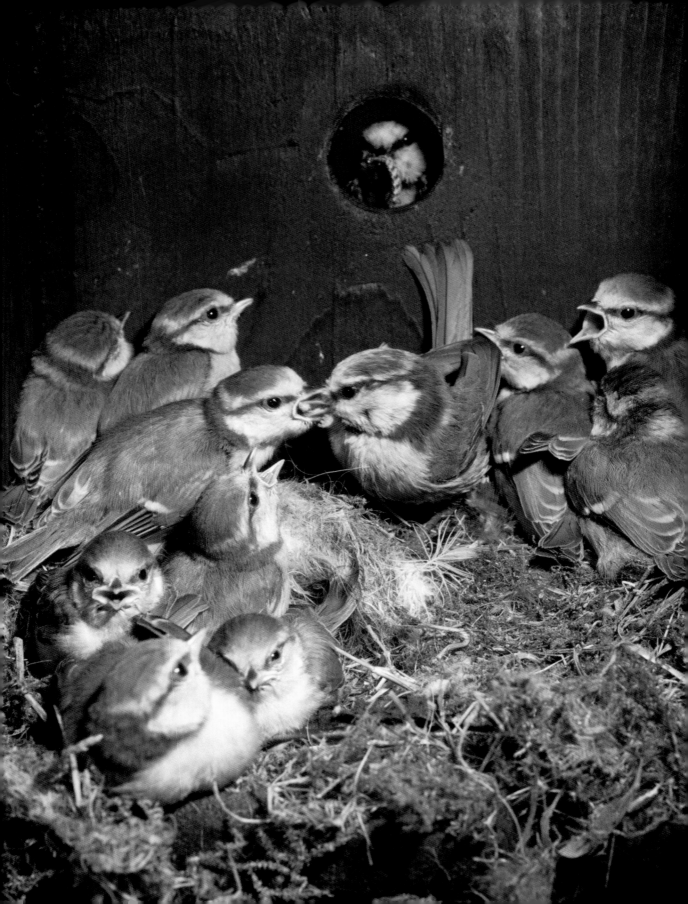

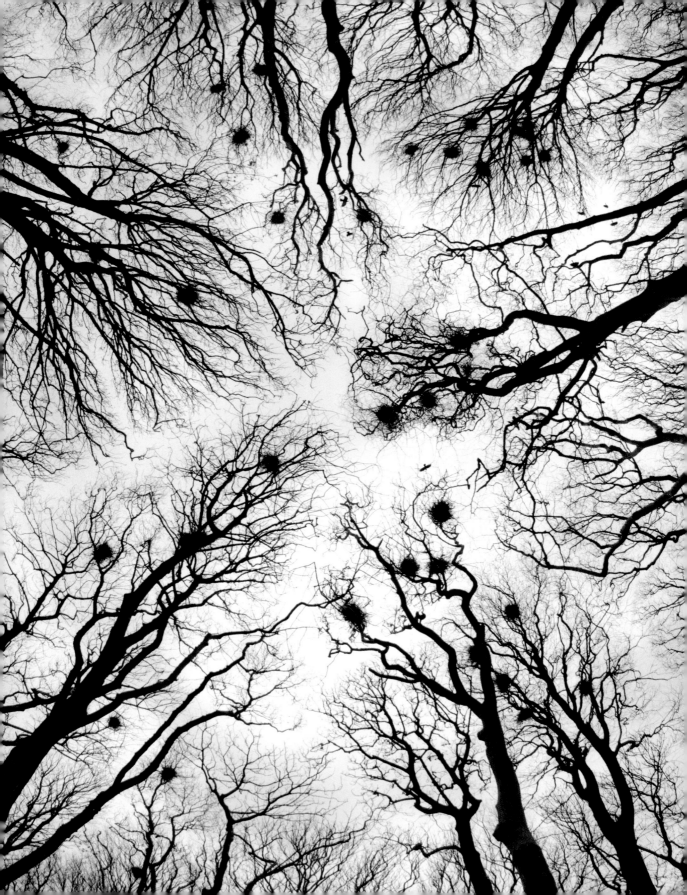

Pied Wagtail/White Wagtail

Motacilla yarrellii/Motacilla alba

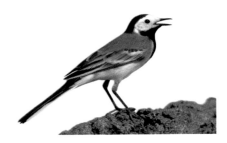

The Pied Wagtail is an attractive little black, grey and white bird with a very long tail. The sexes differ, and some seasonal plumage variation exists. The summer adult male has overall black upperparts and white underparts, with a black throat and breast and a smoky tinge to the flanks. The head is black and marked with a large and contrasting, white facial mask. Note the white wingbars and the white outer tail feathers, most obvious when the bird is in flight. The winter adult male develops a white throat, and the black on the breast is less intense. The adult female is seasonally similar to the adult male, but the upperparts are grey. The juvenile and first-winter are similar to the female but with more subdued markings, a black rump, white barring to the wings and a yellowish flush to the face. The White Wagtail (spp. Alba) is similar to the Pied Wagtail in its seasonal variations, but has a grey (not black) back and rump; the underparts are cleaner white.

This is the most familiar member of the wagtail family, owing to its ability to adapt to human habitation. Its flight is generally undulating and low to the ground. The nest is a cup of grass and twigs, placed in a hole or crevice.

FACTFILE

Length: 17–19cm (6¾–7½in)
Wingspan: 25–30cm (10–12in)
Habitat: generally found on open ground, preferring areas of short grass such as parks, farmland, coastal grassland and car parks
Food: feeds primarily on small invertebrates
Status: widespread and common resident breeding species, present year-round throughout most of the region. Pied wagtail (spp. Yarrellii) is mainly restricted to Britain and Ireland; white wagtail (spp. Alba) occurs in mainland Europe. Northerly populations migrate south for the winter, and some geographical overlap occurs at this time
Voice: the call is a loud 'chissick'

Previous Page Left Young Blue tits clamour to be fed **Right** Rooks build their large twig nests in clumps of tall trees
This Page Above White Wagtail, summer male, spp. Alba breeds occasionally in Britain but is more typically encountered there as a passage migrant along coasts **Opposite Top** White Wagtail, summer male. The black markings on the head contrast markedly with the grey back
Opposite Bottom Pied Wagtail, winter female. Note the flanks that are darker than in spp. Alba

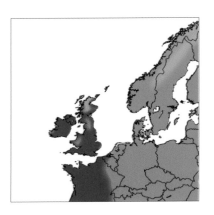

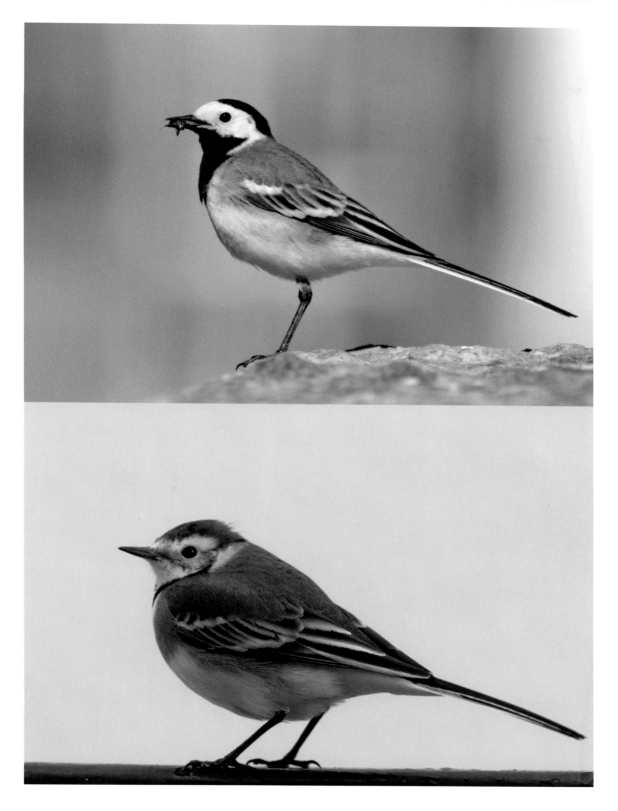

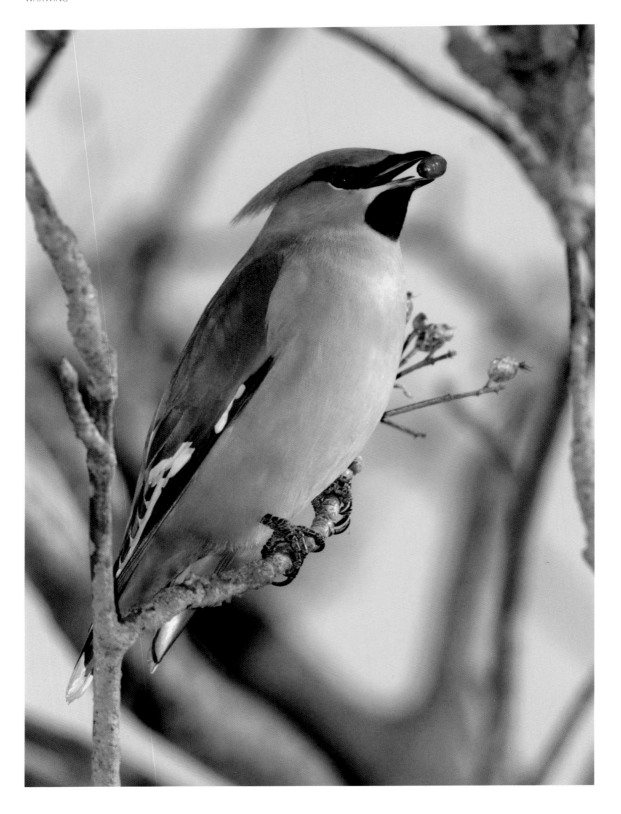

Waxwing
Bombycilla garrulus

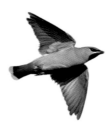

The Waxwing is a colourful songbird, the sexes of which are similar but separable with care. The adult male has primarily pinkish-buff plumage, darkest on the back and nape, and palest on the belly. The rump is light grey and the undertail is chestnut. A number of distinctive and colourful markings adorn the bird, the most distinctive being the obvious long crest feathers. Note the black throat and face mask, and the bright yellow-tipped dark tail. Also note the conspicuous black-and-white barring, yellow markings and red wax-like projections to the wings. The adult female is similar to the adult male but has a narrower yellow tip to the tail. First-winter birds recall the adult but lack the white feather margins and red projections to the wings. In flight, the outline recalls that of a Starling, with rather short triangular-shaped wings.

Revered by many, this colourful species is most commonly seen during the winter months when it migrates in search of winter fruits and berries; numbers vary from year to year. Flocks frequently turn up in urban parks, gardens and even supermarket car parks when natural resources in the countryside become depleted.

FACTFILE
Length: 18–20cm (7–8in)
Wingspan: 32–38cm (12½–15in)
Habitat: favours coniferous pine forests during the summer months. Disperses to other habitats in winter in search of food, and often frequents parks and gardens containing trees and shrubs with plentiful winter berries
Food: feeds primarily on insects during the summer months, fruits and berries during the winter
Status: breeding range extends eastwards from northern Scandinavia. Best known in our region as a migrant winter visitor, present mainly November to March; numbers and range depend on the severity of the weather and food availability. Commonest in winter in eastern mainland Europe, but range extends to eastern Britain
Voice: utters a trilling whistle

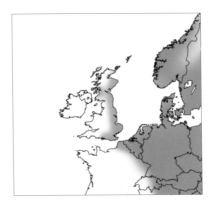

Above Broad, triangular wings give flying birds a distinctive outline
Opposite Berry-laden trees and bushes act like magnets for hungry Waxwings in winter

Chats and Flycatchers
Muscicapidae

Once thought to be the miniature versions of thrushes, this group, which includes such famous birds as robins and nightingales, are now separated into their own family. In common with thrushes, they have large heads and big eyes, which help them forage in shady undergrowth. All species have a similar foraging habit: they perch motionlessly, scanning for invertebrate movements and then fly out to grab what they spot. The robin often searches from the top of a gardener's spade, ready to flit down to the ground to catch what it spots, while the stonechat forages from the top of a gorse bush and the northern wheatear from the top of a boulder. These are not hard-and-fast rules: nightingales also hop along the ground, while common redstarts forage amid foliage. Flycatchers, meanwhile, specialize in catching flying invertebrates in mid-air, which stonechats and others also emulate.

All species feed mainly upon invertebrates, with some, such as robins, taking significant quantities of berries in the autumn. Many British members of this family, though, are summer visitors, retiring to tropical Africa for the winter; these include nightingales, common redstarts, both spotted and pied flycatchers and whinchats.

Their nests are often hidden carefully away. The common redstart and the flycatchers use tree-holes and the robin a depression in a bank, often among vegetation. Black redstarts and northern wheatears use rock crevices, while whinchats and stonechats hide their nests on or close to the ground.

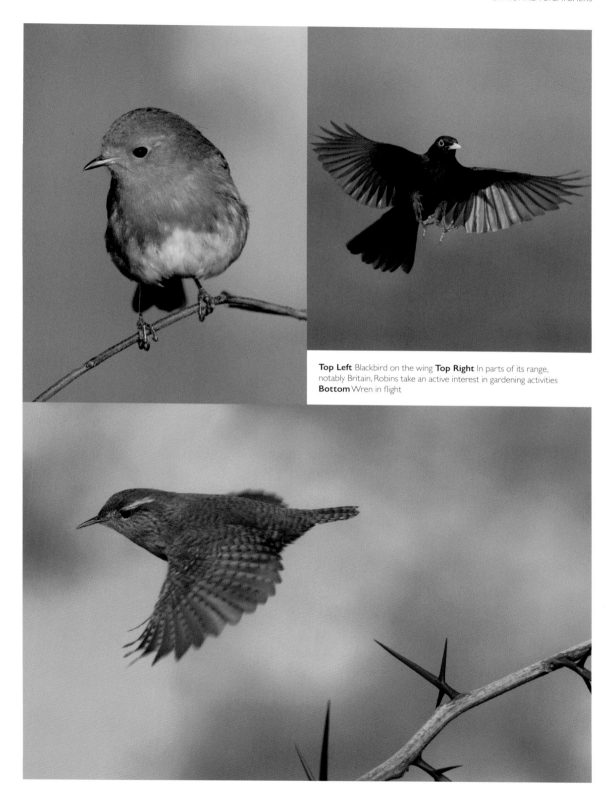

Top Left Blackbird on the wing **Top Right** In parts of its range, notably Britain, Robins take an active interest in gardening activities **Bottom** Wren in flight

Wren

Troglodytes troglodytes

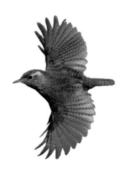

The Wren is a tiny, round-bodied bird with a short tail and dark brown plumage. The sexes are similar. The adult has mainly dark reddish-brown upperparts, the wings and tail displaying subtle barring. The underparts are greyish-white, lightest on the throat and breast and with a buff flush to the flanks. The head is marked with a conspicuous pale supercilium. The long, thin bill is grey-brown and slightly downcurved, and the legs are reddish-brown. The juvenile is similar to the adult. Isolated populations on remote islands to the north of the British Isles are typically darker and more rufous than birds that occur further south.

The Wren is a busy little bird that spends most of its time skulking in low vegetation in search of insects. Typically, it holds its short tail erect when perched in the open. The male constructs a number of dome-shaped nests of grass and leaves to attract the female, one being chosen and the rest discarded. Its numbers suffer badly in severe winters, and birds sometimes roost communally in tight groups during harsh winter nights.

FACTFILE

Length: 9–10cm (3½–4in)
Wingspan: 13–17cm (5–6½in)
Habitat: favours areas of thick undergrowth and can be found in a variety of habitats including woodlands, parks, scrub and coastal cliffs. A familiar garden species
Food: feeds primarily on insects and spiders, occasionally seeds
Status: common and widespread resident breeding species, present year-round in much of the region. Birds in the extreme north and east migrate south for the winter
Voice: a vocal bird whose song is loud and warbling, ending in a trill. Utters a loud rattling call in alarm

Above The Wren in flight, its vibrant song is extraordinarily loud for such a small bird **Opposite** Although the species is common, its numbers crash in particularly cold winters and it can take several seasons for the population to recover

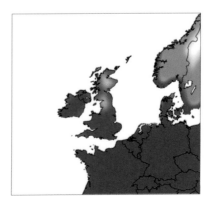

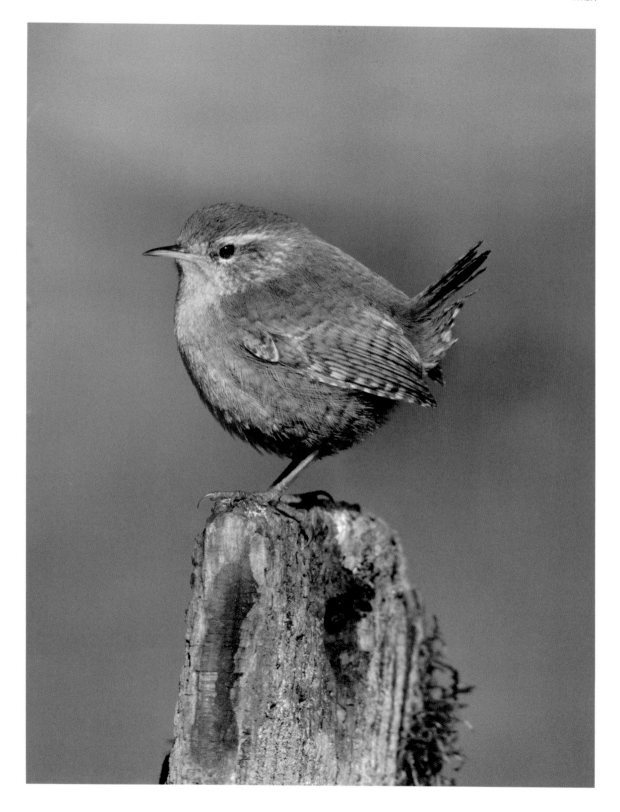

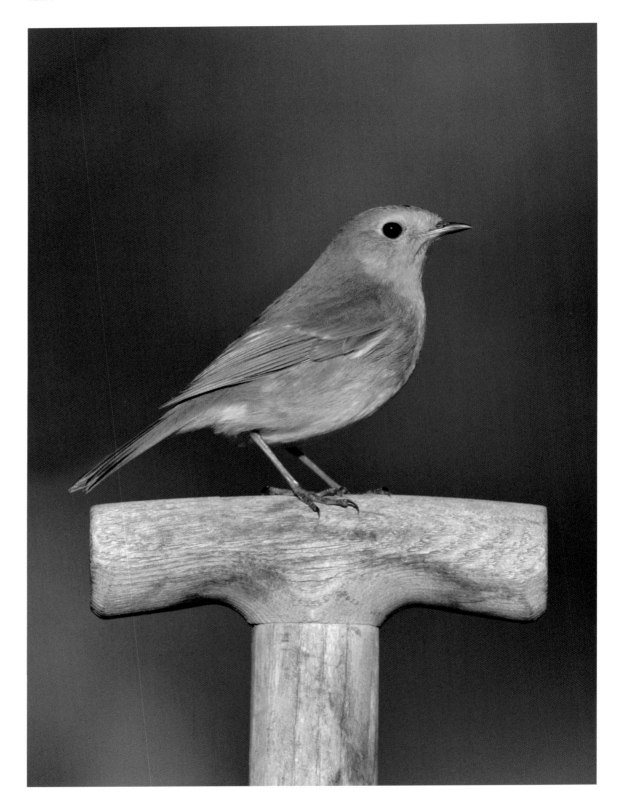

Robin
Erithacus rubecula

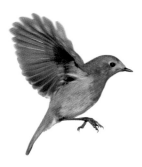

The Robin is instantly recognizable and one of the region's best-loved birds; in Britain in particular it is a familiar and surprisingly tame garden regular. The sexes are similar. The adult has a rotund body with reddish-brown upperparts and a faint buff wingbar. The face, throat and breast are conspicuously bright orange-red, separated from the upperparts by a subtle band of blue-grey. The remaining underparts are pale buff and clearly separated from the brightly coloured breast. The eyes and small bill are dark, and the legs are dark brown. The juvenile lacks the bright orange-red colour of the adult, having brown upperparts marked with a series of pale buff spots and teardrop-shaped streaks. The underparts are pale buff with darker spots and crescent-shaped markings.

The Robin is a perky little bird that likes the damp and shady areas of woodland and garden habitats. It can be particularly bold, especially in the winter months, becoming very tolerant of people and even hand-tame at times. It is a highly territorial species, particularly in the spring, fighting off intruders and rivals aggressively. It constructs a cup-shaped nest of grass, moss and leaves in a suitable hollow or crevice.

FACTFILE

Length: 13–14cm (5–5½in)
Wingspan: 20–22cm (8–8¾in)
Habitat: favours deciduous and mixed woodland, parks and gardens in rural and suburban areas
Food: feeds on a variety of invertebrates, larvae, fruits and seeds
Status: common and widespread resident breeding species, present year-round throughout most of the region. Birds breeding in the extreme north and east migrate to more temperate areas of the region for the winter months
Voice: song comprises a rather melancholy series of whistles and warbles, delivered by both sexes during the winter. Utters a sharp 'tic' in alarm

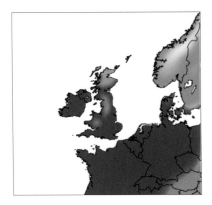

Above Sometimes hovers if it spots a potential meal, such as an insect moving on the foliage of a bush **Opposite** Often uses perches to scan the ground for the movement of an unsuspecting invertebrate

Thrushes
Turdidae

There are six species of 'typical thrush' in Britain. The robins and chats used to be considered to be thrushes but are now part of the flycatcher family. Thrushes are medium-sized birds with strong legs, which they use for feeding on the ground, usually making a series of short runs followed by pauses during which they watch and listen for prey. Thrushes have comparatively large eyes so they have good vision in poor light, allowing them, when necessary, to feed in deep shade. This, perhaps, also enables them to sing very early in the dawn chorus, as well as late at night. Our breeding thrushes have loud, extremely varied and often very beautiful songs, which dominate the atmosphere of the garden right through from mid-winter to the height of spring.

The blackbird is our commonest and most widespread thrush, a staple of gardens, parks and woodlands. Not far behind are the two spotted thrushes: the mistle and song thrushes. The Song Thrush (see page 95) typically forages over small lawns and within woods, while the Mistle Thrush (see page 96) usually forages far out at the centre of large fields and open areas. Thrushes are omnivores, eating all kinds of invertebrates including, in the song thrush's case, snails, but in the autumn they revert to a diet dominated by berries.

Three other species are visitors to Britain. The ring ouzel is a close relative of the blackbird, but nests at higher elevations, usually above 300m (984 feet), often in quite treeless terrain. In the autumn, large flocks of redwings (see page 92) and fieldfares (see page 91) – along with continental populations of blackbirds and song thrushes – arrive from the Scandinavian peninsula to stay for the winter.

All thrushes build large, open-cupped nests, typically with a mud lining. They lay three to five eggs, often blue in colour. Blackbirds will sometimes bring up two or even three broods.

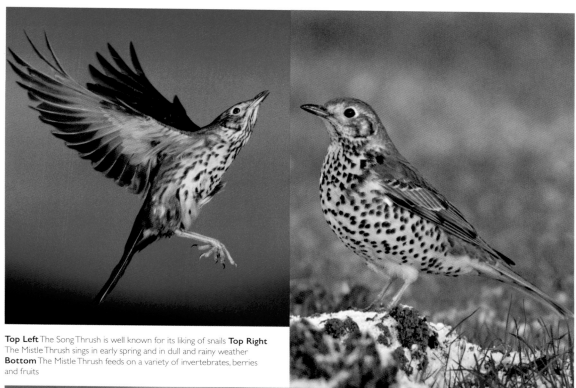

Top Left The Song Thrush is well known for its liking of snails **Top Right** The Mistle Thrush sings in early spring and in dull and rainy weather **Bottom** The Mistle Thrush feeds on a variety of invertebrates, berries and fruits

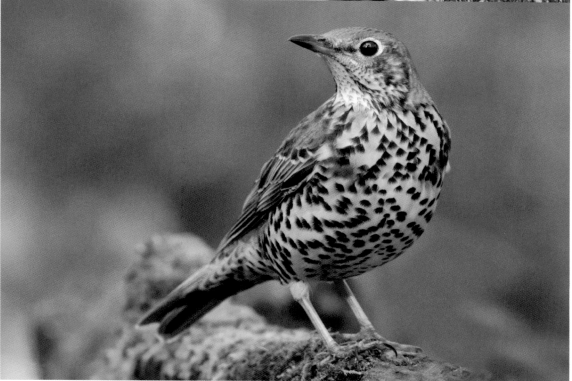

Blackbird
Turdus merula

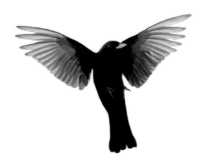

The Blackbird is a common ground-dwelling thrush and a familiar garden visitor. The sexes differ. The adult male has uniformly black plumage with a subtle glossy sheen when seen in good light. Note the bright yellow bill and the yellow eye-ring surrounding the dark eye. The legs are dark. The first-winter male is similar but has a dark bill and a less well-defined eye-ring. Adult and first-winter females have dark brown upperparts and tail; the underparts are paler with a reddish suffusion, subtly spotted and marked with streaking on the breast. The bill is dark, but marked with yellow at the base of the lower mandible. The juvenile resembles the female but with pale yellow spots adorning the back and underparts.

The Blackbird is an abundant and relatively easy species to observe, particularly in urban environments, where it becomes quite tolerant of human presence. It is a regular garden visitor. Its nest is a robust cup of mud, grass and leaves, generally located in a dense shrub or hedgerow.

FACTFILE
Length: 25–28cm (10–11in)
Wingspan: 34–39cm (13¼–15¼in)
Habitat: wide range of habitats including woodlands, farmland, scrub, heaths and coasts. A regular garden visitor in both rural and urban areas
Food: feeds on a variety of insects, worms and other invertebrates; also fruits and berries
Status: widespread resident breeder, present year-round throughout most of the region. Breeding populations from the extreme north and east migrate to the more temperate zones in the south and west, swelling populations in these areas in winter
Voice: male is a consummate songster, having a varied repertoire of fluty and musical phrases. Utters a harsh, repetitive 'tchak' at dusk or in alarm

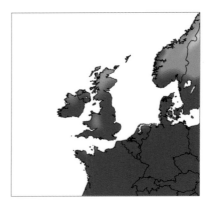

Above Male taking flight **Opposite Top** Blackbird males are conspicuous in the garden, feeding on lawns and alarm-calling loudly if danger threatens **Opposite Bottom** Female blackbird perches, in search of worms and other invertebrates

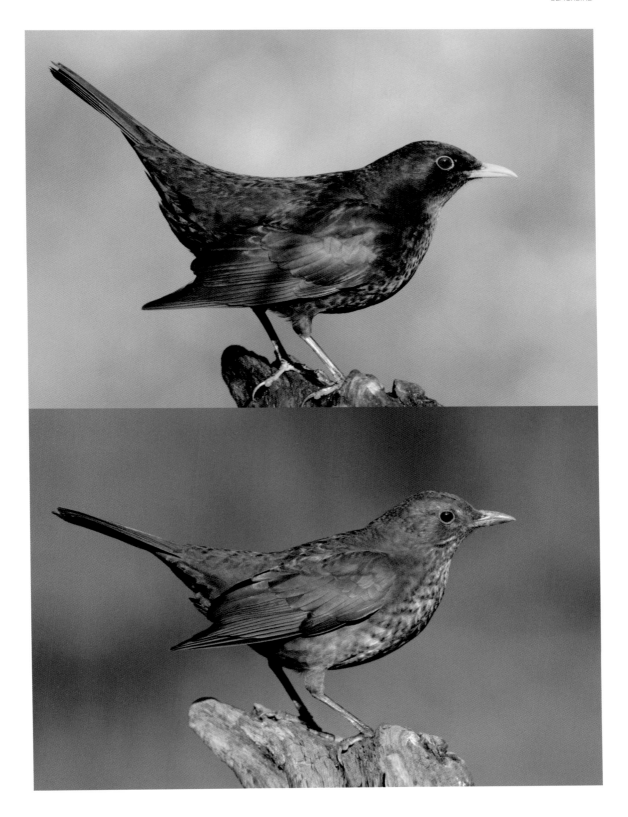

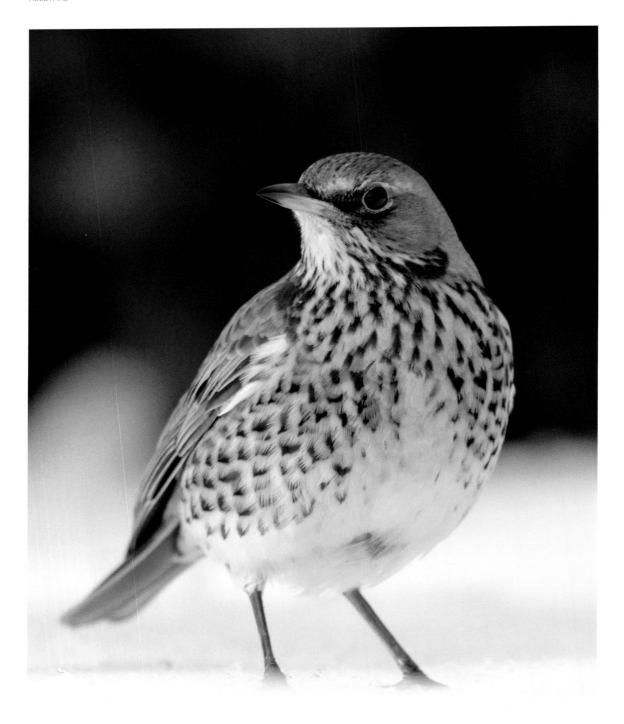

Fieldfare

Turdus pilari

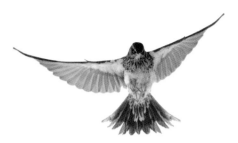

The Fieldfare is a large, colourful thrush that forms sizeable flocks during the winter months. The sexes are similar. The adult has a chestnut-brown back and a grey rump. The tail is black and the head is blue-grey and marked with a pale supercilium and dark lores. The underparts are flushed with orange yellow, grading to whitish on the belly and adorned with conspicuous dark spots on the breast and flanks. The bill is yellow with a variable amount of brown at the tip, and breeding males may develop an all-yellow bill. In flight, the grey rump and white underwings are diagnostic. The juvenile is similar to the adult but with noticeable pale spots on the wing coverts.

The Fieldfare is a common breeding species in central Europe and Scandinavia. Birds from the north migrate south and west in autumn; winter numbers and range depend on weather severity and the availability of food. They form large flocks that feed on fruit and berry crops in hedgerows and trees. The nest is a robust mud-lined cup of grass and leaves.

FACTFILE

Length: 24–26cm (9½–10¼in)
Wingspan: 39–42cm (15¼–16½in)
Habitat: favours open woodland and adjacent farmland, parks and gardens
Food: feeds on a variety of insects, worms and other invertebrates; also fruits and berries
Status: resident breeding species throughout much of northern Europe. Birds from the north and east migrate south and west during the winter months. Primarily a winter visitor to the British isles and western France, mainly from October to March
Voice: the fluty musical song is generally delivered in short bursts. Call is a harsh 'chackchack-chack', sometimes uttered at night when on migration

Above The white underwing is a character shared with the Mistle Thrush, but the colourful plumage allows easy separation **Opposite** A covering of snow makes feeding difficult and birds often seek out disturbed or sheltered areas where they can forage on bare ground or leaf litter

Redwing

Turdus iliacus

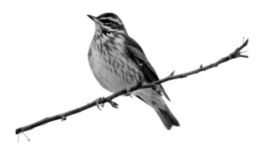

The Redwing is a small, well-marked thrush that is particularly vulnerable to harsh weather. The sexes are similar. The adult has mainly grey-brown upperparts. The underparts are pale with a conspicuous orange-red flush to the flanks and underwing, and are neatly marked with numerous bold dark spots. The head has bold facial markings that include a conspicuous pale supercilium, dark eye stripe and pale patch below the cheek. The bill is blackish-brown with a yellow base, and legs are yellowish-brown. The juvenile is similar to the adult, but with more subdued colouration on the flanks and pale spotting on the upperparts.

The Redwing is best known in the region as a winter visitor; it forms large nomadic flocks at this time, often mixed with Fieldfares. It feeds largely on berries and fallen fruits and is vulnerable to harsh weather; mortality rates can be high during severe winters. The nest is a mudlined cup of grass and moss.

FACTFILE

Length: 20–22cm (8–8¾in)

Wingspan: 33–35cm (13–14in)

Habitat: favours open countryside, open woodland, farmland, parks and mature gardens

Food: feeds on insects, worms and other invertebrates; fruits and berries in the autumn and winter months

Status: common and widespread winter visitor across much of the region, mainly October to March. Breeds in Iceland, Scandinavia and further north and east

Voice: song comprises whistling and fluty phrases delivered in short bursts. Call is a high-pitched 'tseep', commonly uttered from migrating birds in flight

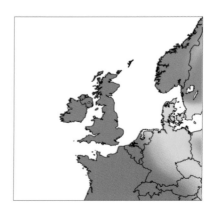

Above The bold patterns on the head and colourful orange-red flanks make identification easy **Opposite** Berry-laden Hawthorn bushes are a magnet for nomadic Redwing flocks in autumn and early winter; typically a bush will be stripped bare within a day or so, forcing the flock to move on in search of alternative food

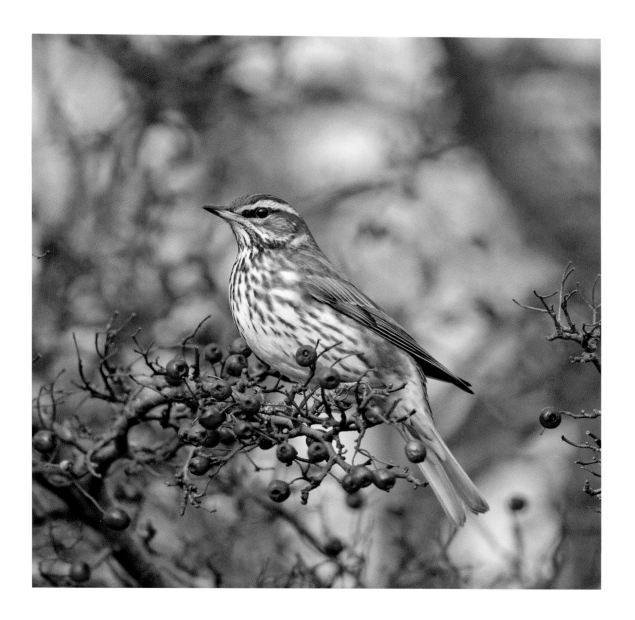

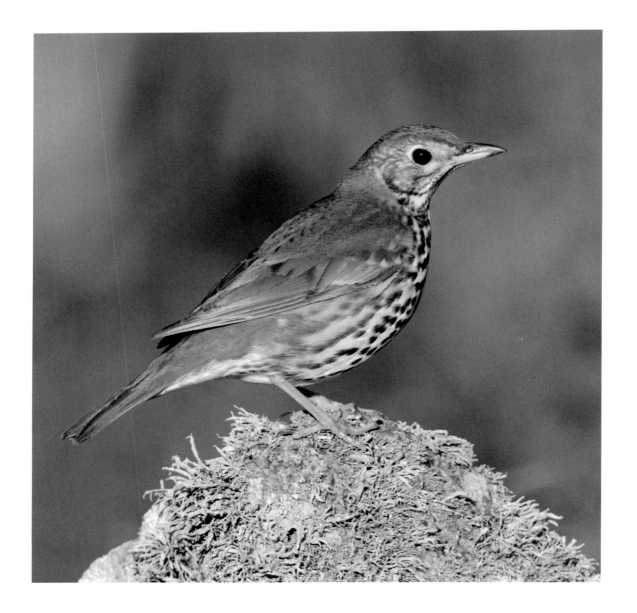

Song Thrush

Turdus philomelos

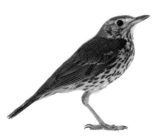

The Song Thrush is a familiar and handsomely marked songbird best known for its beautiful song. The sexes are similar. The adult has primarily warm brown upperparts, the wing showing a faint orange-buff bar. The head is subtly marked with a pale eye-ring, pale throat and thin, dark moustachial stripe. The underparts are pale with a yellowish-buff tinge to the breast, and are marked with a series of bold, dark arrowhead-shaped spots (unlike the rounded spots in the similar Mistle Thrush). The bill is dark and the legs are flesh-coloured. In flight, note the obvious and diagnostic orange-buff underwing coverts. The juvenile is similar but the markings and colouration lack the definition of the adult.

The Song Thrush is a familiar garden visitor, well known for its liking of snails. It often uses favoured rocks and stones as 'anvils' on which to smash the shells, holding the shell in its beak and delivering a swift hammering blow. It constructs a cup-shaped nest of grass, lined with mud or wood pulp.

FACTFILE

Length: 20–23cm (8–9in)

Wingspan: 33–36cm (13–14in)

Habitat: favours habitats offering a mixture of open ground and dense vegetation, trees and shrubs, such as woodland, parks and mature gardens

Food: feeds on insects, snails, worms and other invertebrates; fruits and berries in the autumn and winter months

Status: common and widespread resident breeding species, present year-round throughout much of the region. Northern and eastern breeding birds migrate south for the winter, the geographical range and numbers dependent upon the severity of the winter

Voice: a renowned songster, with a loud and musical song of short phrases each of which is repeated three or more times. Call is a thin 'tik', most commonly delivered in flight

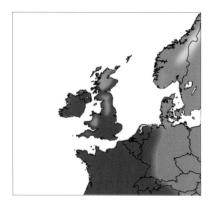

Above Compared to a Mistle Thrush, a Song Thrush is a smaller and altogether more dainty bird **Opposite** The underwing coverts are buffish-orange while those of a Mistle Thrush are white

Mistle Thrush

Turdus viscivorus

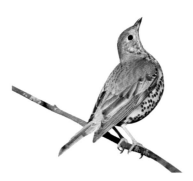

Superficially similar to Song Thrush, the Mistle Thrush is appreciably larger with a plumper appearance. The sexes are similar. The adult has primarily grey-brown upperparts with a subtle white wingbar. The underparts are pale, flushed with orange-buff on the flanks and heavily marked with rounded bold black spots (arrowhead-shaped in Song Thrush). The bill is blackish-brown and the legs are yellowish-brown. In flight, note the diagnostic white underwings and white tips to the outer tail feathers. The juvenile is similar to the adult, but the back and head are marked with white spots.

A Mistle Thrush's flight is powerful and direct, with a series of rapid wing-beats followed by a brief closing of the wings. It habitually sings in early spring and in dull and rainy weather. The resident population is boosted during the winter months by birds that have migrated from further north and east. Its nest is a large cup of vegetation, typically constructed in the fork of a tree or similar visible location.

FACTFILE

Length: 27–29cm (10½–11½in)

Wingspan: 42–48cm (16½–18¾n)

Habitat: favours open woodland, parks, orchards and mature gardens

Food: feeds on a variety of invertebrates, berries and fruits

Status: resident breeding species found year-round in the west of the region. Northern and eastern populations migrate south for the winter months

Voice: song comprises loud and fluty notes, delivered in short phrases and long pauses. Utters a loud rattling call in alarm

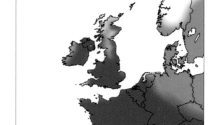

Above The Mistle Thrush habitually sings in early spring **Opposite** The body looks stocky and plump, and the spots on the underparts are bold and distinct

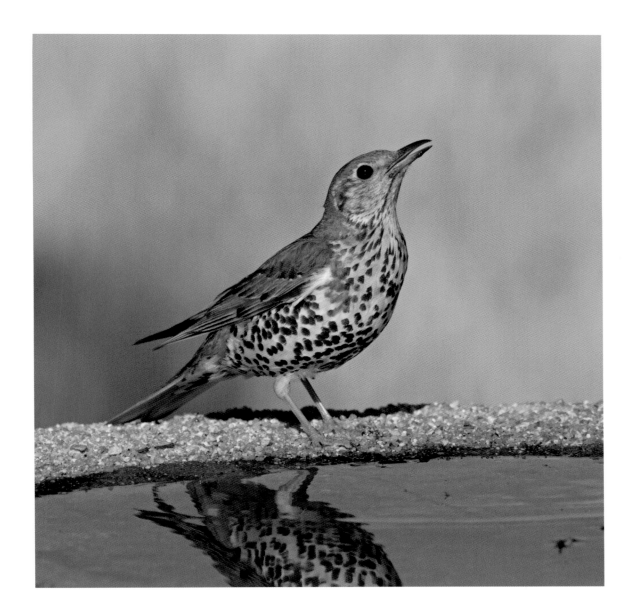

Warblers

Sylviidae, Cettiidae, Phylloscopidae, Acrocephalidae and Locustellidae

The warblers are a group of small, restless and soberly coloured insectivores that largely feature in the British spring and summer, when their many loud and persistent songs fill the airwaves of every habitat from woods to marshes. They do, however, generally avoid busy human environments, so are not as well-known as many other small birds. Almost all are long-distance migrants, wintering in the Mediterranean or crossing the Sahara to Africa.

Warblers were once all lumped into a single family, Sylviidae, but recent research has blown apart the notion that all warblers are related, and the thirteen or fourteen breeding species are now split into five different families. However, many birdwatchers aren't used to these distinctions yet and treat the warblers as a communal entity, as they are here.

The warblers are famously difficult to see and, often, to identify. There are two reasons for this. Many feed in a way that requires delving into the depths of vegetation where insects lurk, meaning that warblers skulk away unseen. In addition to this, most are plainly coloured to fit in with their habitats, with the leaf warblers, including the Chiffchaff, Willow Warbler and Wood Warbler, flitting around among leaves, and the wetland-loving warblers feeding in dense waterside vegetation. The loudmouthed Cetti's Warbler is a particularly awkward species to see. Warblers are also, with a few exceptions, good at hiding their nests.

The Cetti's Warbler is our only warbler in the family Cettidae. One of only two truly resident warblers in the UK (the other is the Dartford Warbler), the Cetti's is a relatively new arrival in Britain, recorded breeding for the first time in 1972. It is mainly found in wetlands, where its loud, almost nightingale-like bursts of song torment birdwatchers. It is frequently polygamous and the male is larger and heavier than the female.

The leaf warblers, in the family Phylloscopidae, are all woodland birds, singing up in the trees but nesting on or close to the ground. In contrast to most warblers their nests are domed. All are migrants, but the Chiffchaff can be seen in Britain all year round; the breeding population almost entirely evacuates the country in winter, but some individuals, perhaps from northern Europe, arrive for the winter.

The Reed and Sedge Warblers are members of the Acrocephalidae family; a third species, the Marsh Warbler, is a very rare nester, not here every year. The two more common birds are wetland species, the Reed Warbler confined to reedbeds but the Sedge Warbler more typical of scrub habitat within or next to wetlands. Both forage deep in vegetation. The Reed Warbler, with its open cup nest built over water, is a favourite host of Cuckoos. Both warblers have very continuous, chirpy, harsh songs.

Two secretive species, with sober plumage, long rounded tails and strong legs, belong to the Locustellidae family. Both have insect-like, persistent songs, the Grasshopper Warbler sounding like a freewheeling bicycle and the rare Savi's Warbler like a mechanical drill. Both are highly secretive transcontinental migrants that winter in Africa.

The warblers of the family Sylviidae are no longer considered to be warblers at all, but are related to a large Asian group called the babblers. The babbling nature of their songs is appropriate enough, although the Blackcap has a powerful, often tuneful song that is much appreciated, especially as this species is an early migrant, arriving in late March. Some continental Blackcaps, mainly from Germany, come here to spend the winter, often appearing in gardens. The other species are all scrub or woodland edge species, the Dartford Warbler being confined to heathland. The Whitethroats are curious for their differing migratory habits: common whitethroats migrate south-west for winter, to cross the Mediterranean from Spain, while lesser whitethroats migrate south-east via Italy or Greece and spend the winter further east in Africa.

All warblers are essentially insectivorous throughout the year, but a major component of their diet in autumn and winter is fruit, in the form of berries. In the autumn, warblers are easy to see coming to blackthorn and other shrubs. These berries help them to put on fat for their migratory journeys. The Sedge Warbler, on the other hand, seems to rely entirely on the flesh of aphids to give it the energy for a possibly single-stage migration all the way to West Africa.

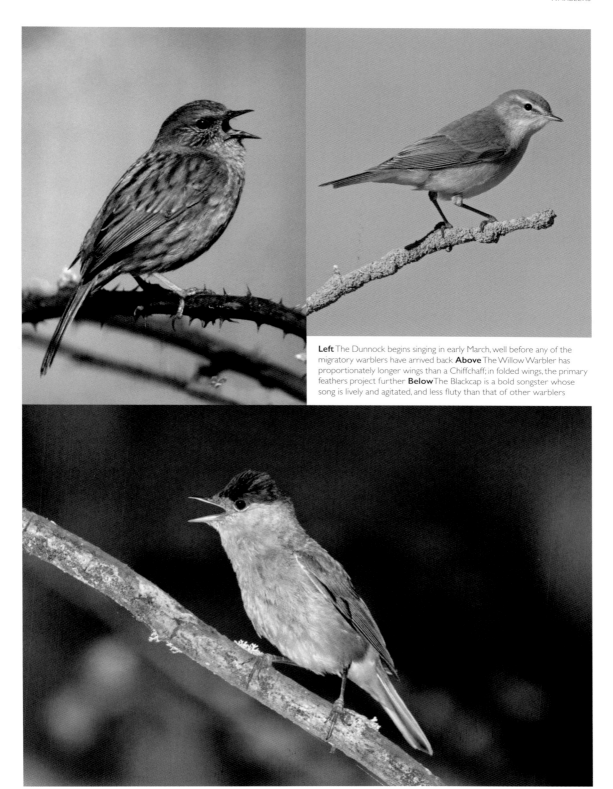

Left The Dunnock begins singing in early March, well before any of the migratory warblers have arrived back **Above** The Willow Warbler has proportionately longer wings than a Chiffchaff; in folded wings, the primary feathers project further **Below** The Blackcap is a bold songster whose song is lively and agitated, and less fluty than that of other warblers

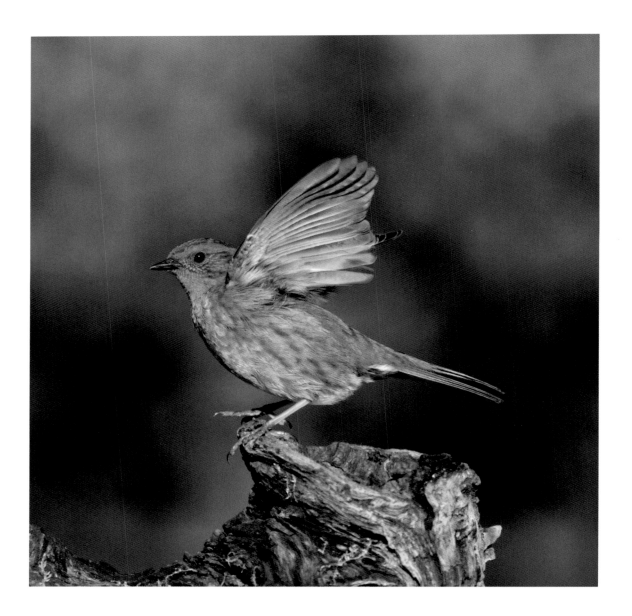

Dunnock

Prunella modularis

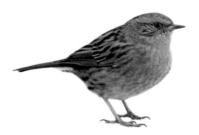

The Dunnock is a common sparrow-like bird with a plump body. The sexes are similar. Although really an accentor, thus not strictly a warbler, the Dunnock shares similarities with this group, both for the shape of its bill and the lively song it utters. The adult has chestnut-brown upperparts with a pattern of darker streaking; note the faint pale wingbar. The underparts are primarily bluish-grey, the flanks displaying bold brown and chestnut streaks. The head is marked with bluish-grey on the face and throat; the crown and ear coverts are streaked with brown. The warbler-like bill is slender and dark, and the legs are reddish-pink. The juvenile is similar to the adult, but is more boldly streaked.

The Dunnock is a rather furtive bird that tends to spend most of its time skulking in deep cover, and is mainly seen on, or close to, the ground. During the breeding season males become much bolder and highly territorial, often singing from a conspicuous perch in the top of a bush or bramble patch. Their courtship and reproductive behaviour is surprisingly complex, with both sexes often engaging with multiple partners. The nest is a sturdy cup of woven plant material in a low bush or hedge.

FACTFILE
Length: 13–14cm (5–5½in)
Wingspan: 19–21cm (7½–8¼in)
Habitat: favours woodlands, hedgerows, scrub and mature gardens
Food: feeds on invertebrates and seeds
Status: common and widespread resident breeding species, present year-round and found in suitable habitat across most of the region. Birds in the extreme north migrate south during the winter months
Voice: utters a lively warbler-like song, delivered in short bursts. Call is a rather weak 'tseer'

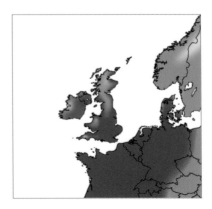

Above Often feeds on the ground, usually beneath a bush or on the edge of cover into which it retreats at the first sign of disturbance **Opposite** In March and April, territorial birds abandon their normally shy and retiring habits and become bold

Whitethroat
Sylvia communis

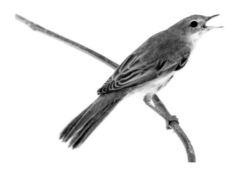

The Whitethroat is the most widespread Sylvia warbler in the region, and commonly seen perched in the open, allowing easy observation. The sexes are similar but separable with care. The adult male has grey-brown upperparts with conspicuous reddish-brown edges to the wing feathers; the head has a blue-grey cap and face, with a bold white eye-ring. The underparts are pale with a pinkish-buff flush, most obvious on the breast. Note the striking white throat and the white outer tail feathers. The slender bill is sandy-brown and dark-tipped, and the legs are pale pinkish-brown. The adult female is similar to the male but the cap and face are tinged with brown, while the underparts are flushed with pale buff. The juvenile recalls the adult female.

The Whitethroat is one of the easiest warblers to observe owing to its bold nature and habit of perching out in the open, often on the highest point of a scrub patch. Its song is characteristic. The male initiates the construction of several nests, the female choosing one and completing the work. The nest is a grass cup in low-lying scrub.

FACTFILE

Length: 13–15cm (6–6in)
Wingspan: 19–23cm (7½–9in)
Habitat: favours open habitats with areas of low scrub cover such as hedgerows, heathland, farmland and coastal grassland
Food: feeds primarily on insects; also fruits and berries
Status: common and widespread summer breeding visitor found in suitable habitats throughout most of the region; present mainly April to August. Overwinters in Africa
Voice: the song is a characteristic rapid coarse warble, often delivered when in flight or perched in the open. Call is a harsh 'check' issued in alarm

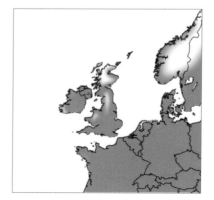

Above Territorial males are very vocal and often deliver their song in flight, particularly at the start of the breeding season **Opposite** Whitethroats keep to cover for much of the time but once in a while a bird will pop up and perch on a prominent twig

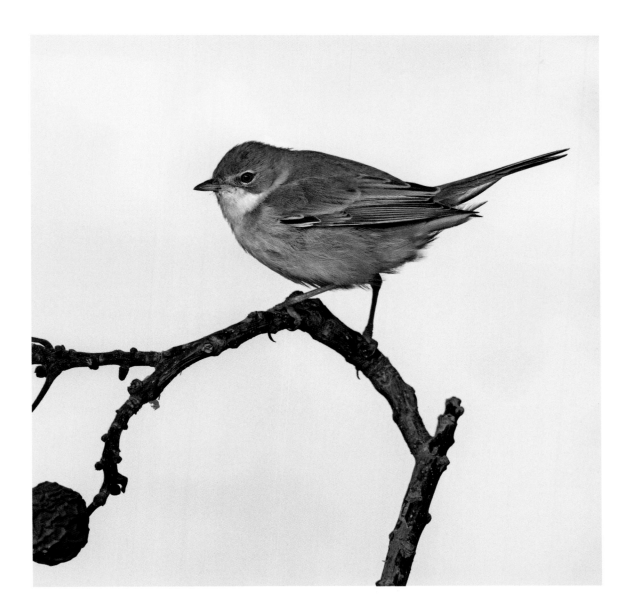

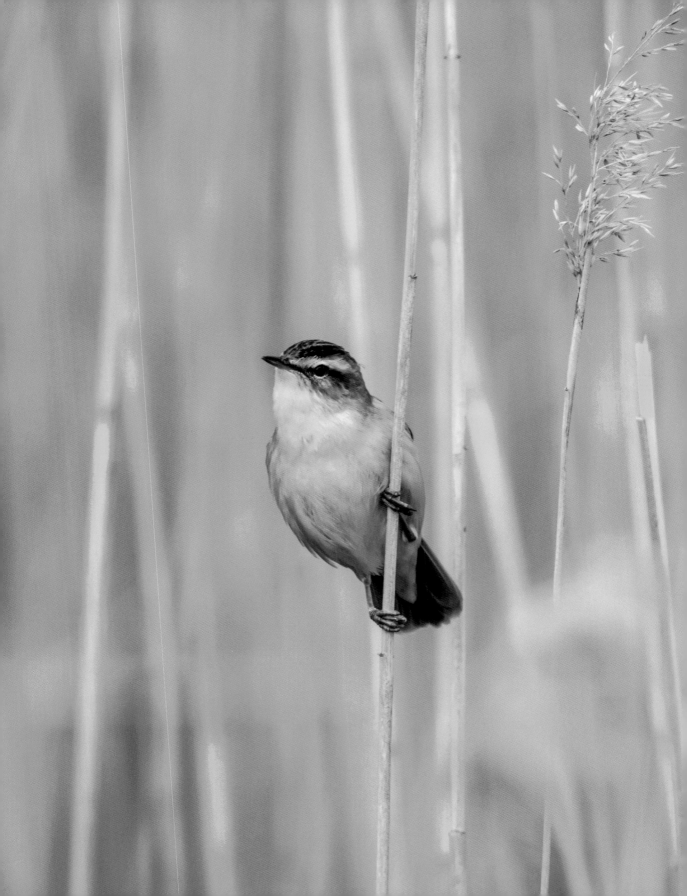

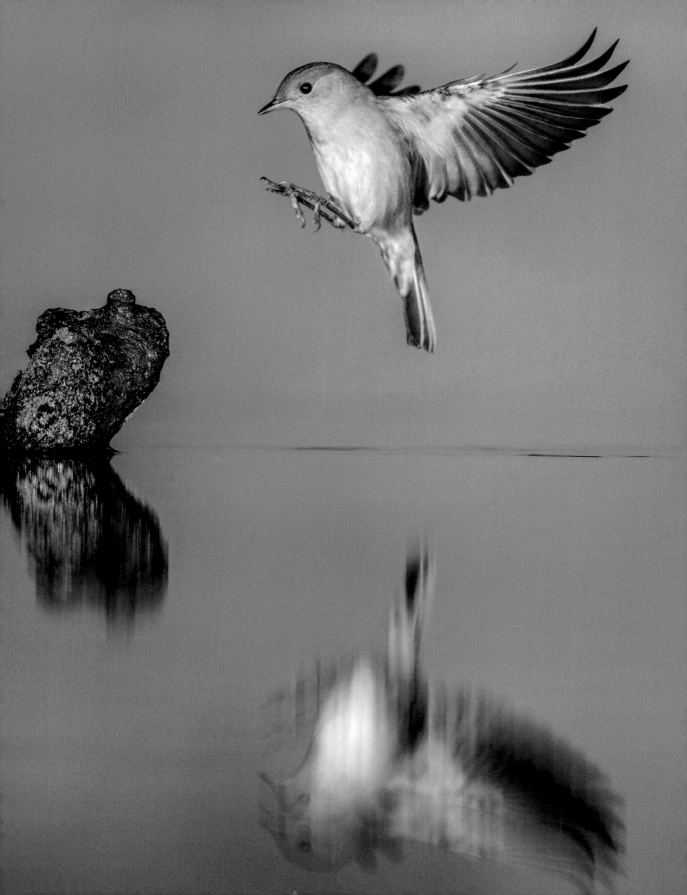

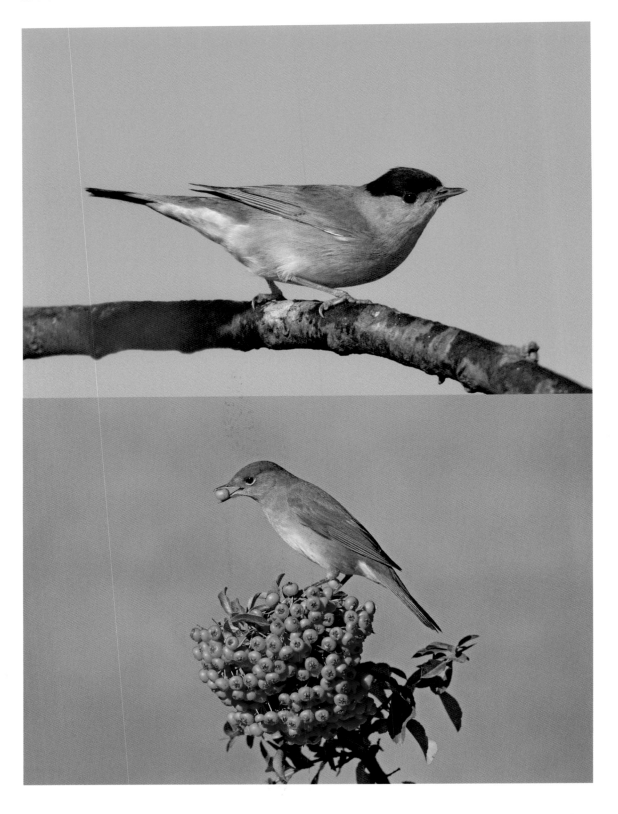

Blackcap
Sylvia atricapilla

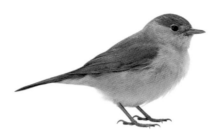

The Blackcap is a distinctive and handsome warbler with a beautiful melodic song. The sexes are separable. The adult male has primarily grey-brown upperparts with a lighter grey face and nape. The underparts are light silvery-grey, palest on the throat and undertail. The head is adorned with a bold and obvious black cap, and a subtle pale ring surrounds the eye. The bill is dull black and the legs are grey. The adult female is similar but has a richer brown flush to the upperparts, and the cap is reddish-chestnut. The juvenile resembles the adult female.

The Blackcap is a relatively common and widespread species, and an occasional garden visitor that can often be observed singing from an exposed perch. It seeks wooded areas with plenty of low undergrowth in which to nest, constructing a thin cup of vegetation within a metre or two of the ground.

FACTFILE

Length: 14–15cm (5½–6in)
Wingspan: 20–23cm (8–9in)
Habitat: favours a range of habitats including deciduous woodland with an understorey of dense scrub, mature gardens, parks, hedgerows and scrub
Food: feeds on insects and berries
Status: common and widespread summer breeding species, present mainly April to September. Most migrate to Africa in autumn, but southwestern parts of our region host an increasing number of overwintering birds
Voice: song is a delightful, rich musical warble, similar to that of garden warbler but lacking the thrush-like tones. Utters a 'tchek' call in alarm

Previous Page Left Closely related to the Willow Warbler, the Sedge Warbler favours a wide range of habitat, including heathland **Previous Page Right** The female Blackcap has a reddish-chestnut cap and a richer brown flush to the upperparts than the male **Above** The female has a reddish-chestnut cap **Opposite Top** The male's black cap is diagnostic among warblers in our region **Opposite Bottom** Overwintering birds in particular will often feed on garden berries, and visit bird feeders

Chiffchaff

Phylloscopus collybita

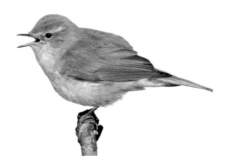

FACTFILE

The Chiffchaff is a small warbler with a distinctive song. The sexes are similar. The adult has a mainly grey-brown head and upperparts. The underparts are pale greyish and flushed with yellow-buff, particularly obvious on the throat and breast. The head is marked with a subtle pale yellow supercilium. The bill is slender. Note the comparatively short primary projection of the wings when at rest, and the dark legs, which allow separation from the similar Willow Warbler. The juvenile is similar to the adult.

Outside its resident range, the Chiffchaff is one of the first migrants to appear in the spring. A busy feeder, it is constantly on the move, foraging in the tree branches for invertebrates. During the breeding season, displaying birds can often be observed perched on branches and fluttering their wings rapidly. It nests in dense cover close to the ground, constructing a feather-lined grass dome.

Length: 10–11cm (4–4¼in)
Wingspan: 15–21cm (6–8¼in)
Habitat: favours mature deciduous woodland with a dense understorey of shrubs
Food: feeds primarily on insects
Status: widespread breeding species, commonest from April to September. Most birds migrate to southern Europe for winter, but the species is present year-round in small numbers in the southwest of our region
Voice: utters a distinctive and repetitive 'chiff-chaff' song that affords the species its English name. Heard most frequently during the spring but can be uttered throughout the summer and autumn months. Call is a soft 'huitt'

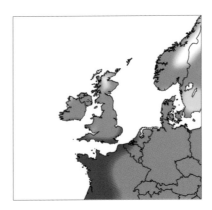

Above Males are very vocal in spring, making identification straightforward

Willow Warbler

Phylloscopus trochilus

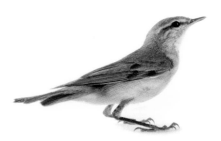

This is a small warbler, similar in appearance to Chiffchaff, but separable with care. The sexes are similar. The adult has mainly olive-green upperparts, and the head is marked with a pale yellow supercilium. The underparts are mainly grubby-white with a yellow flush to the throat. The slender bill is brown and the legs are orange-brown. Compared to a Chiffchaff, note the overall brighter colouration, the more obvious supercilium, the lighter-coloured legs and the longer projection of the primary feathers. The juvenile recalls the adult but is paler and more yellow overall, particularly on the underparts.

The Willow Warbler is a common warbler, and a relatively short-staying breeding visitor. The male defends its territory aggressively, chasing off rivals and other songbirds. It performs an elaborate, fluttering courtship display and nests on the ground in thick cover, constructing a grass dome.

FACTFILE

Length: 11–12cm (4¼–4¾in)
Wingspan: 17–22cm (6¾–8¾in)
Habitat: inhabits areas of woodland including coppices and scrub. Particularly favours birch woodland and willow scrub
Food: feeds on insects and other invertebrates
Status: summer migrant breeding species, common and widespread throughout the region in suitable habitat; present mainly April to August. Overwinters in Africa
Voice: utters a repetitive, descending tinkling phrase that ends in a flourish. Call is a disyllabic 'hueet', similar to that of the Chiffchaff

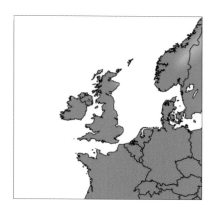

Above The pinkish-brown legs as well as the song help with identification

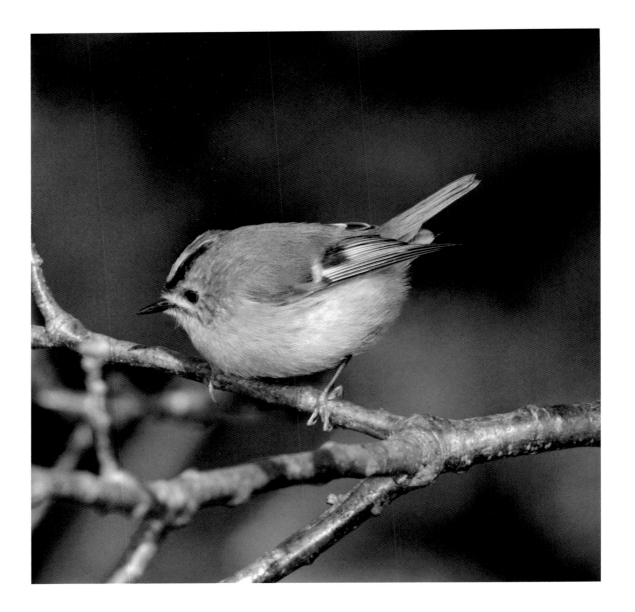

Goldcrest
Regulus regulus

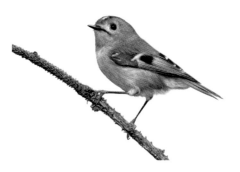

The Goldcrest is a tiny warbler-like bird with a rather squat and rounded body; it is the region's smallest bird species. The sexes are often separable. The adult male has dull greenish upperparts; the underparts are uniformly yellow-buff. Note the two pale wingbars, the subtle light-coloured eye-ring and the striking black-bordered orange and yellow crown. The small, needle-like bill is black. The adult female is similar to the male, but the crown colour is pure yellow. The juvenile resembles the adult but lacks the distinctive crown markings and colours until the autumn.

The Goldcrest is a tricky bird to observe at times, owing to its size and habit of foraging for insects in the top of the tree canopy. Its distinctive call is often the first sign of its presence. Numbers are boosted in more temperate areas in the winter months by an influx of winter migrants. It constructs a nest of moss, lichens and cobwebs, generally in a coniferous tree.

FACTFILE

Length: 8–9cm (3–3½n)
Wingspan: 14–16cm (5½–6in)
Habitat: a woodland species that favours conifers, but also found in deciduous woodland, areas of scrub, parks and rural gardens
Food: feeds primarily on small insects and their larvae
Status: common and widespread resident breeding species, present year-round throughout much of the region. Numbers are boosted outside the breeding season by birds migrating from further north and east of our region
Voice: song is a series of high-pitched notes and phrases, ending in a flourish. Call is a thin 'tsee-tsee-tsee'

Above Although the crest on the crown is colourful, it can be hard to spot if the bird in question is feeding in the canopy, above the observer
Opposite Feeds in the manner of a warbler, searching for invertebrates on twigs and among foliage

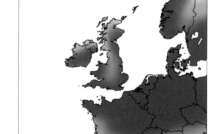

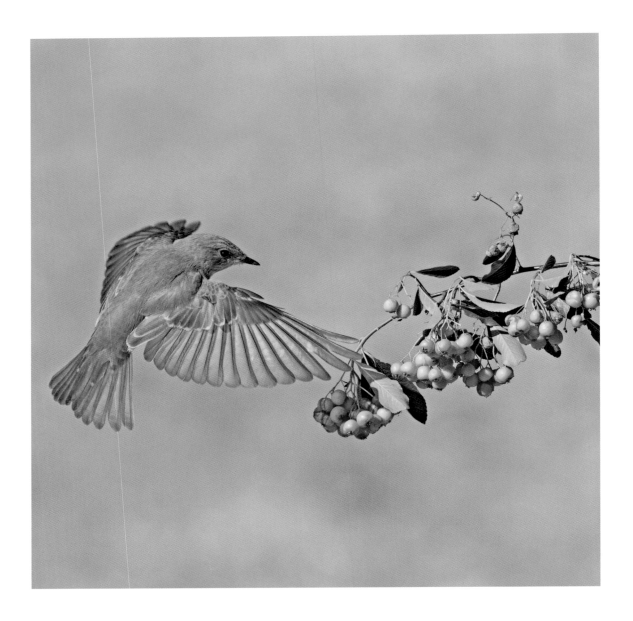

Spotted Flycatcher
Muscicapa striata

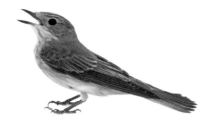

The Spotted Flycatcher is a lively but rather elusive, drab-coloured bird, and the larger of the two flycatcher species commonly seen in the region. The sexes are similar. The adult has rather nondescript grey-brown upperparts, the crown marked with dark streaks. The underparts are pale greyish-white and flushed brown on the flanks, the breast adorned with subtle dark streaking. The fine bill, eyes and legs are dark. The juvenile is similar to the adult but has light spots on the back and dark spots on the throat and breast.

The Spotted Flycatcher feeds by making frequent sorties for flying insects from favoured perches, which it sits on in a characteristic upright posture. It is a rather secretive bird during the breeding season; combined with its rather drab appearance this makes it easily overlooked. It constructs a finely woven, cup-shaped nest from grasses and plant material, typically in a tree fork, wall creeper or suitable crevice in a building.

FACTFILE

Length: 14–15cm (5½–6in)

Wingspan: 23–25cm (9–10in)

Habitat: favours open woodland, parks and gardens; commonly nests in residential gardens and adjacent to habitation

Food: feeds primarily on flying insects, which it catches on the wing

Status: summer breeding visitor, widespread throughout the region in suitable habitats; present mainly May to August. Also seen on migration. Overwinters in Africa. Numbers have declined in recent years

Voice: song is rather quiet and comprises simple high-pitched call-like notes. Utters a buzzing 'tsee' call

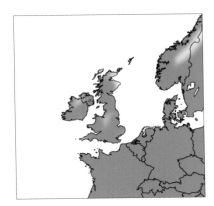

Above The plumage is rather plain overall but note the streaked crown and subtle pale wingbars **Opposite** Sometimes hovers momentarily while in pursuit of an insect

Tits
Paridae and Aegithalidae

There are six species of tit in Britain plus one, the Long-tailed Tit, which is in a different family, but is an honorary member of the group owing to its habit of commonly associating with other tits in flocks, being of similar diminutive stature and equally acrobatic when foraging. Nevertheless, the Long-tailed Tit is distinct in having pink in its plumage and quite different breeding habits.

The tits are among Britain's most familiar and best-loved birds. Two species, the Blue Tit and Great Tit, are colourful, bold and abundant everywhere from urban gardens to deep forests. Their habit of nesting in holes has enabled them to become among the best-studied birds in the world, because the birds are easily caught, DNA-profiled, ringed and monitored. The other tits also nest in holes, but Willow and Crested Tits will excavate theirs for themselves, not relying on the actions of decay or the efforts of woodpeckers. Competition for holes is intense and, where there are many Blue and Great Tits, a Coal Tit may find itself having to use holes on the ground, among tree roots for example.

The nests of tits consist of a platform of moss lined with hair. However, the Long-tailed Tit makes something quite different: a dome of soft materials placed in a branch fork, close to the trunk, rather than in a cavity, often in a thorny bush. It is made of moss bound with cobweb strands, insulated with feathers and camouflaged with fragments of lichen. This remarkable structure can take three weeks to build.

Most tits attempt just one brood a year – unusual for such small birds. They carefully time breeding so that the young hatch at the same time that there is a coincidental bloom in the number of caterpillars in the woodland canopy. This is mass production. The Blue Tit lays one of the largest clutches of any British bird, usually in double figures. For a couple of weeks, a parent Blue Tit may visit a nest 500 times a day, each time bringing in one caterpillar. For the spring and summer period, tits will indulge in a completely insectivorous diet, but when autumn comes this reverts completely to vegetarian, consisting of nuts and seeds, plus a few berries. The whole gut has to adapt, elongating to cope with the harder-to-digest plant material. Some tits, including coal, crested, marsh and willow may use autumn days to store away food for later consumption. They seem to remember their hiding places, an indication of the high intelligence level of many members of this family. Once again, the Long-tailed Tit is different. Its diet is largely insectivorous, right through the winter.

Tits gather into flocks in the autumn and winter. Many bird species, including tits, treecreepers and goldcrests, join 'nuclear' feeding flocks of Long-tailed Tits roaming the woodland and scrub. Long-tailed tits are very unusual because they remain in family units; flock members consisting of an adult male and female, their young from the year's breeding, plus a few blood relatives, stay together and roost at night in a huddle. Other tits generally gather in flocks while feeding during the day, but roost separately.

Tits are among the first birds to start singing in the spring. It only takes the switch from decreasing to increasing day-length for the chiming songs of Great Tits to fill the chilly air. By mid-January, Blue, Great and Coal Tits will be noisily defending their territories for the breeding season to come.

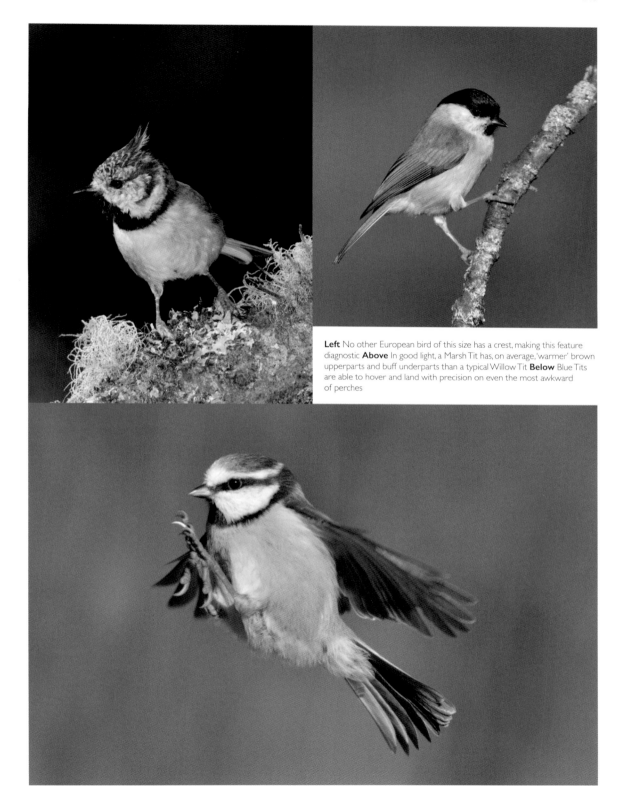

Left No other European bird of this size has a crest, making this feature diagnostic **Above** In good light, a Marsh Tit has, on average, 'warmer' brown upperparts and buff underparts than a typical Willow Tit **Below** Blue Tits are able to hover and land with precision on even the most awkward of perches

Blue Tit
Cyanistes caeruleus

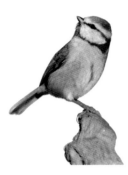

The Blue Tit is a colourful little bird and a regular visitor to garden feeders. The sexes are similar, and separating them is tricky, but males are generally more brightly coloured than females. The adult has a compact body with a greenish back; the wings and tail are blue and the underparts are bright yellow. Note the subtle white wingbar, and the central dark streak to the underparts. The head is mainly white, but boldly marked with a conspicuous bright blue cap and a dark blue (almost black) collar connected to a thin dark eye stripe and small bib. The dark bill is small and stubby, and the delicate legs are bluish. The juvenile is similar to the adult but with more subdued colours; it generally lacks any blue in its plumage.

The Blue Tit is an inquisitive and endearing little bird and a garden favourite. It naturally seeks tree holes in which to nest and readily uses purpose-built nest boxes, constructing a cup-shaped nest lined inside with hair and grasses. Rarely venturing far from the safety of cover, its flight is swift and agile on rapid wing-beats.

FACTFILE
Length: 11–12cm (4¼–4¾in)
Wingspan: 18–20cm (7–7¾in)
Habitat: favours areas of deciduous woodland, parks and gardens. A common visitor to garden tables and feeders
Food: feeds on invertebrates, fruits and seeds
Status: common and widespread resident breeding species, present year-round throughout the region, but absent from remote offshore islands and parts of Scandinavia
Voice: call is a chattering 'tser err-err-err'. Song includes whistling and trilling elements

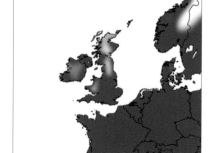

Above The white face and supercilium are neatly framed by black and blue, giving the bird a smart appearance **Opposite** Aerobatic and manoeuvrable in flight

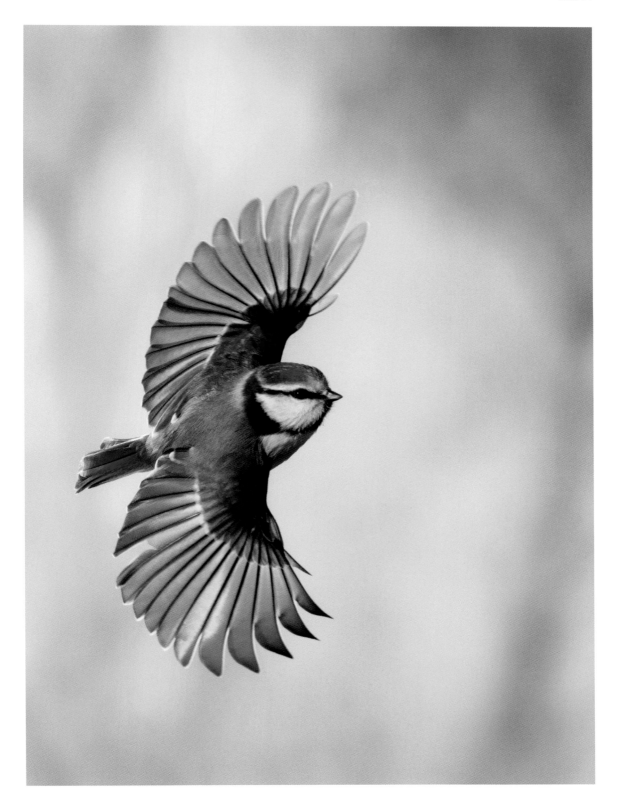

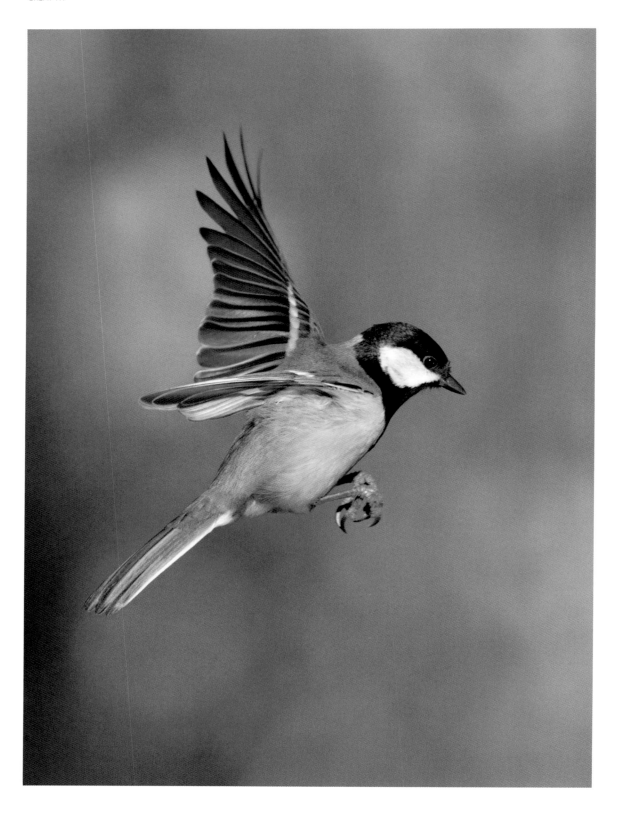

Great Tit
Parus major

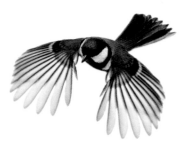

The Great Tit is a colourful woodland bird and a familiar garden visitor. The sexes are similar but separable with care. The adult male has a greenish back and the upperwings are blue with an obvious white wingbar. The underparts are yellow with a central bold black stripe that runs from between the legs across the belly and breast to connect with the black throat, collar and cap. A large white triangular cheek patch is framed by the black head markings. The black bill is small but robust-looking, and the legs are blue-grey. The adult female is similar, but the central black stripe is much narrower and more broken, especially between the legs, and the head and throat are less glossy. The juvenile has much duller and less well-defined plumage, but with hints of adult colouration.

The Great Tit is a rather bold species and a common sight in rural and urban gardens, readily coming to feeders. It has the largest European distribution of any member of the tit family. It frequently forages on the ground or in low-hanging branches, and its flight is fast and agile on rapid wing-beats. The Great Tit seeks tree holes or suitable gaps in walls and buildings in which to nest, and is an enthusiastic user of nest boxes. The nest is a cup lined with hair and feathers.

FACTFILE
Length: 14–15cm (5½–6in)
Wingspan: 22–25cm (8¾–10in)
Habitat: favours areas of deciduous woodland, parks and gardens. A common visitor to garden tables and feeders
Food: feeds on invertebrates, fruits and seeds
Status: common and widespread resident breeding species, present year-round throughout the region; absent from remote offshore islands
Voice: utters a sharp 'tche-tche-tche' call in alarm. Song is a diagnostic 'teacher-teacher-teacher'

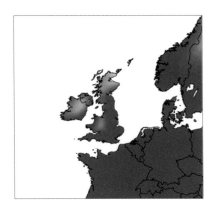

Above The bright yellow-green plumage and bold pale wingbar are striking features in flight **Opposite** The white cheek patch is a striking feature and one that allows easy identification, even with a partial view of a bird

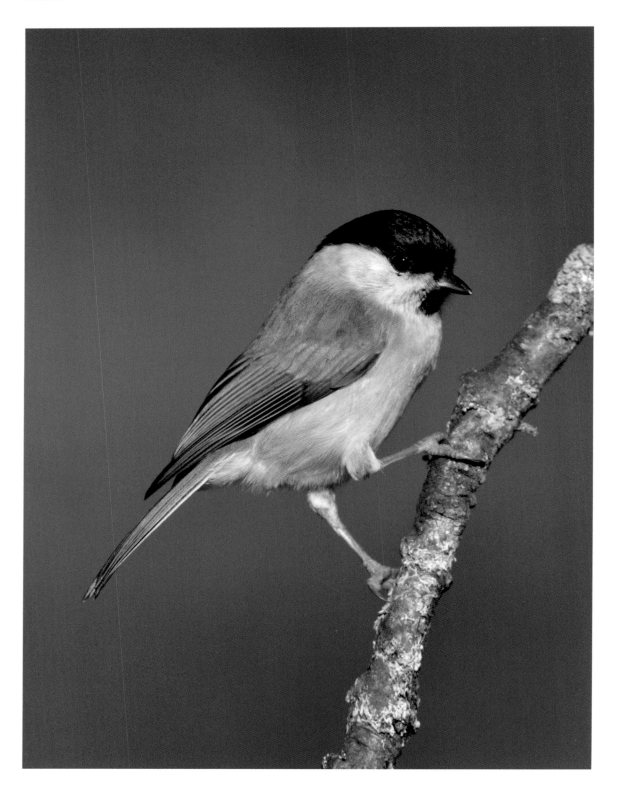

Marsh Tit
Poecile palustris

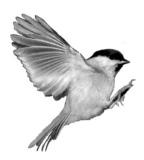

The Marsh Tit is a feisty little woodland bird, very similar in appearance to Willow Tit and the more commonly encountered species of the two. The sexes are similar. The adult has uniform grey-brown upperparts; the underparts are grey-buff. The head is marked with a bold black cap that extends to the dark eye. The cheeks are whitish and the throat is marked with a small black bib patch. The black bill is stubby and a small white spot at the base is sometimes visible. The legs are delicate and bluish. Compared to the similar Willow Tit, note the glossy sheen to the black cap (discernible in good light), the smaller black bib and the lack of a pale wing panel. Note also the more slender-looking neck. The juvenile recalls the adult.

Extremely subtle differences in plumage make the Marsh Tit difficult to separate from the Willow Tit when encountered in most circumstances in the field. Habitat and voice allow confident separation with experience. It nests in existing holes in tree trunks and stumps, often enlarging them when necessary, and constructing a cup of plant material lined with hair. The species can pair for life and inhabits the same territory throughout the year. It occasionally visits bird tables and feeders, but less regularly than other species of tit.

FACTFILE

Length: 12–13cm (4¾–5in)
Wingspan: 18–20cm (7–7¾in)
Habitat: inhabits deciduous woodland, parks and gardens
Food: feeds on invertebrates, seeds, nuts and berries
Status: a common resident breeding species, present year-round throughout most of the region, with the exception of Ireland and the extreme north
Voice: call is a loud 'pitchoo' sneeze; utters a loud and repetitive 'chip-chip-chip' song

Above Marsh Tits are much more familiar visitors to garden bird feeders than Willow Tits, although visits are typically brief **Opposite** The narrow black 'bib' and glossy sheen to the cap are both good features for comparison with a Willow Tit; Marsh Tits are much more familiar visitors to garden bird feeders than Willow Tits, although visits are typically brief

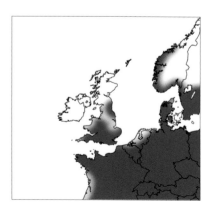

Coal Tit

Periparus ater

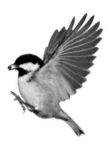

The Coal Tit is a tiny bird that is associated with coniferous woodland. The sexes are similar. The adult has bluish-grey to grey-brown upperparts, with two white wingbars; the underparts are pale pinkish-buff. Some subtle geographical plumage variation occurs, and birds from different areas of the region can display yellowish, green or brown tinges. The head and chin are black and marked with a triangular white cheek patch, running from the base of the bill and below the eye; note the diagnostic narrow white patch on the nape. The small bill and the delicate legs are black. The juvenile recalls the adult but with less well-defined markings and more subdued colouration. This is the species of tit most commonly associated with coniferous woodland. The Coal Tit feeds acrobatically, and is noticeably more agile than other tit species when foraging in the outer reaches of branches and treetops. It nests in tree holes or suitable crevices, and also uses nest boxes.

FACTFILE

Length: 10–11cm (4–4½in)

Wingspan: 17–21cm (6¾–8in)

Habitat: favours coniferous forests and plantations, but also widespread in mixed and deciduous woodland

Food: feeds on insects and spiders; also some seeds. A regular visitor to garden feeders

Status: widespread resident breeding species, present year-round and common throughout the region in suitable habitat

Voice: call is thin and piping. Utters a 'teechu-teechu-teechu' song, reminiscent of the Great Tit, but weaker, higher-pitched and more rapid

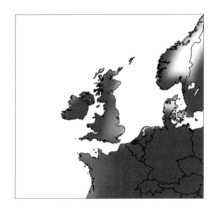

Above A Coal Tit is a compact little bird with the size and proportions of a warbler, but a proportionately large head and stubby bill **Opposite** At bird feeders, Coal Tits typically collect an item of food and then quickly retreat to cover to eat it

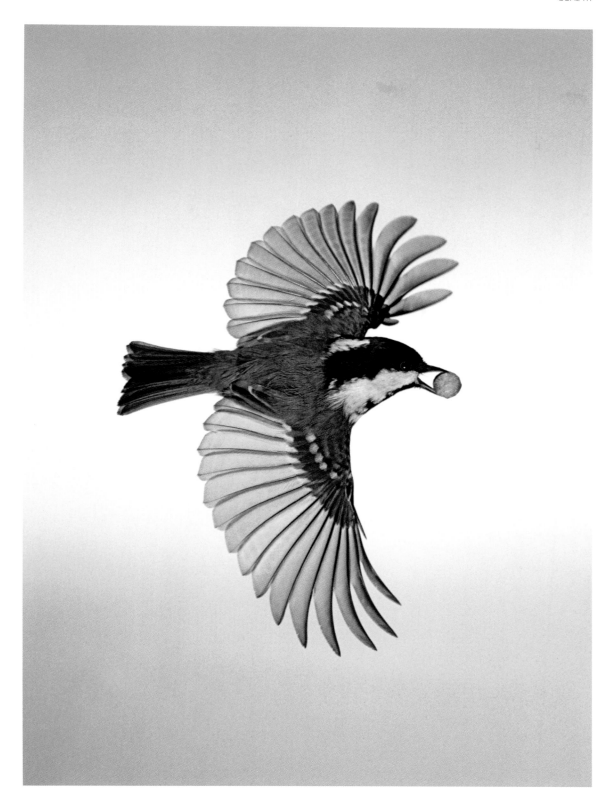

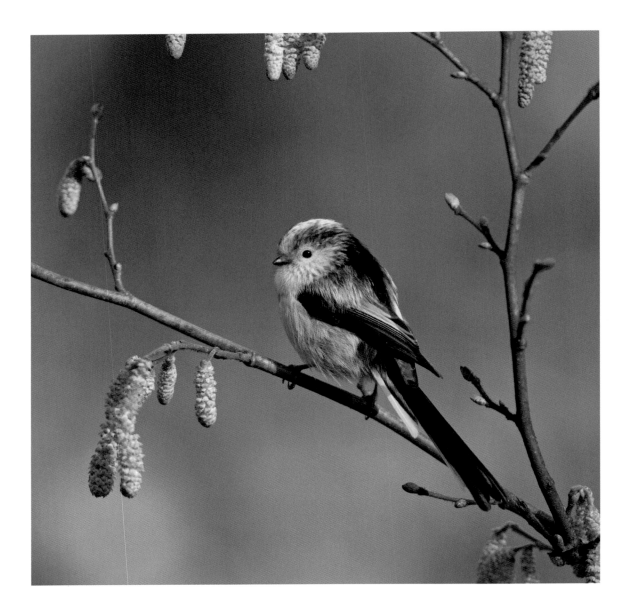

Long-tailed Tit

Aegithalos caudatus and *Aegithalos rosaceous*

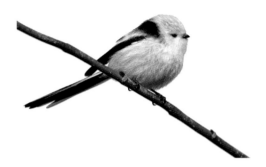

The Long-tailed Tit is an endearing, fluffy-looking bird with a rounded head, plumpish body and long tail. The sexes are similar. At first glance, adults from most of the region appear to have mainly black upperparts and tail with white underparts. Closer inspection reveals a pinkish chestnut patch on the 'shoulder'; the underside and flanks are also flushed with pink. The head is predominantly white, with a bold black band running above the eye to the mantle. The eye is dark and the stubby little bill is black. The legs are delicate-looking and dark. Birds from Scandinavia have an entirely white head. Juveniles of all races lack the pinkish plumage elements, and have a dark wash across much of the face.

A Long-tailed Tit's flight is undulating and agile on rapid, whirring wing-beats. It is often seen in small agitated groups, particularly during the winter months, that never seem to remain in one place for long. It visits garden tables and feeders in rural areas, but is less regular in its appearance than other tit species. Its nest is an intricate ball, woven from moss, lichen, feathers and spiders' silk, and is commonly placed in a bush or hedgerow.

FACTFILE

Length: 13–15cm (5–6in)

Wingspan: 16–19cm (6–7½in)

Habitat: favours deciduous woodland, hedgerows and areas of scrub

Food: feeds primarily on insects and other invertebrates; some seeds in the winter months

Status: widespread and fairly common resident breeding species, present year-round throughout the region in suitable habitat

Voice: contact call is a rattling 'tsrrr' and thin 'tsee-tsee-tsee'. The soft song is easily missed

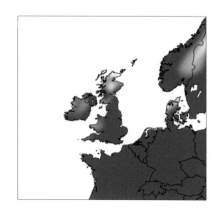

Above The rounded body shape and proportionately long tail mean that identification of the species is straightforward **Opposite** Both Long-tailed Tits, the *Aegithalos caudatus* (above) and *Aegithalos rosaceous* (opposite) can be found in Europe, with some sightings of *caudatus* in the UK. However, *rosaceous* is darker and more commonly found in the UK

Woodland birds

Much of Britain's semi-natural vegetation cover is woodland, so it is not surprising that many of our commonest birds are associated with it. Several of our familiar garden species, including Blue, Great and Coal Tits, Blackbirds, Robins and Chaffinches have spilt over from woodland or woodland edge.

Woodland, of course, is not a uniform habitat. Britain holds many species of trees and shrubs, intermixed in different ways according to climate, soil type, topography and history, so no wood is exactly the same as another, either in its botanical makeup or its birdlife.

Every wood also has different sections, like a house with many rooms. Dense woodland is different to the clearings within it, and the edge of a wood often carries more variety than the depths of a wood. Woods are storeyed, too, with the floor, understorey and canopy each providing different conditions for birds. So, for example, a Wood Warbler nests on the woodland floor but often feeds in the canopy and might sing in mid-storey. A Great Tit might feed on caterpillars in the canopy in June, but on the ground in December.

The mix of trees is fundamental to which birds live in a wood. Some, such as Crossbills, Coal Tits, Goldcrests and Siskins are found mainly in coniferous woodland, particularly when breeding. Crested Tits prefer old Caledonian forests of Scots pine, while Crossbills prefer spruce. On the other hand, Lesser Spotted Woodpeckers and Hawfinches only occur in deciduous stands. Marsh Tits, despite their name, seem to prefer deciduous trees with an understorey, particularly of holly. Many birds are fussy while others, such as Great Spotted Woodpeckers and Treecreepers, seem to thrive in any mix of trees.

Deciduous woods provide very different resources at different times of year. In the spring and summer the canopy provides enormous quantities of insects – a single large oak tree may hold 30,000 caterpillars – while in autumn and winter much of the produce eventually falls to the ground. Many birds, including tits, finches and nuthatches depend greatly on levels of seed and nut production, which vary from year to year. The Jay is similarly reliant on a good acorn crop to store away in its territory in case times become difficult. Bramblings rely on a good crop of beech to get them through the winter.

Treecreepers, Nuthatches and Woodpeckers are all unusual for their habit of feeding off the surface of the bark. This provides a reliable source of invertebrate food almost throughout the year for a treecreeper, while Nuthatches and Great Spotted Woodpeckers join in with the widespread switch from animal to vegetable food in the autumn.

The woodpeckers make many more holes than they need, and these, along with wear and tear and rotting, provide cavities for a wide variety of birds, from tits to flycatchers. Demand always exceeds supply. Most other species nest low down, where the vegetation is thickest; rather few nest high in the canopy, although Goldcrests do. Jays are mid-canopy nesters and become very secretive in the breeding season. They are prolific nest predators, far worse than Magpies.

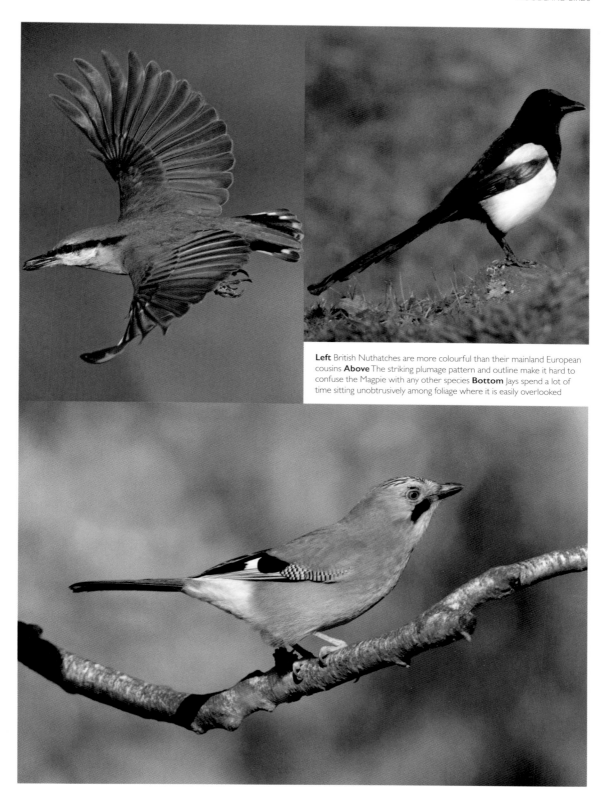

Left British Nuthatches are more colourful than their mainland European cousins **Above** The striking plumage pattern and outline make it hard to confuse the Magpie with any other species **Bottom** Jays spend a lot of time sitting unobtrusively among foliage where it is easily overlooked

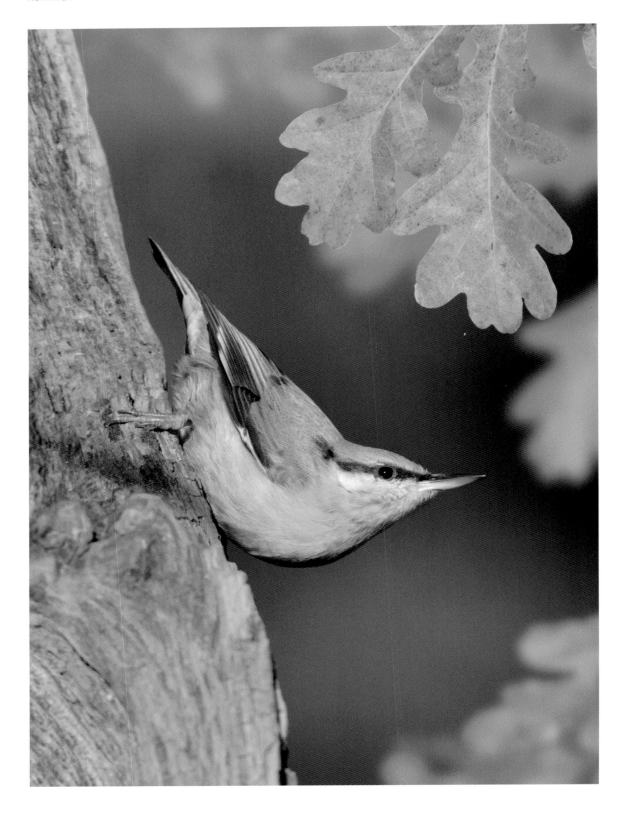

Nuthatch

Sitta europaea

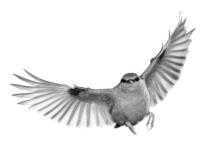

The Nuthatch is a rather stout-bodied and short-tailed woodland bird. The sexes are similar but can be separated with care. The adult has primarily blue-grey upperparts, including the nape and crown; the underparts are mainly orange-buff. The head is marked with white cheeks and a bold black eye stripe, which runs from the base of the bill, through the dark eye and past the ear coverts. The robust dark bill is rather long and sharply pointed, and the legs are sandy-brown. The male can sometimes be separated by the more intense reddish-buff tinge to the rear of the flanks. The juvenile is similar to the adult female but with more muted colours and a less well-defined eye stripe.

The Nuthatch is a familiar bird of woodland habitats. It is commonly seen descending the trunks of trees head-first, and the only species in the region to do so. It feeds by using its chisel-like bill to dig insects out of tree bark and to split open acorns and other seeds it wedges into bark crevices, storing food for the winter months. A very sedentary bird that pairs for life, it nests in tree holes and typically lines the entrance with mud to reduce the size of the hole.

FACTFILE

Length: 12–14cm (4¾–5½in)

Wingspan: 23–27cm (9–10½in)

Habitat: associated with deciduous and mixed woodland habitats, parks, gardens and other areas with mature trees

Food: feeds on insects, seeds and fruits

Status: common and widespread resident breeding species, present year-round across much of the region, with the exception of Ireland, the extreme north of Scotland and Northern Scandinavia

Voice: song commonly comprises a loud series of 'pee-pee-pee' notes. Utters a loud and insistent 'zwitt' call in alarm

Above On average males tend to have more richly colourful underparts than females **Opposite** Powerful feet and claws provide a confident grip when climbing up and down tree trunks

Treecreeper
Certhia familiaris

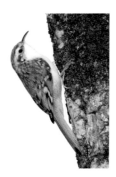

The Treecreeper is a furtive little woodland bird with a downcurved bill and long brown tail. The sexes are similar. The adult has mainly brown upperparts, marked with lighter blotches and darker streaks; this provides superb camouflage against tree bark. Note the broad zigzag markings on the wings. The underparts are silvery-white with a subtle buff tinge towards the rear end of the flanks. The head has a grubby-white supercilium. The dark brown bill is long, thin and conspicuously downcurved. The legs are light brown; note the long toes and extended hind claw. The juvenile is similar to the adult but has subtle spotting on the underparts.

The Treecreeper is an unobtrusive bird that feeds by spiralling around tree trunks, starting at the base and working its way up before flying to the next tree when it reaches the top. It keeps its body held close to the trunk and creeps on its short legs, using its long tail for support. It is a rather sedentary bird that roosts (sometimes communally) in bark crevices. It nests in crevices and behind tree bark.

FACTFILE
Length: 12–13cm (4¾–5in)
Wingspan: 18–21cm (7–8in)
Habitat: mature deciduous and mixed woodland habitats
Food: feeds primarily on insects and spiders, occasionally seeds
Status: resident breeding species, present year-round. Common and widespread in suitable habitats throughout most of the region
Voice: song comprises a short series of high-pitched notes terminating in a trill. Utters a shallow, high-pitched 'tseert' call

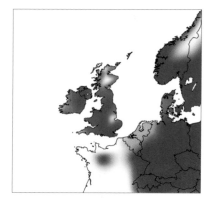

Above Stiff, bristly tips to the tail feathers provide rigid support for climbing birds **Opposite** The plumage is overall cleaner-looking than a Short-toed Treecreeper and the bill is proportionately shorter

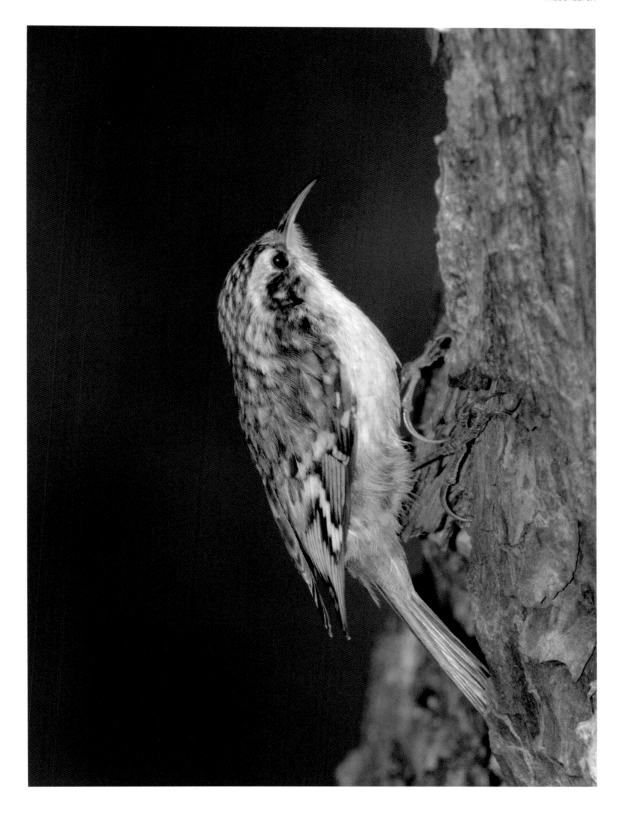

Crows

Corvidae

The Crow family contains several well-known formidable species, many of them intelligent and adaptable. They are larger than most songbirds – indeed the Raven, as big as a Buzzard, is one of the world's largest Passerines – and several of them are noisy, aggressive and abundant. They are characterized by bristle-like feathers covering their nostrils, by long, strong legs and feet and by their stout, multi-purpose bills. In most species the plumage is black, with variations such as the grey head and nape of the Jackdaw, the glossy colouration of the Rook and the ash-grey mantle and breast of a Hooded Crow. However, the Magpie is boldly black-and-white and the Jay is decidedly colourful; abroad, the 134 species are similarly divided into black and gaudy.

The thick, straight bill of most members of the family allows them to be omnivores, eating a combination of meat and vegetable items. The Jay is an extreme example, spending the autumn days collecting and caching thousands of acorns, while switching in spring to a diet including insects mixed with the eggs and nestlings of birds. The Red-billed Chough is the closest to an exception, using its long, curved bill to probe into soil for a largely invertebrate diet. Along with the Jay, the Carrion Crow often caches food, though usually for short periods of time.

Crows build large, bulky nests of sticks, often strengthened with mud and soft material such as hair and feathers. Most build platform nests, but those of the Magpie have a roof. Crows have only one brood a year, of between two and eight eggs. They often live in pairs throughout the year, but their social lives can be very complex. In the case of Magpies, Carrion and Hooded Crows, the population consists of non-breeding flocks as well as pairs. Rooks and Jackdaws nest in colonies, and while Jackdaws are exceptionally faithful to their mates, a rookery is full of attempted extra-pair matings.

Crows are well-known for their cawing sounds, but their vocabulary is far richer than most people realize. The Jay makes a loud screeching noise but will also 'sing' with high-pitched elements and excellent mimicry.

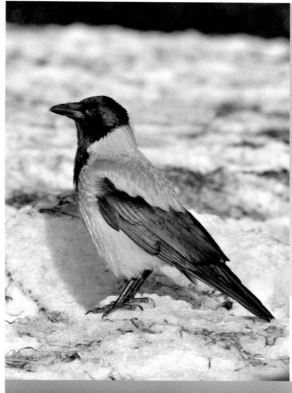

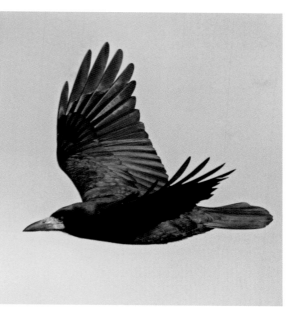

Left Hooded Crows are hardy birds adapted to harsh environments and can tolerate snow and ice during the winter months **Above** The broad wings and splayed primaries give the Rook excellent control and manoeuvrability in flight **Below** Jackdaws found from northern Scandinavia eastwards have paler heads than birds from elsewhere, and a variable pale half-collar

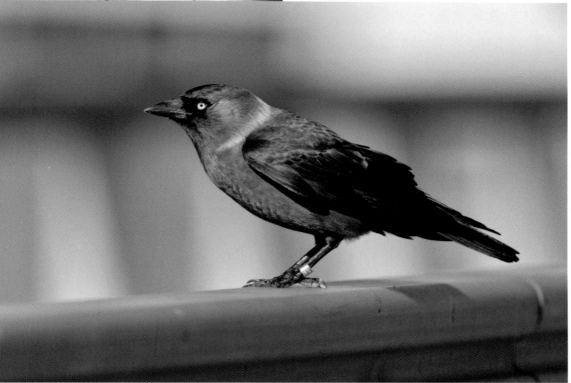

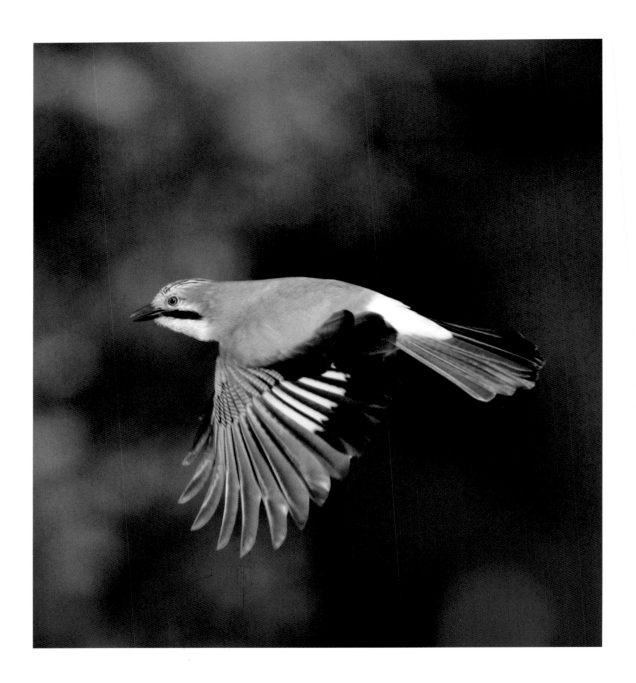

Jay

Garrulus glandarius

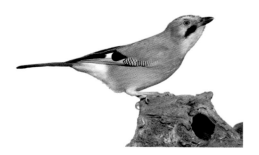

The Jay is a handsome and furtive woodland bird, commonly heard more often than seen. The sexes are similar. The adult has predominantly pinkish-buff plumage; the rump, undertail and lower belly are white. The longish tail is black, and the broad rounded wings display black-and-white on the primary flight feathers. A beautiful patch of blue, with black-and-white chequer-board markings is situated on the upperwing coverts. This feature is obvious both in flight and on the folded wings of standing birds. The head has a pale forecrown with dark streaks, and a black 'moustache'. The bill is dark and the legs are flesh coloured. In flight, note the conspicuous white rump and contrastingly dark tail. The juvenile is similar to the adult, but the streaking on the crown and moustachial markings are less obvious.

The Jay is a wary bird that takes flight at the slightest hint of human presence, its disappearing white rump often accompanied by the raucous alarm call. An individual Jay may bury thousands of acorns during the autumn as a food larder for the winter months. It nests in trees, constructing a lined twig pile close to the trunk. It is a sedentary breeding species in the main, but some irruptive migration can occur when the crop of acorns is poor.

FACTFILE

Length: 33–35cm (13–13¾in)

Wingspan: 52–58cm (20½–22¾in)

Habitat: associated with mature deciduous woodland, particularly where oaks predominate. Also found in parks, and an occasional garden visitor

Food: acorns form an important component of the Jay's diet. Also feeds on invertebrates, seeds, fruits and the eggs and chicks of other birds

Status: widespread resident breeding species, present year-round throughout the region in suitable habitats

Voice: utters a diagnostic harsh and far-carrying raucous call

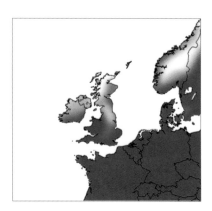

Above Plumage colours are subtly understated except for the striking chequered blue patch on the wings **Opposite** With even a partial or distant view, the white rump is the species' most striking feature in flight

Magpie
Pica pica

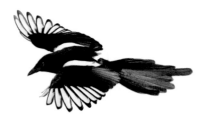

The Magpie is a common bird, its distinctive long tail and black-and-white plumage making it instantly recognizable. The sexes are similar. The adult has mostly glossy black plumage with a contrasting white belly and patch of pure white on the shoulder of the closed wing. The bill is black and powerful, the culmen noticeably curved. The legs are dark. In flight, note the broad, short wings and the black-fringed pure white primaries. Also note the long black tail, which gives the bird a diagnostic outline. In good light, a beautiful bluish-green iridescent sheen is commonly visible. The juvenile is similar to the adult.

The Magpie is a widespread and familiar bird. An opportunistic feeder and an enthusiastic scavenger, it is often seen on roadsides taking advantage of roadkill and it possesses an amazingly well-developed road sense. It nests in trees, constructing a robust platform of twigs, often with a protective dome, which is frequently used year after year. It is commonly observed in small groups outside the breeding season.

FACTFILE
Length: 45–50cm (17¾–19½in)
Wingspan: 52–60cm (20½–23½in)
Habitat: favours lightly wooded habitats including open woodland, parks, gardens, farmland and urban areas
Food: a versatile species that feeds on a variety of carrion, invertebrates, seeds and fruit. Also a notorious nest raider, taking the eggs and young chicks of smaller songbirds
Status: common and widespread resident breeding species, present year-round throughout the region
Voice: utters a loud, rattling alarm call

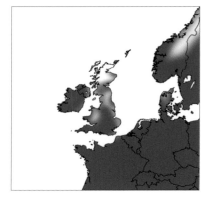

Above Flight is often accompanied by the Magpie's chattering call
Opposite Bold white markings contrast with the otherwise mainly black plumage; in good light, note the bluish sheen to the wings

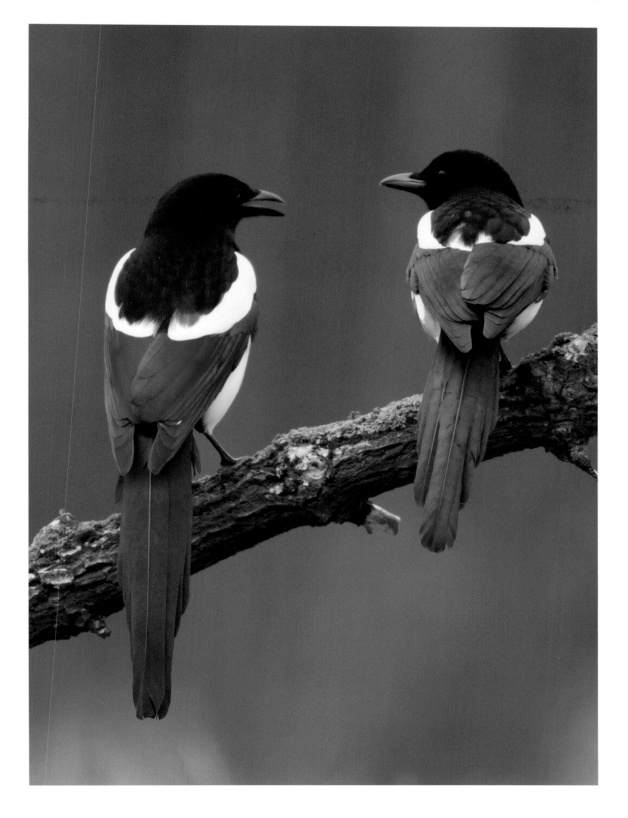

Carrion Crow

Corvus corone

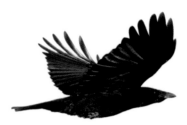

The Carrion Crow is an iconic member of the crow family and the most likely corvid to be encountered either singly or in pairs. The sexes are similar. The adult has uniformly black plumage that displays a glossy sheen when seen in good light. The black bill is large, stout and powerful, and note the feathered base which allows separation from the adult Rook. The eyes and legs are also black. In flight, the wings are broad, with long, finger-like primary feathers at the wingtips. The tail is rather square-ended. The juvenile is similar to the adult.

Far less gregarious than the similar Rook or Jackdaw, the Carrion Crow is a rather wary bird that is widely persecuted. Flight is strong and direct. Pairs are typically faithful throughout the year, and the species generally only forms flocks at winter roosts and during springtime displays. It nests in trees, constructing a well-lined twig platform.

FACTFILE

Length: 43–50cm (17–19½in)

Wingspan: 90–100cm (35½–39in)

Habitat: traditionally associated with open farmland, but nowadays also found in a variety of rural and even urban habitats

Food: an omnivorous and opportunistic feeder, its diet includes invertebrates, grains, carrion and the eggs and nestlings of other birds. A regular visitor to refuse tips and a skilled bin raider

Status: common and widespread resident breeding species, present year-round throughout much of the region. Largely absent from Ireland, northern Scotland and Scandinavia where its cousin the Hooded Crow predominates

Voice: utters a raucous 'creeaa-creeaa-creeaa' call

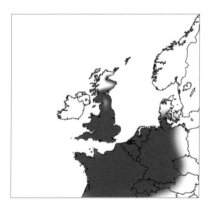

Above The wing-beats are powerful but fast level flight looks overall rather laboured

Hooded Crow

Corvus cornix

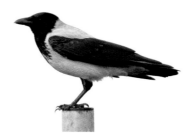

Formerly treated as a geographically separated subspecies of Carrion Crow but now given full species status. Structurally similar to Carrion Crow, the adult has mainly grey body plumage, displaying a subtle lilac tinge in certain lights.

The Hooded Crow is a wary species that is generally far less gregarious than other corvids. Interbreeding with Carrion Crow does occur where the ranges of the two species overlap. An opportunistic feeder, its varied diet allows it to take advantage of a number of food sources from carrion to live prey and scavenging refuse. It nests in trees, constructing a well-lined twig platform.

FACTFILE

Length: 43–50cm (17–19½in)

Wingspan: 90–100cm (35½–39in)

Habitat: occurs in a wide range of mainly rural habitats including farmland and moorland; coastal areas are a particular favourite during the winter months

Food: an omnivorous and opportunistic feeder, its diet includes invertebrates, grains, carrion and the eggs and nestlings of other birds

Status: northern and eastern counterpart of Carrion Crow and a resident breeding species, present year-round. It ranges from Ireland and northern Scotland to Scandinavia and eastern Europe

Voice: utters a raucous 'creeaa–creeaa–creeaa' call

Above Like their Carrion cousin, Hooded Crows are inventive feeders and some have learned to drop seashore molluscs from a height in order to smash their hard, protective shells

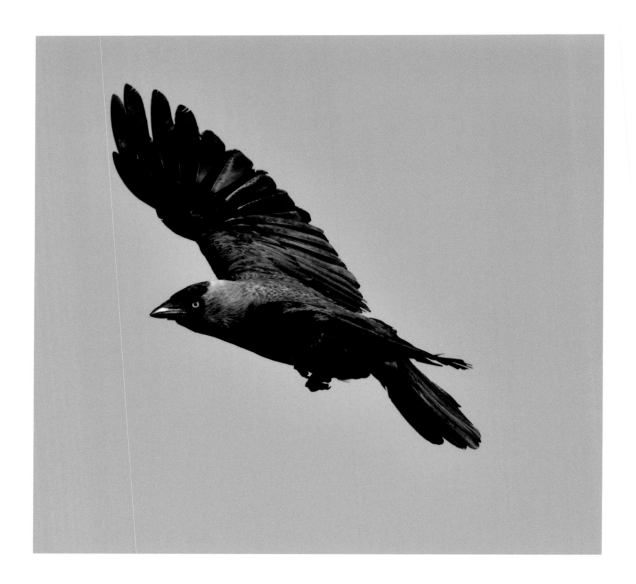

Jackdaw

Corvus monedula

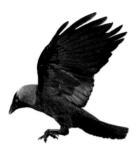

This the most common and widespread small corvid in the region. The sexes are similar. The adult at first glance appears to have uniformly dark charcoal-grey plumage. When seen in good light or under closer inspection, the plumage is darkest on the upperwings and crown, and the nape and throat are lighter silvery-grey. The eye is pale blue-grey, almost white, the robust bill is black and the legs are dark. The juvenile is similar to the adult, but the eye is darker and duller and the plumage displays a brown tinge.

The Jackdaw is a familiar and successful species that is capable of adapting to a range of environments and exploiting most food sources. It is often bold and approachable in urban environments. It nests colonially in a variety of locations including rock crevices, trees, old buildings and even chimney pots. It constructs an untidy, soft-lined platform of twigs.

FACTFILE

Length: 31–34cm (12–13¼in)

Wingspan: 67–74cm (26–29in)

Habitat: a versatile species, found in a variety of rural and urban habitats, from coastal cliffs and farmland to gardens and urban parks

Food: omnivorous, and can exploit most food sources

Status: common and widespread resident breeding species, present year-round throughout the region, with the exception of the extreme north

Voice: utters a sharp and often repeated 'chack'

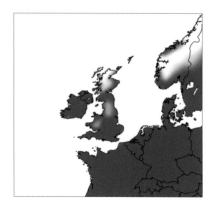

Above This is the smallest of the dark corvid species with a relatively stubby bill and a diagnostic pale eye in adult birds **Opposite** Aerobatic and manoeuvrable in flight, and capable of soaring and hovering briefly too; often seen in flocks outside the breeding season

Rook
Corvus frugilegus

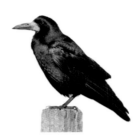

The Rook is a common and gregarious farmland bird, often encountered in large flocks or at nesting colonies. The sexes are similar. The adult has uniformly black plumage that can display a purplish iridescence when seen at certain angles and in good light. The eye is dark and the large bill is dark grey, almost black. At the base of the bill, a diagnostic light-coloured bare skin patch allows certain separation from similar corvid species. The rather peaked crown is also a useful aid to accurate identification. In flight, note the broad wings, the long, finger-like primary feathers at the wingtips and the rounded tail. The juvenile is similar to the adult, but lacks the bare skin patch at the base of the bill and can be confused with a Carrion Crow.

Primarily a ground feeder, the Rook uses its long bill to probe the ground for beetle larvae, earthworms and seeds. It nests in large colonies in the tops of tall trees, constructing large and untidy twig platforms. These colonies are usually loud and raucous. Winter roosts can number many hundreds of birds, and populations are boosted in more temperate regions at this time by migrants from further afield.

FACTFILE
Length: 43–48cm (17–19in)
Wingspan: 81–99cm (32–39in)
Habitat: associated primarily with agricultural land and adjacent woodland areas
Food: diet traditionally comprises a mixture of soil-dwelling invertebrates and agricultural seed. Like most corvids, it is an opportunist feeder and occasionally visits garden tables and scavenges open bins
Status: widespread resident breeding species, present year-round throughout most of the region, except the far north where birds migrate to avoid extreme weather
Voice: utters a repetitive raw 'kaw-kaw-kaw'

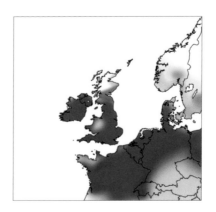

Above The bill is proportionally very long by the standards of other black corvids; bare skin at the base is an adaptation to their ground-probing feeding habits **Opposite** In spring, displaying birds are very vocal; when calling they typically stretch their necks out and raise their tails

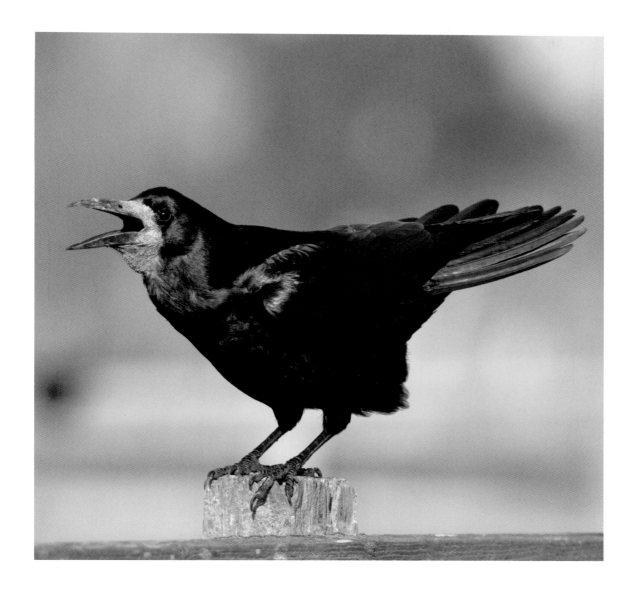

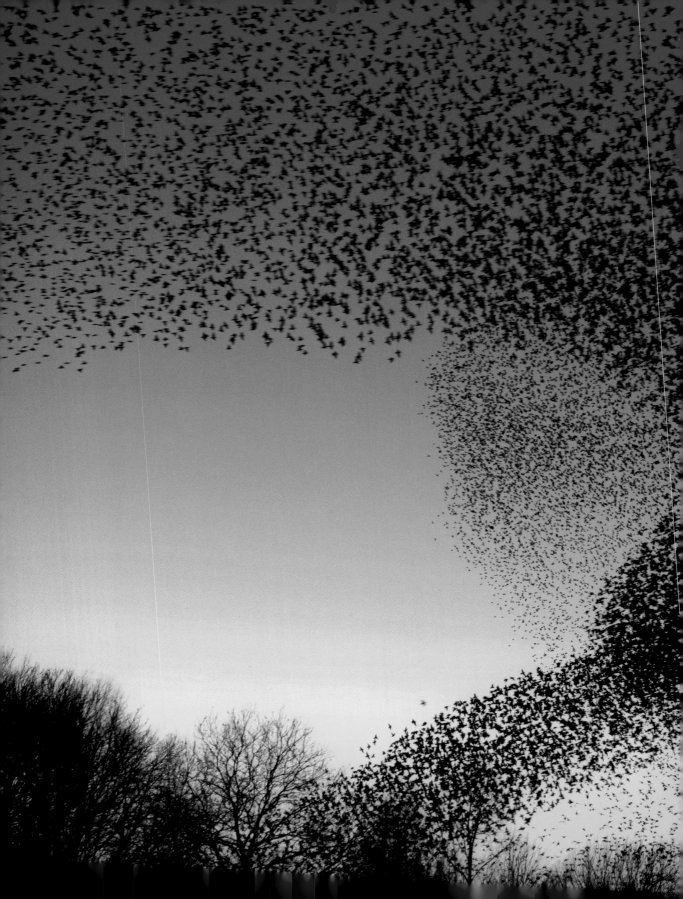

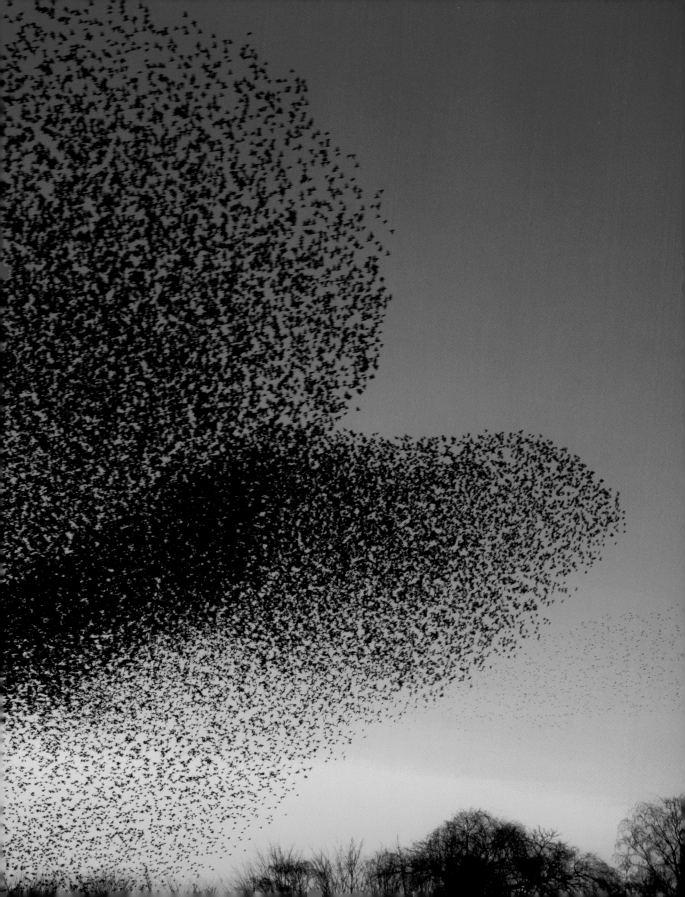

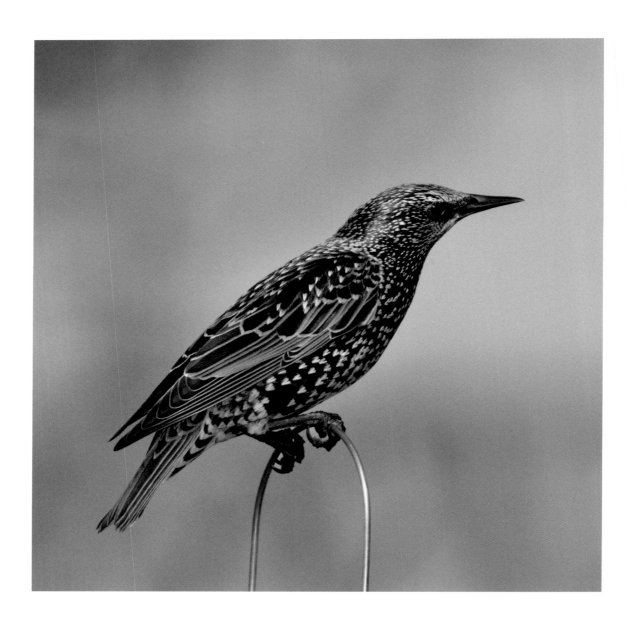

Starling
Sturnus vulgaris

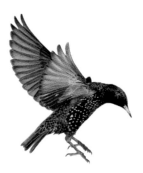

The Starling is a common sight in rural and urban areas and an extremely vocal bird, uttering a range of sounds. The sexes are similar but usually separable with care during the summer. The summer adult has entirely dark plumage with an obvious oily sheen and an iridescence that includes green, bronze and blue tones when seen in good light. The bill is yellow and the legs are reddish. The bill of the male has a blue base to the lower mandible, and the female generally displays some spotting on the underside. The winter adult is beautifully adorned with strikingly contrasting pale feather tips. These take the form of white 'V'-shaped marks on the breast, bronze spots on the head and back and bronze edges to the wing feathers. The bill is dark. The juvenile has uniformly grey-brown plumage with a dark bill, acquiring adult plumage in the main by the autumn, but often retaining the grey-brown to the head and neck. By the first winter the plumage is indistinguishable from the adult. In flight, note the diagnostic short triangular-shaped wings seen in all birds.

The Starling typically forms large flocks outside the breeding season. Numbers in western Europe are boosted in autumn by birds that have migrated from further east and north to avoid harsh winter weather. Hundreds of thousands of birds congregate at popular roosting sites such as lowland marshes, the flying flocks forming huge clouds in the sky at dusk; this display can be spectacular. Its nest is a grass platform in a tree hole, nest box or building

Previous Page A spectacular murmuration of Starlings **Above** Although the species is still common and widespread, numbers of breeding and wintering birds have declined significantly in Britain in particular **Opposite** A solitary Starling is an unusual sight and most are found in sizeable flocks

FACTFILE

Length: 20–22cm (8–8¾in)

Wingspan: 37–42cm (14½–16½in)

Habitat: an adaptable species that occurs in a variety of habitats from lowland farmland, marshlands and open countryside to coastal regions and urban areas

Food: feeds on insects and other invertebrates, seeds and fruits

Status: widespread and abundant resident breeding species, present year-round in most of the region. Numbers are boosted in the winter months by birds migrating here from further east and north

Voice: an enthusiastic mimic and lively songster. Song includes mimicry of other bird song and man-made sounds. Also utters various clicks and descending whistles

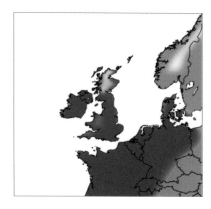

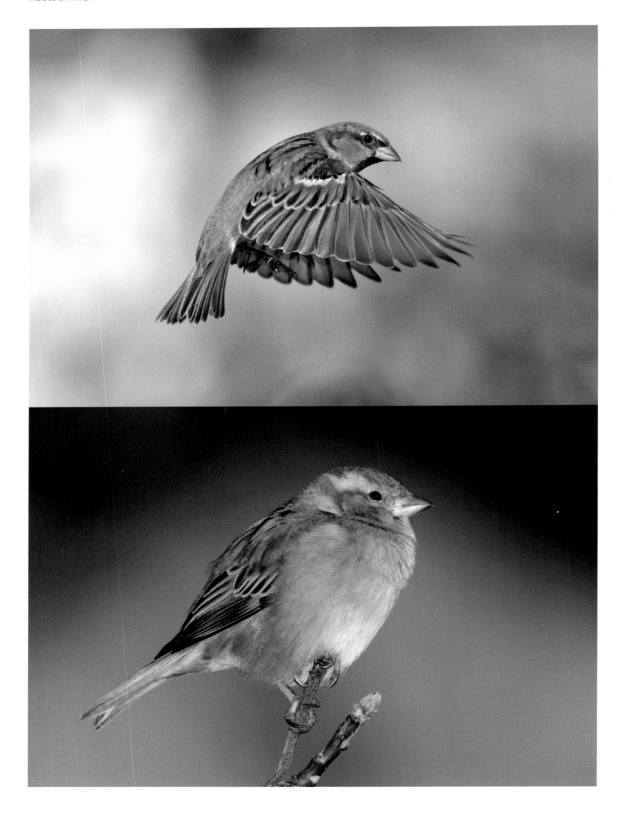

House Sparrow
Passer domesticus

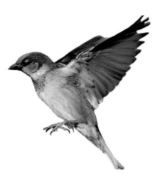

The House Sparrow is a familiar species that shows a distinct affinity with human habitation. The sexes are dissimilar. The adult male has mainly chestnut-brown upperparts, marked with a series of dark streaks; note the bold white wingbar. The head is distinctively marked with a grey crown and cheeks, with chestnut brown beneath the crown and on the nape. The underparts are primarily pale grey with a large and contrasting black patch on the throat and breast. The bill is short, robust and varies seasonally in colour from black to brown; the legs are reddish. The adult female is more plainly marked: the upperparts and the head are mainly brown, the back is marked with buff streaks. Note the pale buff supercilium behind the eye. The underparts are uniformly pale grey. Juvenile plumage is similar to the adult female but has less well-defined patterning; it becomes indistinguishable from the adult by the first autumn.

The House Sparrow is often seen in small groups around bird tables and feeders, perched on roofs and wires or taking dust baths. It can become surprisingly bold in some urban areas, and often hand-tame in locations such as urban parks and outdoor restaurant seating areas. The species usually pairs for life and will use favoured nesting sites several years running. It constructs a loose nest of grass in a building crevice or hole.

FACTFILE
Length: 14–15cm (5½–6in)
Wingspan: 24cm (9½in)
Habitat: favours areas of human habitation and occurs in villages, towns and around farms
Food: feeds on a variety of items including seeds, kitchen scraps and invertebrates. Regular visitor to garden bird tables and feeders in many areas
Status: widespread resident breeding species, present year-round and common throughout most of the region in suitable habitats. Its numbers have declined severely in recent years
Voice: utters a variety of sharp chirping calls

Above At the height of the breeding season, a male's bill is black; bib size and intensity determines dominance in a flock **Opposite Top** The male pale wingbar is striking in flight **Opposite Bottom** The female plumage is buffish-brown and rather nondescript

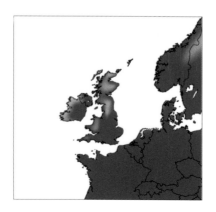

Tree Sparrow
Passer montanus

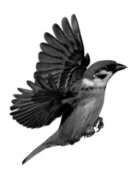

This is the rural counterpart of the House Sparrow and broadly similar in appearance. The sexes are similar. The adult has primarily streaked brown upperparts, with two obvious white wingbars. The underparts are pale greyish-white, the flanks showing a buffish tinge. The head is boldly marked with a chestnut cap, a small black bib and white cheeks with a central black patch. The black bill is rather stubby and stout-looking; the legs are pale brown. The juvenile is similar to the adult but displays more subdued and less well-defined facial markings.

The Tree Sparrow is rather timid compared to its cousin the House Sparrow, and less tolerant of human habitation. It favours more rural environments and can be found in flocks with finches and buntings during the winter months, typically feeding on the ground. A sociable species, it breeds in small, loose colonies and readily takes advantage of nest boxes.

FACTFILE
Length: 13–14cm (5–5½in)
Wingspan: 20–22cm (8–8¾in)
Habitat: variety of habitats including open woodland, parks and wooded suburbs. Particularly attracted to arable farms and grain spills
Food: feeds primarily on seeds and invertebrates
Status: local resident breeding species, present year-round throughout the region except in the extreme north. Its numbers have declined severely in recent years
Voice: it utters a chirp similar to that of the House Sparrow. In flight, it also commonly delivers a sharp 'tik-tik'

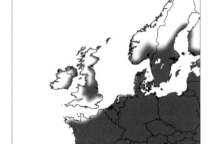

Above Hovering birds reveal obvious pale wingbars **Opposite** The chestnut crown and white-framed black check patch allow easy separation from a male House Sparrow

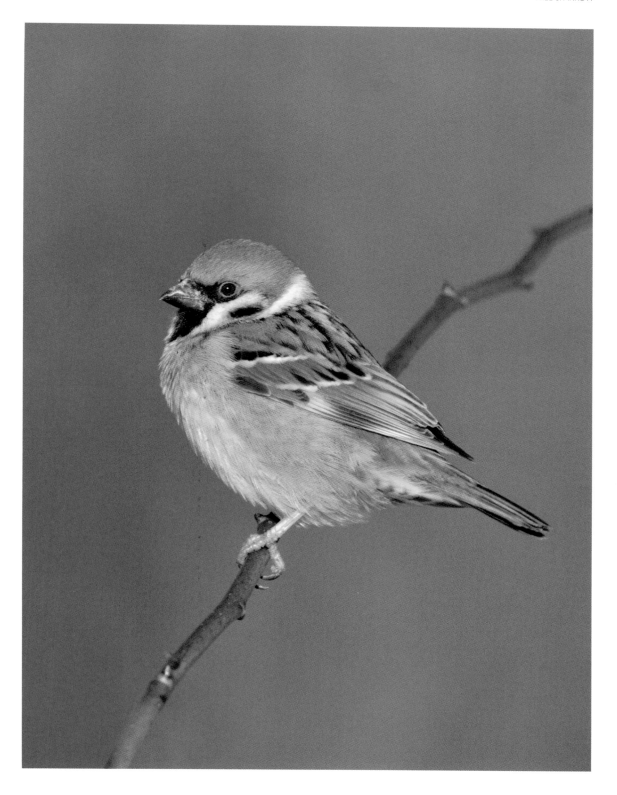

Finches
Fringillidae

The finches are small, restless and often colourful birds that are highly adapted to eating seeds. They are often specialized to harvest particular seed crops; Goldfinches, for example, are associated with thistles, Crossbills with conifers and Hawfinches with hard tree seeds.

The Finch bill has two grooves on the roof, one either side of the mid-line. When dealing with a seed, the finch lodges it in one of these groves, and then brings the cutting edge of its lower mandible to bear on the husk, piercing it and then, using its tongue, peeling it away in a similar action to a tin-opener. The kernel is thus exposed and the husk discarded. This de-husking technique is common among finches but the dimensions and shapes of their bills are often very different. The Hawfinch has extra projections on the mandibles that bring enormous pressures to bear on anything from acorns to olive nuts, while the Crossbill opens up the scales of conifer cones by the act of shutting its crossed bill and forcing them open.

There are twelve species of finch in Britain, most with some kind of affinity with seeds. Apart from those mentioned above, Redpolls are birch specialists, Parrot Crossbills are drawn to pine, Siskins to spruce (and alders) and Bramblings to beech mast. Linnets and Twites take very small seeds from farmland and wayside weeds; Greenfinches and Chaffinches are generalists. Bullfinches are unusual for taking many soft fruits in the breeding season (and ash seeds in the winter).

Finches are extremely sociable, occurring in flocks throughout the year, only the Chaffinch being highly territorial in the breeding season and feeding its young on insects. Autumn brambling flocks sometimes number in the millions, especially on the continent. This species, along with the Chaffinch, Siskin and Redpoll, is highly migratory, with large numbers coming to Britain to spend the winter, in the latter three cases augmenting the British resident population. Goldfinches sometimes leave Britain to winter on the continent.

Finches are famous for their neatly constructed nests, a cup of moss, hair and other materials. The goldfinch nest is lined with thistledown. Anywhere between two and seven eggs are laid, which usually hatch at the same time. A curious aspect of finch breeding behaviour is that pairs often nest close together, with several in the same tree or group of trees. These are known as 'neighbourhood groups'.

The bright plumage of finches comes to the fore in the late breeding season by means of a clever trick known as 'abrasion'. When birds moult in the autumn, the tips of the feathers are often dull, while just inside the tips the feathers are colourful. As the winter progresses, wear and tear ensures that the outer tips are ground away, exposing the colourful subterminal parts. Despite being worn, the plumage looks bright and crisp, without the need for an energy-sapping spring moult.

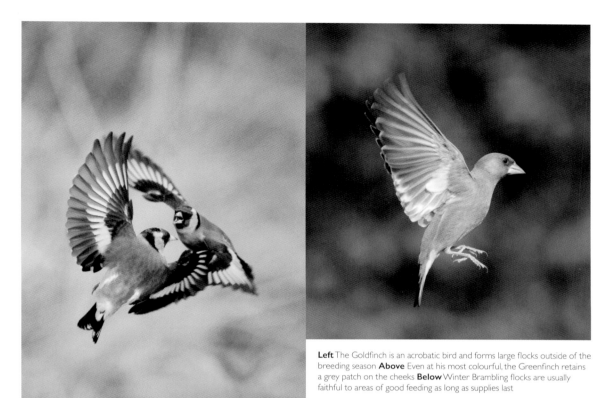

Left The Goldfinch is an acrobatic bird and forms large flocks outside of the breeding season **Above** Even at his most colourful, the Greenfinch retains a grey patch on the cheeks **Below** Winter Brambling flocks are usually faithful to areas of good feeding as long as supplies last

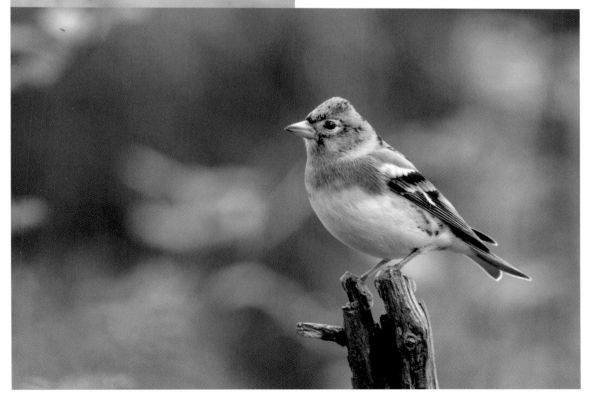

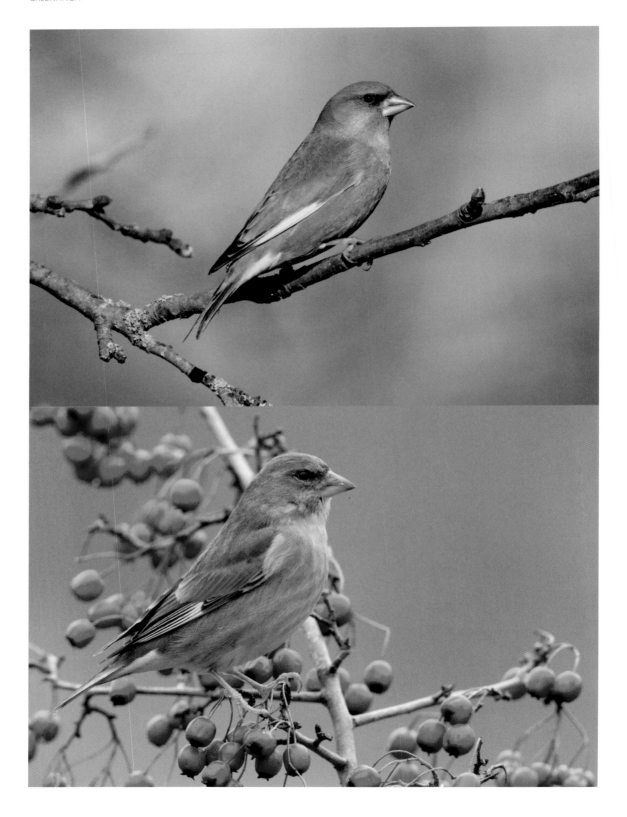

Greenfinch
Chloris chloris

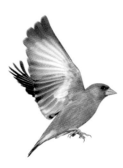

The Greenfinch is a brightly coloured finch with a large conical bill. The sexes differ. The adult male has intense yellowish–green plumage overall, darkest on the upperparts. Grey patches adorn the sides of the face, neck and wings; note the striking bright yellow patch to the edge of the wings, and the yellow sides to the base of the tail (most obvious in flight). The intensity of the plumage colour increases as winter progresses, and pale feather tips wear away. Note the pale stout-looking bill and the pale legs. The adult female is similar to the adult male, but the plumage is muted, with less yellow on the wings and tail; there is usually faint streaking on the back, although this is variable. The juvenile is similar to the adult female, but with more conspicuous streaking all over.

The Greenfinch is a widespread species and a familiar garden resident. It is an enthusiastic visitor to garden bird tables and feeders, and pecking-order quarrels often break out. The nest is a cup of grass and twigs placed in the fork of a tree or bush.

FACTFILE
Length: 14–15cm
Wingspan: 25–27cm
Habitat: favours lowland habitats, including woodland edges, hedgerows, parks and gardens
Food: feeds on seeds, berries and fruits, with invertebrates in the breeding season
Status: resident breeding species, common, widespread and present year-round across much of region except northern Scandinavia; here it is a summer visitor
Voice: song is rather varied, ranging from rapid, trilling whistles to well-spaced, wheezing 'weeeish' phrases, sometimes delivered in flight. Call is a harsh 'jrrrup' uttered in flight

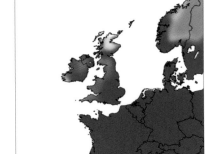

Above In flight, note the pale underside to the flight feathers and the yellow-green sides to the base of the tail **Opposite** All birds show a striking yellow bar along the edge of the folded wing

Goldfinch
Carduelis carduelis

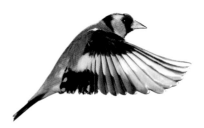

This is a colourful finch with unmistakable markings. The sexes are similar. The adult has upperparts that comprise a buffish-brown back and black wings and tail, marked with a series of white patches and a striking yellow wingbar. The head has a bold black-and-white pattern and a large red facial patch. The underparts are whitish and display a pale buff flush to the flanks and breast. The pale bill is relatively long and conical, and the legs are flesh-coloured. In flight, note the broad yellow wingbar, the white feather tips to the black upperwings and the white tips to the tail feathers. The juvenile is buffish overall with an unmarked head and an obvious yellow wingbar.

The Goldfinch is an acrobatic bird that generally feeds by extracting seeds with its bill directly from the heads of favoured plants such as Wild Teasel and thistles. It is readily attracted to garden feeders and tables and forms large flocks outside the breeding season. The nest is a cup of grass and moss hidden among the outer twigs of a tree.

FACTFILE

Length: 12–13cm (4¾–5in)

Wingspan: 21–25cm (8–10in)

Habitat: lowland areas, favouring scrub, hedgerows, woodland margins and mature gardens

Food: feeds on seeds and particularly fond of teasel, thistles and daisies

Status: common and widespread breeding species found throughout the region, except for the north. Present year-round in most areas, although local dispersal and general southerly migration does occur in autumn

Voice: song is a rapid, cheerful twittering. Utters a tinkling, trisyllabic call

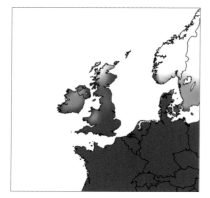

Above In flight, the yellow wingbars are a striking feature **Opposite** The white-framed red face and yellow on the wings make for a colourful appearance

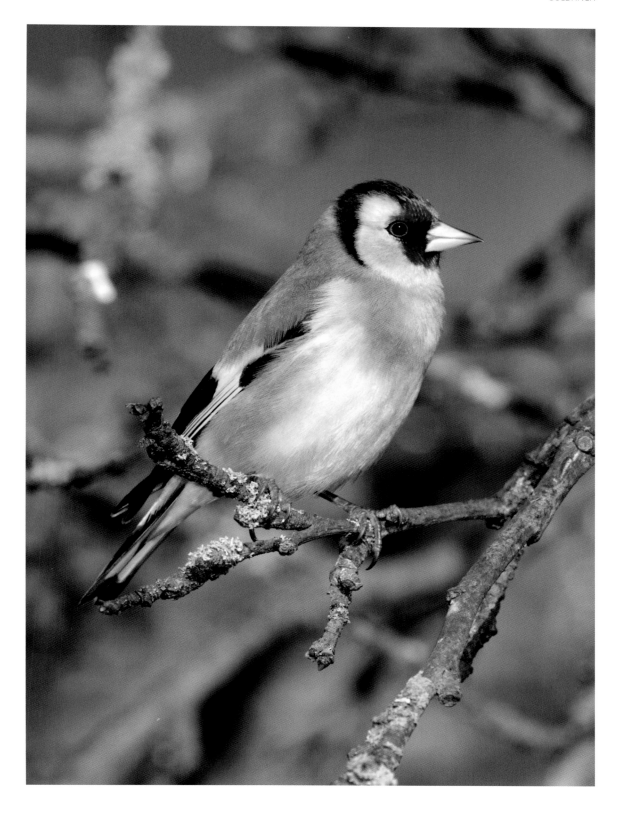

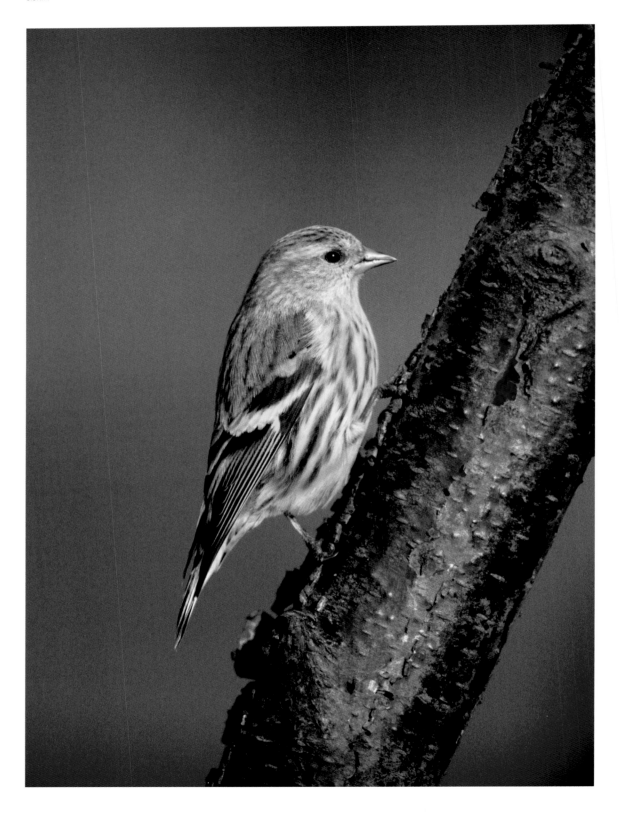

Siskin

Spinus spinus

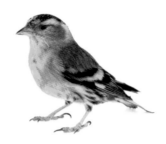

The Siskin is a brightly coloured little finch, easily recognized by the yellow elements of its plumage; the colours are most intense during the breeding season. The sexes are similar but separable with care. The adult male has streaked bright yellowish-green upperparts, with dark wings and yellow wingbars. The head is adorned with a contrasting black cap and bib. The underparts are pale whitish and boldy marked with dark streaking on the flanks and an intense yellowish-green flush on the breast. Note the bright yellow rump and yellow triangular patches on the base of the tail. The bill is conical and finely pointed. The adult female is similar but the colouration is subdued overall and it lacks the black cap and bib markings. The juvenile displays the wing and tail patterns of the adult, but has mainly streaked, grey-brown plumage overall, paler on the head and underparts.

The Siskin feeds primarily on the seeds of trees such as spruce, alder and birch. It extracts them directly with its tweezer-like bill, hanging acrobatically from the cones and twigs. It occasionally visits garden feeders where it shows a fondness for peanuts, but generally it is a more reluctant visitor than many of its counterparts. It nests high up in the outer twigs of conifers, constructing a moss-lined cup of twigs and grass.

FACTFILE

Length: 11–12cm (4¼–4¾in)

Wingspan: 20–23cm (8–9in)

Habitat: favours coniferous forests in the breeding season, but more widespread in the winter, with a preference for alder and birch woodlands, and mature gardens

Food: feeds primarily on the seeds of spruce, alder and birch

Status: locally common breeding species in the north and east of the region, and present year-round except in the extreme north where it is a summer visitor. In its resident range, and in western Europe, numbers are boosted in winter by birds migrating from further north and east

Voice: song comprises a series of warbling, twittering phrases. Utters a disyllabic 'speeoo' whistling call

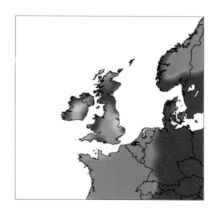

Above Colourful and unmistakable during the breeding season, with a dark cap and broad wingbars **Opposite** Plumage is overall pale, with streaked underparts and the species' trademark yellow wingbars

Chaffinch
Fringilla coelebs

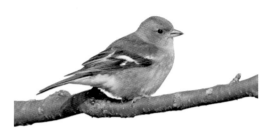

The Chaffinch is one of the most common and widespread species in the region. The sexes differ. The adult male is a colourful bird, with the plumage colours most intense in the breeding season. It has a chestnut back, a dark tail with white outer feathers and black wings with two contrasting white wingbars. The head has a blue-grey crown and nape, and the face and throat are pinkish-orange. The underparts are pinkish-orange, most intense on the throat and breast and fading towards the belly and vent. The stout, triangular bill is blue-grey during the breeding season and grey-brown at other times. In flight, the extensive white on the wings and tail is striking. The adult female has mainly buffish-brown plumage overall, darkest on the upperparts; note the two pale wingbars. The juvenile is similar to the adult female.

During the winter months the Chaffinch forages for seeds on the ground; it is also a familiar garden bird that is readily attracted to feeders. Outside the breeding season it forms loose flocks, and numbers in western Europe are boosted by migrant birds from further north and east. It nests in a beautifully constructed cup of lichen and moss, placed in the fork of a tree or bush.

FACTFILE

Length: 14–15cm (5½–6in)

Wingspan: 25–28cm (10–11in)

Habitat: variety of habitats including woodlands, farmland and parks; a familiar garden visitor

Food: feeds on seeds and invertebrates

Status: common and widespread throughout. Present year-round in much of the region but Scandinavian populations migrate south and west for the winter months

Voice: song is a descending trill that finishes with a flourish. The call is a distinctive 'pink pink'

Above The female's plumage is drab by comparison with a male but shows the same striking white markings on the wings **Opposite** During the breeding season male Chaffinches use a prominent perch from which to sing and watch for danger; if a threat is identified, an insistent and persistent alarm call is uttered

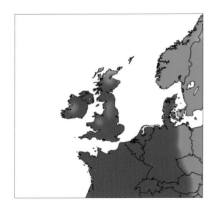

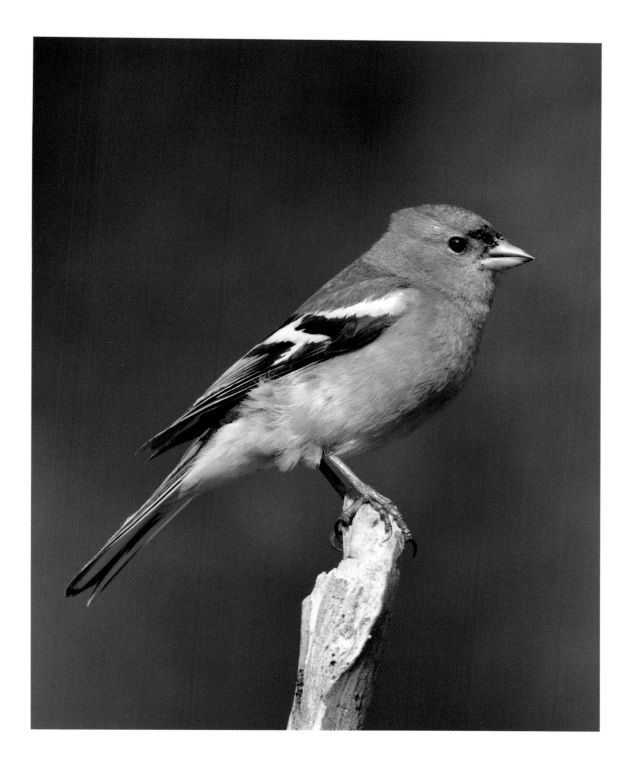

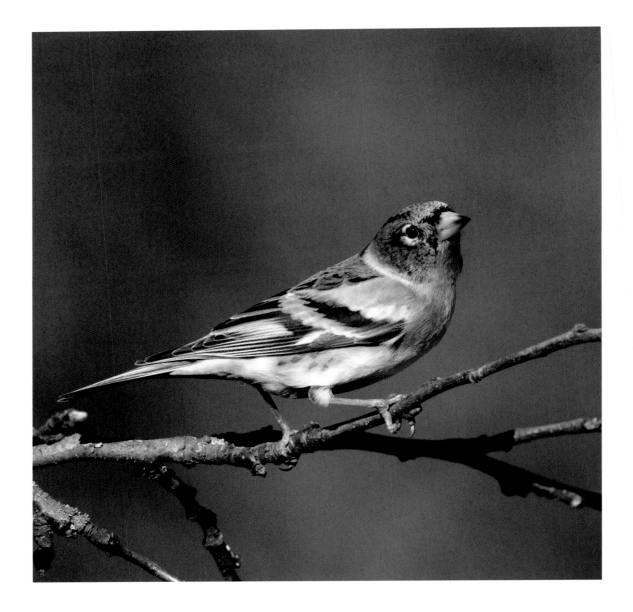

Brambling
Fringilla montifringilla

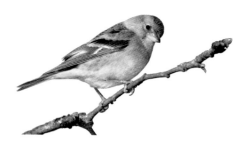

The Brambling is a handsome finch. The sexes differ and seasonal plumage variation occurs. The winter adult male has a dark head and back, the feathers displaying grey-buff fringes, which gradually wear off. The wings are dark with pale feather margins and whitish-orange wingbars. The lesser wing coverts are orange, the colour extending to the throat and breast, and grading to white on the belly and vent. Note the dark spots on the flanks and the triangular, dark-tipped yellow bill. The summer adult male is similar but the hood, back and bill are black or blackish. The adult female is similar to the adult winter male but with muted colouration overall; the pale fringes on the back feathers are more obvious. The head is grey-brown and marked with dark lines to the nape and sides of the crown. The immature is similar to the winter adult but with subdued colouration, although the sex cannot always be reliably determined. In flight, the obvious white rump is a good aid to identification of all birds.

Best known as a winter visitor, the Brambling's numbers and distribution at this time are affected by the food supply in its summer range. With a particular liking for Beech seeds, it will linger until supplies dwindle, forcing it to move south and west. Outside the breeding season, it can form large flocks.

FACTFILE
Length: 14–15cm (5½–6in)
Wingspan: 25–26cm (10–10½in)
Habitat: variety of open and wooded habitats, showing a preference for locations where beech proliferates
Food: feeds on seeds in winter, particularly those of beech. Diet includes invertebrates during the summer months
Status: summer breeding visitor to Scandinavia, present mainly May to September. Elsewhere, best known as a winter visitor, mainly October to March. Numbers vary each year depending on weather and food availability elsewhere
Voice: song is seldom heard in the region, but comprises a series of buzzing notes. Call includes a harsh, wheezing 'jseeerrp'

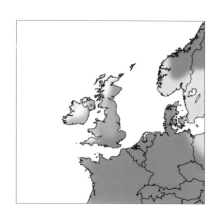

Above Even though female Bramblings are less colourful than males, they share the same orange colour on the wings and flanks; the precise hue is subtly unique to the species **Opposite** In winter, males have more strikingly marked and richly coloured plumage than females

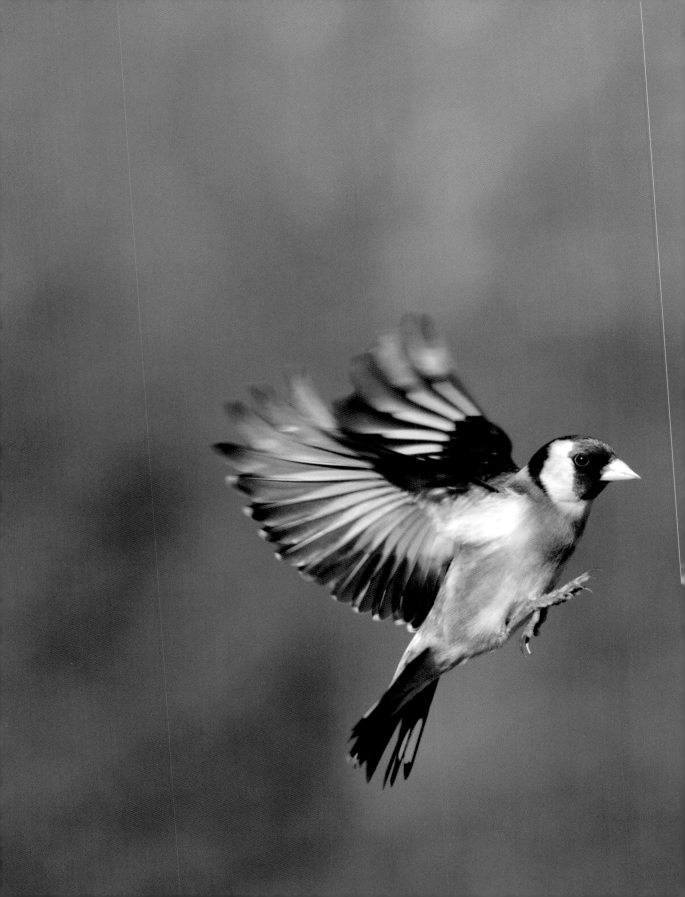

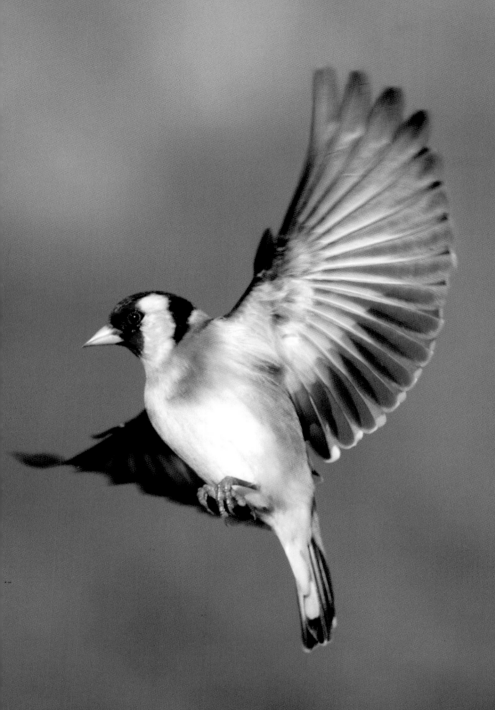

Bullfinch

Pyrrhula pyrrhula

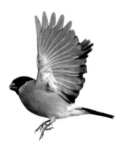

The Bullfinch has a plump body and distinctive plumage. The sexes differ. The adult male has a blue-grey back and nape; the tail is black and the black wings display a broad white wingbar. The head has a bold black cap and bib, contrasting with the rosy-pink face, breast and belly. The vent and rump are white and the stubby bill is dark. The adult female is similar to the adult male, but the rosy-pink elements of the plumage are replaced with dull pinkish-buff. The juvenile is similar to the adult female but lacks the black cap and is generally buffish-brown. In flight, the white rump is obvious and diagnostic in all birds.

The Bullfinch is a rather timid species that seeks the sanctuary of deep cover, and is heard more frequently than it is seen. When encountered it is commonly seen in pairs. It feeds on the buds, seeds and fruits of trees and is an occasional visitor to garden feeders in rural areas. It nests in deep cover, constructing a platform of twigs.

FACTFILE

Length: 16–17cm (6–6¾n)
Wingspan: 25cm (10in)
Habitat: a species of mainly rural areas, found in deciduous woodland, hedgerows and mature gardens
Food: feeds primarily on buds, seeds, berries and fruits
Status: a common and widespread resident breeding species, present year-round throughout the region in suitable habitats
Voice: the song is rather quiet and seldom heard, consisting of slow, fluty notes. The call is distinctive a soft, monosyllabic piping 'pew', sometimes delivered by a pair in duet

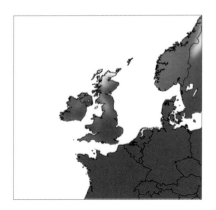

Previous Page Goldfinches in flight **Above** The white rump of the Bullfinch is an obvious feature in flight, contrasting with the dark tail **Opposite** The female is usually seen in the company of a male and the pair is often site-faithful throughout the year

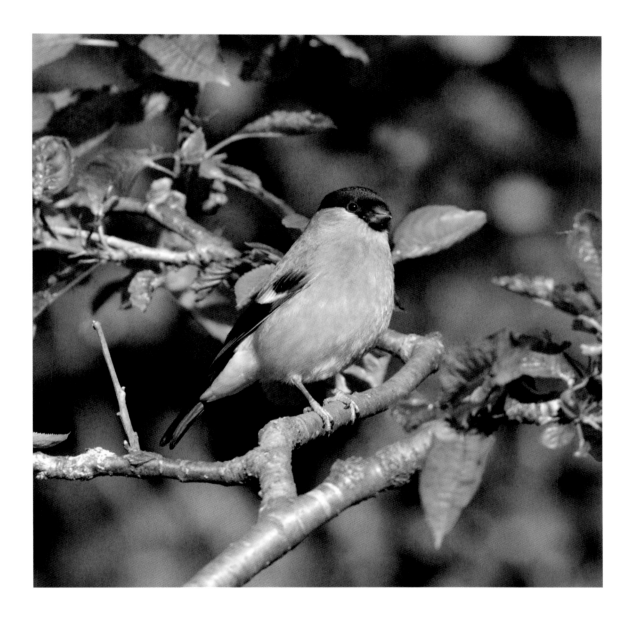

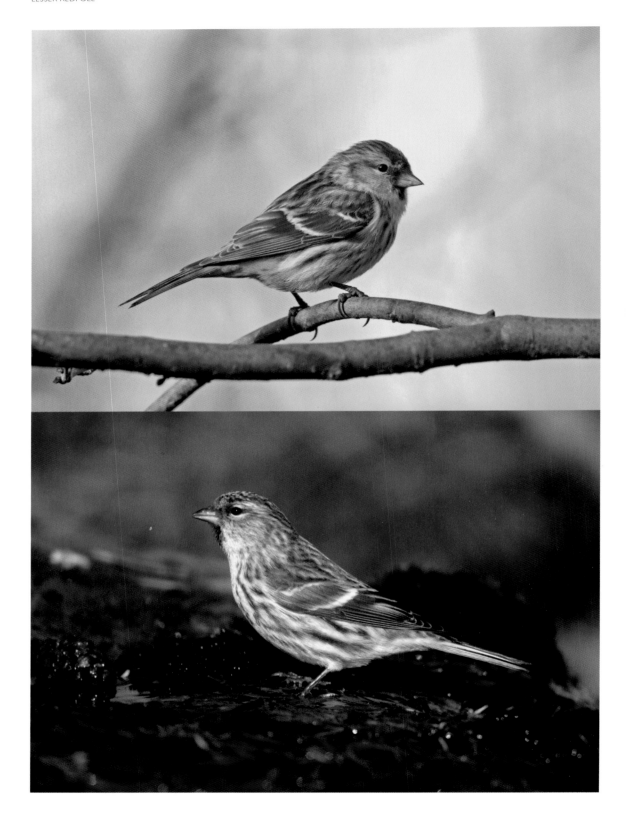

Lesser Redpoll

Acanthis cabaret

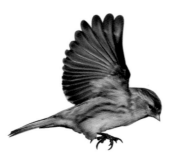

The Lesser Redpoll is a compact little finch with a small yellow bill. The sexes are similar but are sometimes separable. The adult male has heavily streaked grey-brown upperparts, darkest on the back, and with pale wingbars. The underparts and rump are pale, heavily streaked, with a pinkish-red flush usually discernible on the breast. The head has a red forecrown, black lores and black bib. The short, triangular bill is yellow. The adult female and immature birds are similar to the adult male but lack the pinkish-red flush to the breast. In flight, note the forked tail and pale wingbars in all birds.

Outside the breeding season, the Lesser Redpoll forms large gregarious flocks, often mixing with Siskins. It is an acrobatic feeder, dangling from thin twigs and plucking seeds from treetop cones with its small bill. It builds a nest of twigs and grass, usually positioned high up in a tree.

FACTFILE

Length: 12–14cm (4¾–5½in)
Wingspan: 20–25cm (8–10in)
Habitat: during the breeding season favours birch woodland, but occurs in areas of both birch and alder at other times
Food: feeds primarily on the seeds of alder and birches
Status: resident breeding species present year-round in suitable habitat throughout the region, except the far north. Some southward migration occurs in areas that experience harsh winters
Voice: song comprises a series of wheezing and rattling notes. Call is a rattling 'chek-chek-chek' uttered in flight

Above In flight the forked tail and pale wingbars can be noted **Opposite Top** The female plumage is streaked brown, with pale wingbars and a yellowish bill **Opposite Bottom** The extent and intensity of red in a male's plumage varies between individuals and increases throughout spring

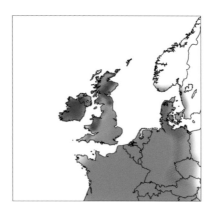

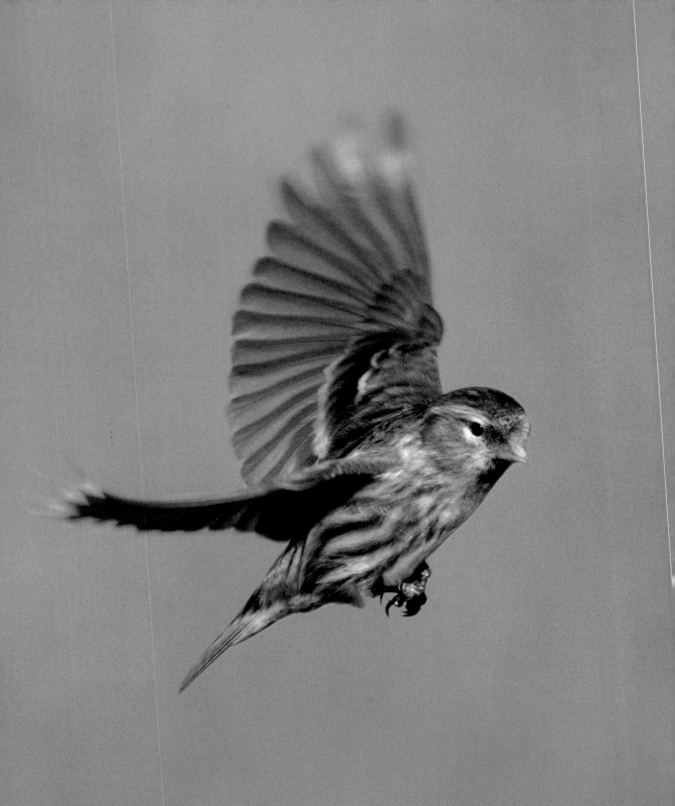

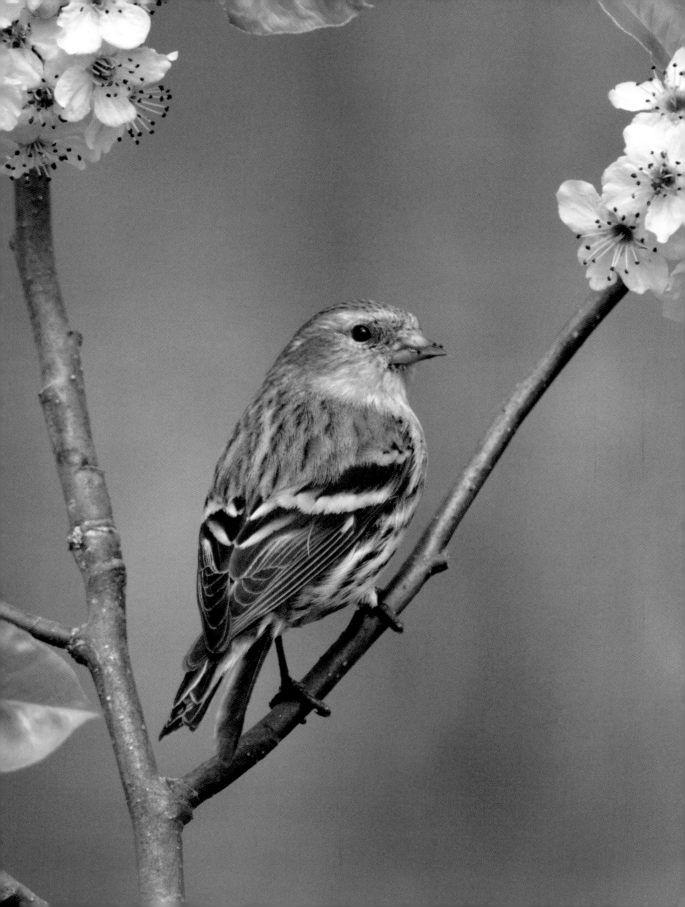

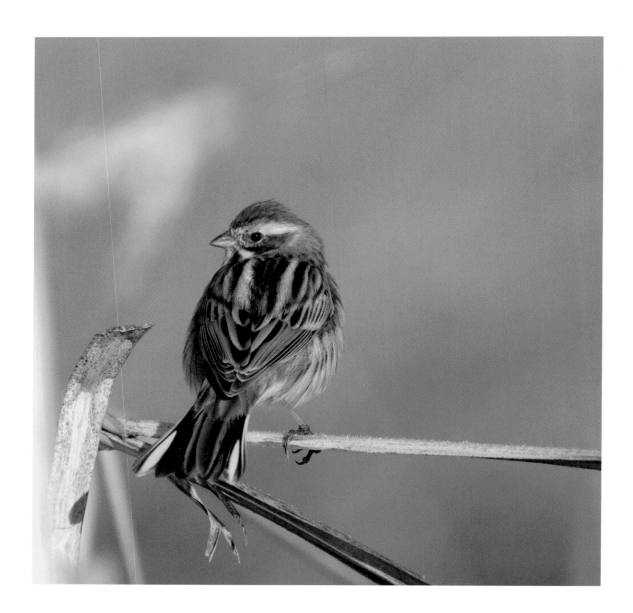

Reed Bunting

Emberiza schoeniclus

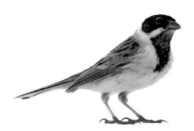

The Reed Bunting is a distinctive bird of wetland margins. Seasonal plumage variation occurs, and the sexes can be separated in the summer. The summer adult male has mainly reddish-brown upperparts marked with dark streaking. The underparts are mostly white with faint streaking. The head, throat and bib are black with a white sub-moustachial stripe and collar. The stubby triangular bill is dark. The winter male and adult female recall the summer male, but the distinctive black-and-white head and throat markings are replaced with a pattern of dark brown and buffish-brown stripes. The bill is greyish in colour. The male can display a suggestion of summer plumage, with spotting to the throat and bib. The juvenile is similar to the female but with even more subdued markings on the head. In all birds, note the white outer tail feathers, which are most obvious in flight.

In the breeding season, the male Reed Bunting uses exposed, elevated perches or fences from which to sing, making observation easy. At other times it is unobtrusive and the species favours the cover of reed beds and field furrows; in winter it sometimes forms small flocks.

FACTFILE

Length: 14–15cm (5½–6in)
Wingspan: 21–27cm (8–10½in)
Habitat: favours reed-bed margins and scrubby wetlands, particularly during the breeding season. Also found on farmland, especially in winter
Food: feeds primarily on seeds and invertebrates
Status: widespread and locally common breeding species. Present year-round in much of the region, but birds from the north and east migrate south and west in the autumn, returning in the spring
Voice: utters a distinctive and repetitive chinking song. Call is a thin 'seeu'

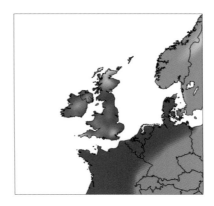

Previous Page Left A Lesser Redpoll in flight **Previous Page Right** A Siskin feeds primarily on the seeds of trees **Above** The male Reed Bunting has whitish underparts and underwings **Opposite** Note the streaked brown plumage and white in the outer tail feathers

Yellowhammer

Emberiza citrinella

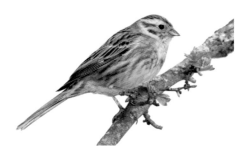

The Yellowhammer is a colourful bunting, the summer male being particularly eye-catching. The sexes are separable, and some seasonal plumage variation occurs. The adult male in summer has a reddish-brown back, the dark feather centres giving it a rather streaked appearance; the rump is reddish-brown. The underparts and the head are bright yellow, the head being marked with faint dark lines. The flanks are adorned with streaking, and the breast has a chestnut flush. The stubby triangular bill is greyish. The adult male in winter has subdued yellow elements to its plumage and the dark streaking on the head and upperparts is more intense. The adult female has brown upperparts, with a reddish-brown rump. The underparts are pale yellow and streaked, and the head and breast are greenish-grey, and are also streaked. The immature is similar to the adult female but the streaking is more intense.

The Yellowhammer is a classic bunting of farmland and open countryside, its distinctive song and bright colouration make identification simple. Outside the breeding season it often forms flocks and mixes with other buntings and finches, typically around grain spills and other concentrations of food. It nests in low scrub or on the ground, constructing a bulky platform of grass and straw.

FACTFILE

Length: 15–17cm (6–6¾in)
Wingspan: 23–29cm (9–11½in)
Habitat: open grassland and farmland with scattered scrub and hedgerows
Food: feeds primarily on seeds and invertebrates
Status: rather sedentary resident breeding species, present year-round across most of the region in suitable habitats. Birds from upland regions and from more northerly and easterly extremes move south and west in the autumn
Voice: song comprises a series of chirping and wheezing phrases. Call is a sharp 'sttut'

Above A particularly colourful female can look confusingly similar to a male with dull plumage **Opposite** The male's bright yellow head and classic plump-bodied bunting shape make for easy identification **Next Page** The precise hue of a male Bullfinch's rosy pink underparts is subtly unique to the species

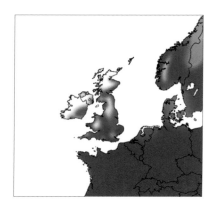

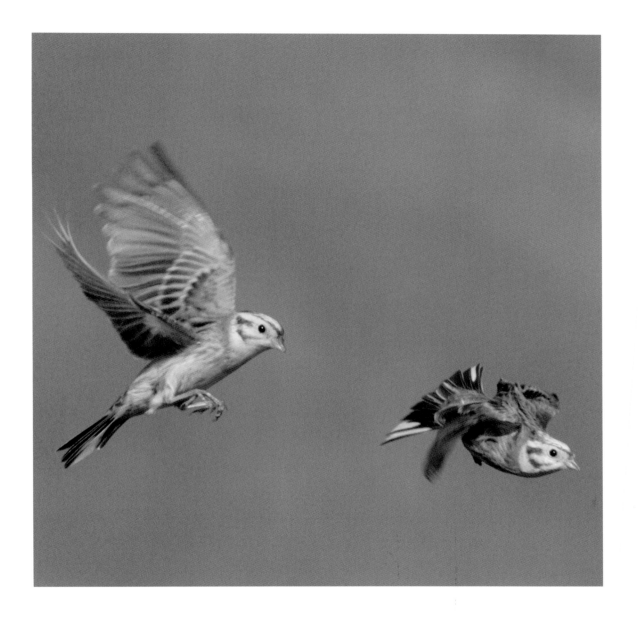

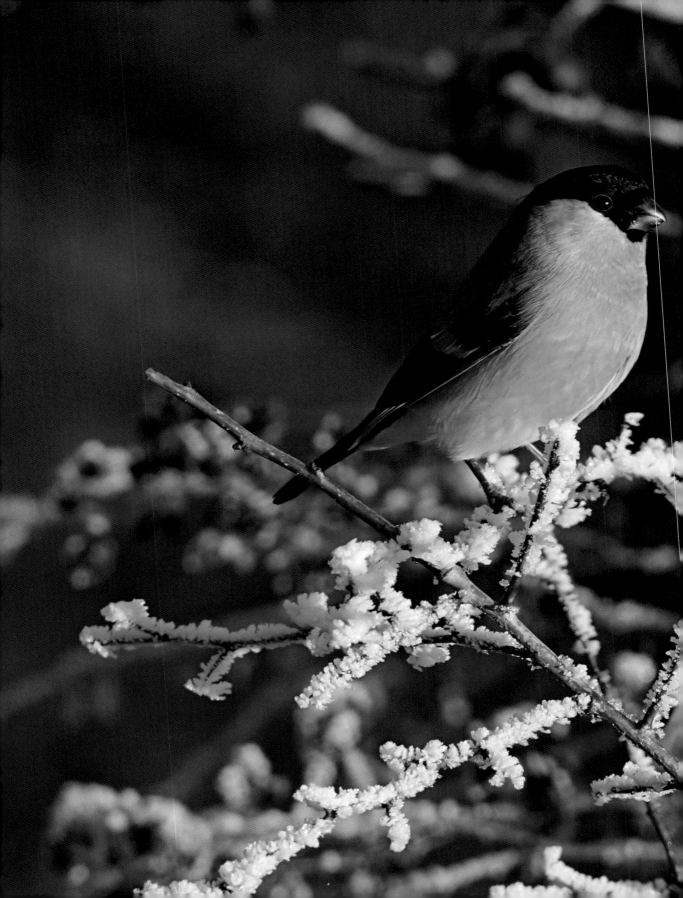

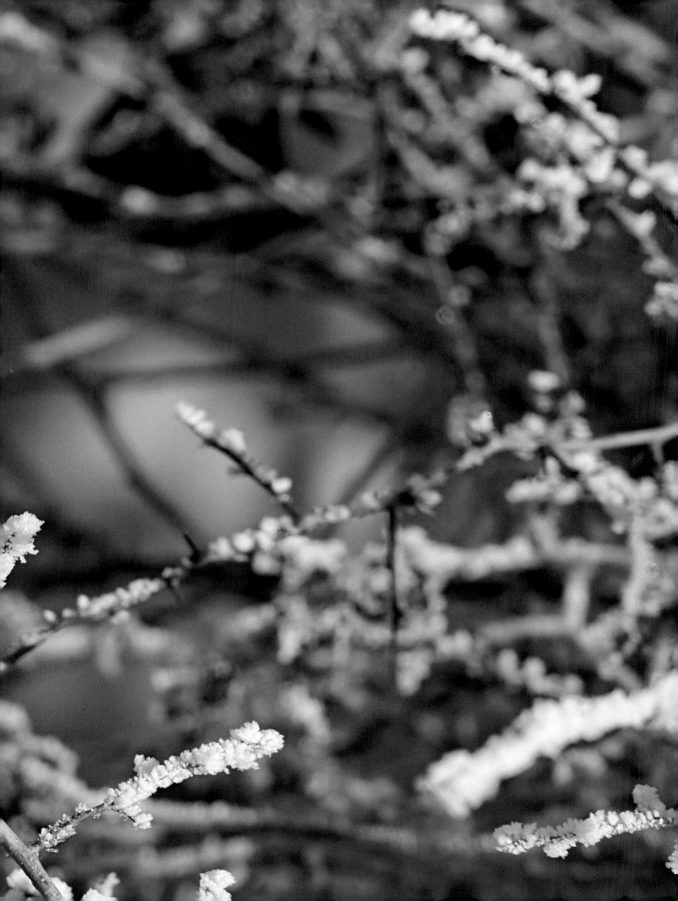

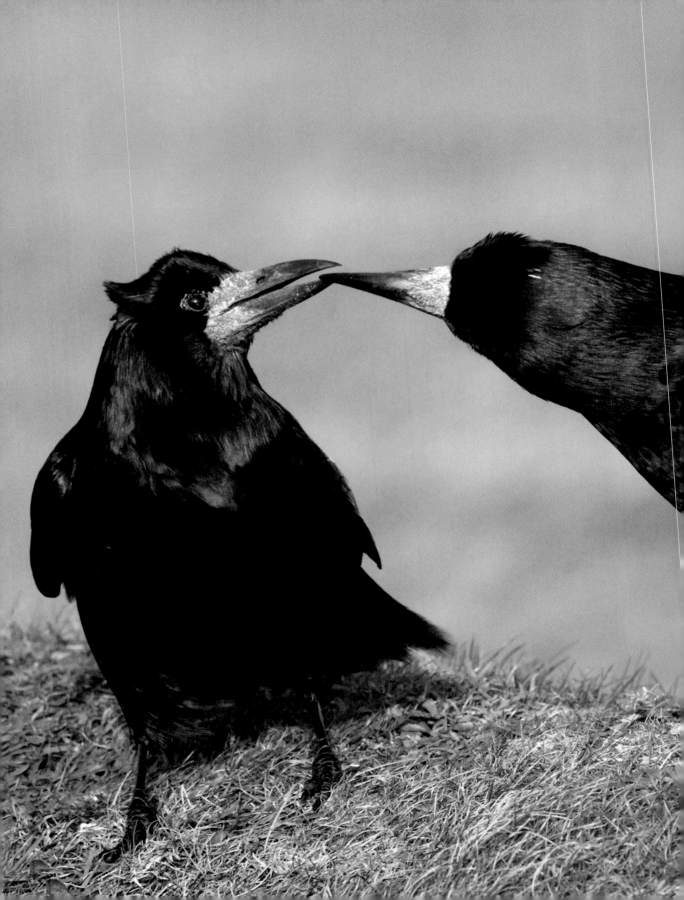

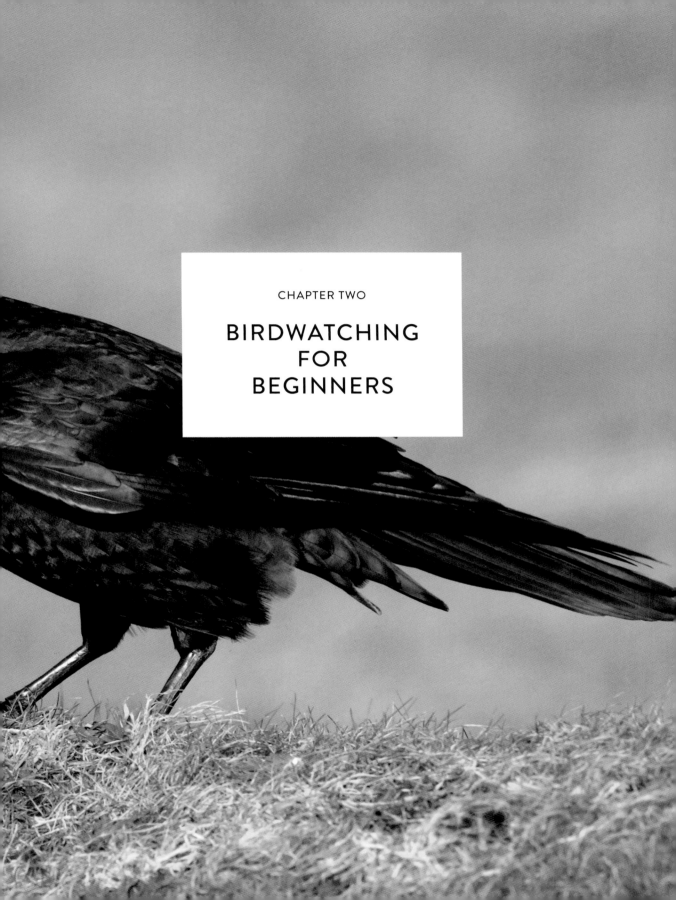

CHAPTER TWO

BIRDWATCHING
FOR
BEGINNERS

THE STUDY OF BIRDS

We share the earth with about 11,000 species of birds. We share the same continents, the same countries, our neighbourhoods, even our gardens. We breathe the same air. But despite this proximity, birds and humans are not similar; the life of a bird and that of a human are quite alien to each other.

In some ways that is not surprising, because our evolutionary path diverged from birds about 300 million years ago. Our differences are unimaginably vast. We are Synapsids, which include, other than mammals, some of the weirdest creatures that ever roamed the earth. Birds are Sauropsids, a group that includes reptiles. The chickadees and bluebirds are more closely related to the great dinosaurs such as Stegosaurus and Brachiosaurus than they are to us.

The upshot is that almost every twist and turn of the life cycle of birds is something of a foreign country. If, miraculously, a human turned into a bird but kept the same consciousness, life would be barely recognizable. A bird's anatomy, movement, senses, lifestyle, reproduction, daily life and survival are all completely different to ours. We cannot really get under a bird's skin.

That, in part, is what makes birds so endlessly fascinating. Even their basic locomotion – flight – is beyond our reach and has been a source of inspiration for centuries. To most birds, it is everyday life. Flying is so easy for them that a Bar-tailed Godwit, for example, can spend a week flying from Alaska to New Zealand without stopping.

Feathers, essentially modified scales, are the definitive trademark of modern-day birds, although we now know that some dinosaurs had them, too. They form an extremely effective insulation, so much so that some species can remain outdoors during the Arctic and Antarctic winters, in temperatures that can plunge to -40°C. Yet birds thrive in the tropics, too, and they can also swim. Feathers are the ultimate flexible covering. For birds, the moult, when new feathers are grown and old ones discarded, is a vitally important process.

Reproduction in birds revolves around the hard-shelled, external egg. For almost every bird, that sets a challenge of siting a nest and sometimes building it, of incubating and then brooding chicks, all of which can be hazardous activities. A few circumvent the rules – some Megapodes use the heat generated by soil fermentation, or even geothermally warmed soil to incubate their eggs – but being tied to this mode of reproduction has wide implications. On the whole, reproduction needs to be quick, and in most species parental care is peremptory and expedient.

Even that most easily appreciated of avian delights, bird song, is not what it seems. It can be a source of harmony within a breeding pair, but more normally it is a competitive breeding signal, typically only used by a male in the breeding season, at least in temperate climates. It is a passive-aggressive proclamation of owned territory and breeding intention, and hard work for the singer. Birds produce their songs not with vocal chords, as we do, but lower down the respiratory tract, where the trachea divides into the bronchi of the lungs. Here lies the syrinx, an organ which varies in complexity among birds. In many songbirds, the song is actually a combination of two songs, a composite of the two bronchi.

Perhaps the most admired of any avian talent is that of migration, the ability to travel vast (or very short) distances, using only what is in a bird's head and what it can perceive. The recent suggestion that birds can 'see' magnetic fields is just one of the wonders that we find hard to fathom. Birds have such efficient body clocks that they can use the sun-compass as our star moves across the sky. Birds remember

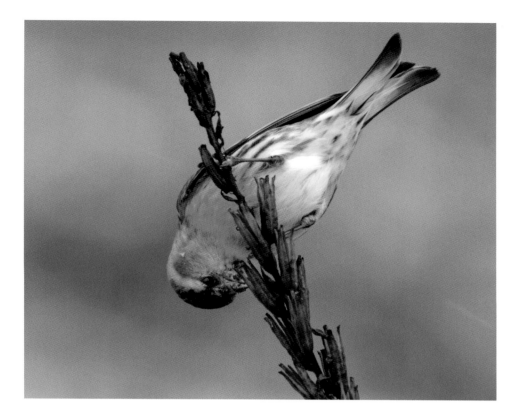

landmarks with astonishing accuracy. Even more remarkably, a bird inherits its migratory pathway – for example a Common Cuckoo chick, raised by a completely unrelated foster parent, leaving on its migration months after its genetic parents have left, nonetheless finds its way to Africa.

Birds are astonishing and different in these and so many ways, so it is perhaps not surprising that people view them as objects of intrigue and wonder. People have been observing birds for centuries, all over the world, and in modern times this has now crystallized into the hobby of birdwatching, one that is happily growing fast all over the world, a delight for all kinds of people. This enthusiasm is sorely needed because, however much we might revere birds, we aren't looking after their world very well.

Ironically, while birds are very different to us, it is their need to share the same continents, lands and air to breathe that has placed them under worldwide threat.

Previous Page Rooks are normally encountered in large flocks or at nesting colonies **Above** A Siskin feeds upside down on the seeds of a plant

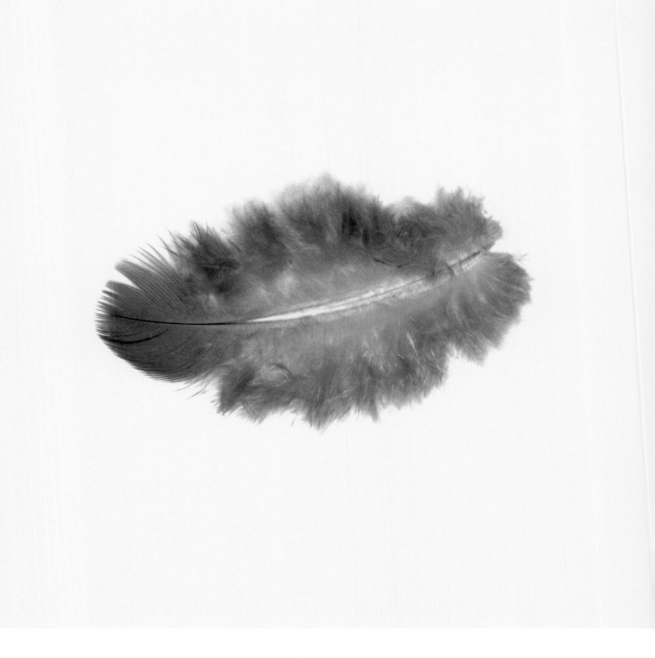

LIFE OF A BIRD

Apart from bats, birds are the only vertebrates capable of flight. The ancestors of modern birds took to the air some 150 million years ago and since that time the ability to fly has allowed them to occupy almost every terrestrial habitat on earth, and many aquatic ones, too.

What Makes Birds Special?

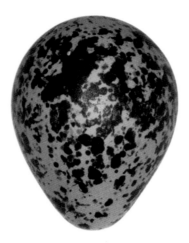

For birds, flight would not be possible without feathers, but these lightweight, tough and resilient structures are also vital for thermal insulation. In addition, contours, shapes, patterns and colours confer species and gender identity on their owners, and camouflage is also important for many species. Unsurprisingly, there are different kinds of feathers on a bird's body that fulfil a range of functions, those associated with flight being structurally different from those that insulate. In common with their reptilian ancestors, birds lay eggs, inside which their young develop. Eggs are laid in nests, which vary from a rudimentary scrape in the ground to an intricately woven basket, depending on the species.

The eggs themselves are protected by a hard, chalky outer casing and the developing chick gains its nutrition from the egg's yolk. Newly hatched birds are vulnerable, and not surprisingly chick mortality is high. The degree to which newly hatched birds can fend for themselves, and the effort invested by their parents in looking after them, varies considerably. With songbirds, and many other bird families too, adults brood and feed their young (which are essentially defenceless at first) until at least the point where they fledge, and often for several weeks after they have left the nest. On the other hand, young gamebirds are active almost from the moment they hatch and leave the nest straight away, though they still depend on their parents to a degree for shelter and protection, and to be guided to good areas for feeding.

Not only are there birds in all the terrestrial habitats of Europe and North America, almost all sources of food are exploited by one species or another. Some birds are purely vegetarian, feeding perhaps on seeds, fruits or shoots, while many more include invertebrates – particularly insects – in their diet during the summer months. A few are strict predators, taking prey that includes other birds. Although some birds lead rather solitary lives except during the breeding season, many species are gregarious and either breed in colonies or spend the winter months in sizeable groups. Complex behaviour patterns allow individuals to rub along with one another.

Opposite A downy feather from a hatchling **Above** A Lapwing egg

The Hatchling

A young bird becomes conscious of its surroundings well before it hatches from the egg. Several days prior to hatching, it will notice the chilling and warming as the incubating parent leaves and returns. More chicks hatch in the morning than in the afternoon, and this suggests that, even in the egg, they already have some kind of diurnal rhythm; this may be as a result of the parents' incubating intermittently during the day, and a long unbroken spell during the night. Doubtless it will also feel its parent turning the eggs at frequent intervals; this is probably done to prevent the egg membranes sticking to the shell, and to aid the uptake of oxygen, though a few species do not turn their eggs.

At first, the developing chick breathes oxygen that passes into the egg through the surprisingly porous eggshell and the albumen (the white); expired carbon dioxide passes in the opposite direction. In the early stages, respiration is by diffusion, but soon a system of blood vessels develop outside the embryo; then the blood takes up the oxygen and carries it into the embryo. Water is also lost through the shell of the egg as the chick develops and, as this happens, the egg membrane contracts and pulls away from the shell at the blunt end of the egg, leaving an air space just inside the shell. Sometime before it hatches the young bird punctures the membrane with its bill. It can then get its nostrils into the air space and breathe air directly through the shell, using its lungs for the first time (although it still relies partly on the external blood vessels). Only after this stage can the young bird begin to call.

Eventually, the time comes for the young bird to break out of its egg. It does this by chipping a ring of holes around the blunt end of the egg. To do this it uses a particularly powerful neck muscle, the hatching muscle, developed at this time especially for this one purpose, to force the head hard against the end of the egg. It also presses against the shell with a small sharpish spike, the egg tooth. This is a small white protuberance near the tip of the upper mandible (some species also have one on the lower mandible), clearly visible on a newly hatched chick; in most species it drops off a few days after hatching. Occasionally one finds a chick that has died in the egg at hatching time to be missing the egg tooth, which provides ample evidence of the importance of this small structure for this one essential job.

Once the end of the egg is well cracked, the chick forces its head against the loosened end and, at the same time, presses with its legs against the other end; the top comes off. The actual period of breaking loose is quite short in most small birds, but may take several hours in some of the larger species whose egg's thick shell seems difficult to break; the effort required appears to be considerable, the baby bird having to rest frequently. Eventually, however, the young chick breaks free to start its life as a nestling.

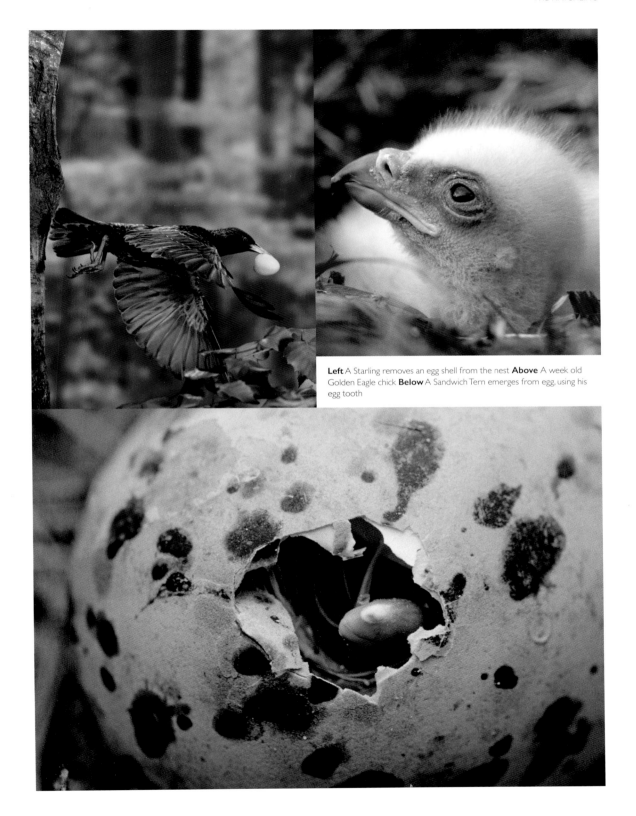

Left A Starling removes an egg shell from the nest **Above** A week old Golden Eagle chick **Below** A Sandwich Tern emerges from egg, using his egg tooth

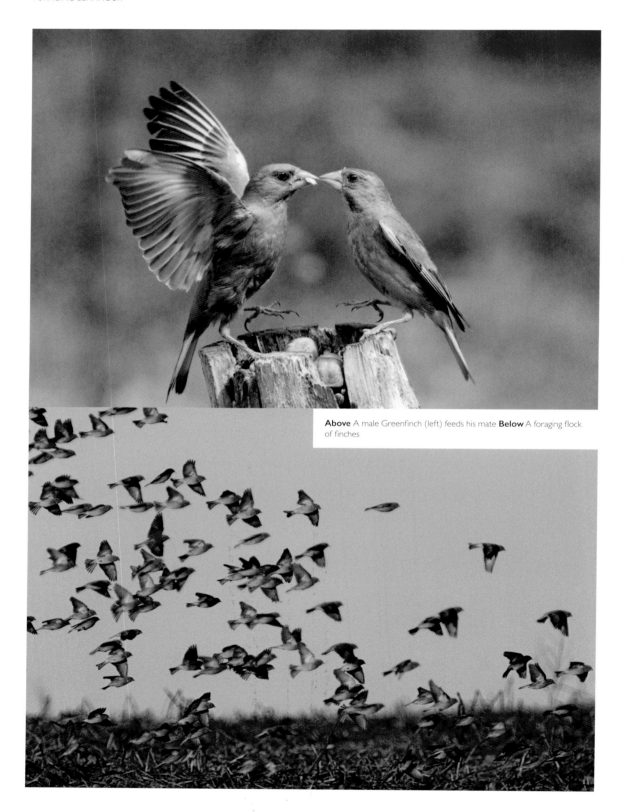

Above A male Greenfinch (left) feeds his mate **Below** A foraging flock of finches

Foraging Behaviour

Learning to feed

Learning to feed for itself is perhaps the most difficult single thing that a young bird has to do, and it is no wonder that so many of them fail the test. Young swifts leave the nest when their parents are away, and fly off by themselves; they have never seen their prey in its natural habitat, and they get no help from their parents. Most birds get some sort of assistance from their parents after they leave the nest. We know very little about how they actually learn to catch their prey.

Even parental tuition cannot cover all situations. Resident European birds may switch from insects in summer to seeds in winter, while the warbler, which leaves a European woodland for an African forest, faces a whole range of changes. The habitats, the prey and the predators all change; all must be learned if the young bird is to survive.

The individual seems to develop its hunting skill in response to reward and failure – continuing to hunt in places where it has been successful and tending to give up on places where it fails to find food.

Flocks and flocking

Many species feed in flocks at rich supplies of food – such as gulls on rubbish tips, seabirds on shoals of fish and vultures, kites and crows at carrion. Many other species hunt in loose flocks – such as mixed parties of woodland birds, flocks of pigeons in fields and gatherings of rooks and jackdaws or of buntings and finches. At least in many of these cases, the young bird may be able to learn the whereabouts of food by watching others in the flock. For many birds there is another advantage in living in flocks. The larger the numbers of birds the more likely it is that one of them will spot an approaching predator before it gets dangerously close. Raptors get closer to prey in small flocks, before the alarm is given, than is the case with large flocks; hence they are more likely to be able to make a kill from a small flock than a large one. Birds spend an appreciable amount of time scanning around for predators, but individuals spend less time on the look-out when they are in a large flock than when in a small one and so they have more time for feeding.

There is, however, a disadvantage to being in a flock. When an individual in a flock finds an item of food, a nearby bird may come and snatch it before the finder can eat it. This is not usually important where small food items are being taken since the bird that finds them can swallow them quickly. But a large worm, or a large seed, which takes some time to deal with, may easily be snatched by another bird. Food stealing of this type is quite common in birds in winter. Robbing often occurs between individuals of the same species. In small flocks there is usually a clear pecking order among the birds in a flock. Individuals know each other. When birds have previously squabbled they remember who won, and a hierarchy develops. The advantages to the winner are obvious, but to the losers the system may have certain benefits: it is better to give up swiftly and avoid injury than to risk a prolonged and possibly damaging battle. In such dominance hierarchies, older birds tend to dominate younger ones and the males usually dominate the females. These hierarchies are probably established partly on the basis of the experience of the birds concerned, but also partly on their size.

In mixed species flocks, larger or more aggressive species often take food from the slower or less aggressive species. Great Tits snatch beech seeds from Blue Tits before the latter can open them and eat the contents. Both Great and Blue Tits rob Coal Tits. As a result, Coal Tits try to avoid direct confrontation; often, at a bird-table, Coal Tits sneak in underneath and wait for the other tits to drop a small piece of food; which they then rapidly grab and fly off with.

Flight

Lift and drag

Flight is achieved by creating lift – an upwards force great enough to counteract the force of gravity on the bird's body. Lift is produced by the wings. When air moves over a stationary wing of an appropriate shape, the air, which is deflected over the upper surface, has to travel faster than the air beneath the wing, because it has further to travel in the same time. The pressure exerted by air passing over the surface of the wing is inversely proportional to the speed at which it is travelling. So, the air that passes above the wing is at a lower pressure than that beneath, and this produces lift. It may seem odd, but most of the lift produced by a wing comes from the passage of the air over the top of it and not from that which passes underneath.

Unfortunately for the bird, there is another force produced by air passing over the wing. As the air hits the wing, the wing tends to be pushed backwards; this force is called drag and this too increases with the size of the wing, the airspeed, and the angle the wing is held at.

Gliding

There are two ways that a bird can glide in still air. First it can launch itself from a high perch and use the potential energy provided by gravity; its movement is comparable with that of a toboggan on a snowy slope. It can maintain its speed for as long as it is above the surface of the ground; but since it is losing height all the time, the length of time that it can stay airborne will depend on the height from which it launched itself.

The second method of gliding is the reverse of this – maintaining height by loss of speed. Such a glide can only take place when a bird has already achieved a reasonable airspeed; it is using kinetic energy. The moment the bird stops flying and starts to glide it is slowed down by drag. As it slows, it loses lift, since lift varies in proportion to airspeed. The bird can maintain its lift by increasing the angle of attack of its wings. However, this in turn increases the drag and so the bird slows down still further. It is not long before the bird has slowed down so much that it has reached stalling speed. Then it can no longer stay airborne. It may seem that such a method of gliding is not much use, but in practice birds use it regularly every day, for

it is the way in which they land. By approaching a branch or other landing site in more or less level flight they can, if they judge it right, slow down to the speed at which they stall, just as they land, thereby minimizing the shock on their legs.

Powered flight

Most birds have to use flapping flight in order to stay airborne. They must produce enough energy to overcome gravity and counteract their rate of sink, so that they stay aloft, and enough forwards force to overcome drag so that they can move forwards. The flying power is produced by the downbeat of the wing. During this movement, the wing twists slightly because the wing bones are at the front of the wing and the pressure of the air against it causes it to rotate. As a result, the wing pushes the air downwards and backwards, propelling the bird in the opposite directions – upwards and forwards. The wing-beat is in fact more complex than this. Because the bird is travelling forwards during the downbeat, the movement of the wing-tip relative to the air is not straight downwards, but angled forwards. This makes it slightly more difficult for the bird to get propulsion from the downbeat than if the beat was *straight downwards*. Propulsion is aided because the large feathers at the tip of the wing are, like the wing itself, supported closer to their front edge than the rear and so, again like the wing, the feather twists during the downbeat. This results in the air being pushed backwards and downwards.

Turning

There are a number of ways in which a flying bird can turn. Any unilateral alteration of the bird's shape results in imbalance in the amount of drag on the two sides of the bird and hence leads to the body turning. This can be achieved by the bird sticking a webbed foot out to one side or turning its tail to one side; species with elongated outer tail-feathers, such as swallows, are particularly adept at rapid turns.

Nevertheless most birds rely mainly on adjustment of wing shape for turning; anyone who has watched a tail-less swallow or martin will know that the bird can still manage well. Slight folding of one wing will reduce the surface area and hence both the drag and

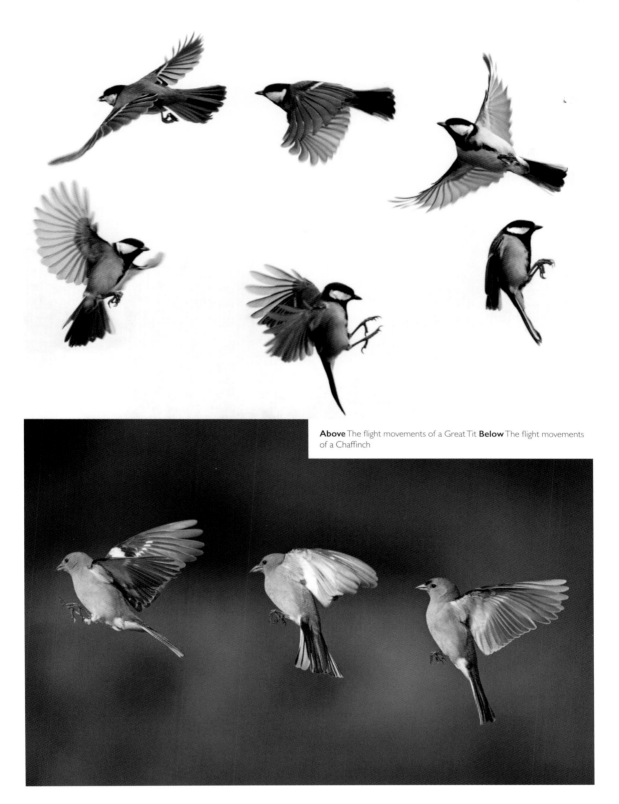

Above The flight movements of a Great Tit **Below** The flight movements of a Chaffinch

the lift on that wing, with the result that the wing will drop slightly and move forwards, relative to the other. Equally, increasing the angle of attack of a wing will result in an increase in both lift and drag, so that wing will be slowed and lifted, relative to the other. Either, or both, of these manoeuvres will result in the bird banking.

Take-off and landing

Taking-off requires a lot of energy. The bird must accelerate to normal flying speed, and gain height; both of these require more energy than normal flight. A small bird such as a sparrow or a thrush alters the angle of its body so that it is flying upwards and increases its wing-beat; nevertheless, taking-off does not seem to be too difficult. This is not the case for all birds, however, and some species have special problems with take-off. Because of their size, very large birds cannot just jump into still air and fly away; they need to have a good air speed before they can easily get enough lift from their wings. There are two ways of achieving this. First, many large birds such as swans need a take-off run in order to get up sufficient speed for take-off. Second, and far easier but not always possible, is for the bird to take-off into a strong headwind; the speed of the wind immediately gives the wing a high airspeed and hence valuable lift. Many birds take-off from perches in trees or on cliffs and this provides another useful way of getting up speed: the bird simply drops off the perch, accelerating with the help of gravity.

Landing is achieved by losing the lift. Ideally this is done in such a way that the bird is flying as slowly as possible at the moment of touchdown, so as to minimize the chances of injury. However, those birds that have some trouble taking-off also have certain problems with landing. Large birds such as swans prefer to land on water if possible since this reduces the likelihood of harm. They can also reduce their speed relative to the ground by coming into land upwind, allowing the wind to give them lift when their land speed is well below their normal stalling speed.

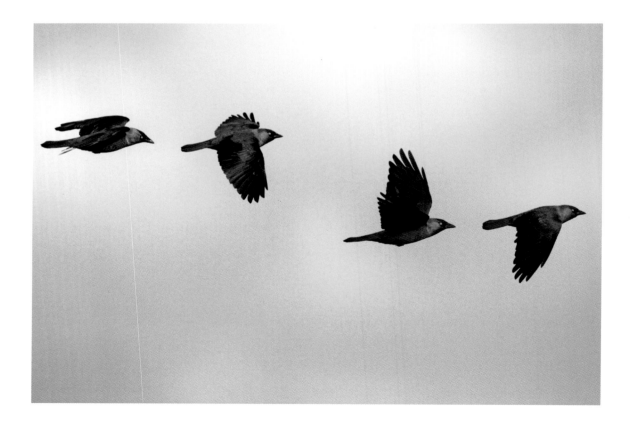

Wing shapes

The shape of birds' wings varies markedly in relation to the type of flight that the species uses. In general birds that need high manoeuvrability have shortish wings, and often longish tails, enabling them to turn swiftly. For example, sparrowhawks, which hunt largely in woodland, have broader wings and longer tails than the falcons, which hunt in the open; they probably fly less swiftly, but they can turn more easily. Another factor that may affect wing shape is the migratory behaviour of the bird. Many species that migrate long distances lay down large quantities of fat as fuel for the journey. For two short, but very critical, periods of the year the birds weigh much more than for the rest of the time. For example, the two species of Willow Warbler and Chiffchaff are very similar in many ways. However, the Willow Warbler migrates to central Africa, undertaking long flights across North Africa while the Chiffchaff goes only to southern Europe and North Africa. The Willow Warbler has a wingspan of over a centimetre more than the Chiffchaff. Is this related to its need to carry greater weight during migration?

Flight speeds

Every bird can vary the speed at which it flies, within certain limits. The speed at which it chooses to fly depends on what it wants to do. If we drive a car very fast along a motorway, we get to our destination sooner than if we drive it more slowly. However, if we want to cover the greatest distance on a given amount of fuel, it is better to drive at a slower cruising speed. It is the same for a bird; if it needs to escape a predator or to make as many journeys as possible to its nestlings, it may make sense to fly as quickly as possible. If, however, it has to make a long migratory flight without many chances to stop and refuel (see page 213), it pays it to cruise at a lower speed because this gives it the greatest range on its fat reserves.

The situation is more complicated for a bird than for a car because the bird is moving through air, which itself may be moving rapidly. If a bird flew at 20km (12 miles) per hour into a headwind of 20km (12 miles) per hour, it would stay in the same place. The ideal air speed for a bird to cover the greatest distance for a given amount of energy varies with the force and direction of the wind; it should fly faster into a headwind and more slowly if it has a tailwind. This is not merely theory: Chaffinches have been shown to adjust their air speed in this way. Precise measurements of airspeeds of birds are not easy to make, and many accounts are greatly exaggerated. Even a swooping Peregrine is unlikely to be travelling at more than about 180km (111 miles) per hour. Level cruising speeds of birds are very much slower than this, and vary with a number of features of wing shape. In general, larger birds tend to fly faster than smaller ones.

Opposite The flight movements of a Jackdaw

Running, Hopping, Walking and Perching

Two-legged animals such as birds and humans need rather large feet if they are to maintain their balance easily, whereas quadrupeds such as cows and horses can manage with much smaller feet. The possession of large feet enables birds to wrap their long toes securely around branches, and so perch easily. Since their legs are placed far to the back of their bodies, many of the birds that swim well are not good walkers. Some of the diving ducks waddle rather ineffectively, and divers and grebes can hardly walk at all.

The length of the leg varies greatly between groups. The two visible sections of the leg, the tibia and the tarsus, have to be more or less the same length, otherwise the bird could not keep its centre of gravity over its feet; it would topple over every time it tried to sit down. Birds with long legs tend to be those that live in open country and need to run well (ostrich, cranes, wild turkey) or those that need to stand in water to feed (flamingos, herons and many waders).

In contrast, birds that hang upside down from the branches or small twigs of a tree while feeding need to be able to grip strongly. They also need their centre of gravity to be as close to their feet as possible; such birds have short legs. Birds that come into this category include the tits, finches and many of the smaller parrots. Birds that spend their time climbing the trunks of trees do not have such short legs. They tend to hang from their splayed feet, often, as in the woodpeckers and treecreepers, supported by stiffened tail feathers, which they use as a prop. Nuthatches have a different method of climbing. They put one foot ahead of them from which they hang, and the other behind them to steady themselves; they do not use their tail for support. This method can be used equally well for climbing *down* tree-trunks, an ability unique to Nuthatches; in this case the bird hangs from the upper, rearmost foot and uses the other one to steady itself.

Pigeons and Sandgrouse (two closely-related families) have very short legs. They spend a lot of their time on the ground, but neither group can run rapidly; they depend on flight for escape. The birds with the shortest legs of all are the Swifts and Kingfishers. Kingfishers use their legs only for perching above the streams into which they dive for fish. Swifts, the most aerial of all birds, use them only for clinging to vertical surfaces or crawling into their nest-chambers.

Most birds need to be able to tuck their legs and feet away in flight so that they do not affect the streamlining. Usually they do this by folding their legs up and tucking them under the belly feathers; however, birds with long legs cannot do this. Species such as Herons, Flamingos, Cranes and the longer-legged Waders have to fly with their legs trailing behind.

Birds that feed on the ground either hop or walk (running is a fast form of walking). Most species, indeed most families, stick to either one method or the other. The Crow family is an exception; some members, such as the Raven, usually walk while others, such as the Jay, usually hop; the Magpie tends to walk if it is moving slowly, but changes to long, bounding hops when it speeds up.

Most birds that spend nearly all their time on the ground, such as Waders, Larks and Pipits, run. Those that hop are primarily arboreal – such as thrushes, tits and finches. When moving from branch to branch, hopping is clearly the best sort of locomotion; the bird half jumps, half flies from a perch and lands on another with both feet together. What is not clear is why such birds do not change from hopping to running when on the ground. It seems as if in some way the adaptations for hopping restrict the ability to run. It has been suggested that the ancestral mode of locomotion for the passerines was hopping, and that walking was a later development. The evidence for this is that in some species, such as the Raven and the Skylark that walk as adults, the young hop for the first few days after leaving the nest.

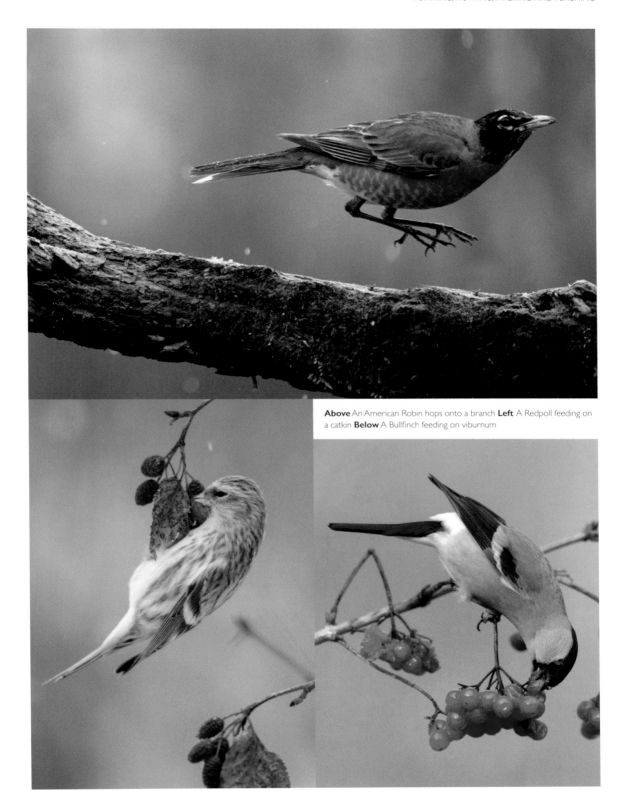

Above An American Robin hops onto a branch **Left** A Redpoll feeding on a catkin **Below** A Bullfinch feeding on viburnum

Bird Song

A bird breathes in air through its trachea (windpipe). At the bottom of the neck, the trachea divides into two tubes, the bronchi, that carry the air to the two lungs. At the junction of these two bronchi lies the syrinx, a complex organ which produces many of the sounds birds make. The bronchi are composed of cartilaginous rings joined to each other by connective tissue. In the area of the syrinx, these thin tissues are modified to form elastic vibrating membranes, the tension of which can be altered by a complex of controlling muscles. As air passes over these membranes they vibrate, and this produces the sounds we hear. The quality of the sound varies with the tension of the membranes. Not all the sounds are derived from the syrinx alone; for example the calls made by some of the swans are, at least in part, the result of complex convolutions of the trachea itself.

The design of the syrinx varies markedly in different species of birds and there is still debate as to the exact way in which many of the sounds are produced. However, it is now clear that in certain species, which produce complex songs such as the Chaffinch, the full song is made up of two separate parts, produced by the membranes in each of the two bronchi. How the bird controls the two sets of sound from the two bronchi is not understood. The musculature of the syrinx is complicated, but birds have been divided into two groups on the basis of these muscles, the oscines and the non-oscines; the former being largely equivalent to the passerines.

The structure of songs and calls

The sounds made by birds are used to convey messages to other individuals. Some of the sounds made, especially some of the songs, are very complex. Birds' hearing is somewhat different from ours and it is likely that they are able to get much more information out of a call than we are able to. Even so, birds can produce a wide variety of different calls to convey different messages. Up to fifteen different types of call have been identified in the Whitethroat. In some species such as the Chaffinch and the Yellowhammer, the individual birds have a smaller number of elements that they put together to make a song. They tend to keep these elements in the same order so that they produce a song that they repeat. They may have more

than one song type, and use just a few over and over again. Such a group of song types is called the bird's repertoire. Each individual has a slightly different voice so that, in many cases, individuals can learn to recognize the songs of neighbouring birds and the calls of their mates or chicks and distinguish them from other birds.

The function of songs and calls

Birds produce calls or sounds in order to convey information to other birds. In certain cases, the same sound may serve two functions. For example the territorial song of a male bird may be used to warn other males to stay away, but at the same time serve to attract a female.

The songs of different species are often clearly different. One of the reasons for this is that songs also provide a valuable way of recognizing a species, so reducing the chance of a bird breeding with another of a different species. This is especially important in birds that are similar in appearance as with some of the warblers.

Some types of sound have characteristics that make them useful under particular circumstances. For example, calls of less than half a second duration, within a certain frequency range, which start and end sharply, are thought to be very difficult to locate. (They certainly are for humans.) It may be no coincidence that a wide variety of different species give alarm calls that have precisely these characteristics. Alarm calls are given to warn mates and offspring of the presence of a predator; at the same time, the bird that gives the call does not want to give its own position away if it can help it. By using a call that is hard to locate, it minimizes the risk to itself and at the same time warns the other birds. The type of alarm call given may depend on the type of predator so further information is supplied to the listener about the particular danger that threatens it.

Opposite A male Chaffinch singing on a branch

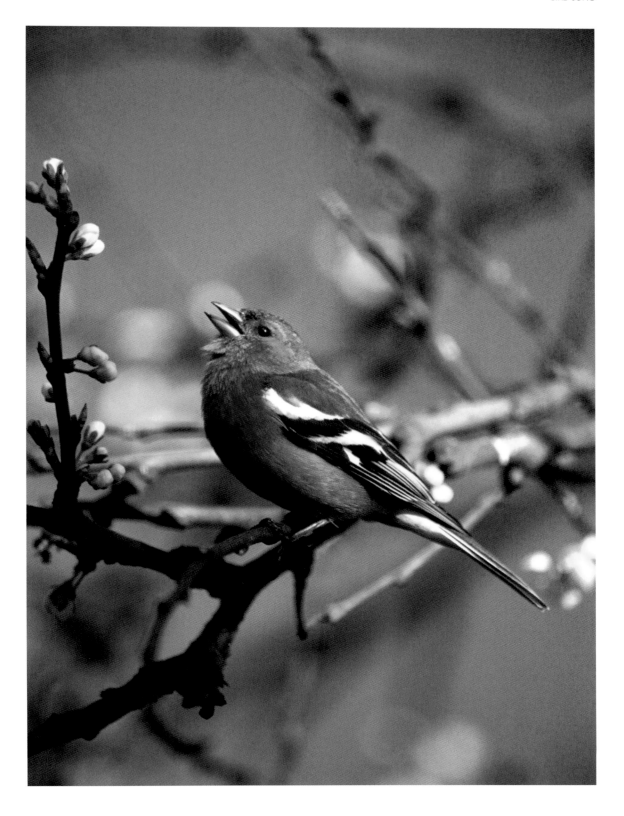

Territories

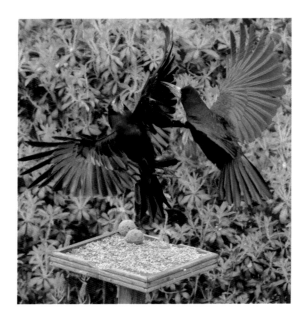

Once a male bird is ready to breed it must find a place to do so – a territory. The purpose of territories varies so much between species that it's hard to define them simply. They are, however, all fairly vigorously defended and some people have therefore defined a territory as any defended area. Most territories are associated with breeding. But a few birds establish territories, briefly, on migration, and others do so in winter quarters; and some birds may defend other areas for other purposes.

Territories vary from tiny spaces just around the bird to areas of many square miles. Even birds living in the same habitat and with roughly similar feeding habits may differ in the types of areas they defend.

In most species, if the individual fails to establish a territory, it will not be able to breed. If a bird fails to obtain a territory, why doesn't it breed without one?

The function of a territory

Three main explanations of the importance of having a territory have been put forward. It is a place where a pair can mate and live without interference; it is an area where the pair can get food for their brood without competition from others of their kind; territories lower the nesting density and this reduces danger from predators.

Interspecific territories

It seems at first somewhat surprising that, usually, a species will only defend its territory against members of its own species. For example, Blackbirds maintain territories against Blackbirds, and Song Thrushes against Song Thrushes, but Blackbird and Song Thrush territories overlap completely. Since the type of food that the two species eat also overlaps, one could have thought that, if food for the young was an important function of territorial behaviour, the Blackbird would have tried to establish a territory that excluded both neighbouring Blackbirds and Song Thrushes; but this does not happen.

Proportion of the year spent on territory

Different species occupy and defend their territories for different lengths of time. Great and Blue Tits, are present for most of the year, but are only strongly territorial in late winter and early spring (although there is some resurgence of territorial behaviour for a brief period in autumn). Blackbirds and Robins hold territories throughout the winter, but they differ in the way they do it. Female Blackbirds remain on territories defended by males, whereas both male and female Robins often defend their territories separately, each keeping to their own. In spring, the females give up their own territories, often mating with a male in an adjacent territory.

Establishing a territory

The young bird, which is trying to stake out a territory for itself for the first time, faces a number of problems. Old birds can usually successfully defend their territories against other birds that try to usurp them; the old adage 'possession is nine-tenths of the law' seems to hold strongly. Even in migrants, the older males seem able to get back to the breeding grounds before the younger ones, and they establish territories that cover much the same areas in successive seasons. The young bird seeking a territory for the first time really only has two options (since he is unlikely to wrest a territory in direct combat); he has either to find one whose previous holder has died or he must try to squeeze in on the border of two others and expand it little by little. He has the best chance if the territories are large and the owners are

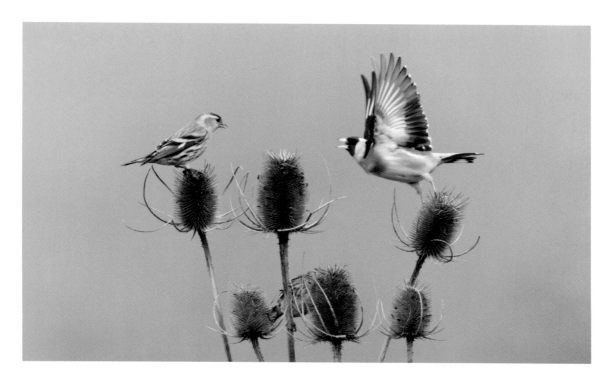

hard-put to defend them easily. If he persists he may have a good chance of becoming accepted by his neighbours. He has established himself.

Maintaining a territory

Once he has successfully established his territory, a bird defends it vigorously against intruders, advertising his presence by song or display. Though there is wide overlap, displays tend to be used more in open country or at close quarters, while song is more important in situations where visibility is limited, such as woodland.

The response of a territory owner to a strange song can easily be seen by playing a tape recording of a song in a territory. The owning male quickly appears and sings at the 'intruder'.

It has been suggested that the reason why birds have several different song types is in order to confuse would-be invaders. Is a bird moving around its territory singing different songs in different places *one* bird or is it several? This type of behaviour may confuse a would-be intruder into thinking there are many birds holding small territories and that it will be difficult to squeeze in there.

It is probably of value to the established individuals to be able to recognize their neighbours. If they are able to do this, then they do not have to waste a lot of time going to see who it is singing on the border of their territories. It may equally be of value to be recognized by one's neighbour since this reduces the chances that he will come charging in every time one starts to sing, just to see who it is.

Usually just singing is sufficient to deter would-be intruders who would like to take over the territory. If singing is not enough and an intruder enters the territory and sings himself, the owner will fly towards him, display to him and chase him off. On the whole, intruders do not push their luck beyond this; physical fights are rather rare. One reason for this is that the established territory holder usually wins such encounters; possession seems to put the defender at an advantage over the intruder. It is not in the interests of the intruder to run the risk of physical injury in a battle if the chances of gaining the territory are slight.

Opposite Rooks fighting over a feeding station **Above** A Goldfinch and a Siskin skirmish over seeds placed in teasel heads

Nests

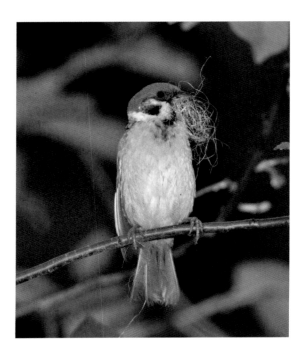

Birds must have a safe place in which to nest and raise their young. The siting of the nest is clearly of great importance. The site must be one where the eggs and young can be kept together, kept dry and kept as safe as possible from predators. Most birds are vulnerable to predators of one sort or another. The best defence is to have a nest that is well concealed; for most small birds this is their main hope of success. For many larger birds, concealment is difficult and the best strategy is to place the nest in a site that is as inaccessible as possible.

Nest site

The nest site itself needs to be chosen carefully. For many species that live in open country or on water there is often little opportunity to make the nest in dense cover. A small amount of concealment by nesting alongside a grass tussock may be all that is possible.

For birds nesting in thicker cover, concealment is easier and remains the most important method of defence used by most small birds, such as warblers. Larger birds try to make their nests inaccessible – in the top of a tall tree (for a Carrion Crow) or on a cliff (for a Raven). This tends to make the birds fairly safe

from most mammalian predators (though squirrels remain a hazard to many birds). But large nests in inaccessible sites, especially trees, tend to be fairly conspicuous; such sites are probably not much use unless the bird can defend itself against other birds. For this reason, rather few small European birds nest in the tops of deciduous trees: even small nests are fairly conspicuous at the beginning of the nesting season before the leaves are out. Some small birds, such as Crossbills, Firecrests and Goldcrests and, to a lesser extent, Long-tailed Tits and Chaffinches nest in the tops of conifers, but these have good cover from foliage throughout the nesting season.

A great many birds nest in holes of one sort or another. All the woodpeckers make their own holes, usually making a new one every year. Many other species nest in holes, including some owls, Redstarts, Jackdaws and Starlings; many of these are dependent on finding old woodpecker nests. The Nuthatch usually excavates its own nest and then carefully plasters resin around the entrance to deter predators. Both Willow and Crested Tits also excavate their own nest-hole, and all woodpeckers excavate their own holes.

Hole-nesting carries certain advantages; most mammals cannot reach the nests (though foxes can sometimes dig out underground nests). Those in holes up trees are safer still; larger birds cannot normally reach the contents of the nest. As a result many birds that nest in holes tend to be more successful at raising young than birds that nest in the open. So why don't all birds nest in holes? The answer is that, whereas birds that nest in the open may have an almost infinite choice of nest-sites, holes tend to be in short supply. They are competed for, sometimes fiercely, and some birds may fail to nest because they cannot find a suitable nest-site.

Type of nest

For birds that nest in exposed sites, the use of nesting material risks drawing attention to the site. Divers, most waders and many gamebirds merely make a modest scrape in which to place their eggs, and use almost no nesting material at all.

Many birds build intricate nests. Even the simple twig nest of the Woodpigeon has to be built carefully.

The birds must find a place on a branch where twigs can be placed so that they will form a firm platform. Many places will be tried and the first twigs are often hard to anchor, but gradually a platform is constructed that is strong enough to hold not just the eggs, but the incubating adult and, later, two large chicks. The pigeons are not highly expert builders; but Crows and Jays interweave the sticks more carefully and make a deep cup, which they line with woven rootlets. The Magpie takes this development one stage further and builds a nest with a strong dome. In this species, the dome probably gives the Magpie protection against raids from other members of the Crow family, though the disadvantage is that it makes the nest larger and therefore conspicuous.

Open, cup-shaped nests are made by many species of passerine birds such as thrushes, finches, and warblers. Most make the outer structure of small twigs and line it with finer material such as hair or feathers. Feathers are a particularly valuable form of insulation and are used by many birds for lining their nests. Unlike ducks and geese, which pull out their own feathers to line the nest, the passerines depend on finding the moulted feathers of other species, or whole dead birds from which they can pluck feathers.

Among the most complex nests built by European birds are those of the Wren and the Long-tailed Tit. The Wren's nest is made of leaves, moss and grass; that of the Long-tailed Tit is constricted from spider's-webs, moss and lichen. The nests are beautifully warm, lined as they are with many feathers; as many as 2,000 have been counted in a single Long-tailed Tit's nest.

The nests of Goldcrests and Firecrests look as if they are just open cup-shaped nests, but they have a ring of feathers protruding over the top of the cup; these act as a thin cover, reducing the amount of heat lost from the nest. This 'door' over the nest is particularly well built in some northern areas.

Some birds use mud for building. Several species of thrushes use mud in the construction of their nest, though only the Song Thrush lines the nest entirely with mud. The House Martin and the Red-rumped Swallow build intricate nests of mud lined with feathers; the birds may fly some distance to collect the mud.

Speed of nest building

Some resident birds may build their nests slowly, taking up to two or three weeks to complete it. Some of the large birds of prey may add sticks to a nest used in previous years, until a very large structure develops.

Some migrants may pair up within hours of arrival on the breeding grounds, and start to build almost immediately, completing a nest within only a few days. The same can be true of resident species which have lost their first nest: a replacement may be built much more rapidly.

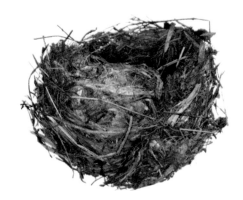

Opposite A Tree Sparrow gathers material for its nest
Above A warbler's nest

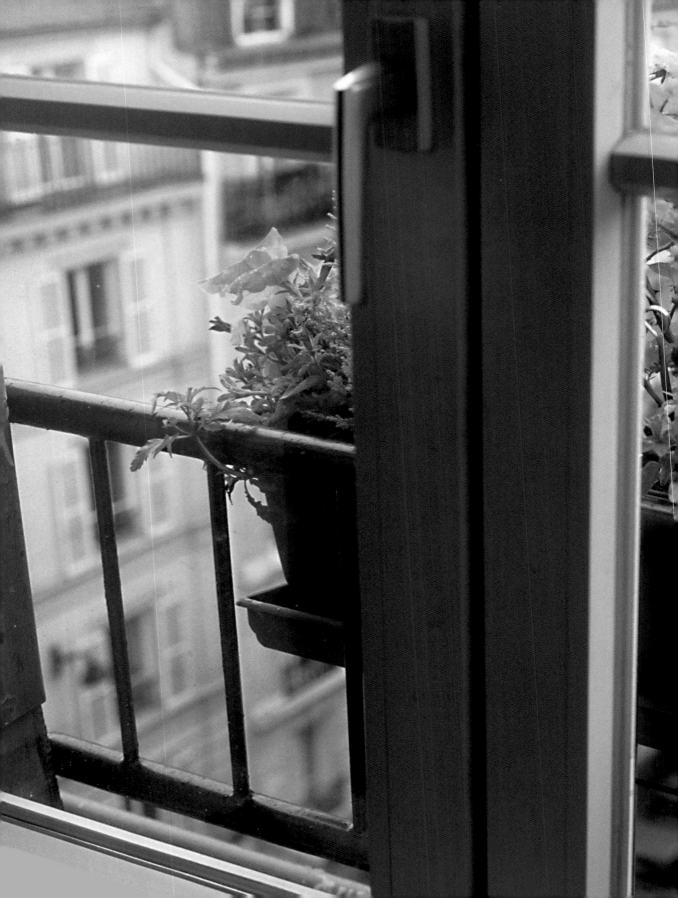

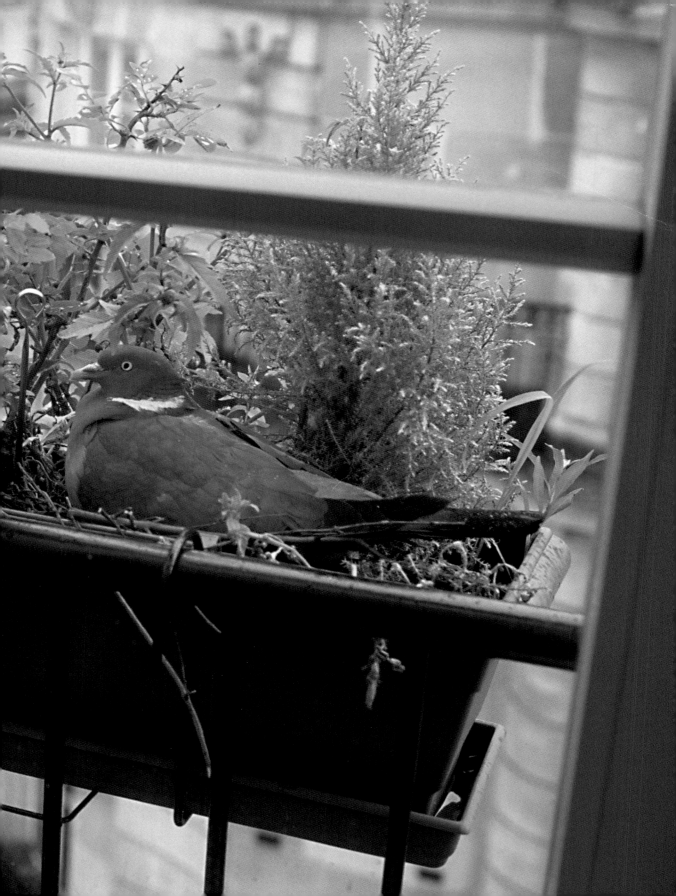

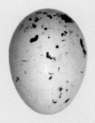

Bullfinch

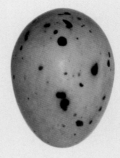

Chaffinch

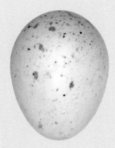

Goldfinch

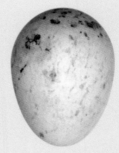

Greenfinch

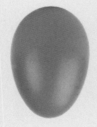

American Robin

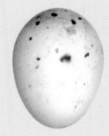

Siskin

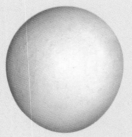

Tawny Owl

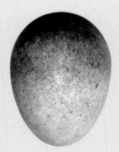

Tree Sparrow

Eggs

Once birds have selected a nest site and built the nest, they are ready to produce the eggs.

Egg size

Two generalizations can be made about the size of eggs in relation to the size of the female's body. First, egg size varies markedly between families, but less so within families. Second, maller birds tend to lay proportionally larger eggs than larger birds do within families.

The somewhat conical shape of waders' eggs means that a normal clutch of four form a neat group if they are positioned so that their pointed ends face inwards. The incubating female could not cover as many eggs of such a large size effectively if they were any other shape. If the Guillemot's single, very pointed egg is accidentally knocked it turns around in a small circle as opposed to rolling any distance; this reduces the chances that they will roll off the cliff edge. Many eggs of hole-nesting species such as the owls and kingfishers are rounder, but it is not known why this should be.

Egg colouration

The eggs of different species are variedly coloured and patterned. The usefulness of some egg colours seems clear, but the value of others is puzzling. The camouflaged eggs of ground-nesting species such as waders and nightjars are obviously adaptive, since they are difficult for predators to find. On the other hand, some species lay eggs that are not well-camouflaged at all – such as the white eggs of Woodpigeons and Turtle Doves and the pale eggs of Pheasants. These eggs are normally covered by the incubating birds (both members of a pair of Woodpigeons taking turns, but only the female Pheasant) and so there is no need for them to be well-camouflaged. The eggs of most hole-nesting birds are white or pale blue, perhaps to make it easier for the parent birds to see them.

Apart from the well-camouflaged eggs of birds that nest on the ground, it has generally proved difficult to correlate the colours of eggs with any particular aspect of the nesting behaviour of a species. The nest itself is necessarily a bulky object, much larger than the eggs, and, in the vast majority of cases, it is the nest that is found by the predator, and not the eggs. Building a nest that is well-camouflaged or inconspicuous is important; inconspicuous eggs are not necessarily advantageous.

In a few other cases, however, the colour of the eggs is known to be important. The parent Guillemot learns to recognize its own egg by the combination of colour and patterning; so it is less liable, in the turmoil of a densely packed ledge, to end up incubating the wrong egg by mistake. The Cuckoo is another species where the colour of the eggs is important.

Interval between eggs

The laying female needs to find a lot of food to form the eggs. In many small species, the female lays her eggs at daily intervals; in those that lay a large clutch, the female may have to find the food required to form one egg every day (since she cannot store all the nutrients required for all the eggs). In some larger birds the interval between the eggs is longer. Canada Geese lay at about thirty-six-hour intervals and swans have a two-day interval between eggs. The Swift, which is dependent on flying insects for its food, also lay its eggs at two-day intervals; but if the weather is bad and therefore food is scarce, it may lay at three-day intervals instead.

Previous Page A Woodpigeon resting in a windowbox
Opposite Eggs from different birds, showing the variety of (relative) size and markings

Incubation

After the eggs have been laid, the parents must keep them warm so that they can develop. Incubation takes quite a long time; the shortest incubation period of any bird is eleven to twelve days; most species take longer than that. In order to hatch the egg, parents must apply heat to it. They cannot do this properly through their thick (and insulating) feathers, so they have to develop a special brood-patch; this is an area of the belly from which the feathers are shed and which develops large blood vessels just underneath the skin. By applying the brood patch to the eggs, the bird can maintain the egg at close to its own body temperature. In some species both sexes develop brood patches; in others only the female does so.

Share of sexes in incubation

The parent must not only keep the eggs warm, but must keep the whereabouts of the nest secret. Nonetheless, the parents usually need to feed, so they must make visits to and from the nest. Going to feed is obviously less of a problem for species in which both parents incubate: one can take over directly from the other. When only one of the parents incubates (usually it is the female), the eggs may chill when left untended; so the bird must keep its foraging trips short, especially in cold weather. It is not always clear why the male does not incubate; differences occur between closely related species. Even when both parents incubate, the female often does the majority; in particular, she often incubates throughout the night as well as taking a share during the day. The parents may switch over every half an hour or so in small species, or only once or twice a day in larger ones. In Shearwaters and Storm-petrels, which only come to the nesting colony at night, the birds only switch over every two or three nights and exceptionally one bird may have to incubate without a break for eight or nine days.

Hatching synchrony

The moment at which the parents start to incubate their clutch has important implications for the brood. In many species the parents do not start to incubate the eggs until the clutch is complete. Where this happens all the young hatch at more or less the same time (synchronously). In some species, especially ones where the young are nidifugous (hatched at an advanced stage), it is very important that the young are ready to leave together or they become difficult to look after. In contrast, some parents start incubation before the clutch is complete, so that the eggs do not all hatch together (asynchronously). For example, many owls, such as the Barn Owl, start to incubate the first egg as soon as it is laid. Since the eggs are laid at roughly two-day intervals and each takes the same number of days to develop, the chicks hatch roughly two days apart. The earlier-hatched chicks are at a great advantage over their later brethren. The larger the chick, the greater its chance of getting the food it needs; if food is in short supply, the first chick to hatch may flourish while the later ones starve to death.

At first sight, this may seem to be an inefficient way of breeding, since it leads to the death of many young. Almost certainly, however, the opposite is the case: it is, for the parents, a way of ensuring that they raise as many young as possible. When food is scarce, the parents raise more young if the small ones die quickly and so do not compete with the largest. If they were all of equal size, then all would be equally emaciated, and none might survive. This habit is often referred to as the brood-reduction strategy. It is most commonly found in birds for which the food supply is unpredictable.

Eggshell removal

Once the chick emerges from the egg the parents' behaviour changes to deal with young that must be fed. In many species the parents have a special duty to the hatching chick: they must remove the eggshells. This is particularly important in species that nest out in the open. In these the startling white of the inside of the shell contrasts markedly with the camouflaged outside. It is dangerous for the parent to leave the eggshells near the nest; these may well draw the attention of predators to the nest-site so the parents pick up the shells and fly with them some distance from the nest before dropping them.

Opposite A Fieldfare, sitting on its mud-lined cup nest, made of grass, leaves and sticks

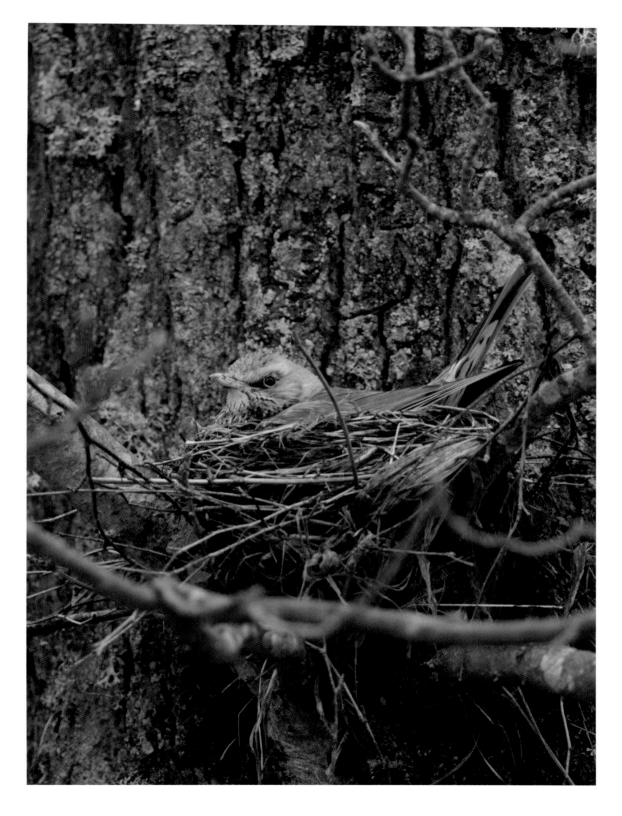

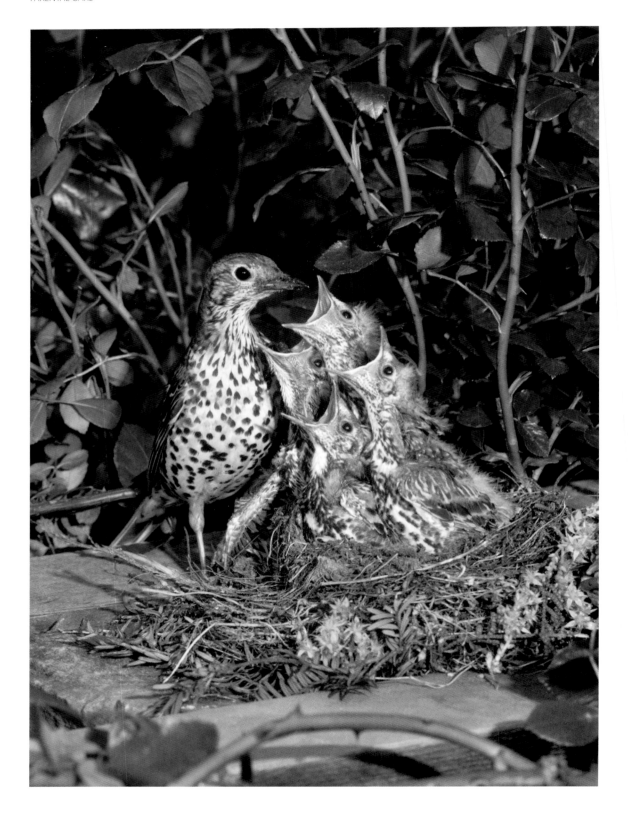

Parental Care

Once the young bird has hatched, the parent must bring it food or lead it to where it can feed itself.

We know rather little about the detailed behaviour of birds with nidifugous young because they are rather difficult to observe. In most species they are led away from the nest within a few hours, a day at the most, of hatching, and for most it is important for them to hatch synchronously. The duties of parents of nidifugous young are mainly to keep them dry and warm, especially when they are very small, and safe from predators. Relatively few bring food to their young. Most take them to good feeding places where they feed for themselves.

Nidicolous (hatched in an undeveloped state) young may still need a lot of brooding – they will not be able to maintain their own body temperature until they are much larger, especially in cold weather. This can pose a problem for the parents in small passerines for which both parents normally collect food for the young. They need to go and hunt for food for the chicks, but the chicks may chill if they are away too long. In warm weather the chicks need little brooding and so both parents can collect food, but in cold weather one of the parents may have to brood the young and this effectively cuts the feeding rate by half. Even though they are kept warm, the young may die of starvation.

It is obviously important to bring to the nest as much food as possible in the time available, and at the same time to reduce as far as possible the amount of effort involved in doing so. Many birds use their crops to bring food back to the nest. They can bring large quantities at each visit, hence they need to make fewer flights between food and nest, and so save energy. Finches bringing seeds, and swallows bringing small insects, would waste an enormous amount of time if they brought in each item individually. A swift, for example, may carry in its huge gape more than 1,500 insects each time it visits the nest. Nevertheless, many insectivorous species, like tits, flycatchers and the bee-eaters, do bring in only a single item on most visits. Apparently, this is because many insects have to be beaten and killed so that they do not sting or bite the young birds. Even the jaws of caterpillars must be broken so that they cannot bite the chick after being swallowed. Since it appears to be too difficult for the adult to hold one prey while preparing another, the items have to be brought in one at a time. But these birds do try their hardest to be efficient: they eat the small prey they find themselves, and take only larger ones to their young.

The size of prey brought in is obviously important. It may be necessary to catch small prey for tiny chicks as they may not be able to swallow larger prey. This is not usually a great problem since many of the parents that bring large food items, such as the birds of prey, can tear them into small portions if necessary.

The quality of the food may also be important. In general it seems that a vegetable diet is not a good one for raising small, rapidly growing young. Almost all birds that feed on vegetable material when adult feed insects to their young. Most finches feed their small young on insects; later they may bring increasing amounts of seeds.

The parents bring food to the nest in response to begging by the chicks; the more begging the chicks do (i.e. the hungrier they are), the greater the likelihood that the parents will work harder to provide more food for them. However, there is a point beyond which they do not seem able or prepared to go. Clearly it is of little value if they endanger themselves too much; if they die, there is little or no hope for the young anyway. As well as bringing food to the nest, most passerines keep the nest clean by removing the faeces, which are produced in a gelatinous sac by the young. These are carried some way from the nest before being dropped so that the site of the nest is not revealed to a predator by a pile of conspicuous droppings.

In almost all species parental care continues for some time after the young have left the nest. There may be a conflict between the interests of the parent and the young at this time. It is in the interests of the young to stay close to the parents, benefit from the safety of the territory and perhaps get fed. In due course the chick will be ignored by the parent, or actively chased away. The parents will then be free to see to their own affairs, which may involve the raising of another brood, undertaking a moult or preparing for migration.

Opposite A Mistle Thrush feeding its young

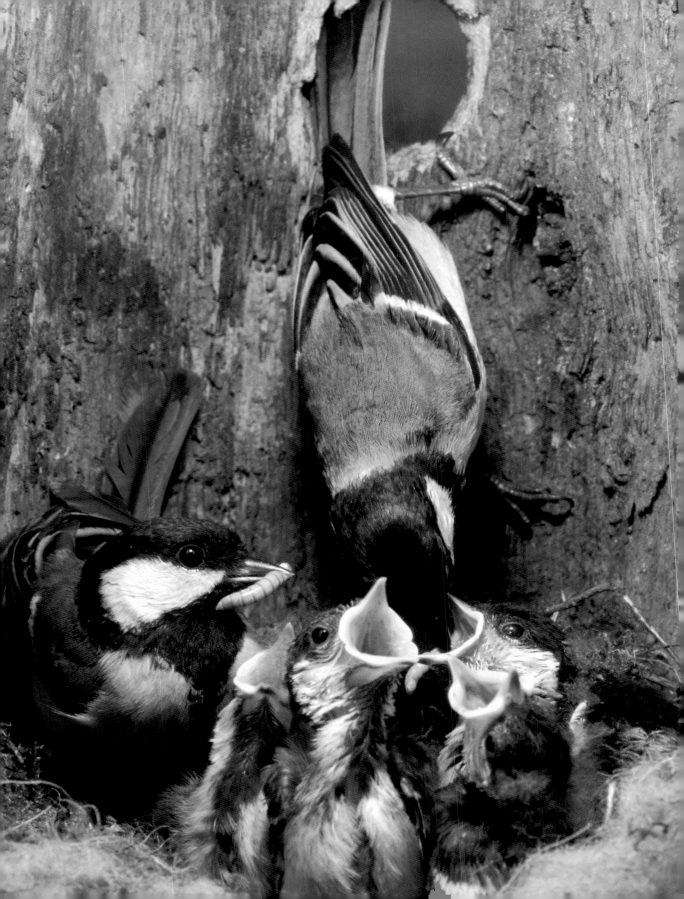

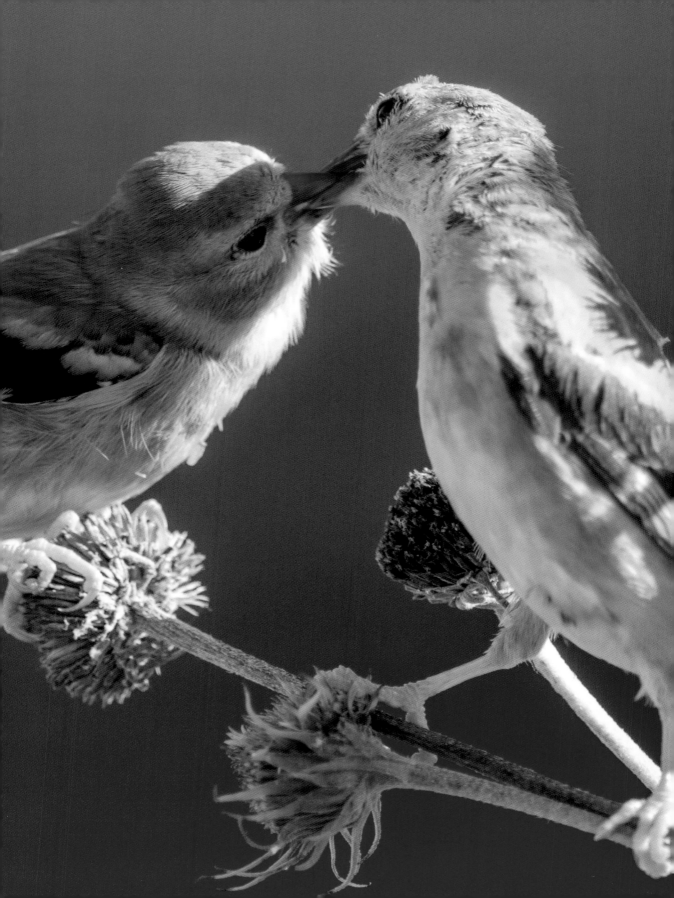

Migration

Flight enables birds to travel great distances, over both land and water, in a short time. Flight enables birds to exploit many places where food is plentiful at certain times of the year, but absent or unavailable at others.

Migration may be defined as 'a regular, large-scale shift of the population between a restricted breeding area and a restricted wintering area'. This is not a completely watertight definition, since, as we shall see, not all migration is between breeding and wintering areas. Nonetheless, it covers the great majority of cases.

Evolution of migration

Migratory habits have arisen as a result of a set of complex 'pros' and 'cons'. In Europe, we tend to think of the swallow as leaving its home and going to a warmer area, with more insects, until home is habitable once more. In fact, this is the wrong way round; it is nearer the truth to say that Africa is the swallow's home and that it comes to Europe for our summer so as to cash in on the rich supply of insects for its young. Certainly this is the way its journeys came about.

Partial migrants

Another group of birds that give us some insight into the evolution of migration are the so-called partial migrants. These are species in which different populations, and indeed different individuals in the same population, show marked differences in migratory behaviour. In Finland, the Robin is almost wholly migratory, whereas in England only a few migrate, and in Spain they are all resident. The tendency to migrate is related to the harshness of the winter – the more difficult it is to survive the winter on the breeding ground, the more advantage there is in being a migrant.

In another partial migrant, the Chaffinch for example, the individuals of the same population differ in their tendency to migrate. In Scandinavia, the migratory tendency seems to be related to the severity of past winters. After a series of hard winters, most of the Chaffinches migrate in winter whereas after a series

Previous Page Left Great Tits feeding their young, they seek tree holes or suitable gaps in walls and buildings to nest, and also use nest boxes, if available **Previous Page Right** American Goldfinch feeding offspring

of mild winters a much higher proportion spend the winter on the breeding ground. What happens is that, in these northern areas, the balance between the advantages of staying put and of migrating is fairly even. During a severe winter the migrants survive better than the residents, whereas in mild winters the advantage lies with the residents. The individual birds are not making a choice; rather, when there is a severe winter, those with the migratory tendency survive better and so leave more offspring (which inherit the same tendency to be migrants), whereas in a mild winter the residents survive better and leave more offspring.

In the Blackbird, another partial migrant, females are more likely to migrate than males, and juveniles more likely to migrate than older birds. This is the opposite of the pecking order noted in birds feeding in winter. Since males are more likely to survive on the breeding grounds than females, and adults than juveniles, the old and the males stand to gain less by migrating than the young and the females. Hence the pattern noted is in keeping with the relative chances of surviving on the breeding grounds. In Germany it has been shown that the tendency to migrate or stay is inherited. Because the advantage of staying versus migrating varies markedly between years, the population of Blackbirds can swing from being mainly migratory to being mainly resident over a few years, depending on the harshness of the winters. These studies show that the migratory habits of some species may vary over even a short span of years. If conditions change permanently, the habits may also change permanently. One species in which this appears to have happened is the Hooded Crow. In the early part of this century, many of them used to migrate southwards in western Europe, coming down as far as the southern end of the North Sea. Nowadays, such sightings are extremely rare. It seems that the migratory habit has become less, possibly because feeding conditions (such as the spread of rubbish tips) have improved.

Migratory species and routes

It is difficult to generalize about those European birds that are migrants. Most insect-eating groups, such as the warblers and swallows, leave Europe for the winter

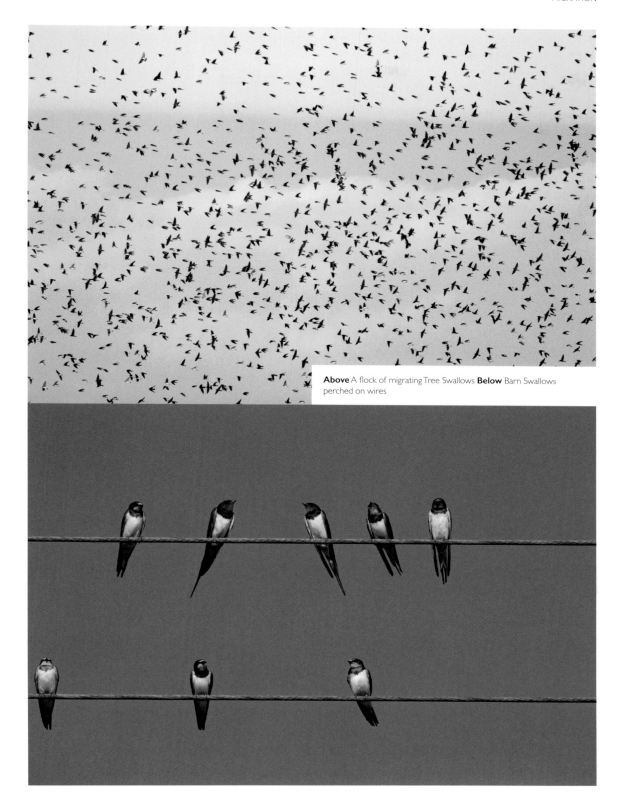

Above A flock of migrating Tree Swallows **Below** Barn Swallows perched on wires

(though Dartford and Fan-Tailed Warblers and Crag Martins are largely sedentary). Other groups that are mainly sedentary contain migrants. For example, the Quail, Turtle Dove, Scops Owl and Wryneck all go to Africa for the winter, while the other gamebirds, doves, owls, and woodpeckers are mostly non-migratory. Most pipits and wagtails stay in Europe; but Red-throated and Tree Pipits and Yellow Wagtails are long-distance migrants.

Ecology of migrants

Most migrants fall into one of two categories. One contains species in which almost all individuals leave Europe for the winter. Although a few of these species go to India and South-east Asia, most go to Africa. Some 600 species of land-birds breed in Europe and Asia, and about 40 per cent of them leave the area completely for the winter (though a few stragglers may stay behind in some cases).

The second category consists of a large number of species that migrate into Europe for the winter, or migrate within Europe. Many migrate particularly to Western Europe (North Sea, British Isles, western France); these areas are much milder than central and northern Europe in winter, thanks to the Gulf Stream, so it is easier both to survive (less food is needed at higher temperatures) and to find food (the land is less likely to be frozen or covered with snow).

Although there is overlap, there are some ecological differences between these two groups of birds. Those that go to Africa include almost all the true insectivores (swallows, swifts, flycatchers) and most of those that rely largely on insects (warblers). Most of those that come into Europe for the winter are ducks, geese and waders from the far north or a long way east in Russia. These birds feed mainly on grass or other vegetable material or invertebrates along the shore or in fields; the last group includes lapwings, starlings and even blackbirds from further east in Europe.

Migratory routes

There are almost as many migratory routes as there are migratory species. In most cases, especially where the birds are night migrants, there are no specific routes on which the birds are concentrated. Most warblers, for example, migrate on a broad front,

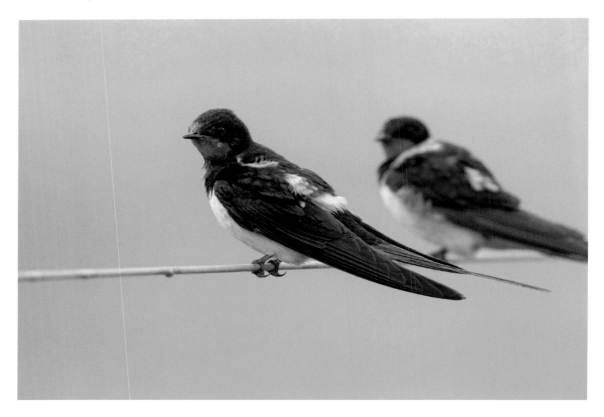

spread out over wide areas of Europe. The same is probably true for many of the diurnal migrants; they do not concentrate in flight lines. Seabirds and sea-ducks often try to keep out over the water, but may become concentrated as they pass certain headlands. Many of the soaring birds concentrate at the short sea crossings; but after that they spread out on much wider fronts.

Some species have no true migratory routes, but nevertheless manage to move to much milder areas for the winter. These are those species that live high in the mountains in summer.

Distances flown in a single flight

Most of the birds that cross the Mediterranean in autumn arrive in North Africa to find it almost at its driest. Almost certainly, for most of them, there is little chance of finding food, especially when one considers how many birds are making the journey. Although some species may stop and try to feed, for many there is no option but to fly on across the Sahara and into the Sahel zone before they reach a reasonable food supply. The shortest distance across the Mediterranean is 14km (8½ miles) and it may be a further 1,500km (932 miles) across North Africa. Many birds must cross these areas of sea and desert in a single flight.

Since many of the smaller birds, such as the warblers, fly at only about 40km (25 miles) per hour, such long distances pose great problems for them; they must expect to have to fly non-stop for perhaps seventy-two hours. At these speeds, even a light headwind may prove disastrous. For example, a 15km (9 mile) per hour headwind would slow a warbler down to 25km (16 miles) per hour and make a 2,500km (1553 miles) journey take 100 hours instead of sixty-two; this might well mean death. On the other hand, if the birds can judge it right, a tailwind would make life a great deal easier for them. We know very little about whether European birds are able to make use of favourable winds for these long flights, but one American species, the Blackpoll Warbler, which flies non-stop from the New England coast to northern South America, a flight of some 4,000km (2485 miles) or more, changes altitude several times on route apparently to take advantage of favourable winds; even with this help, it still takes over 100 hours to make the journey.

Fat reserves for migration

To be able to make these long flights, the migrant birds have to lay down fat reserves. Fat is a particularly good source of energy for a flying animal because it produces more energy per gram than stores of protein or carbohydrate. In addition, as it is used up, one of its by-products is water; for a migrant, which is on the wing for two or three days at high altitude, and without the opportunity to drink, this may be crucial.

The numbers of migrants

The scale of migration is sometimes difficult to comprehend. The number of birds that leave Europe and western Asia for Africa each year is very large indeed (and the figures given below do not include those birds that migrate into or within Europe). In many European countries, bird censuses have been undertaken and these, coupled with measurements of the extent of the relevant habitats, can be used to obtain the approximate numbers of breeding pairs and their offspring. Rough estimates (in millions) for a number of common species in Europe are as follows:

Willow Warbler 900
Sand Martin 375
Tree Pipit 260
Spotted Flycatcher 250
Swallow 220
Blackcap 200
Garden Warbler 200
Lesser Whitethroat 150
Wheatear 120
Redstart 120
Whitethroat 120
Ortolan Bunting 120
House Martin 90
Yellow Wagtail 70
Whinchat 45
Pied Flycatcher 30

Opposite Barn Swallows preparing to migrate **Next Page** A large gathering of swallows resting during migration

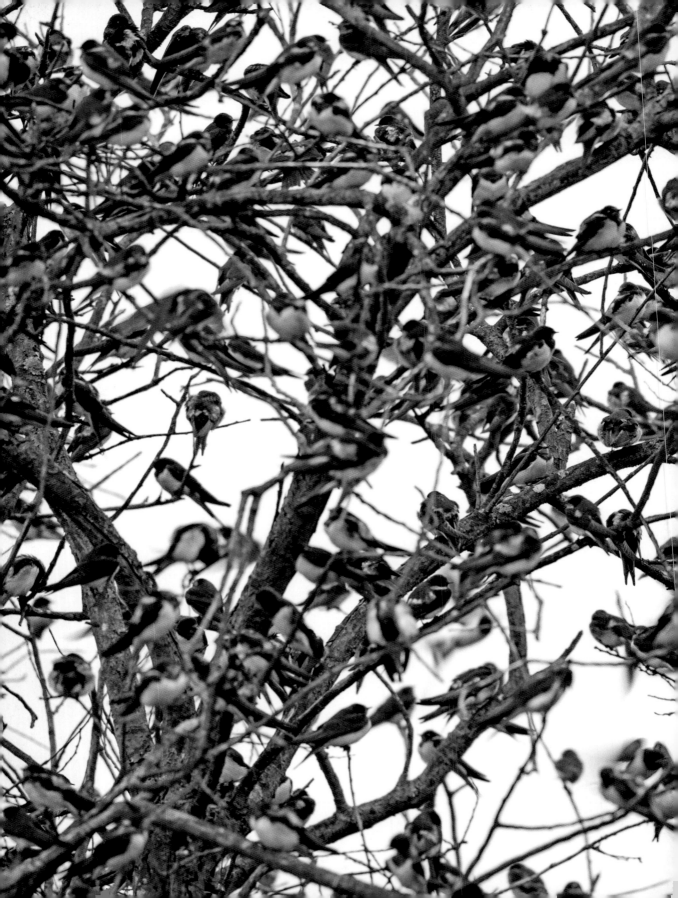

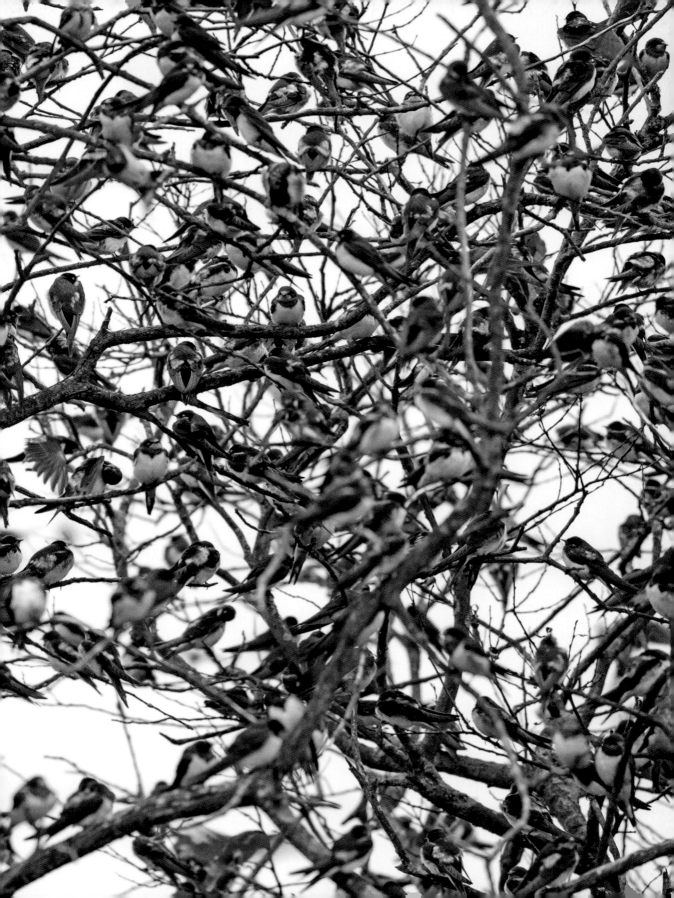

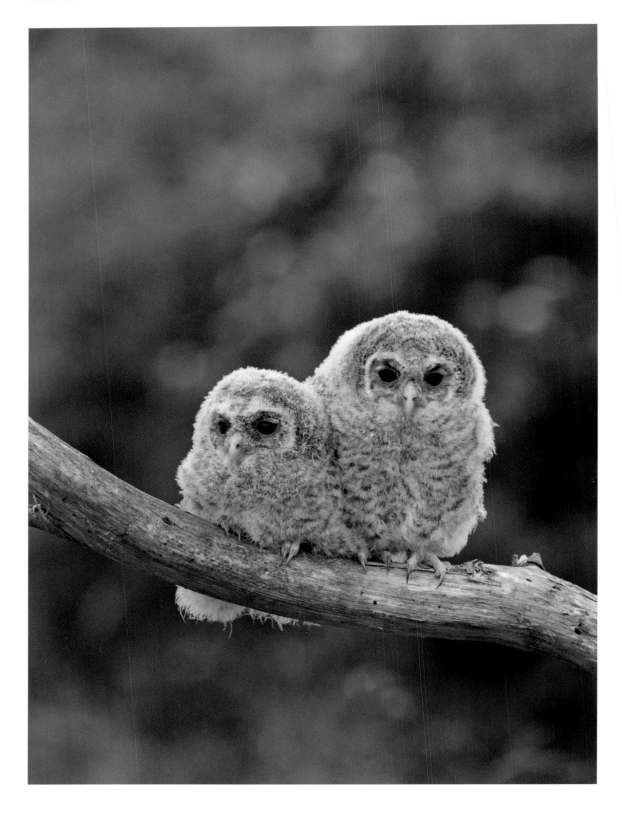

Population

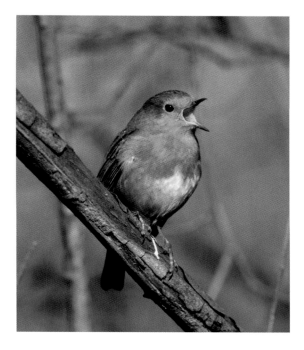

Stability of numbers

In nature, the populations of most species remain remarkably stable. This does not mean that there are no changes in numbers – populations may decline after a very cold winter, for example – but over a longish period of years the numbers remain more or less the same. There are usually one or two pairs of Blackbirds or Robins in our gardens, seldom none or many pairs.

These casual observations are borne out by detailed studies of particular species; such populations tend to fluctuate remarkably little. Similarly, although the numbers of smaller birds, such as tits, fluctuate a little from year to year, sometimes even doubling or halving between years, over the longer term the numbers remain fairly stable. In the tits and some other seed-eating species, the numbers fluctuate in proportion to the seed crops available during the winter. When there is a good crop, survival is good; when the crop is poor, so is survival. The reason why most bird

Opposite Tawny Owl chicks often leave the nest before they are fully fledged. This is normal and they are still attended by their parents
Above A European Robin singing on a branch

populations are stable is that the number of birds born into the population is matched by a similar number that die.

Potential rate of increase

This stability of populations is surprising when we consider the remarkable potential birds have for raising young. A Blackbird can have three broods, each of three or four young, in a single season; and a Robin can have two broods, each of five young. If all of these young and their parents were to survive to the next year, there could be seven pairs where there had been only one the previous year. If, in their turn, all these birds and their offspring survived and bred for a mere four years, there would be 2,401 pairs where there had been but one.

We all know that this does not occur. But what does happen to this enormous production? As we have seen, most of these nests fail, or the young die during their first few weeks of life. Many others, together with some of the parents, also perish before the next breeding season. Although in the long term the number of young birds that survive long enough to breed matches the number of adult birds that die, there are inevitably differences from year to year between these two numbers. As a result, populations often increase or decrease slightly between years.

The potential for extremely rapid increases in numbers is not, of course, normally realized. Numbers are kept in check. However, such calculations are not just figments of the imagination. Under exceptional circumstances, such as when a species is introduced to a new area, birds may increase very rapidly indeed. Several species that were introduced from Europe to other parts of the world have shown dramatic increases in numbers. In the United States, eight Pheasants were introduced to an island in the State of Washington; after six breeding seasons there were 1,989. Both Starlings and House Sparrows have shown similar rapid changes in numbers after being introduced to the New World. Either 120 or 160 starlings were released in New York in 1890 and 1891. By 1950 they had spread across the whole of the United States and were estimated to have increased a million-fold!

Long-term changes in numbers

Although, in the short term, populations may be remarkably stable, long-term changes occur in many species. The number of White Storks breeding in Western Europe has declined markedly during this century. This is apparently because of the draining of the wet meadows, which the storks use for hunting, though changes in their winter quarters (in Africa) may also have had an effect. Another species that seems to have declined as a result of changes in its winter quarters in Africa is the Whitethroat. Its numbers show a very sharp decline during the mid-1970s; this has been associated with the series of droughts in the Sahel area of Africa where the birds spend the winter.

Changes in habitats can also lead to a change in numbers. The numbers of pairs of Great Tits breeding in a Dutch wood increased over a period of thirty years. The wood was a young plantation when the study started but it had matured into rich woodland by the end of the study. Apparently the carrying capacity of the wood increased as the trees grew up.

One of the most remarkable changes in the population of any species in Western Europe during the last century has occurred in the case of the Collared Dove. This species has spread from the east and colonized most of Western Europe during the last forty or fifty years. It first nested in Britain in 1955, yet by 1972 – just seventeen years later – there may have been 40,000 pairs! It is now so common in many areas as to be virtually uncountable. It is not known why this bird has increased so strikingly, but it lives in close association with humans and seems to have, quite suddenly, found that this habitat was a very suitable one.

Immigration and emigration

A very high proportion of the deaths of young birds occur during the late summer, soon after they become independent. Since birds are small and dead ones are rapidly consumed by other animals, this loss is mainly noticed as a drop in numbers. The birds simply disappear. Many people find it hard to believe that so many young birds die before reaching breeding age. They suggest that when young birds disappear from an area, they have not died, but have emigrated to other areas. Birds do, of course, move between areas: any piece of habitat has both immigrants and emigrants. However, emigration (as opposed to death)

is not likely to be the explanation for local drops in numbers. This is because, in most species, local populations tend to fluctuate in synchrony with one another. For example, Blackbirds tend to have good breeding success in years when the ground is damp for long periods (so the parents can easily get food for the young). Since such conditions tend to obtain over wide areas at the same time, Blackbirds over wide areas have good or poor breeding success together. The disappearance of the young from one area is likely to be accompanied by similar disappearances in other areas. The birds cannot be emigrating from all areas at the same time.

Of course, ebb and flow on a local level can sometimes have an effect. In an area of mixed woodland and suburban habitat, for example, breeding success of tits will tend to be higher in the depths of the forest than in somebody's garden, where sources of disturbance (like children) or predators (like cats) abound. After a typical breeding season, the woods will be thronged with young and mature tits, and many of them, under pressure from competition for food, may naturally stray into gardens beyond the forest.

Population regulation

We have seen that bird populations are usually stable over quite long periods of time and that, in spite of there being a large production of young, most of these die before reaching breeding age. What factors affect the way in which these numbers balance? The answer is that populations are regulated largely by their own numbers. Such numbers affect the survival of the individuals present.

The fact that birds produce more young than seem to be needed to maintain their numbers is one of the most important aspects of their biology. Without this overpopulation they could not quickly increase in numbers when conditions are favourable. This is not only useful when the opportunity occurs, such as when the Collared Dove spread rapidly into new areas, but it is essential to all populations. From time to time, all populations encounter poor conditions and their numbers decline. The fact that they are able to produce so many young enables them to make good their numbers as soon as better conditions prevail. Many species go up and down in numbers quite frequently; if they could not rapidly increase in the good years, they would become progressively scarcer.

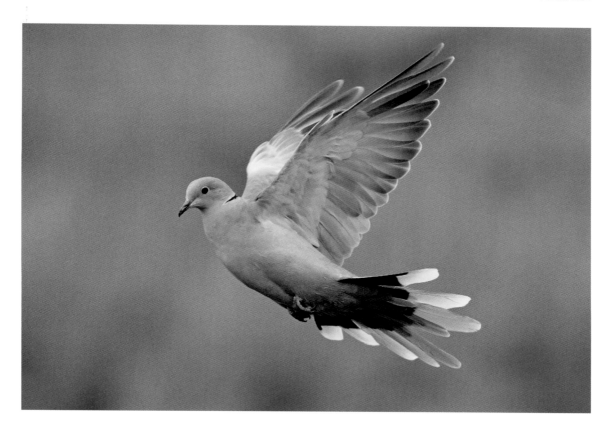

The basis for evolution

Overproduction is the very basis on which evolution operates. Charles Darwin was the first to point out how many young animals fail to reach adulthood and he realized the importance of this. There is great variation between individuals, and they compete for the opportunity to survive to breed. Those individuals that are fittest will be those that survive to leave offspring, which will, in their turn, bear many of their parents' characteristics. Thus, over many generations, the characteristics of a species can change to enable it to cope with a changing environment; eventually new subspecies and new species may evolve. Darwin called this process natural selection.

Survival rates

The number of birds in a population depends on the survival rates of the individuals and the success they have at raising young. We have seen that many young birds die before they reach breeding age (see page 217), and that the annual survival rates of breeding adults varies markedly between species – from as low as about 30 per cent of Blue Tits to as high as about 70 per cent in the Jackdaw. Such information is often presented in different ways: an annual survival rate of 95 per cent is the same as an annual death rate (or mortality) of 5 per cent (100–95). These figures are also sometimes presented as proportions of a unit (1.0) so in this example a survival rate of 0.95 or a mortality of 0.05 (1.0–0.95).

Above A Collared Dove coming into land **Next Page** A flock of Goldfinches, Greenfinches and Tree Sparrows fills the sky

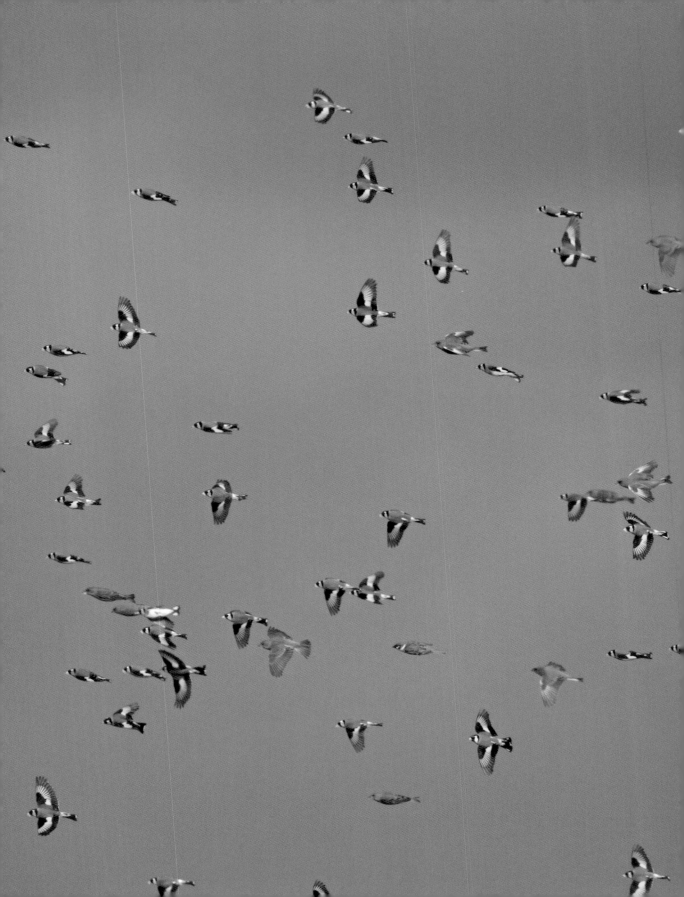

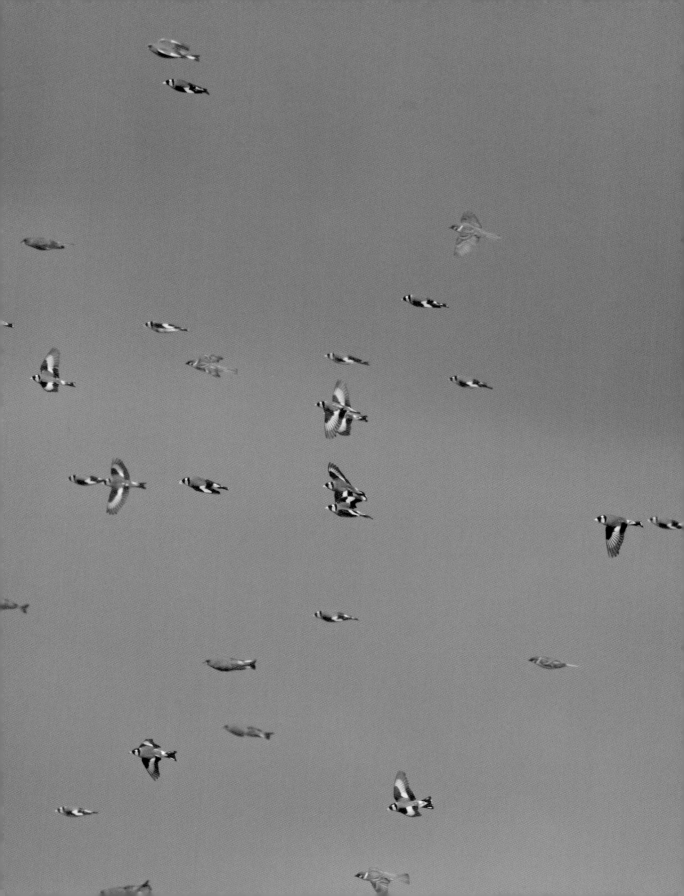

Protection and Conservation

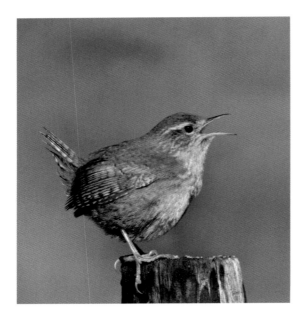

As we have seen, birds will quickly make good their numbers after some natural disaster. They have been doing so for millions of years. Hence there is no real reason to worry about most species if their numbers drop sharply after some difficult period such as a very cold winter. Even birds such as Wrens, which are very sensitive to cold winters, can quite quickly make good their numbers after bad periods. What does matter to such species is any change in habitat; this may affect survival rates or reproductive rates. A change in habitat is likely to be permanent and so the balance of numbers may be permanently affected.

Humans have had a greater effect on the landscape than any other agent since the Ice Age. Many natural habitats have almost disappeared. There is almost no truly natural woodland left over most of Europe, and much concern is now being shown over the rapid disappearance of tropical rainforests. In an attempt to prevent too great a loss of wildlife, many bodies are now concerned with various aspects of conservation. There is a great shortage of resources for such activities, and of land for nature reserves; so it is imperative that we make the best use of what is available by making sure that we understand the key needs. In one sense, this is stating the obvious; but it is by no means always clear what the priorities should be.

Protection of individuals

It is necessary, perhaps, to stress the difference here between caring for individual birds and being concerned for the well-being of populations as a whole. Cold winters result in an increased mortality of individuals, but they do not endanger the population. Should we therefore interfere with nature by providing food to help the weaker individuals to survive since the populations of most garden birds decline markedly in cold winters, even though a lot of people feed them?

For species that have only small populations in restricted areas, a natural disaster may have a more marked effect and even lead to the extinction of some local populations. The species may then be absent, briefly or for a long time, until such areas are recolonized by birds from elsewhere. The more reduced and dissected populations become, the longer recolonization may take. It might never happen. Putting effort into reducing the effect of natural disasters on such species may allow them to cling on enabling their population to recover in better times.

The protection of rare species takes up a great deal of the conservationist's time. One difficulty is that it is not always easy to define what is a rare species and what is not. It could be argued that there are no rare birds in Britain. All the species that the British consider rare are, in fact, reasonably common somewhere else in Europe. None of them could be considered extremely rare on a global scale. All are birds that are on the edge of their range – a place where, almost by definition, a species finds it difficult to survive. In this sense, perhaps, birdwatchers are like gardeners, forever trying to persuade species to flourish in places where they cannot easily do so.

Above Left A Wren sings, perched on a post **Opposite** Goldfinch feed by extracting seeds directly from plants like this teasel

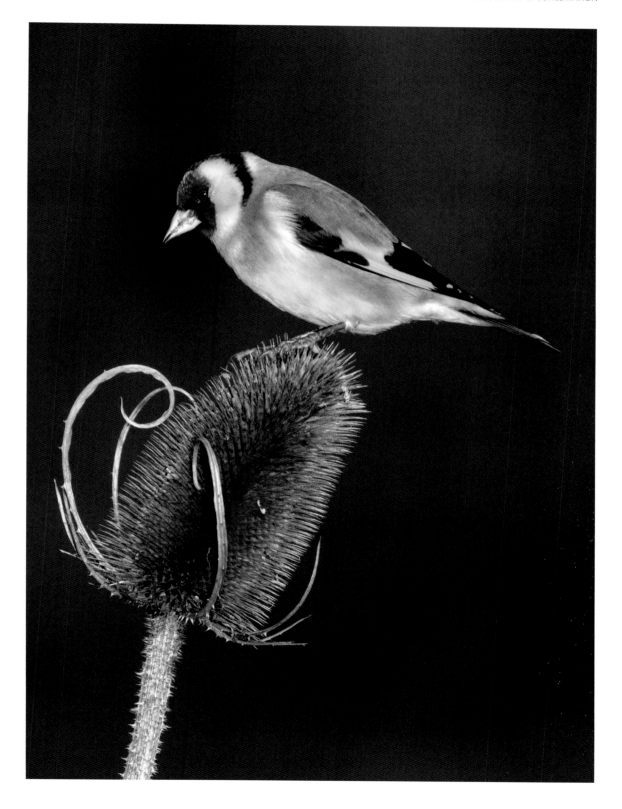

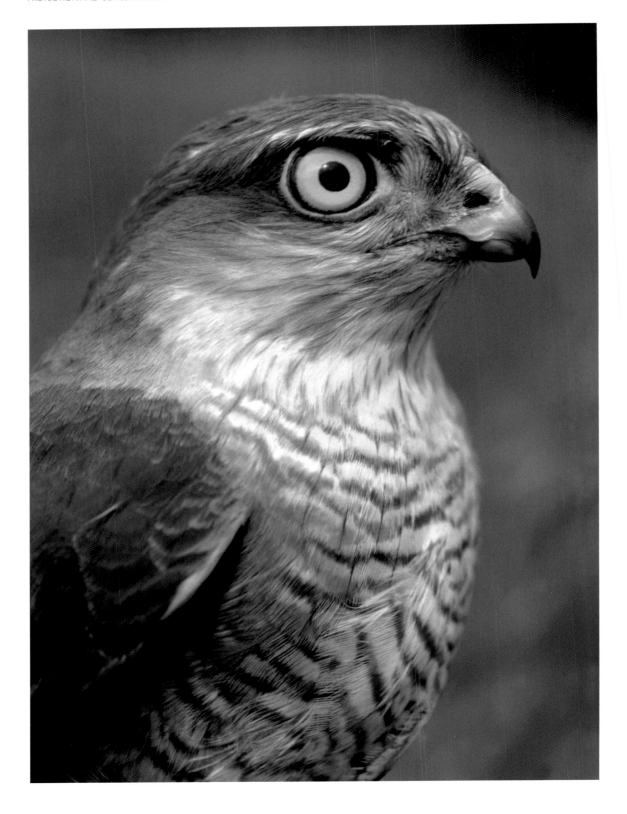

Protection of habitats

In contrast to the fact that healthy populations may need little or no protection, the preservation of suitable habitats is of prime importance. Even small environmental changes may be important because they tend to be permanent, rather than happening once in a while as is the case with natural disasters. To this end, it might be more important to our garden birds to plant trees and bushes for them, or to buy and protect more woodland, than to provide food for them in winter.

In recent years there has been greater recognition of the problems that arise from trying to protect a single species. Conservation now tends to put much of its emphasis on preserving representative areas of a wide range of habitats. In many cases this has the desired effect of protecting many of the rarer birds anyway, and brings the added bonus of giving protection to all the other flora and fauna that occur in such habitats.

Even so, there are problems associated with trying to maintain natural habitats. Even if one can obtain and give protection to large areas this does not guarantee success, since it is not possible to keep the birds in such areas in total isolation. Certain threats to bird populations cannot be eliminated just by setting up reserves. Many species have been affected by the use of poisons aimed primarily at insects, but which also poison birds. These, such as DDT and related substances (often referred to as the chlorinated hydrocarbons), are applied to fields to protect crops. Since they do not break down readily, they have slowly spread into all habitats, partly by the movements of animals carrying them. For example, a Finch may eat the treated seeds, fly to roost in the woods, where it is eaten, chemicals and all, by a Sparrowhawk. Chemicals have also been washed out of the soils and carried down rivers into the seas, where they have built up in the marine food-chains and hence in the seabirds. Plastics and other pollutants that do not break down find their way into the food-chains and nests of birds all around the globe, causing sickness and death. Such is their persistence, and so great the quantities used, that they have even been found in the Antarctic – many thousands of kilometres from where they were originally applied.

Opposite A Sparrowhawk has large eyes and exceptional vision
Next Page Left A Marsh Tit and a Great Tit forage on sunflowers seeds
Next Page Right Dried sunflower heads offer the perfect snack for peckish finches, tits and nuthatches

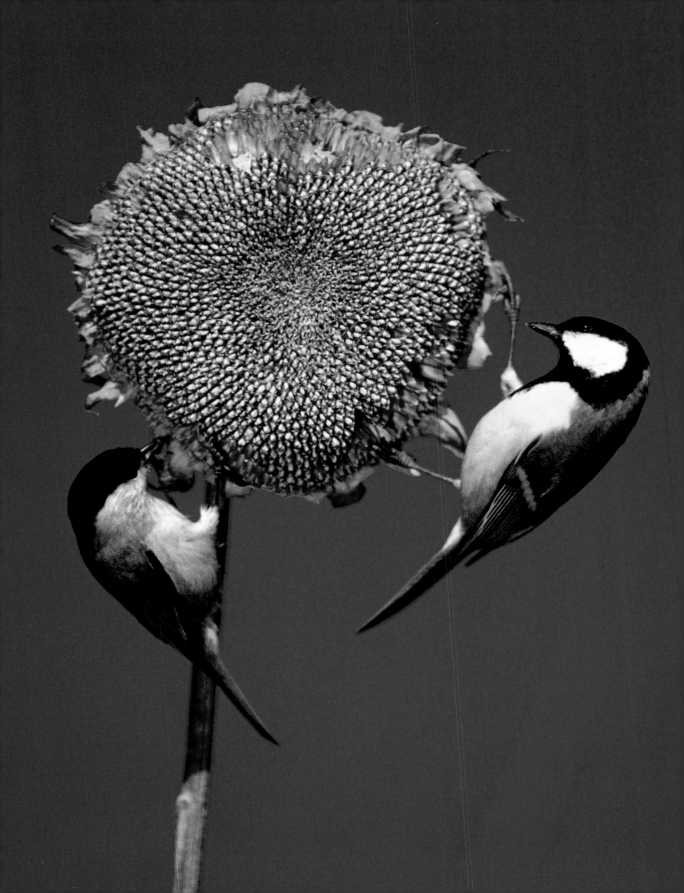

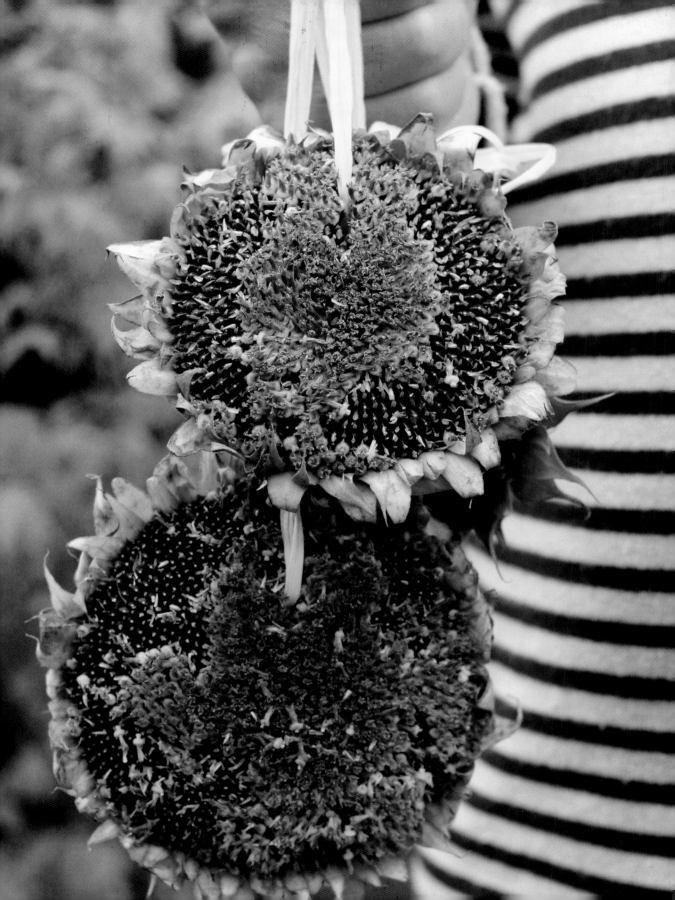

The Changing Scene
A Brief History of European Habitats

European habitats have changed markedly during the last 15,000 years or so, since the peak of the last glaciation. This glaciation was not an isolated incident. During the last two million years there have been several glaciations, interspersed by warmer periods. Indeed there is every reason to suppose that we are living in just one such inter-glacial period and that yet another Ice Age will, in the course of the next few thousand years, descend on Europe. During these glacial periods, the Arctic ice-cap covered vast areas of Europe, extending down to southern Britain and much of central Europe. These areas were of little or no interest to birds. To the south lay the Arctic tundra, usable, as it is today, by waders, geese and a few other species during the summer months.

The habitats that we see today in northern Europe were not eliminated during the Ice Ages, rather they moved southwards and northwards with the changes in climate. As the climate got colder, the plants in any given habitat would die out on the northern edge, but spread on the southern edge. As the climate warmed up, this pattern was reversed. Botanists have built up a good understanding of the movements of the habitats. Ornithologists do not have comparable information on the birds, but it seems reasonable to assume that these stayed in the habitats that they prefer today, and that they too moved as their habitats shifted back and forth.

About 6,000 years ago the habitats stopped moving northwards. They settled into a pattern which, if things had followed the pattern of the previous inter-glacials, would have remained unchanged until the ice began to move southwards once again. But the current inter-glacial (if that is what it is) differs from all previous ones in that a new factor intervened to make other changes to the habitats. Humans arrived in ever-increasing numbers, affecting habitats as never before.

The natural habitats and the arrival of humans
Before humans arrived, most of Europe was covered by a forest of oak, ash, beech, spruce and pine. River valleys were clogged with fallen trees and debris, and so wide areas were flooded, forming extensive marshlands. Only the tops of mountains, the far north where the tundra still exists today, and some drier areas in the south, were forest free. Grassland was almost non-existent. The only open lowland areas, apart from marshes, were sand-dunes and temporary clearings where there had been fire or where large trees had fallen and left small glades.

Until about 5,000 years ago, Mesolithic people lived in tune with their habitat. They had a niche, which was rather like that of other predatory mammals, and had only limited effects on the forests and the marshes. Marked changes occurred with the advent of the Neolithic agriculturists. These people were not nomadic hunters, but settlers who cleared patches of forests in order to grow crops. At first they were only able to clear the lightly wooded ridges, but later, with improved tools, they were able to deal with the larger trees of lowland forests. As the size of their flocks of grazing animals increased, so did the size of the clearings. Grassland started to appear.

Today, in many parts of Europe only a tiny proportion of the original forest remains. Only in recent years has any attempt been made to reverse the trend by re-afforestation, though the new forests are often of alien tree species. Even those forests that have survived have been greatly changed, for humans have removed many of the valuable species and the largest trees. Such losses affect the bird population directly, because these are the very trees that tend to produce the heaviest crops of seeds.

The birch and conifer forests of the far north are probably little altered. Elsewhere, only one or two areas of almost natural forest remain in central Europe. Some of the scrub forest in the drier parts of southern Europe, or on mountains near the limit of the tree-line, may be fairly unchanged, though many have been heavily felled or grazed.

Humans did not make a great impression on the marshes until much later, for to do so required more organization and technical skill than tree-felling. First, the main streams of the rivers were cleared to make them suitable for navigation. Later, it became possible to speed up the flow of minor streams and tributaries, and reduce the flooding of the lowland meadows,

Opposite The Downy Birch, one of the few original trees of the natural forestland

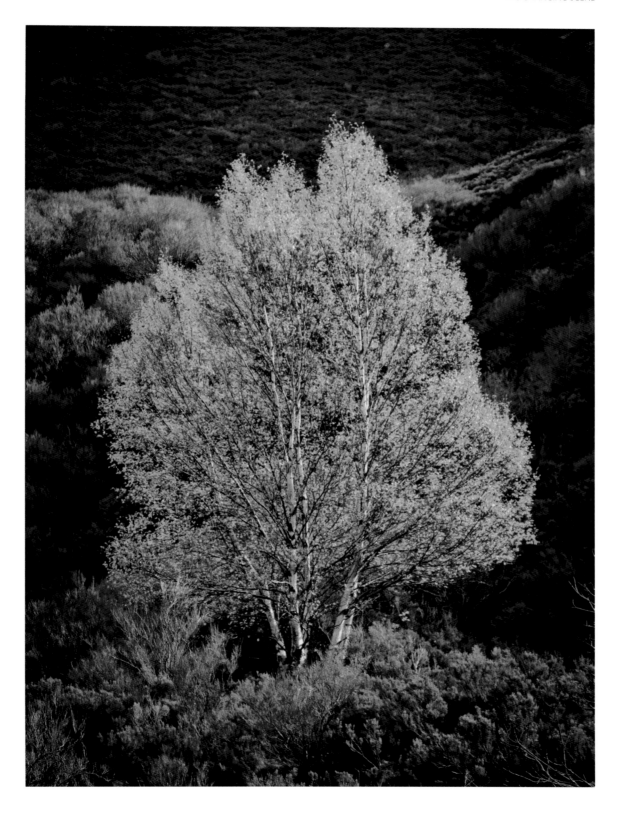

which were valuable for farming. Marshland has now been even more seriously reduced than forest. Parallel with the extensive removal of forests and marshes, there has been an enormous expansion of open country of all sorts. Primarily this has been for agricultural purposes, but a varied range of heath, moor, grassland and other open country now exists where there was virtually none before.

Changes in birdlife

The changes that humans have made to the environment have been covered in some detail because they have had very profound effects on the bird fauna of Europe. Indeed they could be said to be the dominant factor in the distribution of many of the birds we have today.

The losses

Perhaps the greatest surprise is to find that very few European birds have become totally extinct as a result of these extensive changes. As far as is known, only the Great Auk and the Demoiselle Crane have disappeared from Europe, and perhaps the Steppe Eagle. Nonetheless, many other species have been greatly reduced in numbers and have disappeared from large parts of their former ranges. The birds that are in greatest danger tend to be the larger ones. Many of these are heavily hunted, but for most species habitat destruction is probably at least as important a factor. Large birds need large territories and a given area of woodland or marsh can support far fewer large birds than small ones. Hence, the danger of local extinction tends to be higher for a large bird species than a small one.

The gains

The changes humans have made have not just brought about reductions. A number of species must have found manmade habitats to their liking. Many of the birds that live in towns and gardens were originally occupants of the extensive forests; many individuals still live there. Such species include the thrushes (the Blackbird, Mistle Thrush and Song Thrush), the tits (especially Great and Blue Tits), Robins, Chaffinches, Greenfinches, and, in larger areas of parks and gardens, Woodpigeons, Great Spotted Woodpeckers and Tawny Owls. These birds may even have preferred woodland edge to the deep forest. Moving into farmland hedgerows

and into gardens may not have seemed a great change to them.

Some very common garden birds, such as the Starling, House Sparrow and Rook are not woodland species. It is difficult to say where they lived before humans opened up the countryside, or to imagine the House Sparrow without people; most of its relations (Ploceidae) live in dry, open savannah country, and presumably it originally did too. It might have survived the last Ice Age in parts of southern Spain, where there was some rather open steppe-like country. Surely, however, it would not occur in most of Europe today were it not for human activities. Much the same may be said of the Rook; this species needs open country for feeding, although it nests in trees. Originally it probably lived on the edges of steppe, nesting in trees and flying out to open country to feed. Like the Rook, the Starling nests in trees; but it feeds, for most of the year, on areas of short grass. However, it also nests in holes in cliffs, and feeds along the shoreline. Was this its natural habitat in Europe when humans arrived? Similarly, in Britain the Chough feeds mainly on the short grass turf maintained by the presence of grazing sheep. Where was it before there were sheep?

The primeval European countryside may also have been unsuitable for the Buzzard, Red Kite, and Kestrel, all nesting in trees, but feeding over open country. Did they exist along the edges of marshes? Where were the grassland habitats for Quails and Grey Partridges? Where would Skylarks, Meadow Pipits or Whinchats have been found? All must have been very much less numerous than they are today. A particular puzzle surrounds many of the aerial insectivores. Nowadays, virtually all the swallows, house martins, and swifts nest in or on buildings. Even the Sand Martin is largely dependent on people for its nest-sites. Most of them are in the banks of gravel diggings; even the small cliffs along river banks that they use are created by the wash from boats. In the primeval, water-logged marshes such vertical banks would have been absent. Of all the European swifts and swallows, only the Crag Martin remains in truly natural sites. Are these species much commoner today than they were before humans appeared on the scene?

Opposite The Tawny Owl is a forest species that has adapted well to the human environment

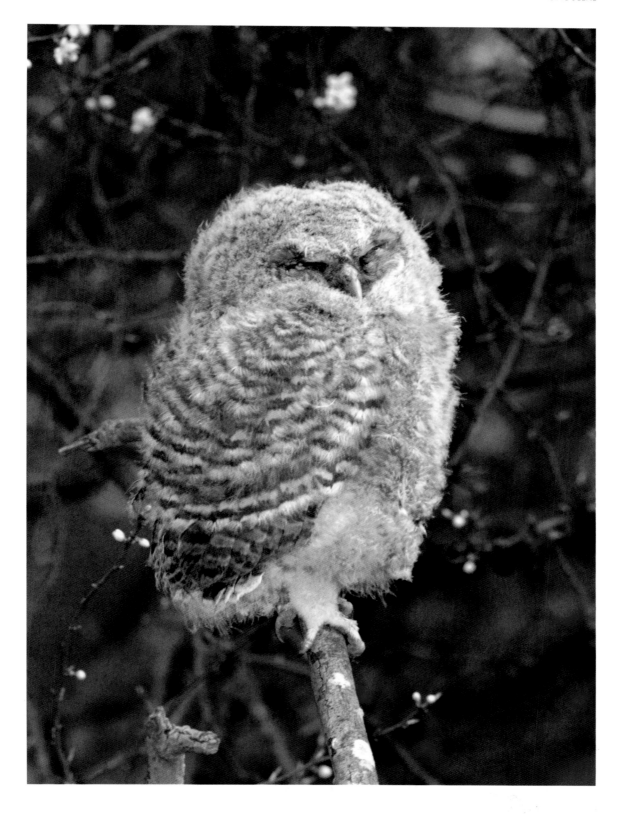

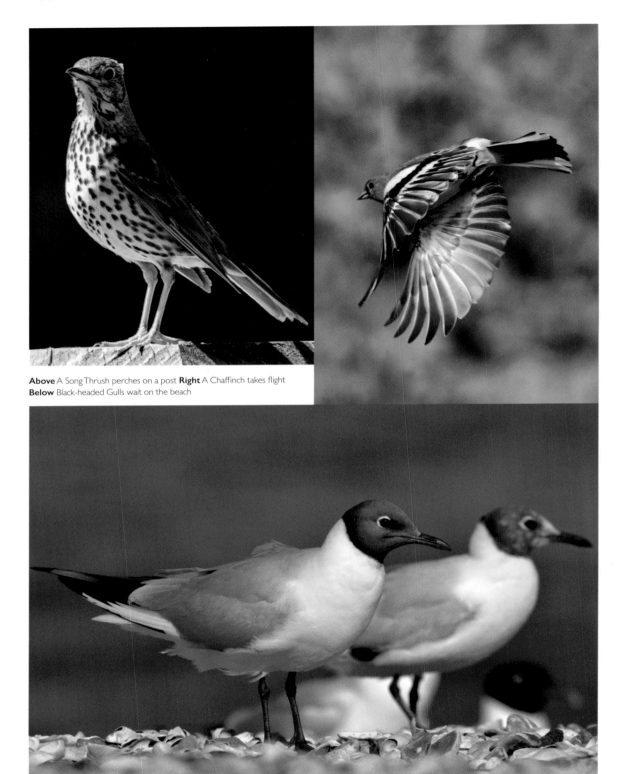

Above A Song Thrush perches on a post **Right** A Chaffinch takes flight
Below Black-headed Gulls wait on the beach

Changes of habits

Some of the birds that occupy human-made habitats may well have been able to colonize them with little or no change of behaviour, since the habitats were sufficiently similar to the ones that they lived in already. In other cases, birds may well have changed their habits somewhat, and this enabled them to increase their numbers markedly. This is what happened with the Collared Dove. Many of the European birds have had 2,000 generations or more to adapt to the changes people have made. Since some small changes can be observed in 100 generations or less, major changes in habits could have taken place since humans started to change the face of Europe. Several species of gull have learned to take food provided by people. Herring, lesser Black-backed, Black-headed and Common Gulls in particular visit rubbish tips in large numbers, and also follow the plough, collecting worms. These species are commoner inland in Europe than they used to be, and many winter further north than they could have done formerly. The provision of these extra sources of food must be an important factor.

Overall change: the future

The result of all these changes is difficult to summarize. We have lost many species from certain areas, though few from the whole of Europe. Many are much less numerous than they once were. Contrariwise, many that were scarce must now be much commoner than they were before humans made their mark upon the scene. To some extent, the changes people have wrought are similar to those that have always been going on; new species have arisen while others have evolved new adaptations to new situations. In one important way however, the alterations brought about by people are different from most of those wrought by nature: they occur much faster. Our increasing technological skills enable us to make ever swifter, more marked changes. In many areas of the world, especially the tropical rainforests, where birds are closely adapted to highly specialized forest types, changes are occurring very much faster than they have in Europe. Such changes bring about huge losses of plant and animal species.

Equally, the future is not particularly rosy for many animals in Europe; changes will almost certainly occur more rapidly in the future than they did in the past. In spite of the growing awareness of the need for a greater ecological conscience, financial pressures are still very powerful and, in emergent, or developing nations, where there are the unsolved needs of rapidly growing human populations, wise long-term planning may be pushed aside by short-term expediency.

It is to be hoped that the growing appreciation of the need for wildlife – not just for its aesthetic merits, but also as evidence of a healthy world – will make our successors more careful and more clever in the ways in which they handle our natural resources than we have been so far. This does not mean that there will be no further changes. Even if we are able to avoid further serious alterations to the world, natural selection will still remain a powerful active force.

Next Page Dogwoods in bloom in California

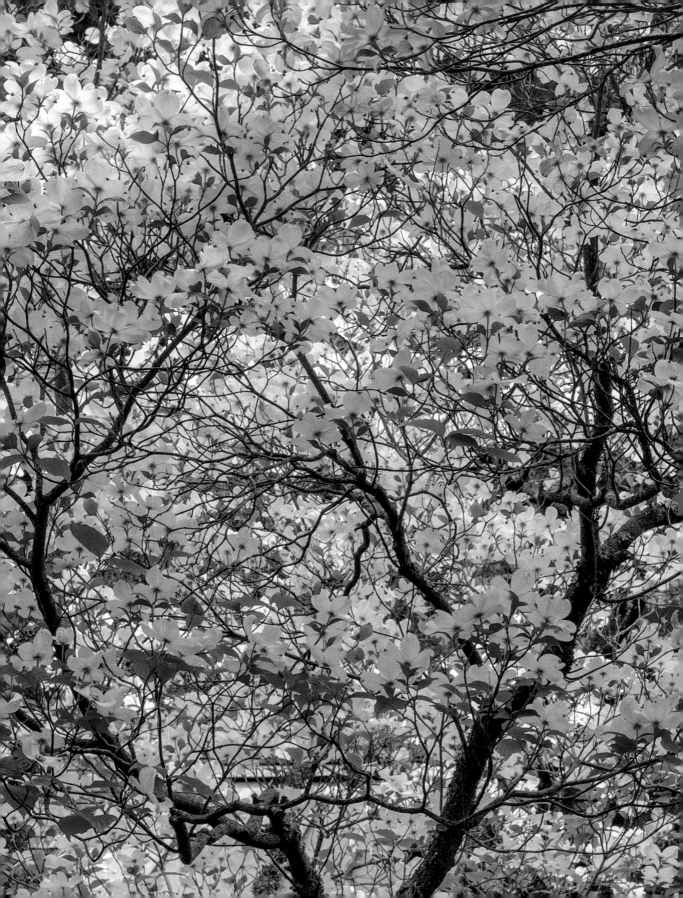

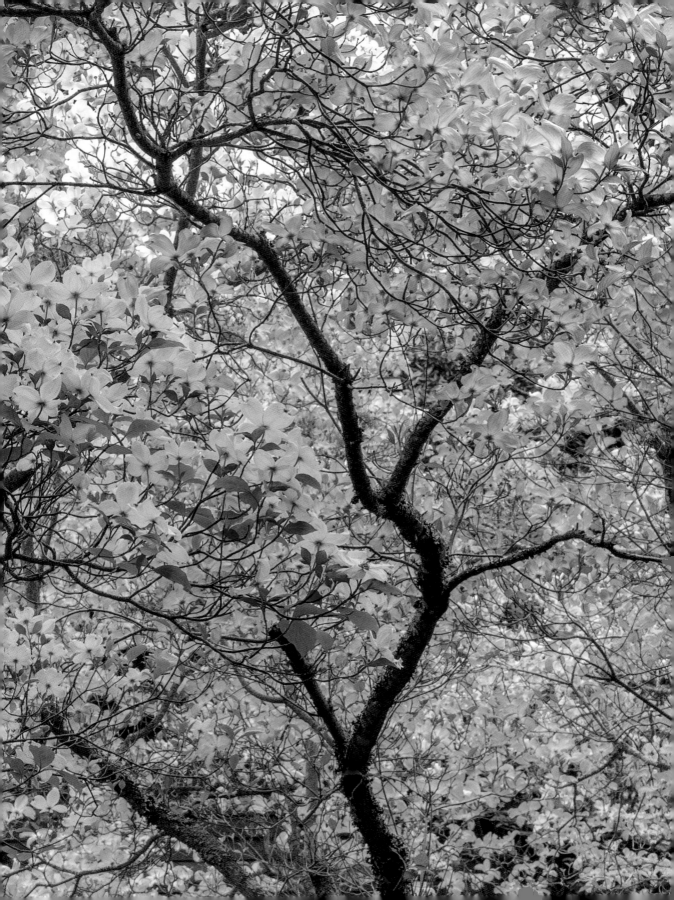

HISTORY OF BIRDWATCHING

As long as humankind has existed, people have watched birds. Birds have had their place in countless human cultures around the globe, worshipped one moment and hunted the next, everywhere from Aboriginal Australia to ancient Egypt. The study of birds is not new. There are descriptions of bird behaviour in the Bible, and even back in the fourth century BC Aristotle realized that something was amiss in the behaviour of the common Cuckoo.

Birdwatching as a hobby, however, is a much more recent development, dating back to the end of the nineteenth century, at a time when most people interested in natural history were shooting, and whose primary concern was for either collecting specimens for its own sake, or for scientific purposes. A less destructive approach to birds was signalled with the formation of the National Audubon Society in the USA in 1886 and the Society for the Protection of Birds (later RSPB) in the UK in 1889, both of which came out of campaigns to restrict the use of feathers in women's fashion, and were largely driven by women. The term 'birdwatching' was coined in Britain by Edmund Selous in his eponymous book of 1901, while Elliott Coues produced his *Key to North American Birds* further back, in 1872. The first US Christmas Bird Count took place in 1900, led by the early wildlife campaigner Frank Chapman.

However, the hobby would never have taken off without three major developments. The first of these was the production of suitable optics. The binoculars we know today originated from an optical system of prisms invented by Ignatio Porro in 1854 and were perfected by the firm Carl Zeiss in 1894. As time went on, binoculars improved, became widely available and eventually cheaper, ready for the real take-off in birdwatching after the Second World War.

The second big development came with field guides. Many books had been published with illustrations of birds, but the real breakthrough came with Roger Tory Peterson's (see page 327) *A Field Guide to the Birds* in 1934. This was the original 'field guide', with similar North American species pictured close together with arrows indicating their salient features. *The Book of Indian Birds*, published in 1941 by Salim Ali, had a similar effect on birdwatching there, while Roger Tory Peterson produced *A Field Guide to the Birds of Britain and Europe*, together with Guy Mountfort and Philip Hollom in 1954. Many field guides followed, and these days there is a field guide to the birds of almost every country in the world.

The third development was leisure time, which grew along with economic prosperity, mainly in the western world at first. In Britain in the eighteenth century, people would routinely work thirteen-and-a-half hour shifts in factories; some of these were young children. There was no time for leisure, except for the highest echelons of society, and it was primarily the wealthy who had much time to look at birds. After the two world wars there was a cultural shift in the west towards mass participation in hobbies of all kinds, of which one was birdwatching.

Towards the end of the twentieth century birdwatching boomed. It did so principally in its heartlands of the USA and UK, but other countries quickly followed, including the Netherlands and Nordic countries. With the advent of international travel, birdwatching tourism began, and even specialized birdwatching holidays (the first tour company was Ornitholidays, a British company founded in 1965). A few people began to go all over the world, seeing hitherto unimaginable numbers of species.

Right up until the end of the twentieth century, a significant proportion of birdwatchers were men. In the last 20 years, however, their dominance has been swept aside and birdwatching has become a mass participation hobby for everybody. It is currently sweeping the globe, too, taking in both Japan and China, for instance, and in emergent countries a growing number of local guides are beginning to make a good living from birding tourism. Such people are also enjoying birdwatching for its own sake, of course.

We can only expect to see birdwatching growing in the years to come. This is to be welcomed in every way, especially when it is aligned with a care for the environment and interest in nature. The latter is essential to guide us through the dangers the planet faces. If our climate emergency cannot be contained, there won't be many birds left to watch.

Opposite An ornithologist wanders in the wood in 1908

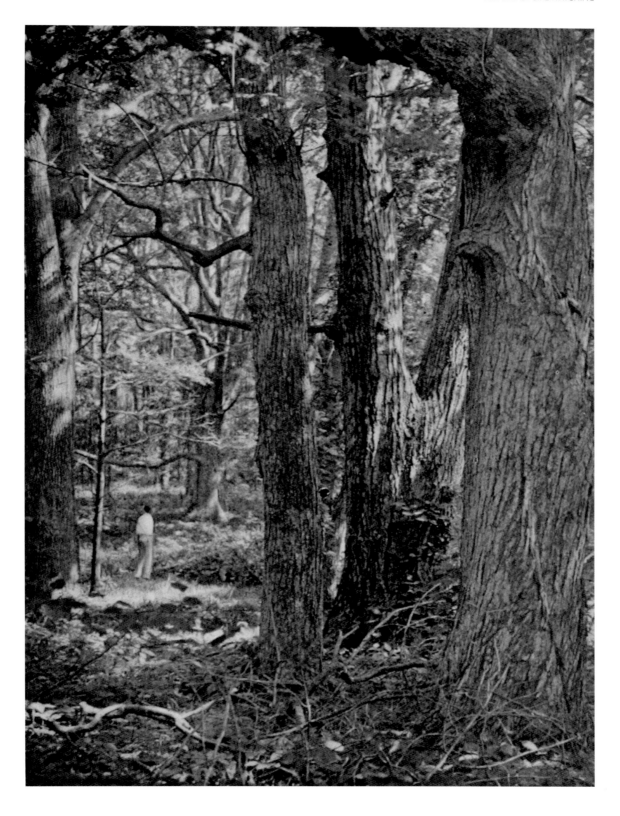

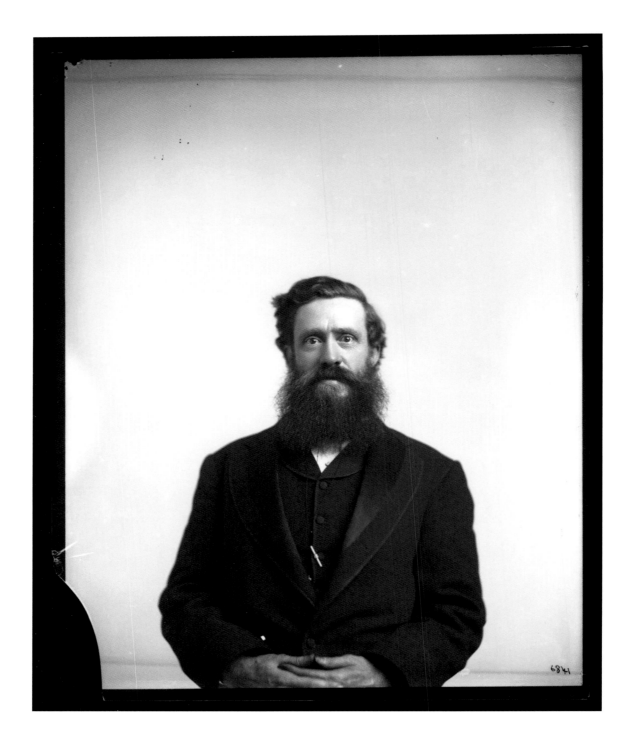

16   TOPOGRAPHY OF THE BODY.

liarly ornamented with feathers of different texture or structure from those of the general plumage ; but an instance of this is seen in our Lewis' woodpecker. The notæum, on the contrary, is often the seat of extraordinary development of feathers, either in size, shape or texture ; as the singularly elegant plumes of the herons. Individual feathers of the notæum are generally pennaceous (§ 4), in greatest part straight and lanceolate ; and

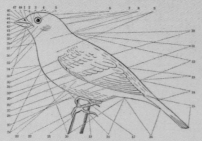

Fig. 4.—Topography of a Bird.

as a whole they lie smoothly *imbricated* (like shingles on a roof). The gastreal feathers are more largely plumulaceous (§ 4), less flat and imbricated, but even more compact, that is, thicker, than those of the upper parts ; especially among water birds, where they are all more or less curly, and very thickset. There are subdivisions of the

§ 38. NOTÆUM. Beginning where the neck ends, and ending where the tail coverts begin, this part of the bird is divided into back (Lat. *dorsum* ; fig. 4, 11) and rump (L. *uropygium* fig. 4, 13). These are direct continuations of each other, and their limits are not precisely defined. The feathers of both are on the *pteryla dorsalis* (§ 8, *b*). In general, we may say that the anterior two-thirds or three-quarters of notæum is back, and the rest rump. With the former are generally included the scapular feathers, or *scapulars* : these are they that grow on the *pterylæ humerales* (§ 8, *b*) : the region of

---

80   PARINÆ, TRUE TITMICE.—GEN. 12.

obvious seasonal or sexual changes of plumage. All but one of our species are plainly clad ; still they have a pleasing look, with their trim form and the tasteful colors of the head.

Subfamily PARINÆ. True Titmice.

Exclusive of certain aberrant forms, usually allowed to constitute a separate subfamily, and sometimes altogether removed from *Paridæ*, the Titmice compose a natural and pretty well defined group, to which the foregoing diagnosis and remarks are particularly applicable. There may be about seventy-five good species of the *Parinæ*, thus restricted, most of them falling in the genus *Parus*, or in its immediate neighborhood. With few exceptions they are birds of the northern hemisphere, abounding in Europe, Asia and North America. The larger proportion of the genera and species inhabit the Old World ; all those of the New World occur within our limits, except two—*Psaltriparus melanotis* and *Parus meridionalis*, which are Mexican, though they have been lately included in our systematic works. The former is a very distinct and beautiful species ; the latter is perhaps only a southern variety of the common Chickadee.

12. Genus LOPHOPHANES Kaup.

**Conspicuously crested. Leaden-gray, often with a faint olivaceous shade, paler or whitish below ; wings and tail unmarked. (All the figures are of natural size.)

Tufted Titmouse. Forehead alone black ; nearly white below ; sides washed with rusty-brown ; feet leaden-blue. Young birds have the crest plain, thus resembling the next species ; but they are nearly white below, the sides showing rusty traces. Largest of our species of the family, 6–6¼ ; wing 3–3¼, tail about the same. Eastern United States, north to Long Island ; "Nova Scotia" (*Aud.*). WILS., i, 137, pl. 8, f. 5 ; AUD., ii, 143, pl. 125 ; BD., 384. BICOLOR.

FIG. 21. Tufted Titmouse.

Plain Titmouse. Plain leaden gray with faint olive shade, merely paler below ; no markings anywhere. 5¼–6 ; wing and tail about 2¾. New Mexico, Arizona and California. CASS., Ill., p. 19 ; BD., 386 ; ELLIOT, pl. 3 ; COOP., 42. . . INORNATUS.

Black-crested Titmouse. Size of the last, or rather less ; similar to the

FIG. 22. Plain Titmouse.   FIG. 23. Black-crested Titmouse.   FIG. 24. Bridled Titmouse.

first in color, but forehead whitish, and whole crest black. Valley of the Rio Grande. CASS., p. 13, pl. 3 ; BD., 385 ; COOP., 43. ATRICRISTATUS.

Bridled Titmouse. Olivaceous-ash ; below soiled whitish ; chin and

---

Opposite Ornithologist Elliott Coues, author of *Key to North American Birds* (1872) **Above** Pages 16 and 80 from Elliott Coues's *Key to North American Birds*

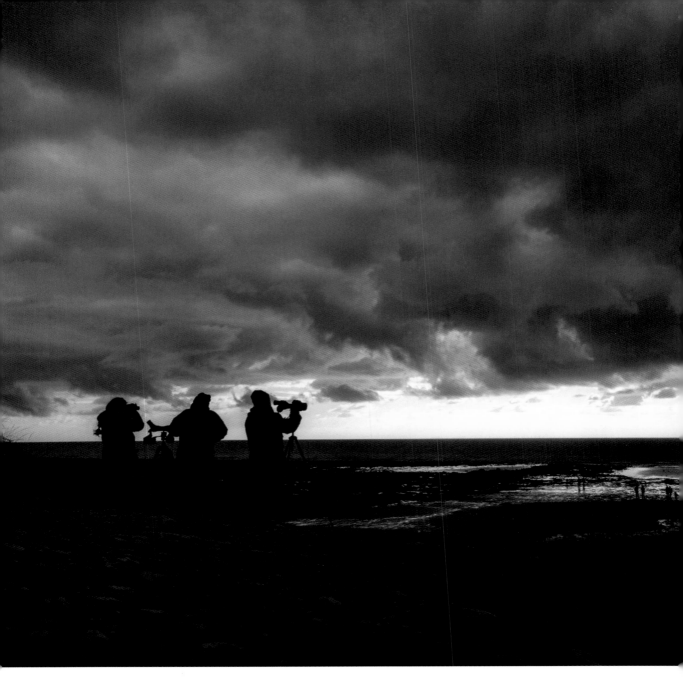

INTRODUCTION TO BIRDWATCHING

If you're thinking of taking up birdwatching, congratulations. Not only will the hobby bring you fun and delight, you are joining an increasing movement around the world who have seen the benefits of looking at birds for their own physical and mental health. Once the preserve of a relatively small section of society, birdwatching is now a pastime for everybody, regardless of background, gender and temperament. Already one of the most popular outdoor pursuits in Britain and the USA, its glory days are still ahead.

There are many reasons why you should take up birdwatching but here, to begin with, is one. Few other hobbies fit so seamlessly into everyday life. You can watch birds when you are gardening, or cooking or when you are washing dishes; you can watch birds while walking or hiking, playing golf or cycling. Birds are there on your commuting trips to and from work; and when you are bored in an office meeting, there are birds outside the window! If you cannot see them, you can often hear them; people have been known to listen and enjoy the bird chorus from a hospital bed.

The ubiquity of birds makes watching them easy, and there are few pastimes that are easier to take up. At the same time, beginning birdwatching is the tip of a wonderful iceberg, with endless possibilities for expanding into something that can become increasingly important in your life.

First steps – identifying garden birds

In theory, you can watch birds without spending any money at all. However, sooner or later you will need a pair of binoculars to help you see birds well enough to put a name to them. To do the latter, you will also need an identification guide, which could be a book – a so-called 'field guide' – or an app (see pages 259 and 389). Both have their merits. For the beginner, a book is probably better and a little more satisfying for browsing through all the possible bird species in your area. The section on Equipment (see page 256) will help with choosing the right binoculars and identification aids.

Most people begin in their gardens, and they soon run into a near-universal problem. Some birds are very easy to identify, such as Blue Tits and Great Tits, but others are much more difficult. Species are also very variable, which means that males and females may look quite different, as is the case with House Sparrows. On the other hand, some species of birds look very similar to each other – a good example is the Song Thrush and Mistle Thrush. Your first foray into bird identification should make you realize that this hobby isn't always easy. It takes time and effort to improve, and you shouldn't be discouraged if you are finding it difficult.

There are ways to overcome these awkward first steps. One is to find an experienced birdwatcher to help, especially if you are getting frustrated. Another is to visit a different place for birdwatching, such as a

pond with ducks and swans, or a nearby wood where you can be refreshed and meet a few more easy species. Eventually, however, if you keep practising and putting in time, you will crack it organically. If you see a bird enough times, the penny usually drops.

However, there is a short cut to proficiency, and that is learning how to look at a bird thoroughly, from top to toe. For anybody who might not have a photographic memory, this takes practice and patience, but it is invaluable. It simply means looking at every part of a bird – the head, the body, the wings, the legs and the tail – trying to remember the colours, patterns and shapes during the time you are observing it. Once you have noted all you can, this gives you the ammunition you need to identify it. The more you note down – in your mind, notebook or phone – the more likely you are to identify it correctly.

Take two examples of how useful this can be. Look at a House Sparrow and ask yourself, what is the pattern on the underside, the breast and belly? You'll see it's plain. Most small birds that resemble House Sparrows have streaked underparts. Similarly, what is the colour of the Robin's forehead (the bit above the bill)? To many people's great surprise, it is orange, the same as the breast. If you practise looking thoroughly at birds, you will notice these small details, many of which are very important. As we will see later, looking at a bird's shape, especially the bill, is often a great clue.

If you wish to improve your observation, there is no short cut to the task of learning the parts of a bird, each of which have technical, but not complicated names. It is easier to say the rump is white, than saying that the 'bit at the base of the tail' is white. The reality is that, among birdwatchers, thorough observation is counterintuitive, and few people are good at it. Most just improve their birdwatching organically.

There is one more first step that will greatly improve your birdwatching skills, and that is to keep looking at familiar birds and learn them thoroughly. If you manage to do this – and then again, it is counter to human nature, as most people quickly get excited and want to see as many birds as quickly as they can – you will eventually become a much better birdwatcher. If you are truly familiar with common and garden birds, you will be much better able to spot something different and unusual.

Opposite Bird watchers at Flamborough Head in the UK

Immersion

None of the first steps mentioned in the section on the previous page is compulsory. Many people enjoy their birds at a certain level and are happy not to strive to become any more proficient at identifying them, while others just seem to have an aptitude for birdwatching and quickly become excellent without seeming to try too hard. It doesn't matter which path you have followed, you will soon enter the next phase of your birdwatching life, which could perhaps be described as immersion. If you spend enough time in places where there are birds, you will eventually begin to understand them.

Birds are wild animals that have evolved to treat humans with extreme suspicion. Some are tamer than others, of course, and you will see birds on any walk you do, but our birdwatching will be richer if the objects of our interest are unaware that we are there. We need to make ourselves inconspicuous by being quiet, slow in our movements and relatively concealed.

Being quiet helps in two ways: we can approach a bird more closely than if we are noisy, and we also clear the airwaves so that we can hear what sounds it might be making (there is more about bird songs and calls on page 251). Obviously, the closer a bird is, the better view we get, and an undisturbed bird is more likely to come into the open. Another advantage of being quiet is that it helps us to become immersed in a place, and to become accustomed to nature's pace. Of course, sociable birdwatching is fine, too, but a bubble of conversation is better than a rabble.

Being still also works in two ways. Most birds have panoramic vision and, more than anything, are adapted to flee when they perceive sudden movements. This means that certain human tics, such as pointing towards a bird, lifting binoculars up too quickly or coughing, need to be avoided where possible. It is also a good tip to move slowly when birdwatching, and not to try to cover too much ground. Once you arrive at a spot, stay there and give the birds a chance to move around and show themselves, especially in the summer when they are breeding. Also, if you find yourself among birds, stay with them. It is often tempting, if you are hiking a trail, to want to see what is round the next corner, but the answer might be nothing. If you are seeing things, get the best out of where you are before moving on. In many parts of the world, birds move around in flocks (in temperate regions this is typical of winter woodlands and anywhere in the autumn), and away from these hubs of activity it can seem to be dead.

As a large mammal it is difficult to be completely concealed from a small, highly alert animal with enhanced senses, but it does pay off to make yourself inconspicuous. If a bird is close, just staying still can help. Birds have colour vision that is several times more sensitive than ours, so wearing neutral is a good idea, too. Another good tip is to stand in the shade on a sunny day. Try not to walk along so that your profile is obvious; don't walk on top of a bank, but below it. Crouching, rather than standing up, can also help.

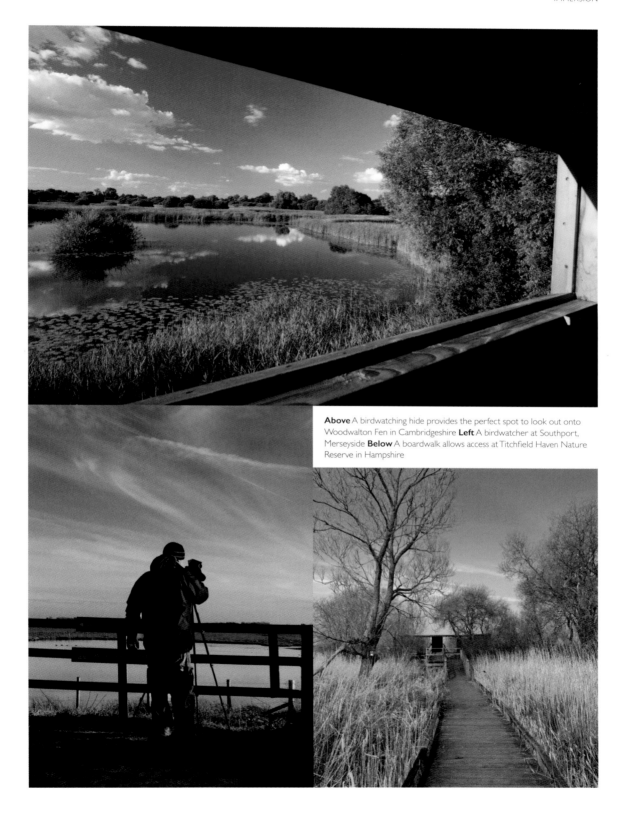

Above A birdwatching hide provides the perfect spot to look out onto Woodwalton Fen in Cambridgeshire **Left** A birdwatcher at Southport, Merseyside **Below** A boardwalk allows access at Titchfield Haven Nature Reserve in Hampshire

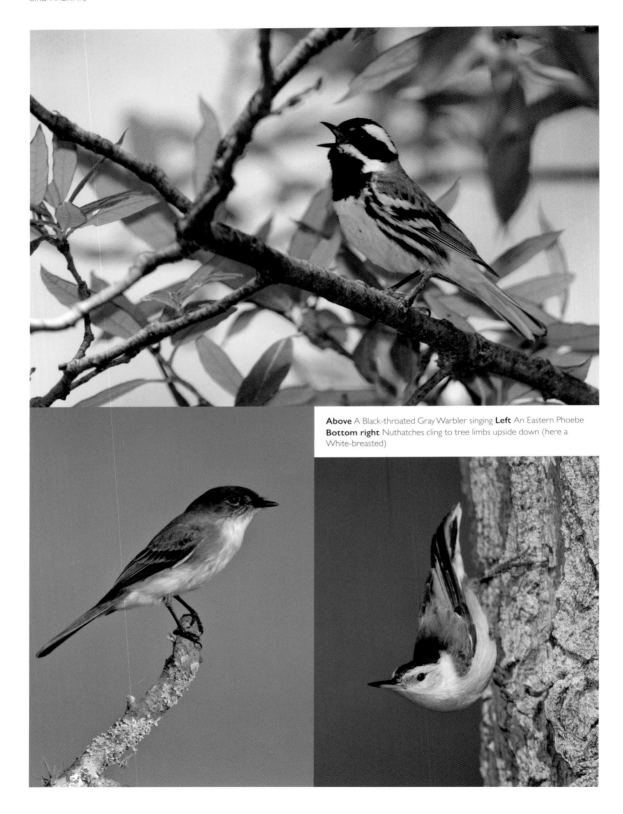

Above A Black-throated Gray Warbler singing **Left** An Eastern Phoebe **Bottom right** Nuthatches cling to tree limbs upside down (here a White-breasted)

Bird Habitats

A beginner will quickly discover for themselves that different species live in different types of country – that is, different habitats. Some of this is obvious even to those who aren't particularly interested in birds, who know that ducks like water and house sparrows like buildings. Almost every species has a preferred habitat. Some are very specific, such as Bearded Reedlings, also known as Bearded Tits, which are found in reed beds and nowhere else. Others cover a broad range, an example being the Wren, which occurs everywhere from gardens to offshore islands. However, even Wrens are only found in the lowest vegetation, usually among thick tangles close to the ground.

Getting to know birds in their respective habitats is a large part of birding. It makes it easier to identify birds because it cuts down the range of possible species. Imagine you see a tit at the top of a conifer tree. Knowing that the habitat of a Coal Tit is coniferous woodland, and that Great, Blue and Marsh Tits prefer deciduous woods helps to narrow the process down, leaving Willow Tits as the only other possibility.

The more time you spend outside birdwatching, the more habitat aware you become. This also means that you can start to predict what you might see before you see it. With experience you can begin to appreciate great subtleties. It becomes possible to predict which birds will be in a particular part of an estuary, or which birds are associated with certain types of tree or types of growth. You will learn that a Lesser Whitethroat prefers taller scrub than a Common Whitethroat. You will detect a juxtaposition of turf, shrub and rocks that helps to sniff out a Ring Ouzel in the hills.

Certain habitats are particularly good for birds, and every birdwatcher should allow themselves the opportunity of visiting them as often as possible. The coast is often richer than inland. If you live inland, however, look for any kind of water, be it a river, a lake or a pond; better still, a freshwater marsh. Woodland is often hard work, good though it can be. Oddly enough, the edge of a wood is usually better than the middle, both for bird species and activity, and the edge of a field is also better than the centre. Not surprisingly, this is known as the 'edge effect'. Another prime habitat is known as scrub, or shrubbery. Along the coast, lagoons and estuaries are usually hotspots, and in the summer rocky coasts are good for breeding seabirds.

There is great joy in appreciating birds in their wild habitats. Not only can you find out where to find birds, but you will learn a great deal about the great outdoors as well, and all the subtleties of landscape.

Times, Weather and Seasons

Birdwatching is a hobby; you don't have to get up early to enjoy it – but it helps. All birds have daily rhythms, and the vast majority are most active in the early morning, just after dawn. The early rising birdwatcher invariably sees more species, hears more species and sees more individual birds, doing more stuff. Part of the reason for this is that there is less disturbance from humans, but the main reason is that birds wake up hungry with the dawn.

On an average day there will still be some appreciable activity roughly into mid-morning, and then a slump. The late afternoon heralds another peak in feeding and moving about, which carries on until dusk. Then nocturnal birds take over, but even their daily rhythm peaks in twilight at both ends of the night.

There are some exceptions. In the middle of the breeding season, birds will simply keep going all day. The same happens in deep winter, when the days are so short that no bird can afford to let up, not even for a few minutes. Another major exception takes place at the coast, when it is the state of the tide that determines what birds do. On an estuary in winter, birds often roost at high tide, but the hour before and after may show spectacular flurries of activity. At low tide the birds might be too far away to see.

Weather affects everything a bird does, and what a birdwatcher does, too. You might think that rain is the biggest problem, but that isn't so – wind is the real disappointment. Not only does wind buffet birds about and cause them to skulk in bushes, but it also makes them much more difficult to see and, above all, hear. In windy conditions, seek a shelterbelt behind a building or some shrubbery – or just stay at home. Rain can promote bird activity, although it isn't always fun getting wet. In warm weather, the periods of morning activity are shorter and end earlier. Severe weather – storms, heavy frost and snow, gales at sea – can disrupt birds and herald unusual sightings.

One of the many joys of living in temperate parts of the world lies in the changing seasons, which provides a broad and colourful canvas for the brush strokes of bird movements. Seasons provide moments – the first Swallow of spring, for example – which define them and lift the spirits. Every season, even the darkest winter days enlivened by Robins and colourful ducks on the pond, by starling roosts and replete estuaries and freshwater lakes, has its signature birdwatching delights. After all, what is the best season for birds swarming into the garden? It is usually the middle of winter, especially after snow and frost.

Many people have no idea of this, but the season of song starts in mid-winter, after the shortest day. Despite the lack of food, birds set up territories and sing lustily right from January onwards, unless the weather is particularly fierce. They will tussle for food at a feeder one moment and proclaim territory the next. The late winter and early spring resound to bird song, which often reduces by May, and the land falls almost silent in June. April and May are the main months of spring migration, when you can go out almost anywhere and see almost anything, especially by the coast, and every species in its breeding finery. For most birds, nesting is done as quickly as possible. Even by late June some birds have finished and are already preparing to leave for their winter quarters, amazing though it may seem.

June and July explode with young birds doing their thing, usually very badly, but they learn fast, and have to. July and August are moulting time, and the latter month heralds the general southward migration, which is much more leisurely than it is in spring.

The delightful things about being a birdwatcher is that you always feel part of the changing seasons. Birds ebb and flow through the year, with different names making appearances like actors in a year-long stage play, and all with their own dramas, too. You can witness this. Over the years you begin to predict what is going to happen, and relish it all the more.

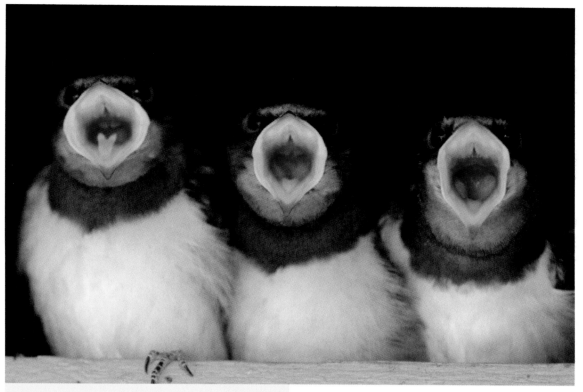

Above Young Swallows wait for food **Below** Birdwatching can mean an early start... **Next Page** ...But the sunrises can be worth it

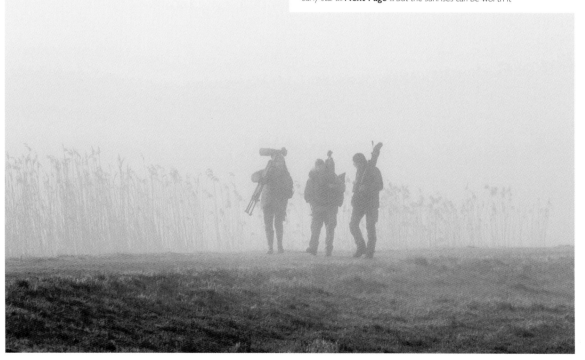

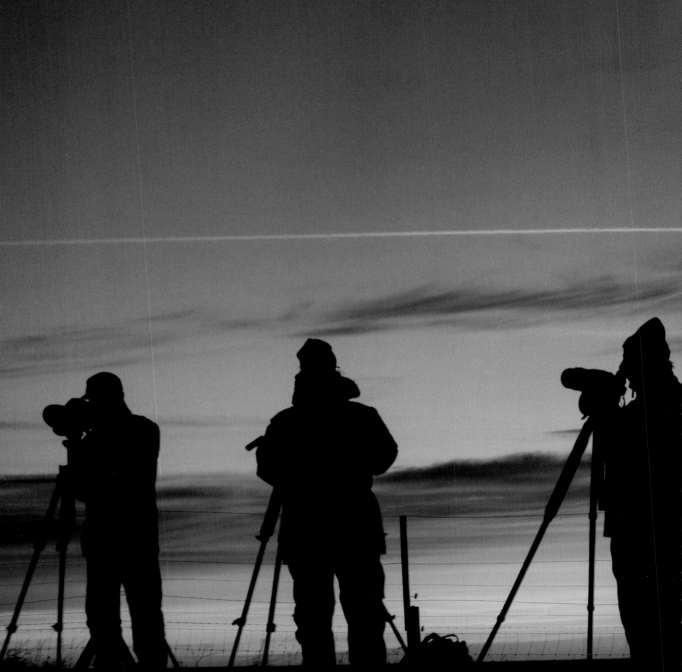

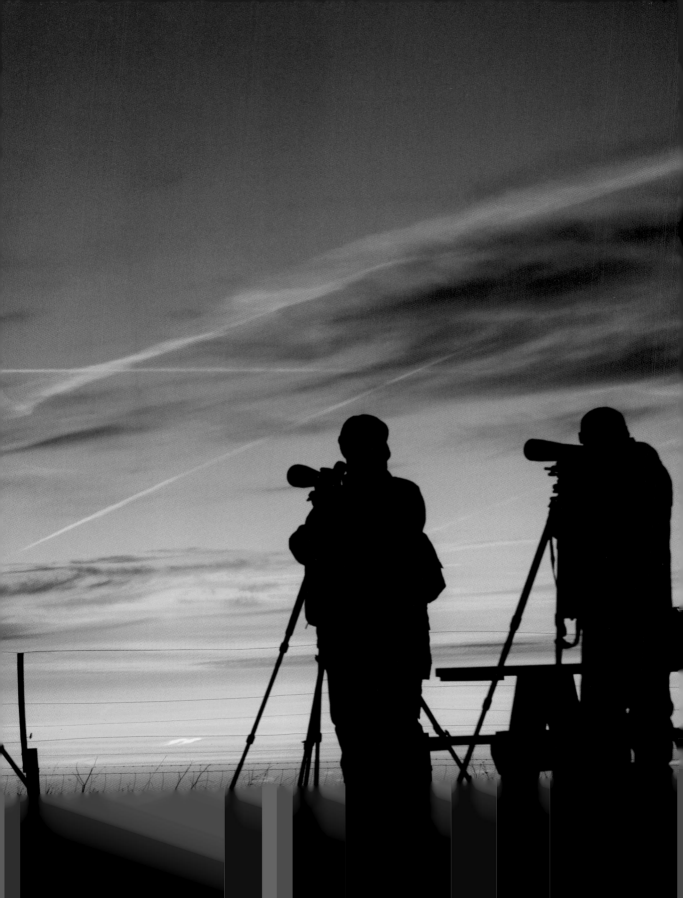

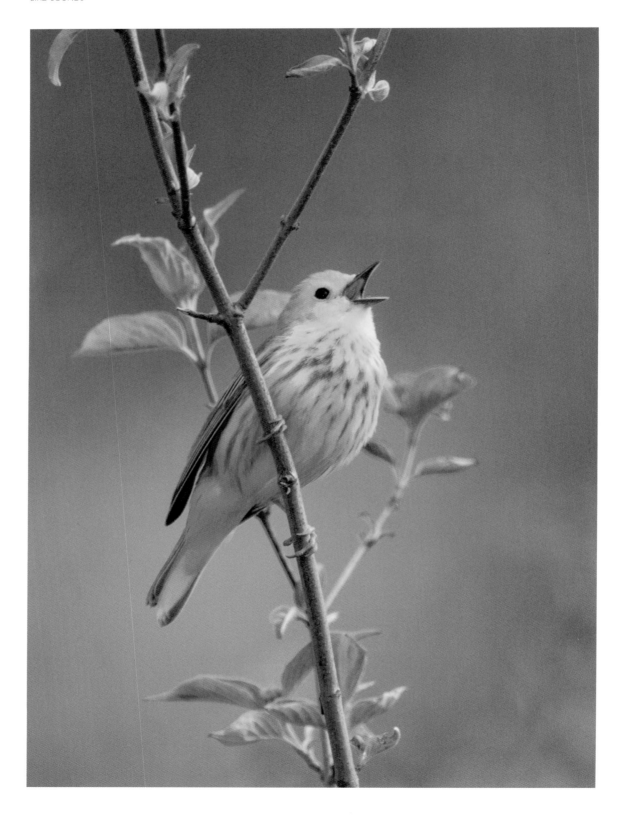

Bird Sounds

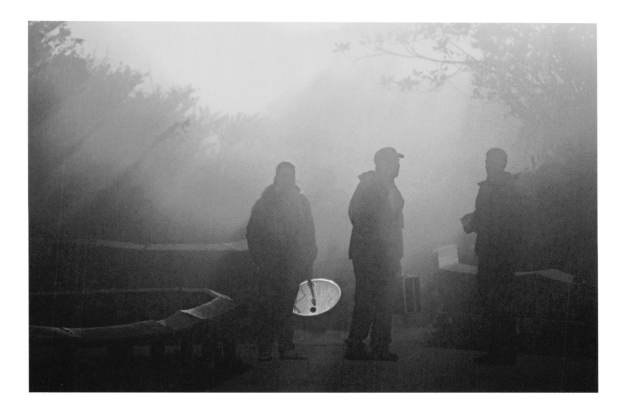

There is no getting away from it; the best birdwatchers are good at recognizing birds from their sounds. Learning bird song, though, is arguably the most difficult aspect of birdwatching.

In some ways, it shouldn't be. After all, people can recognize hundreds, or even thousands, of different human voices without thinking about it. It is certain that all of us have the capability. People might say they cannot cope with bird sounds, but that could simply be a lack of confidence or commitment. After all, most people can recognize a cuckoo, a crow, a gull and so on.

Learning the bird songs and calls in your neighbourhood is as much a task as learning a foreign language. But, as with the language, you can at least pick up words and phrases, and know more each day. It's the same with bird sounds. It is also important to recognize the difference between a 'song' and a 'call'. A 'song' is the territorial voice of a breeding male bird, and is often quite complex, at least a 'sentence' or

'phrase'. On the other hand, 'calls' are the everyday vocabulary of birds, keeping in contact or being alarmed. Most calls are just one or two syllables, 'words' if you like.

The garden is possibly the best place of all to pick up bird sounds. After all, your garden will only draw a small range of species in, and being resident there, you will hear many of them again and again. One good tip is to listen to an unknown sound and then do your very best to see the songster and identify it; this will give you a visual and aural image at the same time.

Many apps (see pages 259 and 389) will include bird sounds to help you learn. There are also a few books specifically on bird sounds on the market.

Opposite A Yellow Warbler singing from its perch on the branch of a tree **Above** Birdwatchers recording bird song at dawn in the Florida Everglades, USA

Types of Birdwatchers

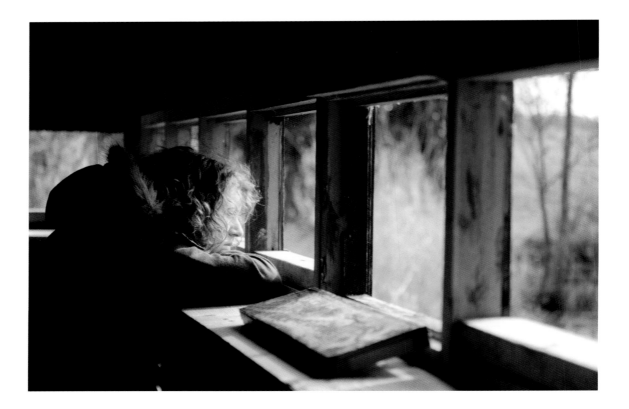

Birdwatching is such a flexible hobby that you can follow it wherever your enthusiasm takes you. You can spend no money at all and watch the birds in your garden, or you can spend all your savings on optics and on foreign trips in pursuit of exotic gems. These differences have spawned a fascinating culture among birdwatchers, with different strands of interest and commitment. It is best not to take these too seriously, and you can always be a member of more than one tribe.

You will soon find out there is a distinction between 'birdwatchers' and 'birders'. On the whole, 'birdwatchers' are the sort of people who love birds and enjoy watching them, invariably in their garden, but also go elsewhere. They will take regular trips to bird reserves; they might even go abroad and watch birds as part of their holiday. The crucial distinction for such people is that this is their leisure; they like being able to identify birds correctly, but this is not their primary focus. They might engage somebody to take them birdwatching and teach them, but they won't normally spend time alone trying to improve their field skills.

Birders (who are called 'Birdos' in Australia and elsewhere) are slightly different. They love birds and birding is leisure, but they care more about the identity of the birds they see or hear and take serious steps towards making a correct identification. They care more if they get something wrong. Visiting good places for birds is an important part of their life. If they go abroad or on holiday, they will consider what birds they might see before they go. They might well have a list of target species, even if only in their minds, and the quality and number of targets they hit will impact on how much they have enjoyed themselves.

As any birdwatcher's experience increases, there are different strands to follow. Many will follow the photography route, or an artistic one. It was once difficult to take a good photograph of a bird, but with the advent of superb, relatively cheap digital cameras, and digiscoping (see page 259) almost anyone can produce stunning images. For many people, a birdwatching trip is only as good as the images from it. Many photographers wow their followers in blogs and online accounts. At the same time, many creative people become artists or sketch-makers, again with online followers marvelling at their skills.

Birdwatching can also lead its followers down the conservation path – hopefully every birder will become more aware of environmental concerns as their commitment deepens, and many people with already deep feelings towards the natural world will gravitate towards watching birds. Hopefully, all birdwatchers of whatever genre will contribute their money towards conservation. For many, however, their main focus will be on the plight of birds and how they may be conserved. Such people will often volunteer to help at their local nature reserve in practical tasks, or with fundraising.

When a birdwatcher leans towards being a birder, they will often specialize, and one of the best-defined tribes is known as a 'patch-watcher'. This is invariably a keen birder who focuses their time on watching and recording the comings and goings of birds (and often other wildlife) at a single location. Such a person may visit their 'patch' as regularly as every week (or even more) and gets much delight in seeing how the seasons advance and how a place differs year on year. Such people often visit at all times of day, and often cherish their 'patch-list' of what they have seen. Of course, such people will enjoy regular days away, and holidays, but the patch will be their focus.

With increased experience, birdwatchers or birders will sometimes gravitate towards such specialized activities as 'seawatching' (watching birds moving over the sea) or 'skywatching' (watching birds flying over) or, self-explanatorily, 'hawk-watching'. Others might seek mainly to improve their bird song recognition.

Every hobby attracts those who go head-over-heels in commitment, even nudging into the subset of eccentricity. It is a matter of regret that birdwatching as a pastime has been indelibly linked in the past with some of these characters, as if there were no other kind. For many years, a small minority of birders, known as 'twitchers', or sometimes just 'listers', attracted attention and even notoriety for their antics,

especially in the press, who love extremes. 'Twitchers' are people to whom the list of birds they have seen, and especially the number they have seen, is everything. Once they have ticked off the birds in their local area, they must then travel to see the rest. When something rare turns up, they arrive to tick it off, sometimes en masse. Occasionally they are so desperate to tick a species off that they trespass, or behave in other antisocial ways, thus cultivating negative headlines.

There is, of course, nothing wrong with twitching or listing, save producing an enhanced carbon footprint. But most birdwatchers don't feel at home at this end of the spectrum.

And while birdwatching does indeed cater for a wide variation in commitment, one observation almost always holds true. It seems, simply, that people who steep themselves in nature and birds are, by and large, friendly souls. The degree of mutual encouragement is remarkable, truly. Rivalries occur, but these are swamped by a general empathy among likeminded 'birdy' people.

To that end, everyone starting out at birdwatching will soon find their own community to join. Local groups of birdwatchers are everywhere, both in the flesh and on the internet, and shouldn't take long to find. Whichever 'tribe' you might be drawn to, you won't be alone.

Opposite A birdwatching hide can be a very rewarding place to spot birds
Next Page Binoculars are an essential tool for most birdwatching pursuits

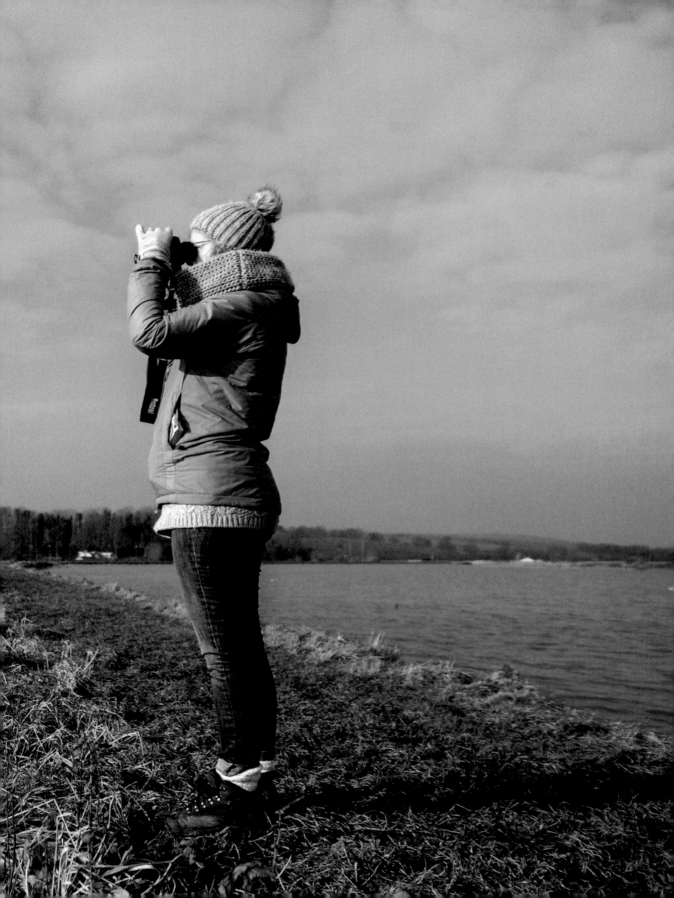

Birdwatching Equipment and Outfitting

As mentioned earlier, it is possible to enjoy birdwatching without buying anything at all, just using your eyes and ears, especially in the garden. People with impaired vision or hearing are not excluded from the hobby; indeed, individuals with vision impairment regularly demonstrate exceptional skills in bird sound recognition. On the other hand, there exists a broad range of equipment to enhance your enjoyment. This section will look at these.

There are only two pieces of equipment that most birdwatchers would consider essential: a pair of binoculars and a field guide.

Binoculars

Binoculars are optical aids that magnify an image. Birds are relatively small and highly mobile, so rather than you trying to approach a bird, your binoculars will give the impression of bringing them closer. Strictly speaking, you could use a monocular instead. However, by virtue of being heavier, binoculars are steadier and focusing feels more natural.

By virtue of being sophisticated optical devices, binoculars are by far the most expensive required outlay for a beginner birdwatcher. Some people try to avoid this by using a hand-me-down from a relative, but binoculars have improved so much in recent years, particularly in the bright images they display, that it is well worth getting a modern pair. Buying new, you should expect to spend several hundred pounds at least, but good binoculars will last some years.

The range of binoculars available can be intimidating to the beginner, but you can save yourself a great deal of hassle by taking some simple steps. Be hands-on, literally. If possible, find your way to a nature reserve shop that sells optics, or go to a specialist shop where you can try models out. There is a lot more to consider than technical specifications. Everybody is different, which might mean that a top of the range pair is useless for somebody because they are too heavy, for example, and the user feels uncomfortable, so they give up the hobby. Binoculars must never be too cumbersome, and they need to feel right. Small details such as grip in the hands and ease of focusing are important. You wear binoculars, so you need to make sure they fit you as a person, taking as much trouble as you would with clothes.

If you wear glasses it is particularly important that you try binoculars out. A binocular has a specification known as 'eye-relief', the distance between eye and eyepiece. It should be at least 15 to 18mm (½ inch). If it's less than 10 to 12mm (¼ inch), the pair won't be suitable.

The moral of the story is that it is best to avoid, if possible, cutting corners and budgets by going online without checking first. The best stockists will encourage you to try different models, because it helps nobody if you buy the wrong pair. As in all forms of transaction, if something is suspiciously cheap, it will probably be a waste of money.

There are some basic binocular specifications that you do need to consider, though. Binoculars are defined by two numbers separated by a times '×', such as 8 × 30. The first figure, the 8 in this case, is the magnification. People are often seduced by high magnification, based on the assumption that the higher magnification, the better the view of the bird. However, too high a magnification leads to two problems: firstly, the binoculars will be larger and heavier, so it is difficult to hold the binoculars still enough to enjoy it. And secondly, high magnification reduces the field of view, which means that you might have difficulty picking up the bird you are trying to see. Make sure that your binoculars have a magnification between 7 and 10. The general consensus among birders is that 8 is about ideal. If you are expecting to spend a lot of time in the open, when birds are often far away, 10 might be better.

The second figure is the diameter in millimetres of the objective lens (the larger lens furthest from the eyes). This is a guide to the field of view – the 'breadth' of what you can see – and also impacts on the brightness of the image, since the wider the objective lens, the more light gets in. In an ideal world, the larger the objective the better, but once again the sheer weight of the column comes in. You won't find many binoculars with an objective of more than 50mm (2 inches), and most are 30 to 40mm (1¼–1½ inches). Optics are so good these days that it doesn't matter.

Opposite Birdwatching in the colder months is often excellent

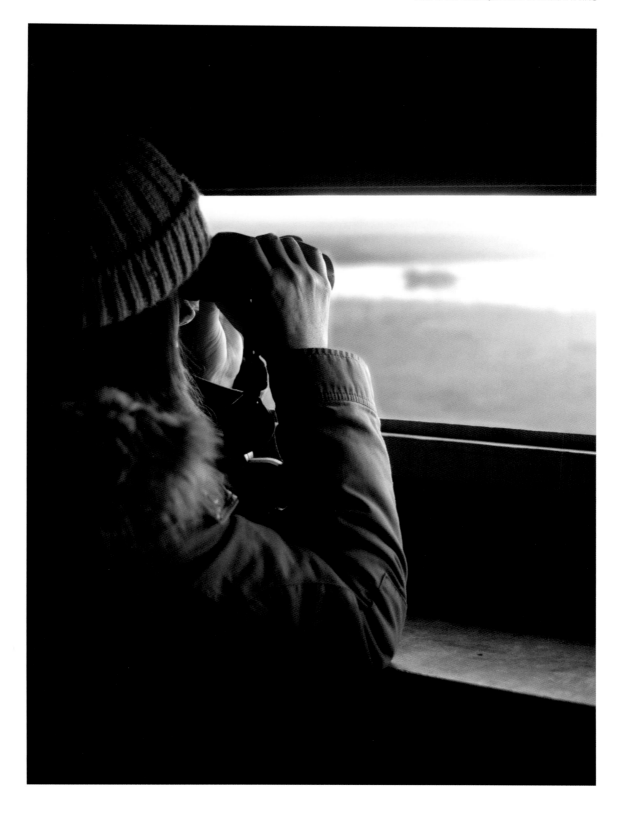

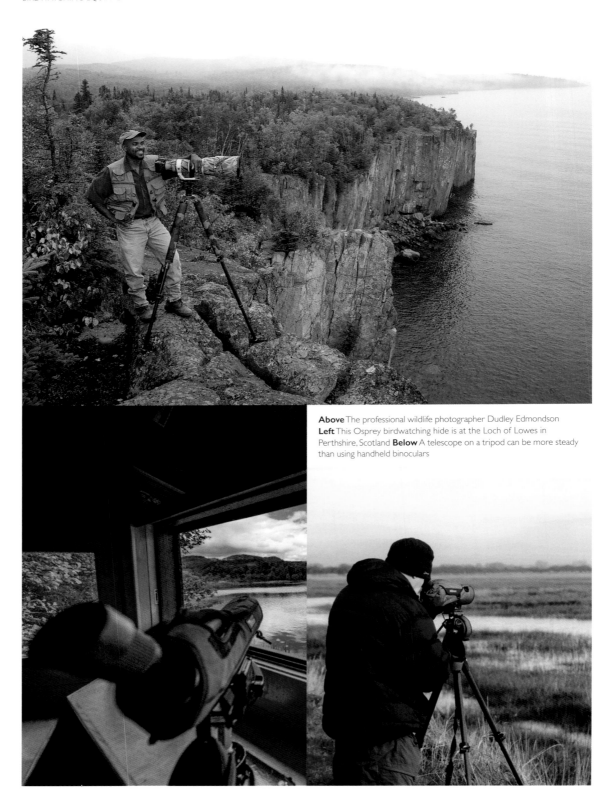

Above The professional wildlife photographer Dudley Edmondson
Left This Osprey birdwatching hide is at the Loch of Lowes in
Perthshire, Scotland **Below** A telescope on a tripod can be more steady
than using handheld binoculars

Two extra types of binoculars are worth considering. Small binoculars (compacts) are very popular if being lightweight is really important, for example for children. These will often have objective lenses of only 20mm (¾ inch), and they do suffer in terms of image brightness, particularly in dark or overcast conditions. However, many people love the fact that you can put them in your pocket or handbag and keep them with you at all times, and in most conditions they are adequate for the task. They are a good option. Another interesting option is binoculars with 'image stabilizers'. These include technology to compensate for movement, including handshake, and can therefore allow for higher magnification. They are invaluable for use on boats and other moving vehicles, and some people swear by them. They have two disadvantages, though: they tend to be heavier than 'normal' binoculars and are expensive.

Once you have your pair, make sure you adjust the binoculars to your eyes, because most people's left and right eyes focus slightly differently. Firstly, adjust the distance between the two binocular barrels to suit the distance between your eyes; this is surprisingly important and often forgotten. You should see one image. Now you need to fine tune to adjust the focus for each eye. First, locate an object, shut your right eye and use the focusing wheel until the image is sharp for the left eye. Then, shut your left eye and adjust the dioptre (the wheel at the base of the right eyepiece) until the image for your right eye is sharp. Then open both eyes to check you have a bright and clear image.

Using binoculars well takes time, but here is a good tip to help you practise. If you are looking at a bird with your naked eye and wish to align your binoculars on it, make sure that you keep your eye on the bird as you bring the binoculars up – don't look down. Practise on moving objects other than birds.

One more tip will be of incalculable use. Clean your binoculars as often as you can, preferably before each field trip. Use a lens cloth, and a soft brush if necessary. If your binoculars are smeared, that's several hundred pounds of good optics not being used!

Telescopes

In today's birdwatching world, many people routinely carry both binoculars and a telescope, sometimes known as a spotting scope (and a camera, too!). The obvious issue with a telescope is that it can be heavy and cumbersome, especially since it invariably requires a tripod. It is possible to buy straps that lighten the load, but for a long walk a telescope isn't always practical. Not many people have a use for a telescope in their gardens.

Spotting scopes are, however, marvellous. They come into their own especially when you have a vista in front of you with birds near and far, or you are watching over the sea. Invariably you can identify more birds with them, at much greater distance, and you don't get tired holding them up, as you would with binoculars. They are also a godsend for a birdwatching tutor who can simply allow somebody to look through the scope without recourse to explaining where the bird is. You can get telescopes of fixed magnification and zoom, the latter usually preferable if you enjoy identifying truly distant birds.

As is the case with binoculars, shop smart and don't be beguiled by magnification; you're looking for birds, not stars and planets. A good scope will start at about × 20 and may zoom to about × 60. Make sure you get an appropriate tripod that will stand up to a moderate wind. A good telescope on a wobbly tripod becomes a bad telescope.

Cameras and lenses are beyond the scope of this book, except to say that photographing birds takes skill and good equipment, invariably a telephoto or zoom lens. These days, many birdwatchers use an attachment for their smartphones allowing them to take pictures through a telescope, often with remarkable results – this practice is known as 'digiscoping'. There are many tutorials online.

Field guides

A field guide is an aid to bird identification using paintings or photographs of the species found in a region or country. The depictions show a bird species in its varying plumages, including male, female, young, breeding plumage and non-breeding (winter) plumage, whatever is appropriate. Most field guides include extra details on the sound a bird makes, tips for identification, habitats and migratory movements. Some interpose similar species for comparison.

The field guide has been a basic tool for birdwatchers for a hundred years, and in that time innumerable guides have been published, especially for Britain, Europe and North America. Up until recently, these have all been books, but these days you can buy apps, too. Apps have the advantage of including bird sounds, and are relatively inexpensive and light. Books have the advantage of being much more beautiful, are better for flicking through to get a feel of what birds are in your area and also for comparisons of the possibilities within large families, such as warblers or ducks.

There wouldn't be so many different guides if they didn't each have something to offer, and choice is personal. You should be able to avoid the bad ones by reading online reviews. You can also browse books at stores and decide what you like. If you are only interested in your garden birds, you can buy guides limited to these.

Notebook

Most birdwatchers enjoy recording what they see. Once upon a time, everybody used notebooks and wrote things down. Some would include sketches and even paintings in their notebooks, and most would record numbers of each species seen and other pertinent facts. These notebooks could be things of great beauty, much treasured as souvenirs of happy birdwatching days.

A lot of birdwatchers still use paper and pen and swear by it. The best notebooks are hardback, preferably with a waterproof cover, and small enough to fit in a pocket. However, technology has changed everything. Now you can record your sightings by smartphone, while you are out and about, adding them to a personal and public database. At present, British birdwatchers usually put their sightings on the BirdTrack app, and these are available automatically for anyone who logs on to the website, so everyone can know what birds are about and track, for example, migratory arrivals. Most of the rest of the world uses eBird, developed in the USA. It uses a similar principle but has many more features, including access to songs and calls.

Clothing and footwear

Few human trappings are quite so personal as clothing, so it's always dangerous to make recommendations. You can wear a tuxedo if you wish (it's been known), a ballgown or the full goth. Nobody minds, least of all the birds. However, if you are leaving the garden and venturing outside, there are a couple of practical needs to bear in mind.

As mentioned, birds have enhanced vision and see more colours more brightly than we do. Therefore, if you wear garish colours you will give yourself away.

Plain dark colours, such as brown or green, will give you a slight advantage. Some people wear camouflage, especially photographers who depend on getting close to their subjects. Some clothing is noisy and, if possible, you should cut this down – waterproof trousers are often the culprits. Whatever clothing you adopt, it's your hobby, and it is important that you feel right when you're birdwatching, otherwise you won't go.

Comfort, we can all agree, is important, and to that end the usual rules apply. Birdwatching often demands that you stay still, sometimes for a long period, in the outdoors, so take steps to ensure that you remain warm. When you set off on a walk, a very good rule is to wear one more layer than you think you will need, and then fit anything extra into your rucksack. A huge range of waterproof jackets are available from outdoor gear shops and specialist retailers. A good smattering of pockets is ideal for notebooks, lens caps, snacks and the like. You might also consider having padded shoulders to ease the weight of your binoculars.

Birdwatching is a year-round activity, so you will often need a warm hat and gloves in winter and a sunhat (and sun cream) in the summer. Birdwatchers are a very accepting group of people and realize that your birdwatching gear is not an accurate reflection of your fashion sense.

Footwear is less accommodating to variety. Most people wear walking boots, the same you'd use for hiking, but trainers are usually fine. High heels can be a challenge.

Opposite Some of the kit you may require to take up birdwatching
Next Page Birdwatching is a richly rewarding hobby and can be sociable, too

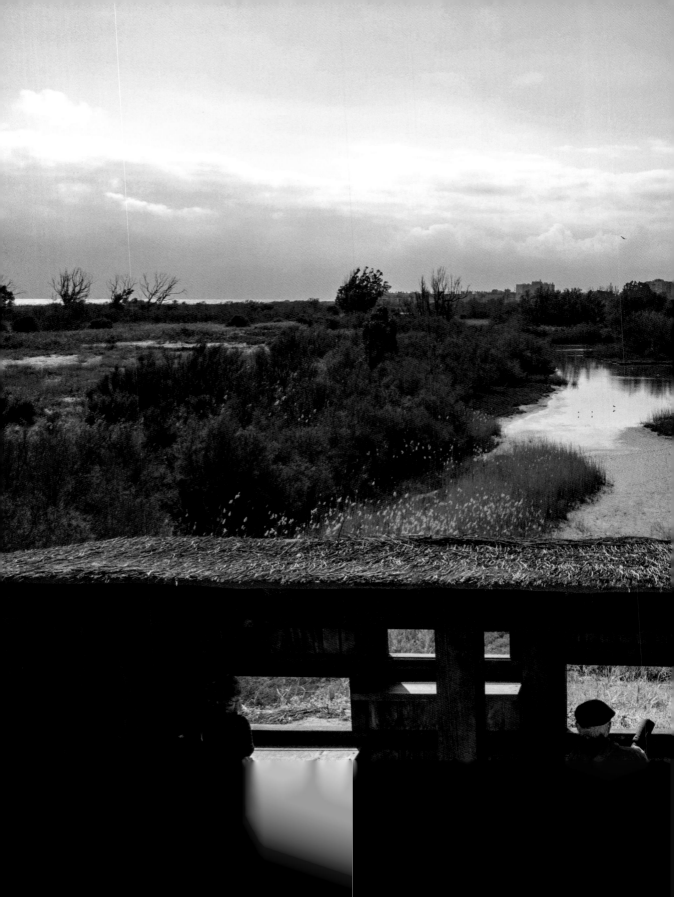

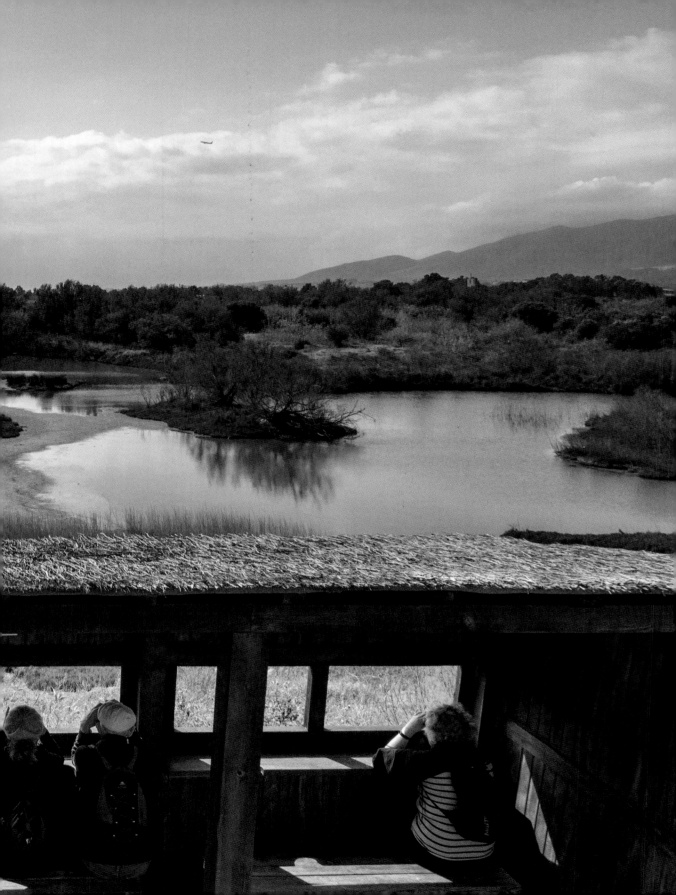

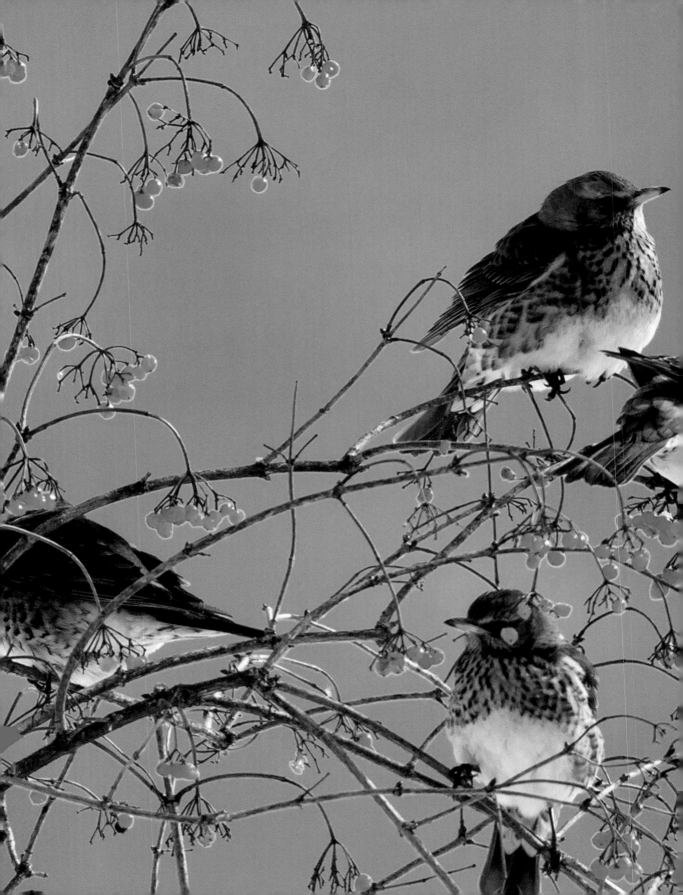

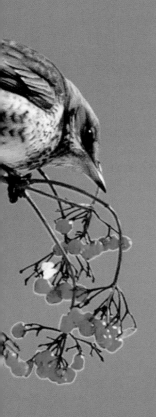
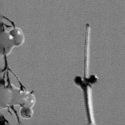

CHAPTER THREE

ATTRACTING BIRDS

THE BIRD-FRIENDLY GARDEN

Birds are a joy to watch, uplifting to listen to and vital to the biodiversity of the world. Creating a bird-friendly backyard helps individuals and species of birds survive, supports other beneficial wildlife such as butterflies and bees and can inspire beautiful garden design at the same time.

Take a little time to stand quietly in your garden, look out of your window or go for a walk in your local neighbourhood or park. Are there any birds around? What is it that brings them to this particular environment? Perhaps they are foraging for insects, seeds or berries, on the ground or in the foliage of hedges, shrubs or trees. You might see them perching on branches, stumps of wood, rooftops or telegraph lines; or a warbling of birdsong from within bushes or climbers, often up high. Certain species of bird might prefer a particular plant or habitat, become more visible or animated at a certain time of year or flock around bird tables or feeders in search of extra sustenance.

What birds are fundamentally looking for is a place for Foraging and Feeding (see page 268) and a space that supports Breeding and Shelter (see page 290). If they can get this in the wild, they will naturally go there but if such habitats can no longer supply what they need to survive, they will look elsewhere. The more closely we mimic nature, by introducing familiar native plants or similar (non-invasive) species, the better chance we have of attracting greater numbers and types of birds to our patch.

With thousands of plant species and their cultivated forms to choose from, guides to bird-friendly Trees and Hedges (see page 272); Flowers, Shrubs and Grasses (see page 277); Climbers and Vines (see page 292); and Woodpiles and Compost Heaps (see page 296) can help. Identify the plants that suit the size, location and purpose of your space, from re-wilding larger landscapes with a broad range of vegetation – including large trees, perhaps – to filling borders or pots with a select offering or two. A bushy vine such as ivy (where it is

non-invasive) or clematis is a good place to start, with potential for fruit, seeds, perches and roosting or nesting spots. Grow one along a fence, a garden wall or even up a small piece of trellis on a balcony. The birds will love you for it.

Birds can also benefit from extra food and shelter during harsh weather or the breeding season, especially with issues such as climate change affecting the weather, seasons, biodiversity and, thus, the provision of natural food and shelter. Consider installing a homemade bird table (see page 284), bird feeders (see page 286), birds baths (see page 287) or even a bird café (see page 289) within your space, or source one from a bird conservation organization (see page 389) to cater for a range of birds or a particular species you want to attract. Make your own nest boxes at the same time (see page 301), designed for safe breeding and adapted into cosy roosts for when winter sets in. Plus, Think Sustainably (see page 306) as you design your green space. We need birds as much if not more than they need us, so plant up and accessorize carefully for the long run. Creating a bird-friendly garden with the environment and all our futures in mind is a great way to add even more passion and vigour to the cause.

Previous page Omniverous Fieldfares (*Turdus pilaris*) feasting on winter berries as grubs and worms become harder to find
Opposite A bright yellow, male American Goldfinch (*Spinus tristis*) seeks out nutritious seeds from a purple coneflower (Echinacea purpurea)

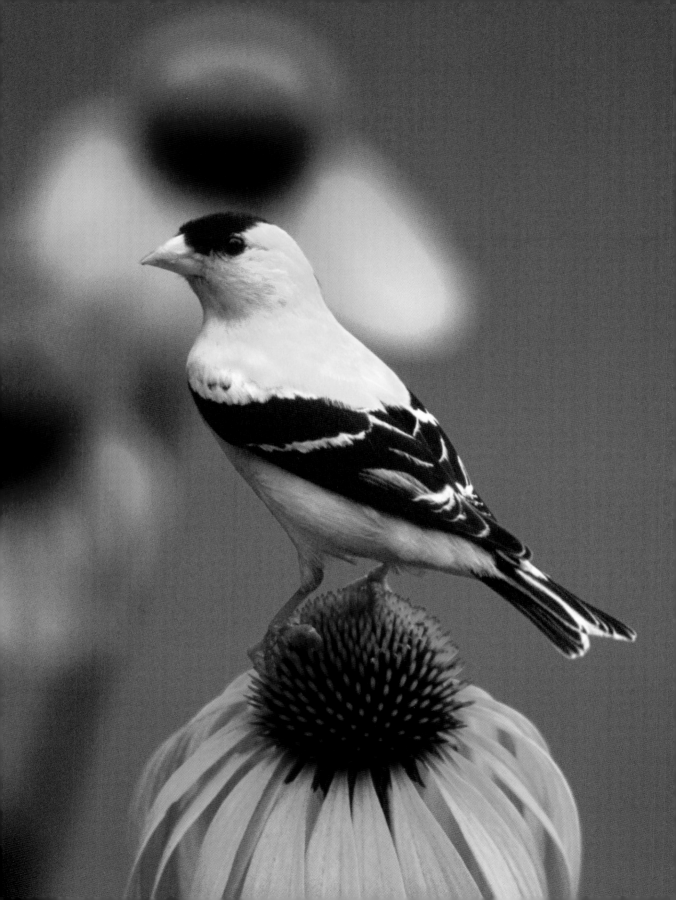

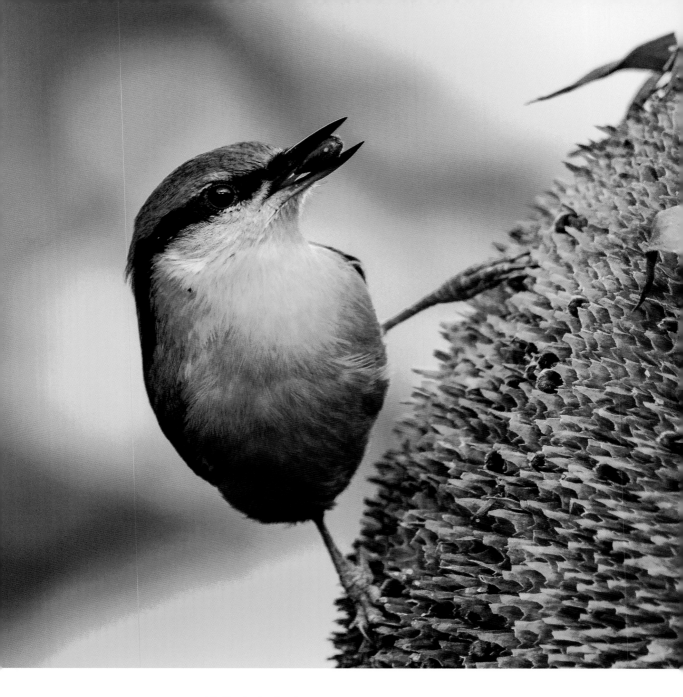

FORAGING AND FEEDING

Entice more species of birds to your backyard or patch with a homegrown seasonal buffet of the kind of food that they eat in the wild including insects and berries. Catering for birds' varied diets and foraging and feeding habits can also be beneficial to plants and your garden, too.

One of the easiest ways to encourage birds to visit your garden is by offering them food. Putting out nuts or seeds in feeders or on tables is one way to do this (see Bird Tables, Feeders and Baths page 282) and can help many birds survive the winter months. But planting or maintaining natural sources of food comes with a range of added benefits: birds get a balanced diet that's ideal for their evolutionary needs in the form of insects, berries, seeds or even sap (sapsuckers) and nectar (hummingbirds); they can forage with the added cover, protection and nesting opportunities afforded by thick foliage, branches or thorns; and a range of foraging styles are catered for, from those that peck on the ground or under bark to those that need to perch, hang upside down or catch their food on the wing.

The symbiotic relationship between birds and plants can also work its magic via the mutual benefit of providing food for birds in return for seed dispersal or insect pest control, which benefits your plants. In addition, some of the most bird-friendly food also happens to be delivered by wonderfully ornamental as well as functional plants from star-flowered serviceberry trees, bright-berried firethorn, light-catching panic grass and scented rambling roses, to lavender, coneflowers, alliums and globe thistles – ideal in a herbaceous border.

Attracting birds to your backyard with plants can also be inspired by simply observing birds foraging and feeding in the wild: insect-eating birds such as nuthatches, tits or chickadees, sparrows, warblers and woodpeckers make the most of a steady supply of leaf, bark and soil-dwelling insects and other invertebrates during the spring and summer months, including common garden pests such as aphids, mosquito larvae and some caterpillars; ground-feeders such as blackbirds, thrushes and robins can be seen hopping around looking for invertebrates in the soil or among grasses or low-lying foliage; blue tits spend a significant amount of time hanging upside down, examining leaves or branches for grubs; while swallows and swifts catch flying insects or floating spiders on the wing.

In autumn and winter, when the days are shorter, the nights are colder and insects more scarce, many birds turn to plant food such as berries and seeds, increasing their likelihood of eating every day and getting the nutrition they need to stay warm or migrate. Larger hips, haws, sloes and cherries attract bigger birds or those that can make use of some seeds, while smaller pickings as found on a rowan tree or holly bush are more easily eaten by blackbirds, thrushes and robins. Seedeaters, meanwhile, such as finches have specially adapted beaks to help them crack through outer casings of seeds, grains or nuts to reach the nutritious seed kernels inside.

Read on for more in-depth, bird-friendly planting descriptions for Trees and Hedges (see page 272), Flowers, Shrubs and Grasses (see page 277), Climbers and Vines (see page 292) and beneficial plants to grow near Woodpiles and Compost Heaps (see page 296).

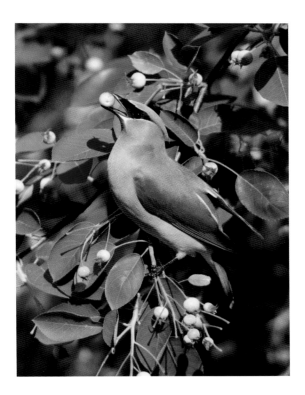

Opposite Help supplement the mainly beetle and caterpillar diet of a hungry Eurasian Nuthatch (*Sitta europeaea*) with a ready banquet of sunflower seeds **Right** The small, fleshy, sugar-rich fruits of the serviceberry tree (*Amelanchier canadensis*) are irresistible to Cedar Waxwings (*Bombycilla cedrorum*) **Next spread, left** Pack mesh feeders with suet pellets to attract acrobatic little Blue Tits (*Cyanistes caeruleus*) **Right** Upright feeders of peanuts are a great way to bring stiletto-beaked Great Spotted Woodpeckers (*Dendrocopos major*) to your backyard

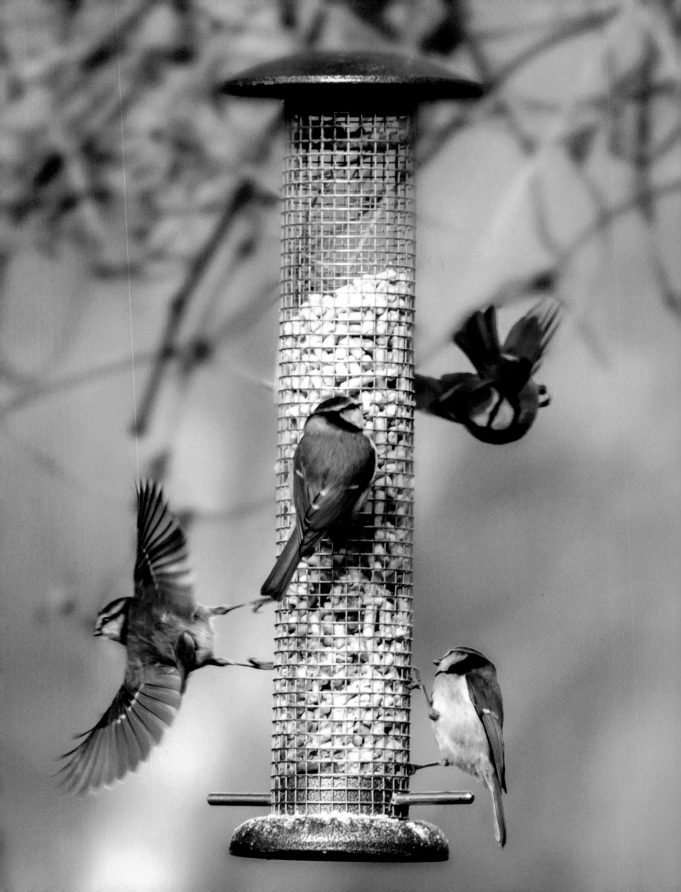

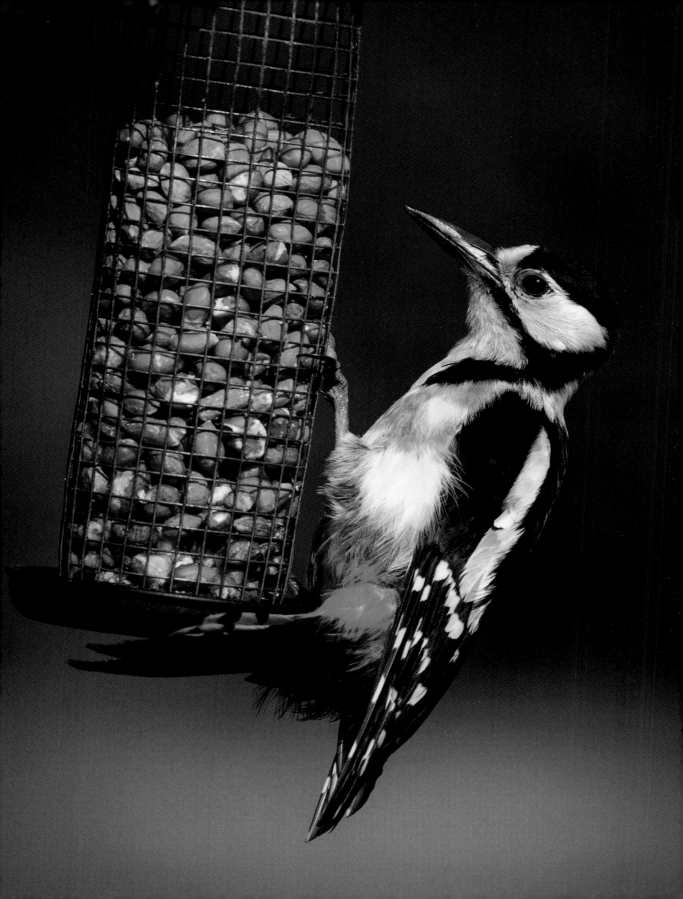

Trees and Hedges

Want to attract more birds to your backyard? Introducing or maintaining trees or hedgerow shrubs is one of the best places to start, as they offer shelter, protection, foraging and food sources and nesting places, as well as ideal posts for perching passerines such as warblers, thrushes, jays and sparrows.

Not only can trees and hedges add welcome, varied height, structure, texture, colour and natural screening to a garden or backyard, they also play host to numerous forms of wildlife including insects, small mammals and birds. Planting or maintaining native tree or hedging species where possible also helps to support the natural ecology and biodiversity of an area. For birds, this means ready access to vital food sources, shelter, nesting sites and materials and perching posts while simultaneously helping to control insect populations or disperse plant seeds for future germination.

Those lucky enough to have a large garden or roaming landscape have a range of options including tall or broad bird-friendly specimens such as oak (*Quercus* spp.), hornbeam (*Carpinus* spp.), maple (*Acer* spp.), pine (*Pinus* spp.), spruce (*Picea* spp.), cedar (*Cedrus* spp.) and cypress (*Cupressus* spp.). Hedging options could be similarly adventurous including layers of beech (*Fagus* spp.), hawthorn (*Crataegus* spp.) and holly (*Ilex* spp.) intertwined with rambling rose or ivy (see page 292 for Climbers and Vines). Combining deciduous trees (flowering and fruiting species that shed their leaves in winter) with conifers (non-flowering, typically evergreen, trees with needles or feathery fronds and cones) and denser shrubs can lend ornamental interest but will also, crucially, support a wider range of birds from insect-, seed- and berry-eating species to ground-roaming foragers and height-loving songbirds.

A well-designed front garden or less spacious backyard can usually accommodate at least one smaller tree or type of hedge, however, potentially bringing hosts of birds such as thrushes, waxwings, finches or warblers to your domain. Graceful birches (*Betula* spp.), gorgeously blooming serviceberries (*Amelanchier* spp.), fruit-laden crab apple (*Malus* spp.) or mountain ash (*Sorbus* spp.) are ideal upfront, while firethorn (*Pyracantha* spp.) and dogwood (*Cornus* spp.) offer autumn colour in beds, borders or along fencing via richly coloured fruits, foliage and stems. Dwarfed cultivars of conifers such as Lawson cypress (*Chamaecyparis lawsoniana*) or Leyland cypress (*Cupressus x leylandii*) are potential candidates for space-restricted hedging if managed well, and give dense evergreen cover and nesting spaces for birds, while hazel (*Corylus* spp.) offers lovely broad leaves and nutritious nuts.

If you're really pushed for space, opt for a dwarf or naturally diminutive tree in a pot and hang a feeder or two from the branches (see page 286). While the tree itself might not produce masses of fruit or a place to nest, passing warblers or songbirds may be on the lookout for an ideal perch and could reward you by returning time after time.

PLANTING SUGGESTIONS

Hawthorn
Crataegus spp.
This ancient hedgerow shrub or tree with its lobed leaves and pretty pink-white late spring flowers provides thorn-protected nesting and shelter, numerous treats for insect-feeding birds and their young, and antioxidant-rich autumnal haws (berries) for birds such as thrushes and waxwings.

Suggested species include English hawthorn (*Crataegus laevigata* – native to UK); European hawthorn (*Crataegus monogyna* – native to UK and Europe); Washington hawthorn (*Crataegus phaenopyrum* – native to US); downy hawthorn (*Crataegus mollis*); and cockspur hawthorn (*Crataegus crus-galli* – native to US)

Mountain ash
Sorbus spp.
Clusters of creamy-white, nectar-rich flowers give way to masses of bright-red, berrylike pomes in autumn providing food for all kinds of birds including waxwings and thrushes, which then help disperse this long-living tree's seeds – an ideal medium-sized species for a front garden or backyard.

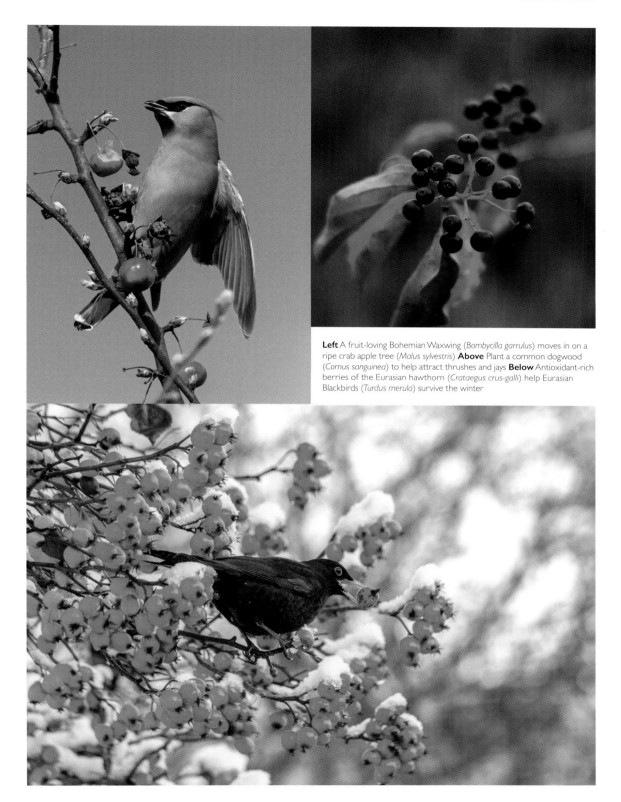

Left A fruit-loving Bohemian Waxwing (*Bombycilla garrulus*) moves in on a ripe crab apple tree (*Malus sylvestris*) **Above** Plant a common dogwood (*Cornus sanguinea*) to help attract thrushes and jays **Below** Antioxidant-rich berries of the Eurasian hawthorn (*Crataegus crus-galli*) help Eurasian Blackbirds (*Turdus merula*) survive the winter

Suggested species include European mountain ash or rowan (*Sorbus aucuparia* – native to UK and Europe); American mountain ash (*Sorbus americana* – native to US) and northern mountain ash (*Sorbus decora* – native to US)

Firethorn
Pyracantha spp.

Shiny evergreen foliage, pollinator-friendly flowers, pendulous red, orange or yellow berry-like pomes to help birds through the winter, angled branches for nesting or training, plus sharp thorns to keep predators at bay and create a natural security barrier give firethorn the edge when it comes to garden hedging.

Suggested species include scarlet firethorn (*Pyracantha coccinea* – native to south-east Europe to Caucasus; naturalized across UK and parts of North America although invasive in some states)

Crab apple
Malus spp.

Crab apple really comes into its own in autumn when spring's showy pink-tinged white blossom, once pollinated by bees, transforms into yellow-green, sometimes red-flushed fruits among golden deciduous leaves. Robins, starlings, greenfinches and thrushes are all fans of this abundant feast.

Suggested species include European crab apple (*Malus sylvestris* – native to UK and Europe) and southern crabapple (*Malus angustifolia* – native to eastern and south-central US);

Hazel
Corylus spp.

One of the few nut-bearing shrubs, large serrated-leaved hazel can be woven into a natural hedge or grown as a small tree adding an uplifting burst of bright green in spring/summer, turning golden-bronze in autumn. All hazelnuts are edible although woodpeckers, jays and nuthatches may well get there first.

Suggested species include common/European hazelnut (*Corylus avellana* – native to UK and Europe); filbert (*Corylus maxima* – native to south-east Europe); American hazelnut (*Corylus americana* – native to North America); and beaked hazel (*Corylus cornuta* – native to North America)

Lawson cypress
Chamaecyparis lawsoniana spp.

A popular garden ornamental or screening choice native to the eastern United States and Japan, this often dwarf conifer in cultivated shades of green, blue or gold provides welcome winter refuge and nesting sites for birds such as finches among dense branches of feathery, flattened, evergreen foliage.

Suggested cultivars include narrow and conical *Chamaecyparis lawsoniana* 'Elwoodii'; more rounded and stout *Chamaecyparis lawsoniana* 'Minima'; dwarf variety *Chamaecyparis lawsoniana* 'Gnome'; and large, stately *Chamaecyparis lawsoniana* 'Colmnaris'

Birch
Betula spp.

Food for birds in the form of seeds from cone-shaped strobili, buds, numerous species of insects and caterpillars and a high sap content plus distinctively coloured, striped and often papery bark, dainty leaves and catkins and an open canopy make birch a great choice for bird-lovers and gardeners alike.

Suggested species include silver or European birch (*Betula pendula* – native to UK, Europe and US); downy birch (*Betula pubescens* – native to UK and Europe); and paper birch (*Betula papyrifera* – native to US)

Serviceberry
Amelanchier spp.

An ideal tree for a front garden thanks to its relatively diminutive size, beautiful star-shaped white flowers and pink to green to gold foliage, the serviceberry is also loved by birds such as finches, blackbirds, robins and waxwings for its deep-red to rich-purple, nutrient-rich, soft and tasty fruits.

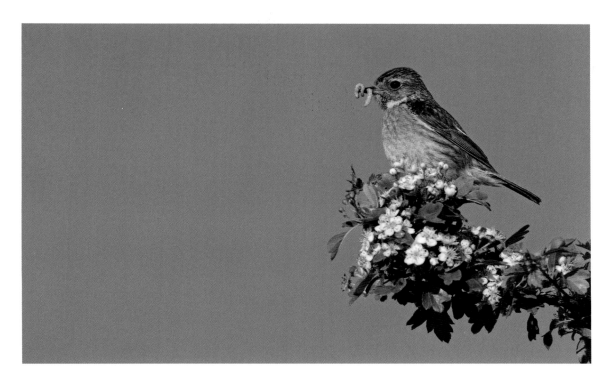

Suggested species include snowy mespilus (*Amelanchier lamarckii* – native to eastern US, widely introduced to UK and Europe); downy serviceberry (*Amelanchier arborea* – native to eastern US); and shadblow serviceberry (*Amelanchier canadensis* – native to eastern US)

Holly
Ilex spp.
Help provide winter food, shelter and protection for birds such as thrushes, finches and robins care of holly's bright-red berries (drupes) and dense, shiny, often prickly evergreen foliage. Holly is dioecious with male and female components on separate plants, so include at least one of each in a border or hedge.

Suggested species include European or English holly (*Ilex aquifolium* – native to UK and Europe) and American holly (*Ilex opaca* – native to south-eastern US)

Dogwood
Cornus spp.
Clusters of insect-attracting creamy-white flowers and fresh green leaves followed by tempting red or black berries provide a ready banquet for birds such as thrushes, bluebirds and jays. Kaleidoscopic autumn leaves or twigs of crimson and gold (depending on species) can also add ornamental colour.

Suggested species include common or bloody dogwood (*Cornus sanguinea* – native to UK and Europe); flowering dogwood (*Cornus florida* – native to eastern US); and Pacific or mountain dogwood (*Cornus nuttallii* – native to western US)

Above Common Stonechats (*Saxicola torquatus*) find tasty grubs within the dense foliage and blooms of trees such as the hawthorn (*Crataegus* spp.), too

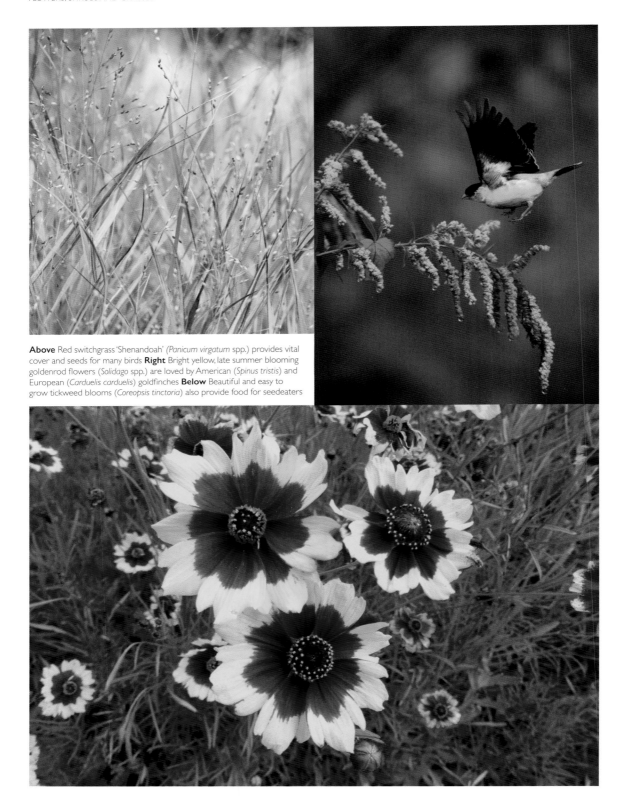

Above Red switchgrass 'Shenandoah' *(Panicum virgatum* spp.) provides vital cover and seeds for many birds **Right** Bright yellow, late summer blooming goldenrod flowers (*Solidago* spp.) are loved by American (*Spinus tristis*) and European (*Carduelis carduelis*) goldfinches **Below** Beautiful and easy to grow tickweed blooms (*Coreopsis tinctoria*) also provide food for seedeaters

Flowers, Shrubs and Grasses

Pack borders or pots with a beautiful display of native and pollinator-friendly flowers, shrubs and grasses to help provide a seasonal pick-and-mix of insects, spiders, worms, fruit, seeds and nectar for the varying diets of different birds. Such plants can also offer vital shelter for ground-feeders.

Flowers, grasses and ornamental shrubs are an obvious choice when it comes to beautifying your garden or patch and can also help attract a host of beneficial creatures including bees, butterflies and birds.

Pollinator-friendly shrubs such as lavender (*Lavandula* spp.) add year-round or seasonal structure, colour and scent plus cover for ground-feeding birds, low perches for songbirds, insects such as caterpillars during spring and a late-summer banquet for seedeaters. Some birds are also known to line their nests with aromatic herbs to potentially create an antibacterial and therapeutic environment for their newborn or fledgling offspring. Flowering and fruiting shrubs such as guelder rose (*Viburnum* spp.) and firethorn (*Pyracantha* spp. – see Trees and Hedges, page 274) also create fragrant and colourful border backdrops as well as a berry banquet for finches and thrushes.

Tall or bushy ornamental grasses such as panic grass (*Panicum* spp.) are softly textural and light-catching and can provide a real feast for grain-eating birds via their plumes, spikes and sprays, plus cover and insects for ground-foragers among lower foliage. Care needs to be taken when choosing the right species of grass for your zone, however: opt for native species of grass where possible; avoid those considered to be invasive (such as the species form of *Miscanthus sinensis*); and choose warm-season or cool-season varieties depending on climate and position. Fresh grass lawns attract birds looking for worms and seeds, while dry grass is ideal for building and lining nests.

Finally, there are the flowering, herbaceous perennials, annuals and biennials with which to create swathes of colour, perfume the air, fill gaps between shrubs, adorn containers of every shape and size and create contrast and movement via a range of foliage, blooms and seed-heads. Grassland or arable wildflowers – many of them from the Asteraceae or daisy family – such as coneflowers (*Echinacea* spp.), cornflowers (*Centaurea* spp.), zinnias (*Zinnia* spp.), black-eyed Susans (*Rudbeckia* spp.), poppies (*Papaver* spp.), asters (*Astereae* spp.) and globe thistle (*Echinops* spp.) are particularly bird-friendly, providing accents of summer colour and cut flowers as well as vital protein-rich seeds for birds through autumn and winter.

Alliums (*Allium* spp.) and teasels (*Dipsacus fullonum*) are also top choices for seed-eating birds and give great winter interest, although the latter can be invasive outside of its native reach. Top of the seedbearers, however, is the mighty sunflower (*Helianthus* spp.), with tall cultivars such as 'Russian Giant' producing thousands of seeds as a ready banquet or to dry and hang out as feeders during the colder months (see Bird Tables, Feeders and Baths, page 282). For nectar-eating birds in more tropical climes choose red-petalled sages (*Salvia* spp.), columbines (*Aquilegia* spp.) and bee balms/bergamots (*Monarda* spp.).

PLANTING SUGGESTIONS

Sunflower

Helianthus spp.
Plant large-headed golden sunflowers for a late summer supply of protein- and essential oil-packed seeds loved by finches, nuthatches and tits. Let birds harvest direct from the plant (protect seeds with muslin until fully ripe) or remove seed-heads and dry them in a warm spot to offer as feeders (see page 289).

> Native species and cultivars include common sunflower (*Helianthus annuus* – native to western US but introduced worldwide) and giant-headed common sunflower (*Helianthus annuus* 'Russian Giant' – native to NA but introduced worldwide)

Coneflower

Echinacea spp.
This long-blooming, easy to grow perennial with its large, downward-drooping and thus cone-shaped daisy-like florets is lovely in borders as a cut flower and is loved by the bees and the birds: the former for its nectar, the latter for the seed-rich spent flowers. Leave *in situ* to provide a ready winter feast.

Suggested species include purple coneflower (*Echinacea purpurea* – native to eastern and central US but introduced to parts of Europe and Asia) and narrow-leaved coneflower (*Echinacea angustifolia* – native to central and southern US)

Cornflower
Centaurea spp.

Once a mainstay of arable fields and meadows, the overuse of herbicides in farming means that annual cornflowers rarely seed themselves naturally. Plant these frilly flowered blue beauties in borders or pots, where small seed-eating birds can also enjoy their bounty in late summer.

Suggested species include common cornflower (*Centaurea cyanus* – native to Europe but naturalized across UK and parts of North America) and mountain cornflower (*Centaurea montana* – native to Europe but now naturalized across UK and North America)

Lavender
Lavandula spp.

This aromatic woody shrub for borders or pots attracts pollinating bees, butterflies and hummingbirds (Americas). Some birds also line their nests with herbs such as lavender, mint (*Mentha* spp.) and curry plant (*Helichrysum italicum*) for naturally antibacterial as well as aromatherapeutic effects.

Suggested species include widely cultivated English lavender (*Lavandula angustifolia* – native to parts of Europe); tuft-flowered French lavender (*Lavandula stoechas* – native to parts of Europe and North Africa); and more broad-leaved spike lavender (*Lavandula latifolia* – native to parts of Europe)

Panic grass
Panicum spp.

This warm-season cosmopolitan grass is long living but slow spreading with a typically dense, columnar form of stiff green stems turning to gold or red in the autumn. Seed plumes ripen from pink to purple and persist well into winter providing protein-packed morsels for sparrows and buntings.

Suggested species include switchgrass (*Panicum virgatum* – native to US, introduced to UK and parts of Europe)

Globe thistle
Echinops spp.

Also known as the blue hedgehog thistle, the steely blue globular flowers on branched or singular stems attract hummingbirds (Americas) and produce a buffet of seeds for birds such as goldfinches, which can also help keep self-seeding down. *Echinops* is also lovely as a cut or dried flower.

Suggested species or cultivars include blue globe thistle (*Echinops bannaticus* – native to UK and parts of Europe – in 'Taplow Blue'); southern globe thistle (*Echinops ritro* – native to parts of Europe, Mongolia and Turkey – in 'Veitch's Blue'); and great globe thistle (*Echinops sphaerocephalus* – native to parts of Europe, Eurasia and the Middle East, and introduced to the US – in 'Arctic Glow')

Teasel
Dipsacus fullonum spp.

A familiar sight in grassland or wasteland, common teasel can also create structure, height and interest in borders with purple-ringed green, prickled flower-heads giving way to brown seed-heads loved by European goldfinches and other birds. Teasel needs careful managing as it can become invasive.

Suggested species include common, wild or fuller's teasel (*Dipsacus fullonum* – native to UK, Europe and temperate Asia; considered invasive in the US as, left unchecked, it can crowd out other species)

Aster
Astereae spp.

This large tribe of typically pink-purple, yellow-centred, daisy-like flowers, including perennial species of aster and *Sympyotricum*, bloom in late summer and autumn and provide food and a haven for year-round or migrating seed-eating birds such as goldfinches, sparrows, nuthatches, buntings and tits.

Suggested species include New England aster or Michaelmas daisy (*Symphyotrichum novae-angliae*, formerly *Aster novae-angliae* – native to North America, introduced to UK and Europe); New York aster (*Symphyotrichum novi-belgii*, formerly *Aster novi-belgii* – native to North America, introduced to UK and Europe); and European Michaelmas daisy (*Aster amellus* – native to Europe and Caucasus)

Tickweed
Coreopsis spp.

Seed-eating birds such as goldfinches love to snack on the tick-like seeds of this low-maintenance, drought-tolerant, long-blooming and cheerful plant. Grow in borders or pots for upright clumps of bright yellow, orange or pink-red flowers, cutting back mid-season to produce more flowers and seeds.

Suggested species and cultivars include large-flowered tickseed (*Coreopsis grandiflora* – native to eastern North America, introduced to UK and Europe); whorled tickseed (*Coreopsis verticillata* – native to eastern North America,

introduced to parts of Europe); and dyer's tickseed *Coreopsis tinctoria* – native to North America, introduced to UK and parts of Europe)

Guelder rose
Viburnum spp.

Fabulously fragrant and frost resistant, species of *Viburnum* can be grown as bushy screens, manageable shrubs, or in pots, providing evergreen or semi-evergreen foliage and balls or sprays of pink or white lacy flowers. The berries are an important food source for some finches and thrushes.

Suggested species include guelder rose (*Viburnum opulus* – native to UK and Europe, Siberia, Turkey and small parts of North America); avoid sterile *Viburnum opulus* 'Roseum', which has beautiful white snowball-like flowers but no berries

Below Plant a mini meadow of bright blue cornflowers (*Centaurea cyanus*) in borders or pots to attract small seed-eating birds **Next spread** Add swathes of grasses and globe thistles (*Echinops* spp.) to extend the seed feast and provide shelter for ground-foraging birds

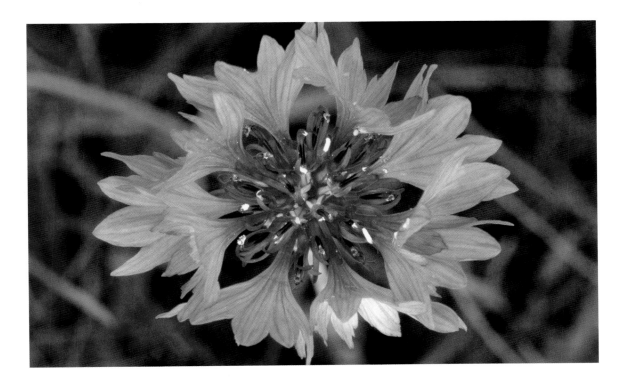

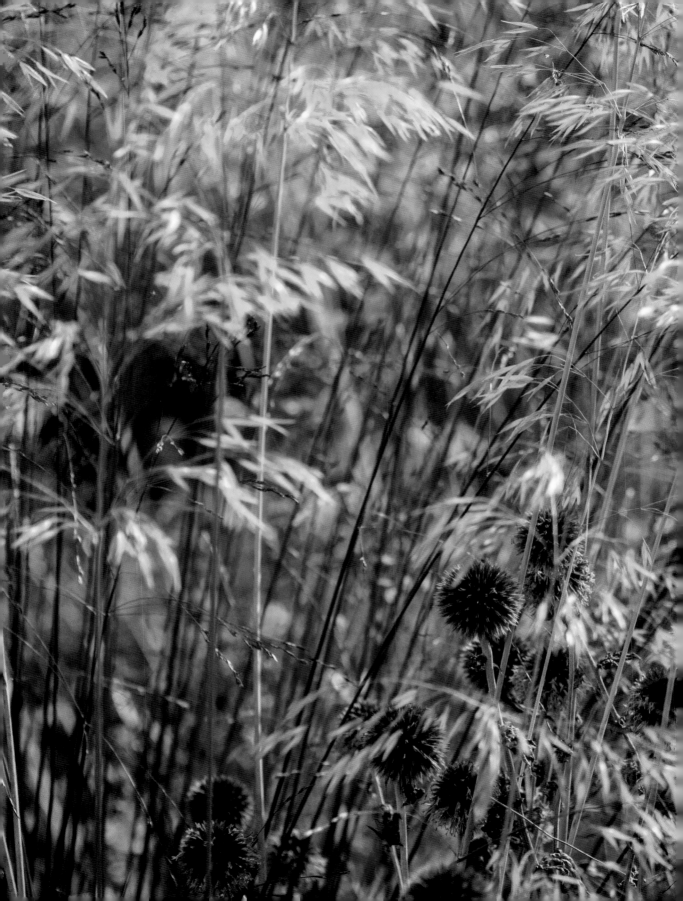

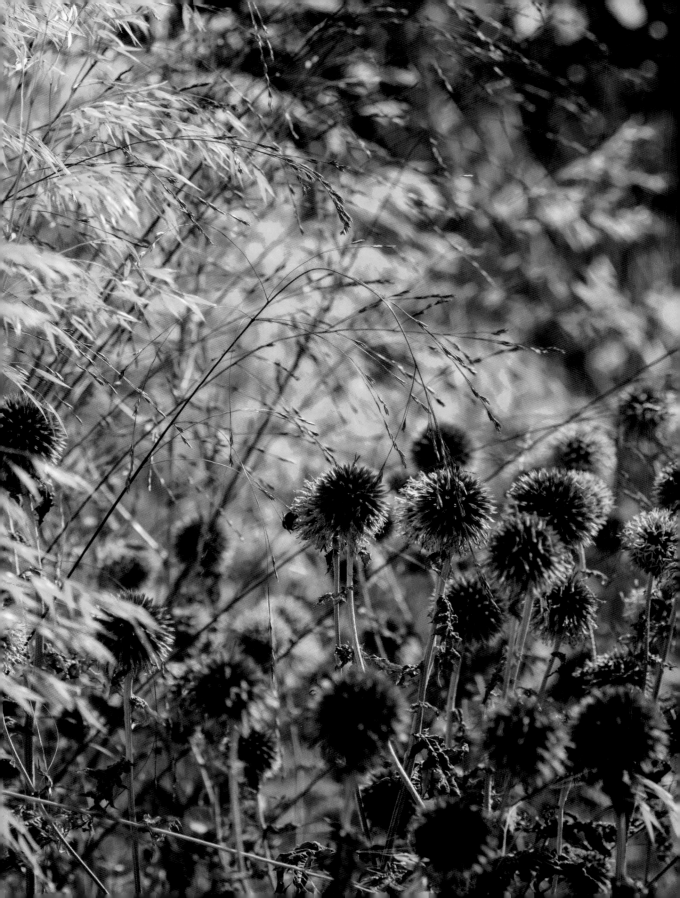

Bird Tables, Feeders and Baths

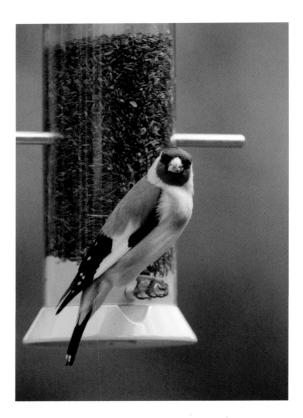

Putting food and water out for birds is a great way to get closer to certain species, observe their fascinating behaviour and help sustain them through the seasons. Choose from a range of bird tables, feeders and baths to suit your space and, by catering for their natural habits, the kind of birds you hope to attract.

Feeding birds through the winter benefits birds the most, as this is the season when natural food supplies are most scarce. Food shortages (in the form of insects, seeds, fruits, sap or nectar) or access to water can occur at any time of the year, however – during exceptionally wet, dry or cold spells, for example, or when there are young to provide for – so refill bird tables, feeders or baths year-round.

What to feed garden birds also relates to the seasons. Birds need high-energy (high-fat) foods during the winter to help them get through long, frosty nights. While in spring and summer they require high-protein food, especially when they are moulting. This includes black sunflower seeds; pinhead oatmeal; soaked sultanas, raisins and currants; mild grated cheese, mealworms, waxworms, mixes for insectivorous birds; good seed mixtures without loose peanuts; soft apples and pears cut in half; or bananas and grapes. Avoid putting out bread, fat or peanuts during this time as such foodstuffs can pose a choking risk to young chicks.

Certain foods and feeders also attract particular species of bird. Ground-feeders such as blackbirds, robins, thrushes, dunnocks and collared doves prefer to feed from a bird table (see Make a Bird Table page 284), platform or safely placed ground tray. Smaller birds prefer a low-roofed table or one where the height of the cover can be adjusted to prevent larger birds taking over. Bird tables or platforms should also be placed away from dense hedges or fences to help avoid cats accessing them.

Birds found flocking around hanging feeders include species of finches, sparrows, tits or chickadees and siskins that like to feed while clinging or perching. Choose a feeder with a perch ring to help facilitate the latter or try fat balls (in winter) or dried sunflower seed-heads hung direct from branches or specially designed feeding stations.

Our feathered friends also need a regular supply of water for drinking and bathing, particularly during winter or a summer drought when natural supplies – from droplets on leaves or the shallow edges of ponds or streams – may be frozen or dried up. Bathing in water also helps birds to preen by loosening dirt so that feathers can be more easily rearranged and spread with oil to help them stay waterproof and warm. Whether they like to take a dip (blackbirds and starlings) or sit in the water to cool off (woodpigeons), watching birds make best use of your bird bath (see Make a Bird Bath, page 287) or garden pond (if you have the room and the inclination to create one) can be quite the delightful performance to watch.

Above Help attract European Goldfinches (*Carduelis carduelis*) with a Niger seed feeder – the yellow base is a draw, too

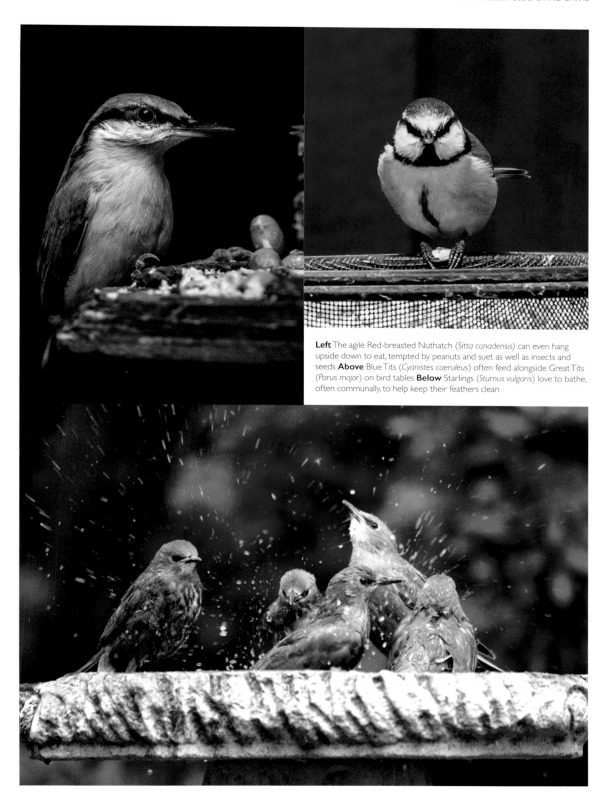

Left The agile Red-breasted Nuthatch (*Sitta canadensis*) can even hang upside down to eat, tempted by peanuts and suet as well as insects and seeds **Above** Blue Tits (*Cyanistes caeruleus*) often feed alongside Great Tits (*Parus major*) on bird tables **Below** Starlings (*Sturnus vulgaris*) love to bathe, often communally, to help keep their feathers clean

Make a Bird Table

Create a raised or hanging bird table to feed ground-feeding birds such as blackbirds, robins and thrushes.

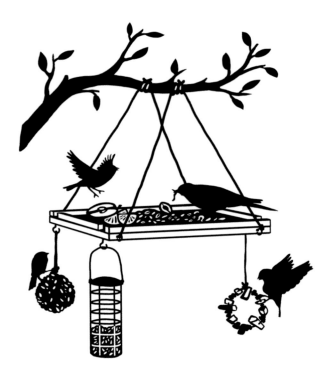

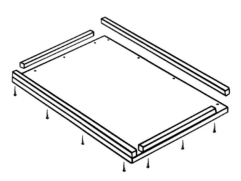

1 Find or purchase a 15mm (0.5in) piece of exterior-quality, sustainably sourced plywood, hardwood (oak or beech) or softwood (pine) timber for the platform element. Ensure that this wood will not split or disintegrate when wet (untreated softwood will naturally deteriorate faster). Sand it smooth to remove crevices that could harbour dirt and encourage disease. Untreated is best but, if treating is required to prolong its life, use a water-based preservative and ensure the wood is fully dry before use.

2 Use a length of sanded 15mm (0.5in) stripwood to create a rim around the edge of the table or platform to help stop food falling or blowing off. Leave a gap at each corner so that rain can drain away. Sand it before attaching and use brass or galvanized self-drilling screws to secure it in place from below: 30mm (1in) long are ideal for the measurements above.

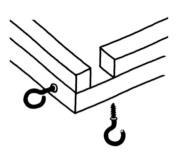

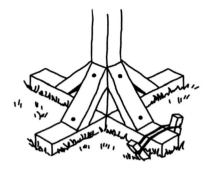

3 Attach 30mm (1in) zinc- or brass-plated screw
   eyes to the side edges of the platform on each
   corner from which to attach a hanging device;
   use light chain, wire or strong cord but ensure
   to hang from two points rather than a central
   point (see main illustration) or the table will
   spin round. Attach further 30mm (1in) screw
   eyes into the base of the platform from which
   to hang nut or seed feeders or fat balls.

5 To make a freestanding bird table, add an
   additional cross-shaped base using self-tapping
   screws (or pre-drill the holes) and diagonal
   supports to secure the base to the post.
   Use pegs and rubber straps to secure the
   base to the ground.

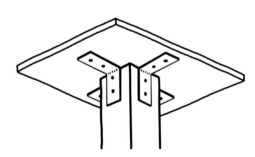

6 Put out a varied banquet of high-quality foods
   and kitchen scraps (dried fruit, mild grated
   cheese, cooked potatoes and pastry), mixed
   seeds, flaked maize, sunflower seeds, pinhead
   oatmeal, mealworms and waxworms (in spring),
   bruised fruit and fat balls or fat cakes (in winter
   or cold spells) to cater for the greatest range of
   species. Include a mix of high-oil seeds such as
   black sunflower, sunflower hearts, peanuts and
   niger seed (this needs a special feeder with
   small slits so that the tiny seeds don't fall out)
   and cereal grains, plus additional insects or
   high-fat ingredients in spring. Avoid split peas,
   beans, dried rice or lentils as only large species
   can eat them dry, and steer clear of mixtures
   containing green or pink lumps, which can
   only be eaten when soaked.

4 Bird tables can also be mounted on
   wooden posts that can be driven directly
   into the ground. Use angle brackets to fix to
   the platform.

Make a Fat Ball

Help birds put on an extra layer of fat and keep active with an energy-boosting buffet of seed, nut and oat-enriched suet balls or cakes.

1 Choose suitable moulds such as paper cupcake cases, small clean yogurt pots or half coconut shells. Pierce the mould to hang from the top (coconut shell) or base (paper cases or yogurt pots) and add a loop of strong twine. Or choose to roll your fat ball using your hands (add twine at rolling stage).

2 Place 150g (5oz) unsalted and unsweetened dry ingredients such as sunflower seeds, oats, chopped peanuts and dried fruit into a large bowl. Use a dedicated bowl (not used for human consumption) if adding ingredients such as mealworms. Avoid adding dried fruit if you have cats or dogs, or peanuts if any risk of allergy.

3 Place a smaller glass bowl over a pan of hot water. Pour 250g (9oz) of beef or vegetable suet into the bowl, turn on the heat and simmer until the suet is melted.

4 Pour melted suet over the dried ingredients and mix well until a clumping consistency is formed. Spoon the mixture into your chosen moulds or use your hands to roll into 5cm (2in) diameter balls, breaking into two to add a loop of twine before firmly pressing the halves back together again. Fat balls or cakes can also be placed on cake pop sticks for placing in plant pots or left as they are to place on bird tables or in mesh feeders.

5 Put moulds or balls on a tray and place in the fridge for several hours or overnight to set. Fat balls, cakes (with paper cases torn off) or filled yogurt pots or coconut shells can then be hung directly from branches or bottoms of a bird table and placed on platforms or in feeders.

6 Don't put out too many fat balls at once as this can attract pests. Make it seasonal and only put out in winter or cold spells. Never feed birds cooking fat from roasting tins or dishes as combined meat juices can be super salty, lead to smearing and create a breeding ground for bacteria. Soft fats such as polyunsaturated margarines or vegetable oils can also smear feathers, destroying waterproofing and insulating qualities.

Below Make sweetly shaped homemade fat balls to attract birds such as the European Goldfinch (*Carduelis carduelis*)

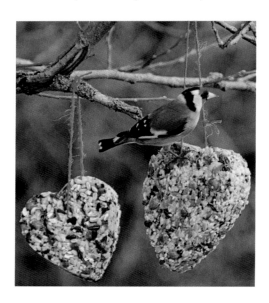

Make a Bird Bath

Give birds a safe and reliable source of fresh water for drinking and bathing, especially vital during hot or cold spells.

1 Source a suitable vessel such as a circular plant pot tray or even an upturned dustbin lid. Choose something as wide as possible with an ideal size and shape being 10cm (4in) deep, at least 30cm (12in) wide and with sloping sides.

2 Choose a suitable spot in an open lawn or border with a good all-round view. Nearby bushes or trees are great for birds to retreat into but avoid enabling predatory cats with a similarly perfect hiding and pouncing spot.

3 Place four bricks on the ground and position your vessel on top, adjusting until stable. Add a handful of pebbles or rocks to help birds get a better footing and avoid slipping.

4 Fill regularly with fresh water, keeping your bath well topped up in summer, hot spells or a drought, and ice-free in winter (knock ice out with a suitable tool or melt it with a little warm water).

Keep it clean

Whatever kind of feeding station you choose, ensure that bird tables and hanging feeders are cleaned regularly (outside, wearing gloves) with a mild (5%) disinfectant solution to help prevent poisoning or disease from contaminated birds, other wildlife or their droppings. Consider moving feeding stations to a slightly different place each month to avoid droppings accumulating underneath. Replace or reduce food to keep it fresh and meet demand. Water containers should also be cleaned if contaminated by droppings and rinsed out daily, especially during the warmer months. Allow them to dry before fresh water is added.

Below Treat bath-loving European Robins (*Erithacus rubecula*) to a regularly topped up body of water in your backyard

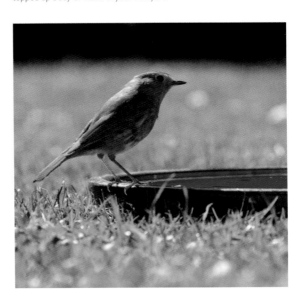

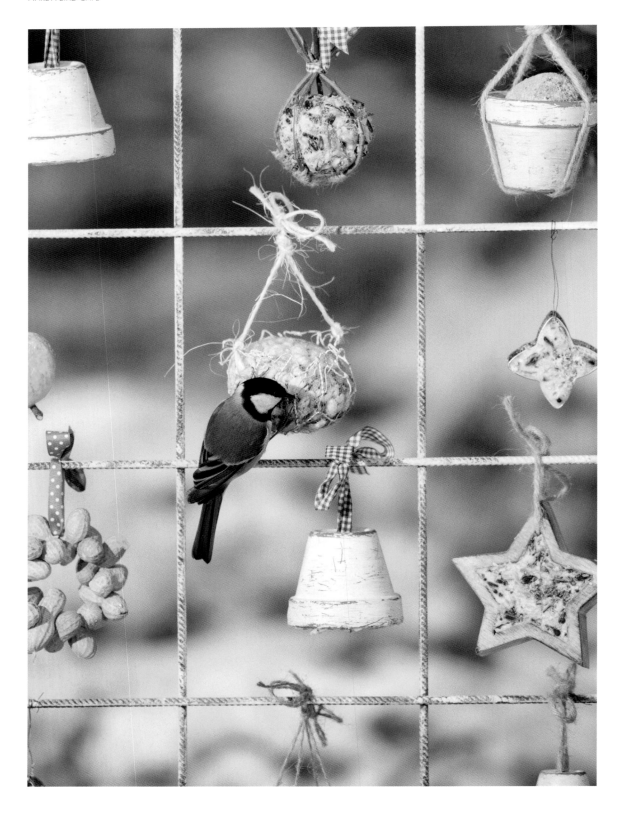

Make a Bird Café

Put out a variety of food on bird tables or
platforms, in tubed or mesh feeders or hanging
direct from trees or feeding stations to attract
greater numbers and species of birds.

Small seeds such as millet
Best scattered in small quantities directly on bird tables
or ground feeders (away from predators). Mostly taken
by house sparrows, dunnocks, finches, reed buntings
and collared doves.

Flaked maize
Has a low oil content and can be dusty and difficult
to hold in mesh feeders so best for bird tables. Loved
by blackbirds.

Peanuts
Crushed or grated nuts attract robins, dunnocks and
wrens, while nuthatches and coal tits often hoard these
nuts. Do not use salted or dry-roasted peanuts; put
whole nuts or large pieces out in spring/summer and
be aware of people with nut allergies.

Sunflower seeds
A great year-round food that's often more popular
than peanuts. Black sunflower seeds have more oil
content than the striped ones, while sunflower hearts
(husked kernels) are less messy to eat. Whole sunflower
seed-heads can also be left on plants (cover with nets
until fully ripe) or removed, dried and threaded with
twine to hang from branches or feeding stations.

Niger seeds
Place these small, black, oil-rich seeds in a special
feeder to attract goldfinches, greenfinches, tits
house sparrows, nuthatches, siskin and great
spotted woodpeckers.

Pinhead oatmeal
This valuable inner part of an oat has often been finely
chopped to make it easier for birds to eat. Suitable for
many birds including wrens, dunnocks, robins,
blackbirds, song thrushes and chaffinches.

Birdseed mixtures
Better birdseed mixtures contain flaked maize,
sunflower seeds and peanut granules. Suitable for
mesh feeders and bird tables and attractive to a range
of species.

Mealworms
Relished by robins and Blue Tits plus insect-eaters
such as pied wagtails. Ideal for feeding birds
throughout the year, although ensure stocks are
always fresh.

Waxworms, ant pupae, insectivorous or softbill food
An expensive option but ideal to attract insect-eating
birds including treecreepers and wrens.

Fat balls or cakes
Balls or cakes of beef or vegetable fat combined with
seeds, oats, peanuts, dried fruit and even mealworms
can really help birds survive the winter. See page 284
for how to make your own.

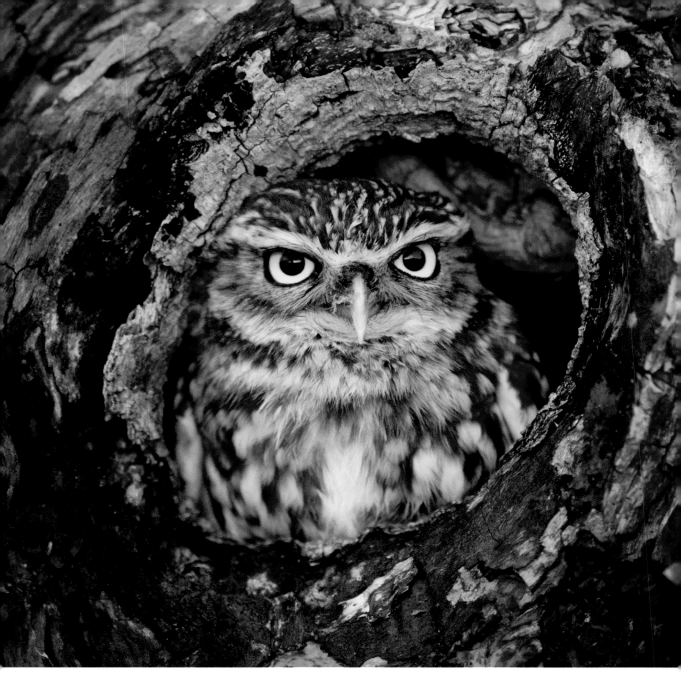

BREEDING AND SHELTER

Combine bird-friendly planting with supplementary nest boxes, roosting pockets and nesting material to give birds safe, year-round and often-vital spaces in which to breed and shelter. Birds need shelter for safety, weather protection, to forage and feast on plant food and to provide an ideal nesting site for raising their young.

Observe birds in the wild and you'll spot them perching in trees, flitting into hedges and shrubs, hopping among thick ground cover or grasses, diving for the protection of a nearby tree or peeping out from holes formed in dead wood, piles of branches, little burrows in riverbanks, the crevices of rocks or the eaves of a house.

The best way to provide ready shelter is by introducing or maintaining a bird-friendly garden (see page 266), combining a good mix of deciduous, evergreen and fruiting Trees and Hedges (see page 272) – where space allows – with a variety of Flowers, Shrubs, and Grasses (see page 277), Climbers and Vines (see page 292), and relatively untouched areas such as Woodpiles and Compost Heaps (see page 296). Many of the best plants for food also offer vital nesting, roosting or sheltering spots for many birds.

Spring is mating and breeding season for most species of birds (although some birds such as collared doves and wood pigeons do it year-round when given ready access to food), usually announced by an increase and heightening of birdsong in mid-winter designed to attract potential mates and protect territory. Breeding times do vary, however, dependent on geography, availability of food and water, the duration of the caring period, brood numbers and nesting sites. The further north a bird's breeding range is, for example, the later its mating season will begin, while migrating birds need to reach their breeding destination before they can even attempt to make a suitable nest.

Different species of bird also locate or build their nests in different ways. Rooks, for example, start early in the season by dropping branches into tall trees to lay the foundations of their large, unruly nests. Blackbirds, robins and song thrushes build nests in the classic design comprising neat cups of woven grasses and small twigs camouflaged with moss and lined with mud. Chaffinches fashion them in the forks of trees using sticky cobwebs as a kind of mortar on which to anchor and combine other materials, while long-tailed tits make intricate and delicate cup-and-dome contraptions, camouflaged with lichens and lined with hundreds of feathers.

Some birds eschew making nests altogether in favour of pre-made cavities in trees or rocks; others fly great distances to source the right materials for their temporary home. Many birds appreciate a little helping hand in the form of a Nest Box (see page 301 for tips on how to make your own) or ready piles of useful twigs, grass, moss, mud, freshly pruned plant clippings, grass and animal fur (avoid this if your pet has recently been treated for fleas or other medical conditions).

In hot or cold weather birds need shelter of different kinds – roosts in which to regulate body temperature or stay dry. Evergreen trees, thick bushes, hedges and reed-beds are great for winter night-time roosts or shade, while tits and wrens can be found roosting in empty nest boxes or supplementary roosting pockets (fill these with straw or wood chippings), huddling together for extra warmth. The greater the camouflage and shelter, the better chance birds have of foraging for their ideal food too (see Foraging and Feeding page 268).

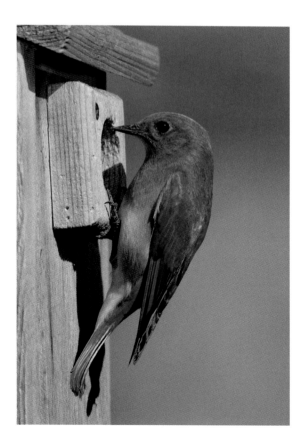

Opposite Help provide birds including the lovely Little Owl (*Athena noctua*) with natural shelter to help them breed and survive
Right Or install a nest box or two to give species such as this Eastern bluebird (*Sialia sialis*) a helping hand

Climbers and Vines

Climbers and vines such as wild rose, honeysuckle and clematis ramble through the understorey or over structures, twine through hedges or cling to the surfaces of trees or walls, creating nesting pockets and shelter for small birds and food in the form of berries, seeds, visiting insects and grubs.

Climbers and vines are a versatile option for all kinds of gardens, as an ornamental covering for fences and walls, to add a trans-season burst of colour and scent in the higher reaches or grown in pots and trained upwards over trellis or a small structure where space is tight – ideal for a balcony or small patio or courtyard.

Birds love them as much in the garden as they do in the wild, nestling into foliage for shelter and protection, picking off ripe berries and haws in autumn and winter, and searching for insects among the ground cover some creeping species of vine provide. Climbers also provide a high perch for songbirds and passing migrating birds.

Wild rose
Rosa spp.
Intertwine rambling species of rose or their single-petalled cultivars through established hedges or train them up walls for a profusion of scented, insect-attracting blooms in summer, vitamin C-rich orange-red hips to help thrushes, waxwings, and blackbirds through the winter, and thorny foliage for shelter.

Native species include dog rose (*Rosa canina* – native to UK and Europe, widely introduced to North America and Australia); beach or Japanese rose (*Rosa rugosa* – native to eastern Russia and Asia, introduced to UK and Europe, considered invasive in parts of US); Virginia rose (*Rosa virginiana* – native to North America); wild prairie rose (*Rosa arkansana* – native to North America); Woods' rose (*Rosa woodsii* – Native to North America)

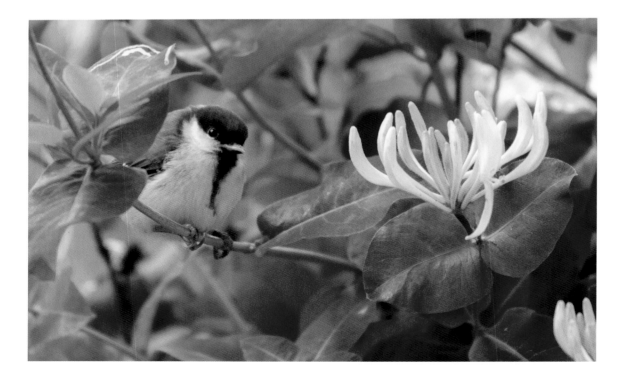

Ivy
Hedera spp.

Give ivy something to climb up and it will repay you with a dense spread of sheltering evergreen leaves plus flowers and purple-black berries in higher spots which ripen in winter providing a vital food source for blackbirds and song thrushes when other food is scarce. Ideal for pots and baskets.

Suggested species include common or English ivy (*Hedera helix* – native to UK and Europe, invasive in some parts of North America)

Honeysuckle
Lonicera spp.

Hardy honeysuckle looks best scrambling through a hedge as per its native habitat but can be trained up a wall, fence, or support. The sweetly perfumed, nectar-rich, exotic flowers attract hummingbirds (Americas) and insect-feeding birds, while bullfinches, warblers, and thrushes love the autumn berries.

Suggested species include common honeysuckle or woodbine (*Lonicera periclymenum* – native to UK and Europe); coral or trumpet honeysuckle (*Lonicera sempervirens* – native to parts of North America)

Blackberry
Rubus spp.

Bird-lovers with larger or wilder gardens that can take a bramble's vigorous, dense, and thorny habit will be handsomely repaid with clusters of white blossom in early spring, shiny red-black edible berries, and flocks of birds that come for the insects, the nutritious fruit, plus shelter and nesting spots.

Suggested species include blackberry (*Rubus fruticosus* – native to UK and Europe); Allegheny or common blackberry (*Rubus allegheniensis* – native to North America, introduced to UK and Europe)

Clematis
Clematis spp.

Choose from hundreds of species, hybrids, or cultivars of twining clematis offering an array of spectacular early or late blooming flowers – some with equally showy wispy seed heads, ideal for lining nests – tangled foliage for nesting within, plus insects and berries for bug- and fruit-eating birds.

Suggested species and hybrids include traveller's joy or old man's beard (*Clematis vitalba* – native to Europe, Middle East, and North Africa and introduced to parts of North America, it can be extremely invasive and is banned in New Zealand); mountain or anemone clematis (*Clematis montana* – native to central and East Asia; winter flowering clematis (*Clematis cirrhosa* – native to Mediterranean Europe; golden clematis (*Clematis tangutica* – native to central and East Asia, introduced to parts of North America); downy clematis (*Clematis macropetala* – native from China to Siberia); evergreen clematis (*Clematis armandii* – native to China and Myanmar); *Clematis florida*; sweet autumn clematis (*Clematis paniculata* – native to New Zealand); first large-flowered hybrid (*Clematis 'Jackmanii'*); leatherflower or vase vine (*Clematis viorna* – native to south-eastern US)

Virginia creeper
Parthenocissus quinquefolia spp.

Given enough sun this show-stopping creeper provides bee-friendly midsummer blooms followed by deep-blue berries on scarlet stems with equally bright-red autumnal leaves. Birds such as bluebirds, woodpeckers and sparrows love the fruit, while tendril-attached foliage is ideal for nesting in.

Suggested species include Virginia creeper (*Parthenocissus quinquefolia* – native to North and Central America, introduced to UK, Europe, North Africa, and Asia)

Opposite Climbing honeysuckle (*Lonicera* spp.) provides a perfect perch for a fledgling Great Tit (*Parus major*) waiting for a parent to bring back food

Next spread For those with a large enough plot, the pretty white flowers (**left**) of Old man's beard or traveller's joy (*Clematis vitalba*) give way to silky seed-heads (**right**), an important food source of goldfinches and greenfinches

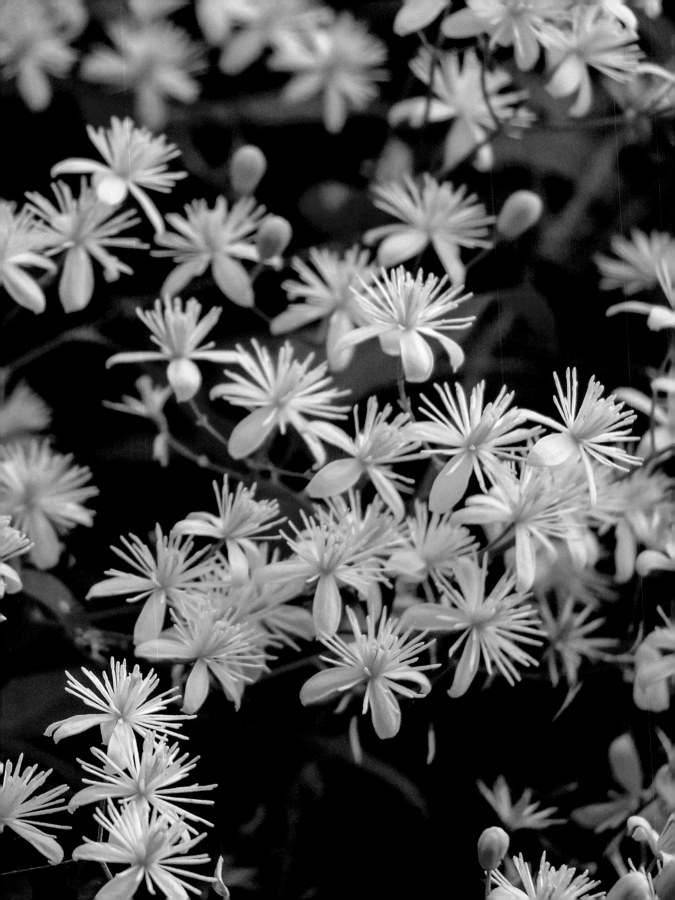

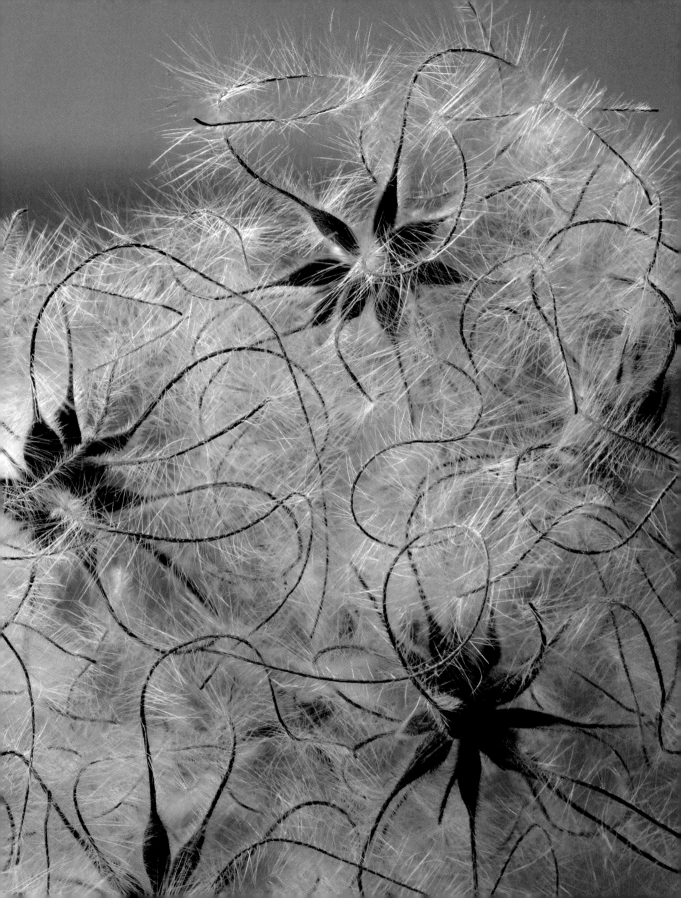

Woodpiles and Compost Heaps

Consider leaving less-cultivated garden areas where dead wood, leaf matter, decomposing plants, weeds and wildflowers can be left in place. This may also be an ideal spot for a compost heap. Birds will come for the many insects, spiders and worms that live there as well as nearby berries or seeds.

Woodpiles and compost heaps in gardens provide rich pickings for birds and other wildlife and can be made even more inviting through the plants and flowers that grow or are introduced there. For larger landscapes or gardens, simply allocate a dedicated area – away from the house if you prefer – where native plant species are allowed to run wild through their natural lifecycles, dead trees can be left to rot undisturbed and fallen twigs or branches collect under hedges or in the understorey along with tree debris and fading or seeding perennials. Such a relatively undisturbed habitat provides a haven for invertebrates such as insects, worms, slugs and spiders; small mammals such as mice and hedgehogs; and amphibians such as toads and newts. They also provide native nectar sources for pollinators such as bees and butterflies and an abundance of food, shelter and nesting places for birds.

This is the perfect place to build or source a composting structure where grass clippings, vegetative food waste, deciduous leaves and pruned plants can be left to rot. Leaving the compost heap open makes for easier turning but also provides insect predators such as robins and blackbirds with ready meals of worms, slugs and bugs. Let weeds, wildflowers and mineral-rich plant species such as nettles (*Urtica* spp.), dock (*Rumex* spp.), yarrow (*Achillea* spp.), wild carrot (*Daucus* spp.), dandelion (*Taraxacum* spp.), comfrey (*Symphytum* spp.), clover (*Trifolium* spp.), cleavers (*Galium aparine* spp.) and borage (*Borago officinalis* spp.) colonize the vicinity to feed beneficial pollinators and their young, and provide shelter and autumn seeds for birds.

Nitrogen-rich plants such as nettles and borage are particularly useful when composting as their chopped leaves can act as an accelerator. When transferred to beds and borders, nutrient-rich compost also attracts earthworms as they pull the goodness down into the ground and send soil up to the surface – good news for plants and birds that benefit from their presence. Just don't transfer the seeds or roots of persistent plants such as dandelions to the heap or you'll end up with a host of unwanted weeds as well as goodness wherever compost is spread.

While open compost heaps are not so viable for smaller backyards or balconies, there's always room for a woodpile, even if it's just a small pile of sticks between planters, a square of logs or an aerated bucket filled with a mixture of soil and wood chippings. You could also part-bury a log or two in a container as a feature. In all cases, select a shady spot and as long as there's a feasible route to it, insects such as woodlice and beetles should move in, hopefully followed by one or two curious feathered friends.

Nettle
Urtica spp.

Nettles attract more than 40 species of insect to their serrated leaves including aphids, ladybirds and caterpillars; plus, it produces a bounty of seeds in late summer providing spoils for insect- and seed-eating birds alike. Throw their nitrogen-rich leaves in the compost heap to help accelerate decomposition.

> Suggested species include stinging nettle (*Urtica dioica* – native to UK and temperate Eurasia, introduced to parts of North and South America and South Africa) and annual nettle (*Urtica urens* – native to temperate Eurasia, introduced to UK, parts of North and South America, Africa and Australia)

Borage
Borago officinalis spp.

Prettify your compost heap or woodpile and add trace minerals to the soil with a colony of bright-blue, star-flowered borage. A magnet for bees and butterflies due to an abundant supply of nectar, the

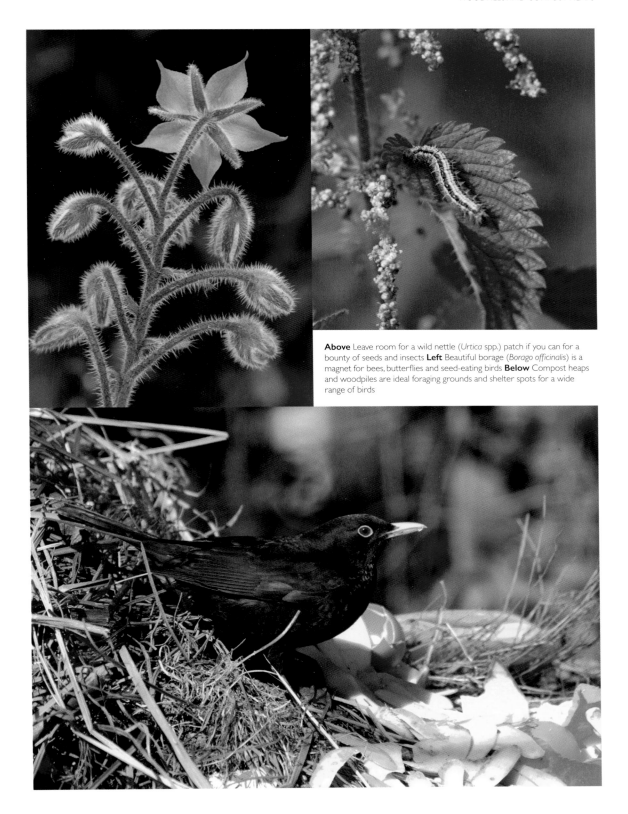

Above Leave room for a wild nettle (*Urtica* spp.) patch if you can for a bounty of seeds and insects **Left** Beautiful borage (*Borago officinalis*) is a magnet for bees, butterflies and seed-eating birds **Below** Compost heaps and woodpiles are ideal foraging grounds and shelter spots for a wide range of birds

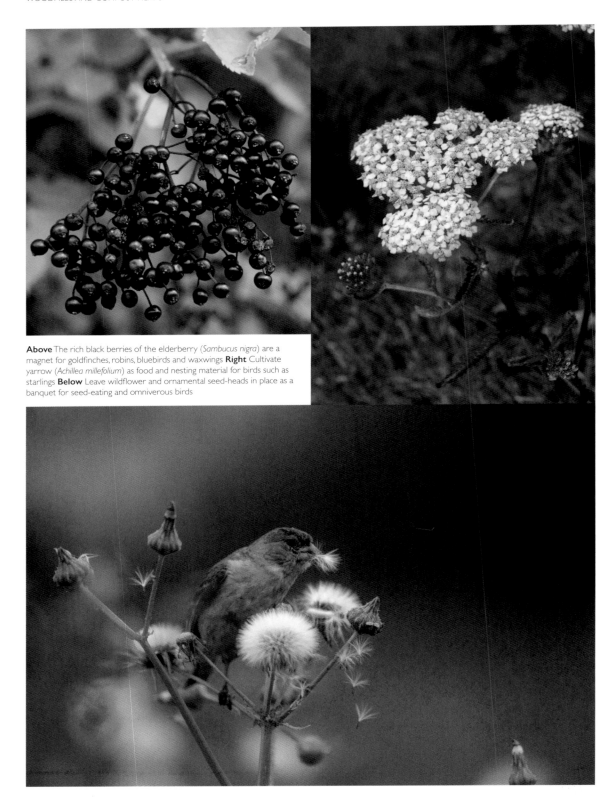

Above The rich black berries of the elderberry (*Sambucus nigra*) are a magnet for goldfinches, robins, bluebirds and waxwings **Right** Cultivate yarrow (*Achillea millefolium*) as food and nesting material for birds such as starlings **Below** Leave wildflower and ornamental seed-heads in place as a banquet for seed-eating and omniverous birds

pollinated flowers then produce a banquet of thistle-like seeds for birds such as finches.

Suggested species include borage (*Borago officinalis* – native to west and central Mediterranean, introduced to UK, other parts of Europe and South America)

Cleavers

Galium aparine spp.

This sprawling annual weed is known for its sticky stems, leaves and round seeds that are dispersed by passing animals, birds and humans. Numerous insects are also attracted to the foliage and tiny white flowers, providing ready meals for bug-eating birds. Avoid composting after seeds have set.

Suggested species include cleavers or goosegrass (*Galium aparine* – native to large swathes of UK, Eurasia and North Africa; introduced to North and South America, Africa and Australia)

Yarrow

Achillea millefolium spp.

A pretty white or pink-tinted, flat-topped perennial wildflower that grows easily on uncultivated land, yarrow provides nesting material for the dwellings of cavity-nesting birds such as starlings and seeds for a variety of songbirds. Mineral-rich yarrow leaves are also useful as a compost accelerator.

Suggested species include common yarrow (*Achillea millefolium* – native to temperate and sub-Arctic North America, UK and Eurasia; introduced to South America, southern Africa, Asia and Australia)

Dandelion

Taraxacum spp.

Birds such as goldfinches, siskins, blackbirds and sparrows eat the seeds, while bees and other pollinating insects come to languish in blooms thanks to the early spring offering of nectar. The yellow flowers also brighten up a log pile patch but avoid placing dandelion roots or seeds in compost.

Suggested species and hybrids include common dandelion (*Taraxacum officinale* – native to UK, Europe and Asia; naturalized throughout North and South America, southern Africa, South America, New Zealand and Australia); red-seeded dandelion (*Taraxacum erythrospermum* – native to Europe, Caucasus and Mongolia; introduced to North America)

Elderberry

Sambucus spp.

Fragrant white lacy flowers followed by clusters of shiny red-black berries deliver an abundant feast of insects and fruits for goldfinches, robins, bluebirds and waxwings. Elderberry foliage also provides shelter while fast-decomposing, activating leaves and twigs can be added to the compost heap.

Suggested species include European elderberry (*Sambucus nigra* – native to UK, Europe and the Middle East; introduced to South America) and American black elderberry (*Sambucus canadensis* – native to southern North America, Central and South America)

Nest Boxes and Roosts

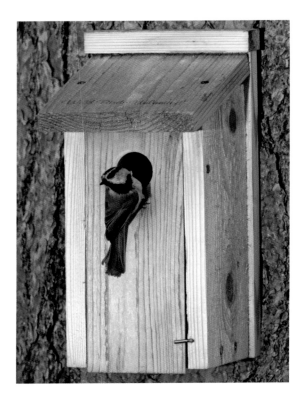

plywood or softwood such as pine serves this purpose well. The box should naturally weather over time to provide an element of camouflage but could be painted a neutral shade of green, brown or grey to allow it to recede into surrounding vegetation, bark or wall. Use an eco-friendly, water-based paint that won't harm birds or the environment; avoid painting around the entrance hole on the inside where birds may peck, and allow it to fully dry for at least a few days before use.

Boxes for tits, sparrows or starlings should be 2–4m (6.5–13ft) up a tree or a wall and (if your garden is large enough) spaced out enough to cater for several territories. House sparrows, house martins and starlings will readily use nest boxes placed high up under the eaves of your house and nest in loose colonies so two or three boxes close together is ideal. Woodpeckers need their boxes to be at least 3m (10ft) up a tree trunk, with a clear flight path and away from disturbance. Robins and wrens prefer open-fronted boxes placed low down, below 2m (6.5ft) and well hidden by foliage but with a clear outlook. If fixing your box to a tree, attach it with a nylon bolt or wire around a trunk or branch rather than a nail; trees grow in girth as well as height so check the fixing every couple of years to ensure fixings, especially wire, are not cutting into the bark. Face nest boxes away from strong sunlight and avoid windy or unsheltered spots.

It's best to put nest boxes up in autumn to give birds time to view a potential nesting place to which they can return in spring; this is important for some species although tits or chickadees do not seriously investigate sites until after winter. Remember that nest boxes can also double up as vital roosts during the cold season but check strict national laws around removing used nests or eggs, even out of breeding season. Roost boxes or woven roost pockets are another easy-to-source option with specially designed nest box cameras becoming increasingly popular for watching breeding and roosting birds in action. If you don't have access to such equipment, try and stay well away or observe from a distance to give birds and their chicks the best fighting chance of survival.

Above A Mountain Chickadee (*Poecile gambeli*) finds a welcome breeding ground and shelter in a safely mounted nest box

Furnish your garden, balcony or backyard with nest boxes and supplementary roosting points to offer birds additional protection from predators and harsh weather conditions, plus a place to safely bring up their young – especially vital when natural shelter and nesting sites are scarce.

Nest boxes are easy to source or make (see Make a nest box opposite), providing a range of small birds with a ready space within which to raise their brood. The key to attracting certain species of bird is to ensure that the entrance hole is the right size for them to easily come and go, but also keep predators or usurping birds at bay: smaller holes for coal tits, marsh tits and blue tits; medium for great tits and tree sparrows; large for nuthatches and house sparrows; and the biggest of all for starlings. Entrance holes also need to be high enough up and perch-free to prevent predators from getting in.

A simple, sloped-roof, closed-front, lid-topped nest box (with entrance hole) made from exterior-grade

Make a Nest Box

Making a nest box for birds such as tits, robins, nuthatches, sparrows and starlings is a fun project and provides such birds with an ideal place to breed and potentially roost.

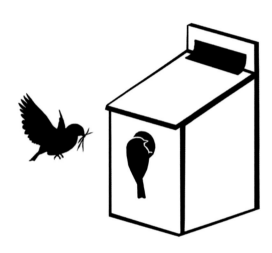

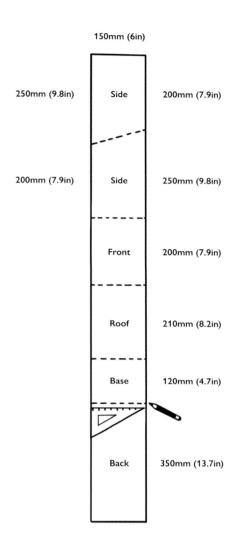

150mm (6in)

250mm (9.8in)	Side	200mm (7.9in)
200mm (7.9in)	Side	250mm (9.8in)
	Front	200mm (7.9in)
	Roof	210mm (8.2in)
	Base	120mm (4.7in)
	Back	350mm (13.7in)

1 Find or purchase a piece of sustainably sourced timber for the main body of your nest box: exterior-quality plywood for a lighter box; hardwood such as oak or beech; or softwood such as pine, but this will deteriorate faster. A long plank 150mm wide (6in) × 15mm (0.5in) thick × at least 1.5m (5ft) that can be cut into pieces is ideal. Ensure that this wood will not split or disintegrate when wet. Untreated is best but if treating is required to prolong life, use a water-based preservative and ensure wood is fully dry before use.

2 Use the diagram plus a set square and pencil to measure and mark your plank into the relevant pieces. These measurements are designed to accommodate the minimum interior box measurement for the use and comfort of the smallest birds, which is 100mm (4in) square.

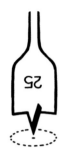

3   Rest the plank on a suitable surface and position it to cut along measurement guides using a saw (a Japanese saw is a great hand tool for small projects or thinner pieces of wood). Sand each piece apart from what will be the inside front surface. Keeping this surface rough will help young birds when they are ready to clamber up. Remember, adults should be in charge of any steps involving sharp tools or materials.

5   Use an appropriately sized spade drill bit or use a hole saw or jigsaw to cut your entrance. Ideal entrance hole sizes are: 25mm (0.9in) for smaller tits or chickadees such as coal tits, marsh tits and blue tits; 28mm (1.1in) for great tits and tree sparrows; 32mm (1.25in) for nuthatches and house sparrows; and 45mm (1.8in) for starlings.

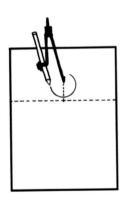

4   Take your front piece and use a set square and pencil to mark out a line 125mm (5in) from its bottom edge with an intersecting line at its central point. Use a compass to mark out the positioning and diameter of your entrance hole. The lowest point of your hole should not extend past your 125mm (5in) guideline to help prevent cats from scooping birds out with their paws.

6   Use a standard drill bit to create a couple of small drainage holes in the base piece to stop the nest box getting damp inside.

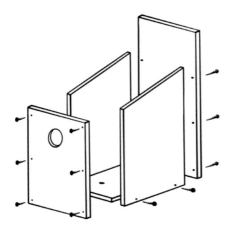

7 Set the roof to one side. Then follow the diagram to attach the sides to the backboard, then the base and finally the front. All should be flush to the base. Use 25mm (1in) self-tapping wood screws, pre-drilling screw holes if required (in harder woods).

9 Position the nest box on a suitable tree, wall or under the eaves (see page 300 for species-relevant advice), facing away from direct sunlight or strong winds if possible, and out of reach of predators such as cats. Birds also benefit from a direct flight path, a measure of privacy and nearby food.

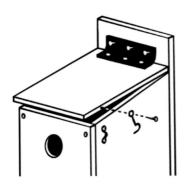

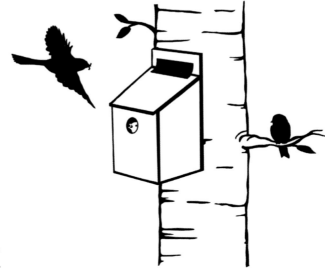

8 Position the roof on top of the front and sides. Create a hinge by nailing on a strip of scrap leather, roofing felt or thin rubber such as a recycled piece of bicycle inner tube. Creating a hinged lid allows for easier cleaning in autumn. If necessary, attach a swing hook box clasp or latch to close.

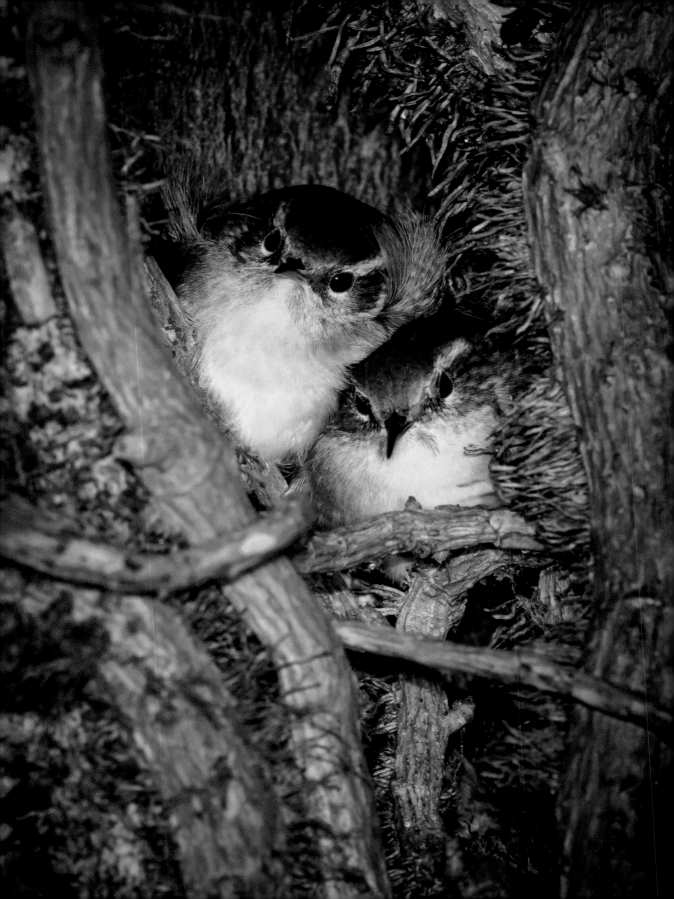

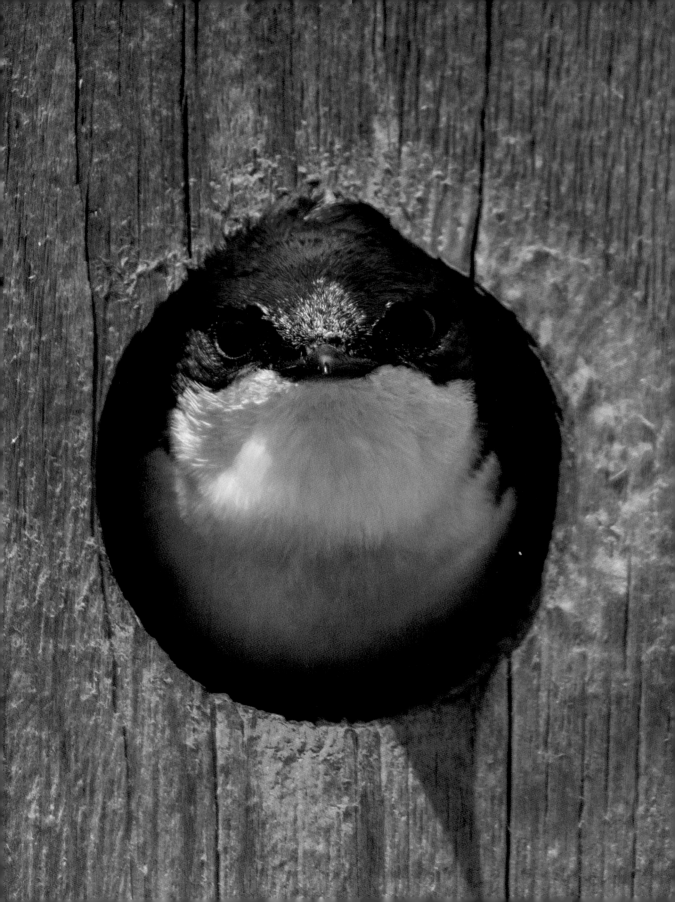

Thinking Sustainably

Birds are hugely important to the world's ecosystems with changes in bird behaviour serving as an early warning sign for pressing concerns such as climate change. Bolstering plant diversity, providing supplementary food and shelter and supporting bird conservation are just some of the ways that we can all make a difference.

In 1859, renowned English naturalist Charles Robert Darwin published his theory of evolution by natural selection: *On the Origin of Species*. A collection of around fifteen species of passerine, now collectively known as 'Darwin's Finches', had a starring role. Known for their remarkable diversity in beak form and function, these variously sized 'finches' (or tanagers, as it now transpires) illustrated how species emerge, change and potentially become extinct in response to changes in the environment, and the importance of biodiversity in the natural world.

This phenomenon is not, of course, particular to the Galapagos Islands, where Darwin observed his 'finches'. Changes in environment happen and are happening all over the world, from entire biomes such as rainforests, grasslands or coastal areas to the ecosystem of your neighbourhood or backyard – with birds often the first to ring such changes, through their dwelling places, feeding habits, breeding times, migration patterns or, in some cases, their decline.

Birds pollinate plants, including a significant number of species used for human medicine or food. They spread seeds and nutrients by dispersing them through their droppings, in turn helping to restore biodiversity where natural habitats may have been seriously affected or destroyed – this includes vital coral reefs. They transform entire landscapes, helping to store carbon, oxygenate the air, transform pollutants into nutrients and keep the climate stable. Plus, they maintain the delicate balance between plant and herbivore, predator and prey and control pests by eating insects and other invertebrates. In short, birds play an essential role in the functioning of the world's ecosystems, as well as being beautiful or inspiring to watch or live among.

But they are also being hugely affected by issues such as climate change: being forced out of natural habitats such as high-altitude forests; moving further north to find suitable dwelling places; migrating earlier or later in the season; or altering breeding patterns to ensure that they have enough food to feed their young, as changes in weather affect the availability of plants or insects. Which is why helping to conserve birds is so important, both in your garden and as part of a global community.

Supporting a national or worldwide bird or wildlife conservation organization such as the Royal Society for the Protection of Birds (RSPB) in the UK or Audubon in the US is one way to help (see page 389 for a helpful list). This includes helping fund global conservation initiatives, volunteering locally, purchasing supplementary shelters or food or taking part in vital bird counts. Attracting birds to your garden, backyard or balcony is another. Provide birds with a place for Foraging and Feeding (see page 268), the right balance of food and suitable shelter for Breeding and Shelter (see page 290) and your flocks should naturally increase. One small flutter for birdkind, one giant soar for birds.

Previous spread, left A pair of Treecreepers (*Certhia americana*) roost through the night among tree-creeping ivy (*Hedera* spp.) **Right** An adult Tree Swallow (*Tachicineta bicolor*) takes shelter in an empty bird box **Opposite** Help conserve endangered birds such as the sweetly singing nightingale (*Luscinia megarhyncos*), one of many species that has been serious affected by habitat loss and climate change

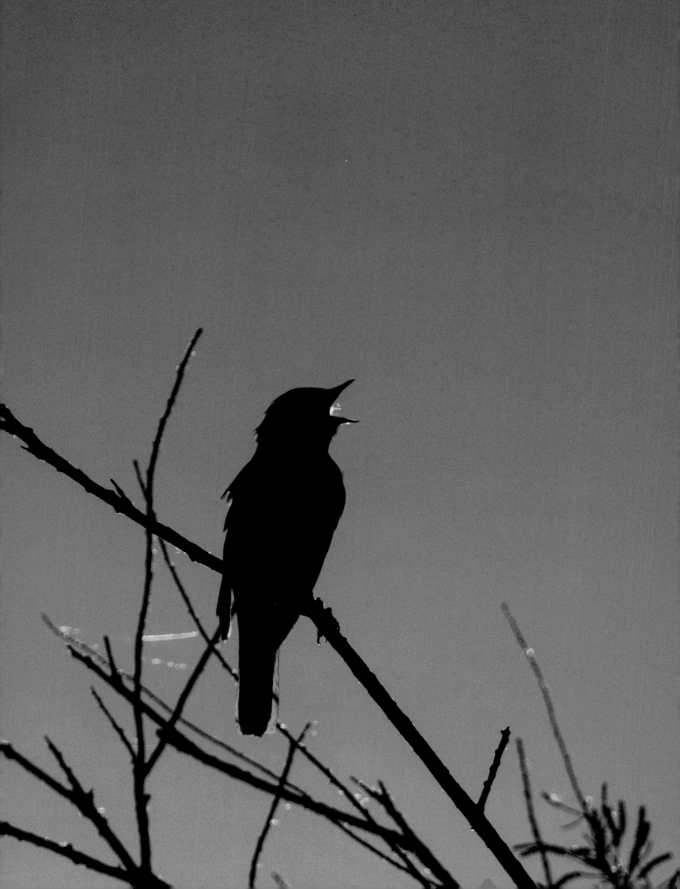

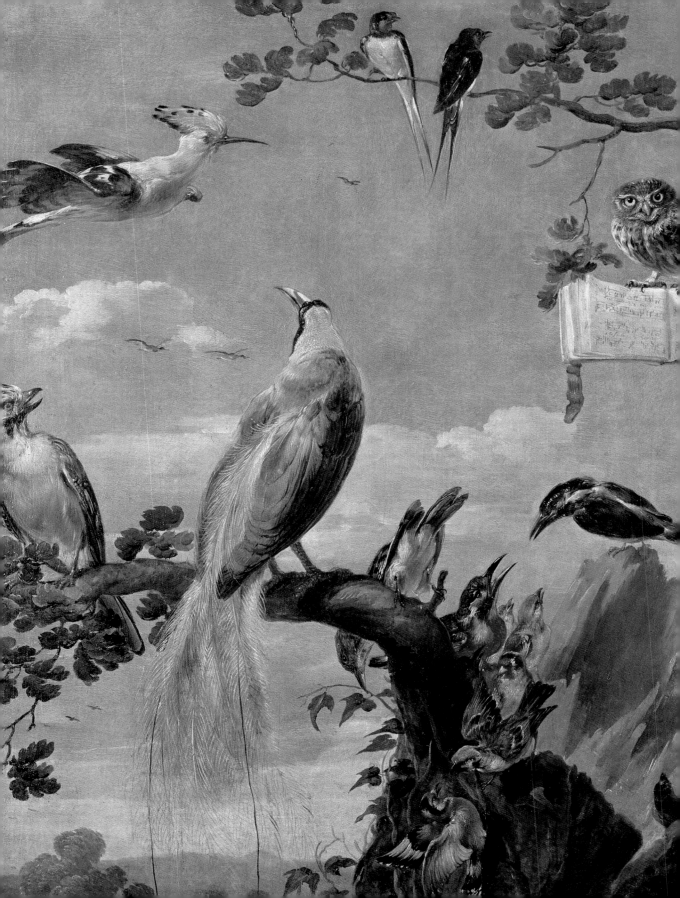

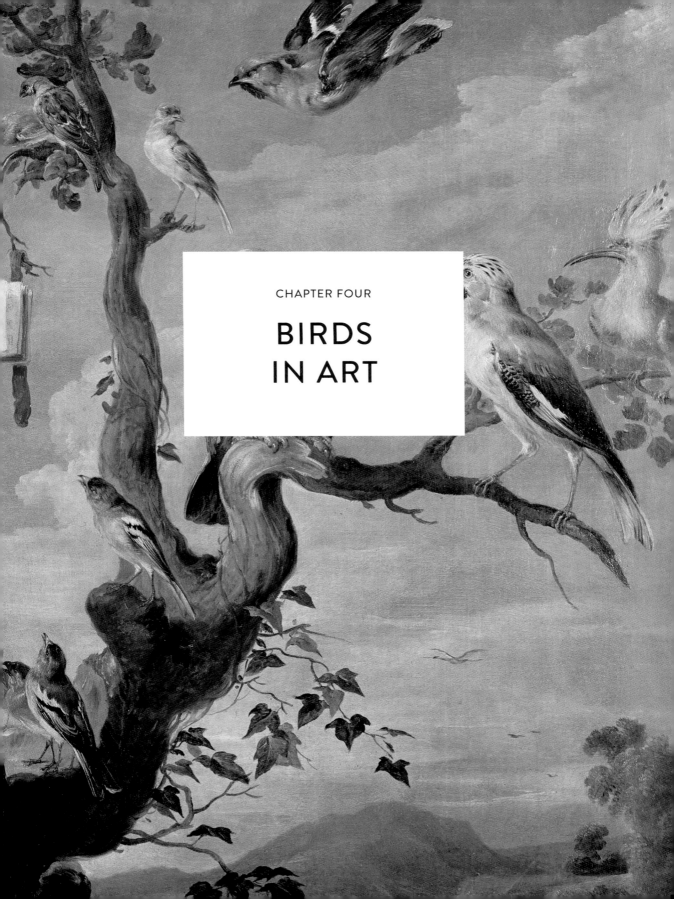

CHAPTER FOUR

BIRDS
IN ART

THE ART OF BIRDS

Birds have intrigued and inspired humans around the world for an estimated 40,000 years, the artistic and scientific documentation of their habits and habitats intrinsically entwined with the record of our own.

As fellow warm-blooded creatures of the animal kingdom we feel a natural affinity for birds and yet are fascinated with their evolutionary adaptations and differences: their extraordinary feathers, colourful or patterned plumes, captivating songs, ingenious nest-building and mating skills, predatory prowess, perfectly formed eggs and their ability to fly sometimes huge distances across the globe. Birds also help maintain balance in our ecosystems in a way that directly impacts our health, food crops, habitats and natural environments. Given this longstanding, intrinsic and mutualistic relationship, the bird as muse features widely in the history of art, over a wingspan of thousands of years.

Fledgling impressions

The first fledgling portrayals of birds date back to Palaeolithic times: the shamanistic, beaked 'birdman' of Lascaux Cave (*c.*15,000 BC) in the Dordogne, France sporting beside him a clear effigy of a small bird perched on a falling staff as he faces off a large bison. In Chauvet-Pont-d'Arc Cave in the Ardéche, an owl stares out from a cave wall – the first image illustrating this bird's unique ability to turn its head 180 degrees? While paintings of giant emu-like birds thought to have become extinct some 40,000 years ago adorn the walls of a cave on the Arnhem Land plateau in Australia.

Birds were later incorporated into art as symbolic representations of freedom, power, royalty, immortality or peace, soaring embodiments of humanity's hopes and dreams, a direct link between Earth and the spiritual realm. As the reach of Ancient Egypt (*c.*3,150–332 BC) and Greco-Roman Egypt (332 BC–AD 629) spread along the wildlife-rich banks of the fertile River Nile, so the teeming population of native and migratory birds including herons, hawks, falcons (relating to the god Horus), ibises (relating to the god Thoth) and geese were incorporated into the higher powers and hieroglyphics of the day. Further east, in the carved caves of Ajanta, India, birds can be found in breathtaking Buddhist frescoes, thought to date back to the Gupta dynasty of the fifth and sixth centuries AD. While, to the west, rock art in the Bighorn Basin in north-west Wyoming and Twin Bluffs, Wisconsin in the Mississippi Valley are rich in eagle-like petroglyphs thought to be the first visual symbols of the legendary Thunderbird, a supernatural being of enormous strength and protective power, widespread in the bird-rich mythology of Native American and First Nations peoples.

As early indigenous and colonial civilizations advanced, so then bird forms and features along with other fauna and flora were also used decoratively and as part of illustrative records. Avian-inspired artefacts from this time include bird-inspired frescoes, statues, ceramics and ceremonial or symbolic headdresses and masks – the latter sometimes adorned with feathers or other bird parts as worn by ancient Mayan, Aztec, Native American, First Nations, Polynesian and Sub Saharan peoples. By the tenth century AD the graceful tradition of bird-and-flower painting had taken root in Tang-era China. Birds were also becoming commonplace in illuminated medieval manuscripts, especially around AD 1250–1350, the popular motif of the European goldfinch symbolizing the resurrection of Christ, fertility and healing.

Previous page *Concert of Birds* (1629–30) by Frans Snyders includes 'legless' birds of paradise (see page 313)

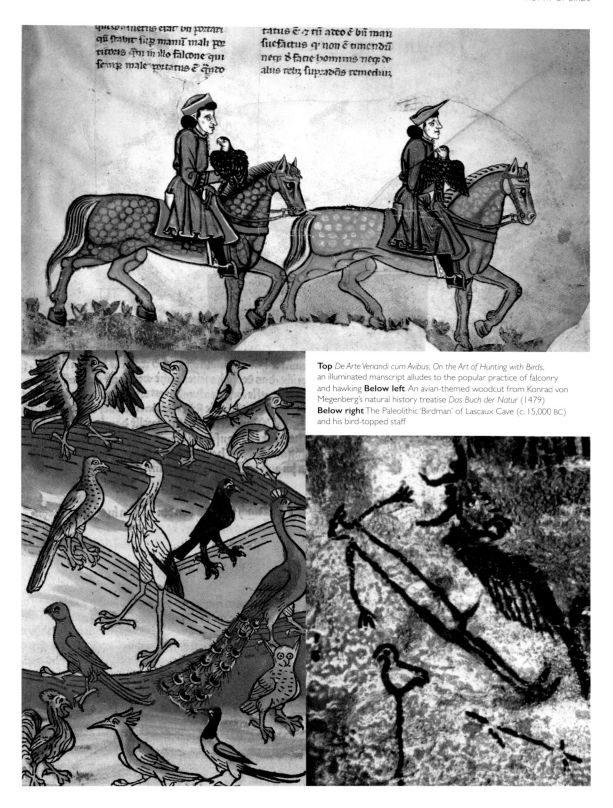

Top *De Arte Venandi cum Avibus, On the Art of Hunting with Birds,* an illuminated manscript alludes to the popular practice of falconry and hawking **Below left** An avian-themed woodcut from Konrad von Megenberg's natural history treatise *Das Buch der Natur* (1479) **Below right** The Paleolithic 'Birdman' of Lascaux Cave (c. 15,000 BC) and his bird-topped staff

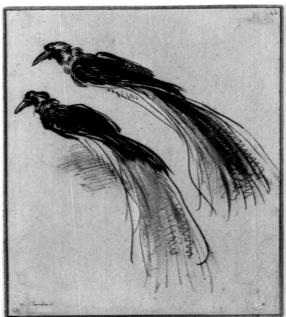

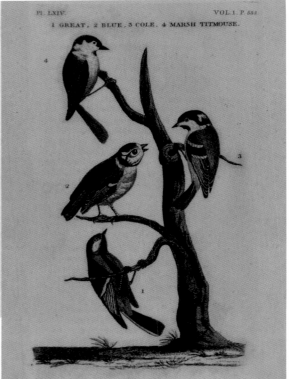

Top left *Two Studies of a Bird of Paradise* (1630) by Dutch artist Rembrandt Harmenszoom van Rijn **Top right** A Great Tit, Blue Tit, Cole Tit and Marsh Titmouse From Thomas Pennant's *British Zoology* (1761–6) **Below** Pages from the ground-breaking *A Natural History of Uncommon Birds* (1743–51) by the 'Father of British Ornithology' George Edwards

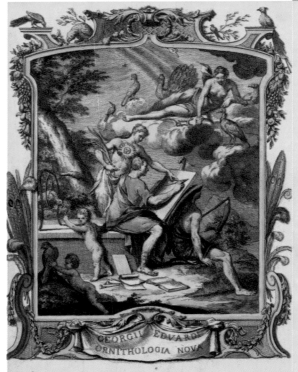

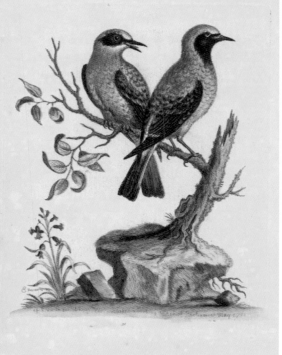

Ornithological forays

With Christianity prevailing across much of Europe, bird-referencing books of the time were either religious or compilations of classical authors such as Aristotle or Theophrastus. That is, until the arrival of what is thought to be the first illustrated ornithological work, *De Arte Venandi cum Avibus* or *On the Art of Hunting with Birds* (*c.* 1240s) by the maverick Holy Roman Emperor Frederick II. Covering a range of experimental and observational content from whether eggs hatch from the warmth of the sun to whether birds use their sense of smell while hunting, the detailed writing is accompanied by over 900 meticulous drawings of birds, and other animals.

Banned by the Church for its scientific lean, it was resurrected in the sixteenth century, joining printed and illustrated versions of Pliny the Elder's first-century *Historia Naturalis* (AD 77; printed 1469) – of which volume ten is entirely devoted to birds; Konrad von Megenberg's *Das Buch der Natur* (1475); Conrad Gesner's *Historiae Animalium* (1551–87), illustrated by Lukas Schan; Pierre Belon's *L'histoire de la nature des oyseaux* (1555) and *Pourtraicts d'oyseaux* (1557); and *Ornithology* (1599–1603) by the globetrotting Italian Aldrovandus, mainly produced using the art of woodcut.

Over in Persia, a manuscript of the witty and profound Sufi poem known as *The Conference of the Birds* by Farid ud-Din Attar (*c.* 1145–*c.* 1221), was exquisitely illustrated with ink, watercolour and gold and silver paintings by Habiballah of Sava, (1590–1610). In Ming dynasty China, birds also featured frequently in literary works, literati paintings and porcelain, while birds such as Manchurian cranes, golden pheasants and Mandarin ducks, embroidered in badges of silk brocade, denoted the rank of scholarly court officials.

The golden age of engraving and still life

By the end of the sixteenth century, engraving was the up-and-coming illustrative technique of the day, as seen in John Jonston's much-translated field guide-style *Historiiae naturalis de avibus* or *Natural History of Birds* (1650–7; or Francis Barlow's *Birds and Beasts in Sixty-Seven Excellent and Useful Prints* (1655), *Birds and Fowles of Various Species* (1658) or his popular illustrations for *Aesop's Fables* (1666).

The turn of the seventeenth century also set the scene for a new genre of still life and wildlife painting, led by Dutch and Flemish painters such as Roelandt Savery – now famed for his images of the dodo (*c.* 1626, see page 375), soon to be extinct – Pieter Holsteyn the Elder and Melchiorde Hondecoeter – the latter attempting to fly his birds across urn-embellished Italianate landscapes with postures of flight for many exotic species that could only have been imagined from their skins.

These imaginings become even more apparent in impossible pairings of South American macaws, Indonesian cockatoos, Eurasian jays and European green woodpeckers in the work of Hungarian-British artist Jakob Bogdani who had a taste for including pops of red in his paintings (1660–9), including the vivid plumage of a scarlet ibis and the cartoonish, red-feathered male northern cardinal. A closer look at the great artist Hamenszoon van Rijn Rembrandt's ink-and-chalk drawing *Two Studies of a Bird of Paradise* (1630), Frans Snyder's *Concert of Birds* (1629–30) or Paul de Vos and Jan Wilden's *Garden of Eden* (1630s) also reveals legless, permanently flying birds of paradise, the skins of these beautiful creatures transported from the island of New Guinea as such, perpetuating the much-rumoured myth that these really were 'birds of the gods'.

Suitably perched

Fast forward one hundred years and such symbolic illusions were cast away in favour of the suitably perched birds of Eleazar Albin's *A Natural History of Birds* (1731–8), patronage provided by the influential Irish doctor, naturalist and collector Sir Hans Sloane. Albin shared his talents with his daughter Elizabeth Albin, now recognized as the first female bird book illustrator, signing forty-one plates as her own.

Sloane also offered his support to 'the father of British ornithology', George Edwards, who used his position as librarian of the Royal College of Physicians to embark on his *A Natural History of Uncommon Birds* (1743–51) and *Gleanings of Natural History* (1758–64). Notable for including a large number of North American birds – via the skins and live species imported from the New World, many of them for the first time – and acute, accurately described observations, around 350 of his descriptions were later used by the great Swedish naturalist Carl Linnaeus for his ground-breaking *System Naturae* (1758). Edwards also engraved his own plates under the tutelage of naturalist and artist Mark Catesby, donned 'the father of American ornithology'. Catesby's *History of Carolina, Florida and the Bahama Islands* (1741–3), including 220 hand-coloured engravings of 109 birds, became the standard work on American birds, plants and other wildlife until the end of the eighteenth century.

Other major contributions to eighteenth-century bird art include Thomas Pennant's *British Zoology* (1761–6), *Indian Zoology* (1769), *Genera of Birds* (1773) and *Arctic Zoology* (1784). Also, John Latham's *A General Synopsis of Birds* (1781–5) including new species from the recently explored land now known as Australia, *Index Ornithologies* (1790) using a Linnaean system to list 3,000 apparently known bird species of the world (although some were later found to be the same species with different names) and his final ten-volume opus, *A General History of Birds* (1821–8) including birds from North America. Pennant also broke ground by employing the female artist Sarah Stone to illustrate some of his plates.

Birds of a New World

At the turn of the eighteenth into the nineteenth century, ornithology received another popularity boost thanks to the innovative intaglio white-line wood engravings and contemporary design of British artist Thomas Bewick's *A History of British Birds* (1797–1804). Over in France, similarly sympathetic bird compendiums included the Comte de Bouffon's *Histoire naturelle, generale et particuliere* (1749–89) with engravings by François Martinet and his team of more than eight artists and assistants, and Jacques Barraband's beautiful representations of exotic birds in François Levaillant's *Histoire naturelle des oiseaux d'Afrique* (1796–1808).

As global exploration gathered pace, so artists began to accompany naturalists on their voyages of discovery, including Sydney Parkinson, who sailed on Captain James Cook's HMS *Endeavour* across the Pacific Ocean between 1768 and 1771 to document flora and fauna collected by Joseph Banks and Swedish naturalist Daniel Solander. Following in his footsteps were doctor-artist William Ellis on Cook's voyage on HMS *Discovery* to New Zealand between 1776 and 1780, George Raper on board HMS *Sirius*, focusing on Australian birds c. 1796–97, Ferdinand Bauer (1760–1826) on the HMS *Investigator* and Scottish convict Thomas Watling (1762–1814) who was sent to the 'land down under' for fraud but became one of Britain's most esteemed wildlife artists.

Across the Atlantic, naturalist John Abbot (1751–1840) was sent to investigate the plants and animals of Virginia by the Royal Society and amassed some 570 specimens in his first two months in the field.

Ornithologist Alexander Wilson followed suit with his *American Ornithology* (1808–14), when he travelled thousands of miles across the land in search of bird species and bird-loving subscribers. His request for support from a Louisville storekeeper and artist by the name of John James Audubon was rebuffed, while simultaneously inspiring Audubon's hugely successful *Birds of America*

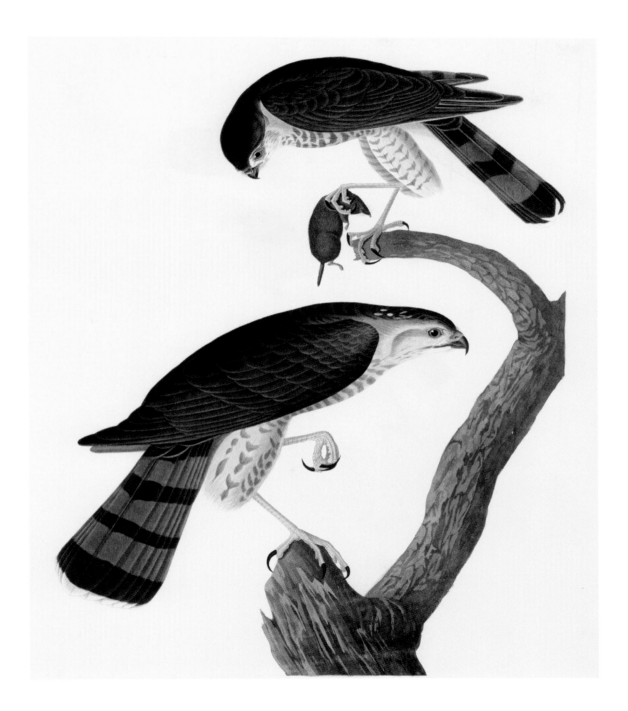

Sharp-shinned Hawk *(Accipiter striatus)* from John
James Audubon's *Birds of America* (1827–38); still
widespread across the Americas

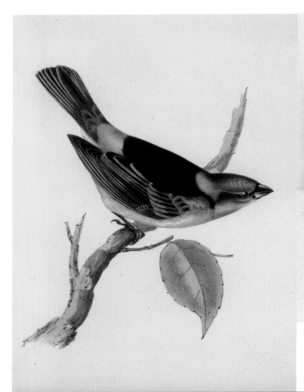

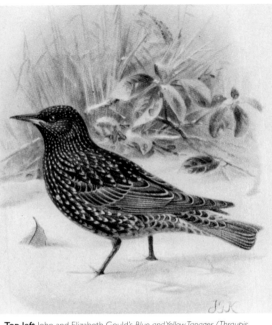

Top left John and Elizabeth Gould's *Blue and Yellow Tanager (Thraupis bonariensis darwinii)* from Charles Darwin's *Zoology of the Voyage of the HMS Beagle* (1809–1882) **Top right** Archibald Thorburn's *Starling (Winter plumage)* from Thomas Alfred Coward's *The Birds of the British Isles and Their Eggs* (1920) **Below** *The Pigeon* (c. 1890) by British artist Joseph Crawhall

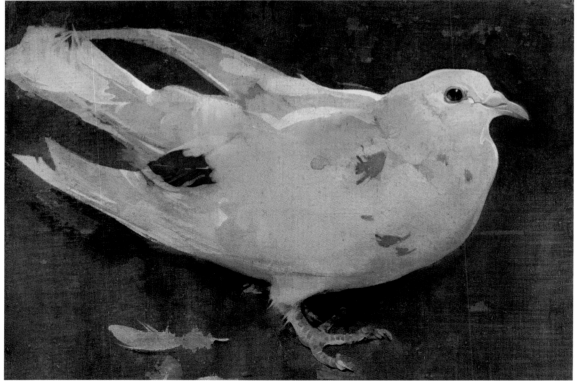

(1827–38, see page 321). Upon finding success in the newly United Kingdom of Great Britain and Ireland, Audubon went on to commission Scottish ornithologist and artist William MacGillivray (1796–1852) to write much of the text.

Flights of fancy

Audubon's artworks were produced using copperplate etching, engraving and aquatint, techniques soon superseded by lithography that allowed artists such as William Swainson (1789–1855) to draw directly onto stone (as opposed to relying on an engraver to transfer a design onto a metal plate) and pull multiple prints in the same run. Lithography also provided the tools to create such avian-inspired masterpieces as *A Century of Birds from the Himalaya Mountains* (1830–2), *Birds of Europe* (1937), part three of Darwin's the *Zoology of the Voyage of HMS Beagle* (1832–6) and *The Birds of Australia* (1840–8) by John and Elizabeth Gould (see page 324); John also created *Birds of Great Britain* (1873) after Elizabeth's untimely death due to the rigours of childbirth and travel. Other female artists making strides at this time include the intrepid Victorian artist Marianne North (see page 326) and her richly observed plants and animals.

John Gould also commissioned Edward Lear (see page 359) and Joseph Wolf to provide illustrations for his books, the former having already produced *Illustrations of the Family of Psittacidae, or Parrots* (1830), the latter having the enviable knack of being able to turn observations of lifeless bird skins into dramatic, soaring illustrations. When William Hart and Joseph Smit worked together to produce watercolours and lithographs for *Exotic Ornithology* (1866–1899), the trade in bird specimens and bird books was fully fledged across all four corners of the globe.

The last half of the nineteenth century saw the production of beautiful plates by artists such as John Gerrard Keulemans and Henrik Gronvold for Gregory Mathews's monumental *The Birds of Australia* (1910–27), but a new raft of bird artists were also producing watercolours of common and garden birds. Joseph Crawhall is lauded for his unlikely masterpiece *The Pigeon* (*c.* 1890) while Leo Paul Samuel Robert (1851–1923) somehow incorporated a bird's-eye view into his work. By the close of the nineteenth century, new techniques including photogravure and three-colour letterpress were coming onto the scene, as seen in Henry Eliot Howard's *The British Warblers* (1907–14).

Fine artists were also exploring new mediums and methods of mark-making, including Swede Bruno Liljefors's (1860–1939) dramatic oil paintings of golden eagles, Eurasian eagle owls and other birds of prey, and his as yet unmatched paintings of birds in flight. There was also Scottish artist Archibald Thorburn's watercolour portrayals of bird feathers and other fine features for Walter Swaysland's *Familiar Wild Birds* (1883) and Lord Lilford's *Coloured Figures of the Birds of the British Islands* (1885–98).

Birdwatching for the masses

Thorburn's latter set of illustrations reached an even wider audience when they were also used for Thomas Alfred Coward's *The Birds of the British Isles and Their Eggs* (1920) and for the pocket-sized *Observer's Book of British Birds/Observer's Book of Birds*, which sold millions of copies between 1939 and the 1970s. Thorburn's self-penned *British Birds* (1915–16) was also one of the first books to illustrate several related species of bird side by side, setting the scene for future field and identification guides.

Fellow artist George Edward Lodge also helped bring the wonder of birds and their habitats to the masses via his delightful paintings for David Bannerman's twelve-volume *Birds of the British Isles* (1953–63) as well as for numerous galleries and private collections. As did birds of prey expert Claude Gibney Davies and Marinus Adrianus Koekkoek, illustrators for *The Handbook of British Birds* (Witherby, Jourdain,

Ticehurst and Tucker, 1938–41) which, due to the clearly depicted plumage, habitat and the male, female and young of each species, became *the* handbook for a growing army of British ornithologists and birdwatchers.

This was joined by the American *Citizen Bird* (1923) dedicated to 'All boys and girls who love birds and wish to protect' them by Elliot Coues and Mable Wright, with enigmatic drawings by the bird painter and tireless traveller Louis Agassiz Fuertes. Soon to add to the roster were the similarly loved wood engravings (1869) of Allan Cyril Brooks, Allen William Seaby (1867–1953) and Charles Frederick Tunnicliffe, the latter of whom created dramatic engravings for Henry E. Williamson's classic tale of *Tarka the Otter* (1932).

Conservation aware

The ability to capture the 'jizz' or 'giss' of a bird – the overall impression of a bird from its shape, posture, flying style, size, colouration, voice, habitat and location – was now embraced by artists such as former cartoonist James Affleck Shepherd (1867–1946) and Eric Ennion (1900–81), a particularly skilled and patient observer of avian life. Many bird artists were also becoming increasingly concerned about, the conservation of wildlife. Leading figures include British painter and naturalist Sir Peter Markham Scott who contributed to *The Birds of the Western Palearctic* (1977) – a handbook of the birds of Europe, the Middle East and North Africa. Scott founded the Wildfowl and Wetland Trust in 1946 and helped found the World Wildlife Fund (now the Worldwide Fund for Nature) in 1961. Another example is Roger Tory Peterson (see page 327), author and illustrator of the *Guide to Birds* (1934), and hailed as the first modern field guide, who was one of the founding inspirations for the twentieth-century environmental movement.

Artists and illustrators such as David Allen Sibley (see page 328) and Jane Kim (see page 330) have then brought the art of ornithology into the twentieth and twenty-first centuries,

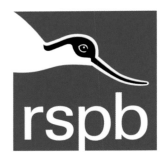

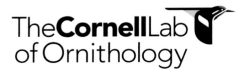

via *The Sibley Guide to Birds* (2000) and Kim's evolutionary *The Wall of Birds* (2015) mural, commissioned by The Cornell Lab of Ornithology in Ithaca, New York.

Figures such as American Modernist artist Charley Harper (page 362) and British bird artists and ornithologists Robert Gillmor (see page 366) and Matt Sewell (see page 329) have also popularized birding via their stylized yet duly observed depictions of our feathered friends. Gillmor's contribution is particularly important for his iconic rendering of an avocet for the RSPB logo, as well as numerous illustrations for books, magazines and exhibitions.

Soaring into the twenty-first century

Today, there are numerous ways to capture the identifying features and spirit of birds from photography and film to contemporary painting and sculpture, printmaking and craft. The invention of photography in 1839, and most especially portable gadgets such as the Kodak Box Brownie, introducing snapshots to the masses from 1900, offered

Top Current RSPB logo. Reproduced by permission of RSPB, © 2020 All rights reserved. Source: RSPB **Bottom** Current Cornell Lab of Ornithology Logo. See the Useful Resources section at the end of this book for further details on these organizations and more, aimed at promoting understanding and conservation of the birds of the world.

new ways to share images of birds from the pioneering work of early English wildlife photographer Eric Hosking (see page 346) and the high-tech hide observations of Bence Máté (see page 356) to Leila Jeffreys' (see page 354) portraits of parrots and pigeons or Thomas Lohr's zoomed-in photos of wings, bellies, and other bird parts (see page 355).

International photography competitions such as Wildlife Photographer of the Year and Bird Photographer of the Year (see page 343) have helped to inspire new and innovative ways to portray birds and the various aspects of their lives while photographic bird identification guides now also sit alongside still-vital illustrated ones. *Collins Life-Size Birds* (Paul Sterry and Rob Read, William Collins, 2016) is a new addition to this beautiful flock.

The advent of the moving image in the late nineteenth century and, more recently, digitalized cinematography, has also inspired such mind-blowing avian insights as David Attenborough's *The Life of Birds* (1998), bringing the sights, sounds and weird and wonderful habits of birds from around the world directly into people's homes (see page 348). Other notable documentaries include *Winged Migration* (2001), a bird's-eye view offered by *Earthflight* (2011–12) and Luc Jacquet's award-winning *March of the Penguins* (2005), illustrating the heart-warming mating rituals and the quest to survive of emperor penguins in the frozen landscape of the South Pole.

The depiction of birds in fine art moved on from the stilted poses of still lifes and classically themed landscapes of the seventeenth century to include Pablo Picasso's iconic paintings and drawings of doves (see page 336); Constantin Brancusi's pared back bronze and marble representations of soaring birds (see page 338); Georges Braque's childlike collages and lithographs of birds in flight (see page 334), and Frida Kahlo's multiple self-portraits with her menagerie of parrots (see page 340). More recent explorations include Mark

Dion's giant walk-in aviary known as *The Library for the Birds* and the background flora and fauna of Kehinde Wiley's arresting portraits.

Last but not least, the aesthetic and symbolic qualities of birds have also been particularly inspiring for printmakers around the world and through time: the poetic tradition of pairing birds and flowers in what is known as Japanese *kacho-e* (see page 333) by artists such as Kitagawa Utamaro, Utagawa Hiroshige and Katsushika Hokusai; the decorative designs of William Morris and C.F.A. Voysey (see page 360) segueing into Art Nouveau designs; or the linocuts of Rachel Newling (see page 368) and Angela Harding (see page 370). Artists such as Taiichiro Yoshida (see page 372), Andy Singleton and Diana Beltran Herrera also enthuse with their bird-inspired artworks crafted from metal, feathers and paper.

While humans may never have the physiological power of flight we can certainly observe birds exercising theirs – via 40,000 years or more of bird art as well as in our backyards – and imagine what it feels like to soar high above it all.

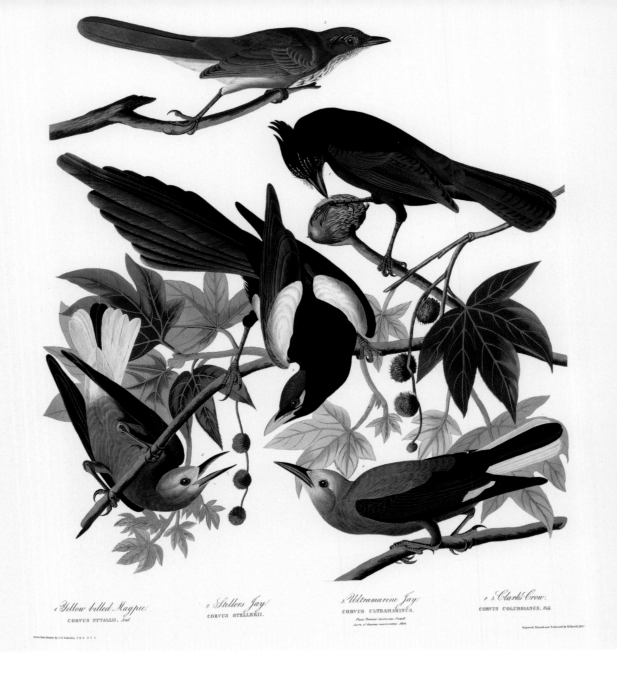

ORNITHOLOGICAL ART AND ILLUSTRATION

Thanks to esteemed ornithologists, natural historians and writers such as Jonathan Elphick (*Birds: The Art of Ornithology*, Natural History Museum, 2014) and Roger J. Lederer (*The Art of the Bird*, University of Chicago Press, 2019) the many-feathered history of ornithological art is finally being given the platform it deserves. From celebrated works such as James Audubon's *Birds of America* to the lesser-spotted forerunners of today's bird identification guides or conservational works, these combined volumes reveal as much about our past and present human nature as they do about the lives of what now amounts to nearly 10,000 known birds, plus all those that were sadly left behind.

John James Audubon

(1785–1851)

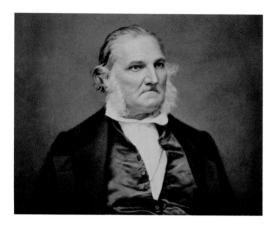

What makes this stunning portal into the natural world even more intriguing is the complex backstory of its creator, self-taught naturalist, painter John James Audubon.

Born in the French colony of Saint Domingue (now Haiti), the illegitimate son of French sea captain and plantation owner Jean Audubon and his chambermaid and mistress Jeanne Rabin (who died during his infancy), the young Audubon was first raised by Sanitte Bouffard, the mixed-race mother of John's half-sister Rose. When the slaves of the island began to revolt, Jean moved his children to Nantes, France, where they then became the wards of his French wife, Madame Bouffard. To avoid conscription into Emperor Napoleon's army at the age of eighteen, he was then sent to America, taking up residence on the family owned estate at Mill Grove (now in the village of Audubon), near Philadelphia. Not only did this opportunity give him the chance to make his own fortune and meet his wife Lucy Bakewell, the 130-acre (53-ha) grounds were a paradise for indulging childhood passions for nature, birds and art. Developing the first known system of ringing birds to track them, by tying strings around eastern Phoebes, and learning to set specimens for drawings took his avian interests to a new level.

Life as a tradesman eventually led him down the Ohio River to western Kentucky where he took up

residence in an abandoned log cabin and set up a dry goods store, hunting, fishing and building up an impressive portfolio of bird drawings in his spare time – although 200 of these were at one point eaten by rats. Although relatively successful, when hard times hit due to rising tensions with the British, he was briefly jailed for bankruptcy. He began drawing deathbed portraits and briefly worked as the first employee of the Museum of Natural History in Cincinnati to pay his way.

To Audubon this was obviously a pivotal moment, where he decided that he may as well follow his true calling rather than prop up a failing business. Leaving his stalwart wife, behind with their two sons, and a new breadwinning role as tutor to wealthy plantation owners, he set off in 1820 down the Mississippi River – with nothing but his assistant Joseph Mason, a gun, his artist's materials and survival skills picked up from Native American communities – to depict all of North America's birdlife with eventual publication in mind.

Audubon's risk paid off. Although away from his young family for months at a time, and rebuffed by some of America's leading scientists for being nothing more than a romantic backcountry upstart presenting birds in unnecessarily dramatic poses, his work was met with high praise across the Atlantic at the height of Europe's Romantic era. Touring England and Scotland in 1926 with 300 drawings to hand, he managed to raise enough funds to publish his work via advance subscriptions, exhibitions, oil painting exhibitions and specimen skins.

Originally engraved by Robert Havell Jnr in aquatint on 'Double Elephant' paper, with 'Ornithological Biographies' of each species later added by Scottish ornithologist and artist William MacGillivray (1796–1852), Audubon's *Birds of America* is now hailed as one of the world's greatest books and works of art of all time. As a keen observer of birds and other wildlife, an early pioneer for the conservation of nature and a man of legendary strength and endurance, his legacy also continues via the crucial work of the National Audubon Society, working in the United States and beyond to protect birds and their habitats, now and for the future.

Opposite *Yellow Billed Magpie, Stellars Joy, Ultramarine Jay and Clark's Crow* from John James Audubon's *Birds of America* 1827–39) **Top** 'American Woodsman' John James Audubon (1785–1851)

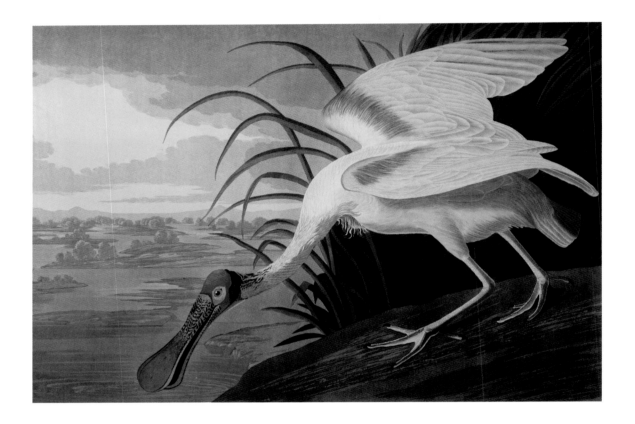

This page *Roseate Spoonbill (Platalea leucoradia)* and **Opposite page** *Snowy Owl (Nyctea scandiaca)*, produced as hand-engraved plates of John James Audubon's original watercolours for his *Birds of America* (1827–39)

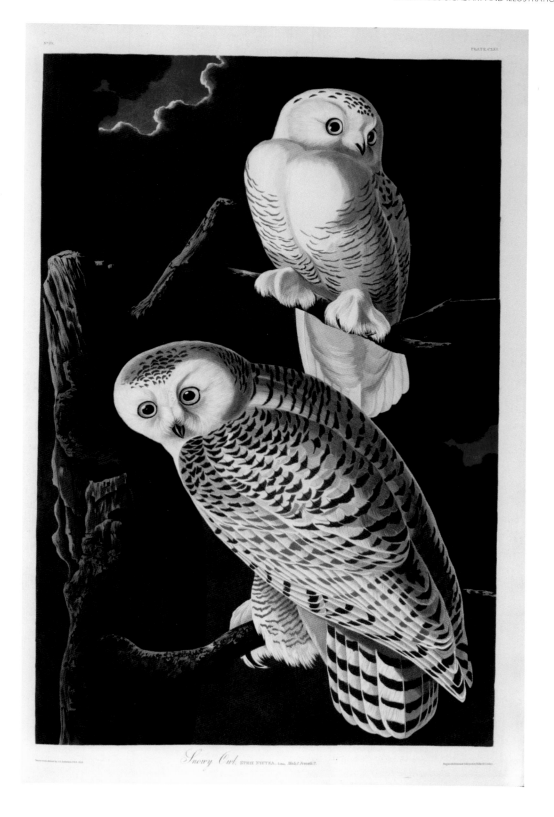

Snowy Owl. STRIX NYCTEA, Linn. Male, 1. Female, 2.

John Gould *(1804–81)*
and Elizabeth Gould *(1804–41)*

Often referred to as 'John Gould and his wife Elizabeth', this ground-breaking couple is jointly responsible for some of the Victorian era's most celebrated illustrated monographs on birds and are, thankfully, now credited as so.

The son of a gardener, a career he also initially pursued, it was John Gould's skill in the art of taxidermy that led to his making, becoming the first curator and preserver at the Museum of the Zoological Society in London. While there he was inspired to compile his first avian publication, *A Century of Birds from the Himalaya Mountains* (1830–2) based on specimens of birds' skins that he was given to mount and curate. John commissioned Elizabeth to draw the illustrations and create lithographs for eighty plates of the book, based on his notes and sketches.

A gifted artist, Elizabeth Gould (née Coxon) was born in Ramsgate into a relatively well-off military family. Marrying John at the age of twenty-four helped her escape a temporary role as a governess and provided a suitable outlet for her creative talents. She went on to illustrate and create lithographs for *Birds of Europe* (1832–7) and *The Birds of Australia* (1840–8) – both also featuring work by a young Edward Lear (see page 359) and part three (the birds volume) of *The Zoology of the Voyage of the H.M.S. Beagle* (1841). For the latter, Elizabeth was drafted in to illustrate Charles Darwin's now famous 'finches' after John Gould helped identify and categorize them.

The Birds of Australia was a particularly landmark publication in Victorian ornithology, featuring some 681 avian species, more than 300 of them new to Western science at the time. The trip forced Elizabeth to leave her young children for two years however, and she sadly died not long after the birth of her eighth child. Although she didn't live to see her Antipodean observations in print, her legacy of more than 800 bird illustrations survives to tell her tale. One of the birds she drew, Mrs Gould's Sunbird (*Aethopyga gouldiae*), is named in her honour. Various species of bird including Gould's Toucanet (*Selenidera gouldii*) are named after John Gould.

Top *Common Cactus Finch (Geospiza scandens) from the* Zoology of the Voyage of the H.M.S. Beagle *(1841)* **Bottom** *Western Wattlebird (Anthochaera lunulata) and* **Opposite** *Gouldian Finch (Erythrura gouldiae), both from* The Birds of Australia *(1840–8)*

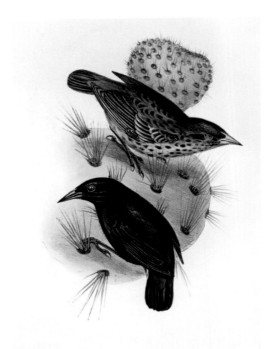

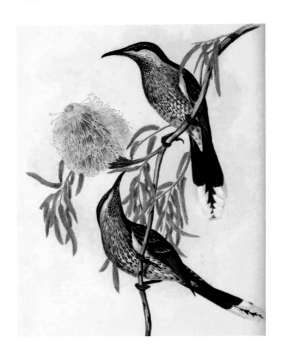

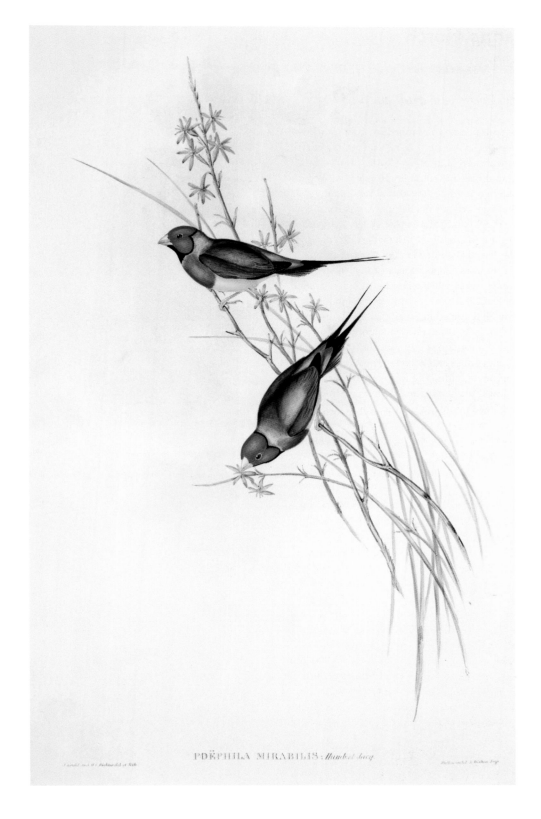

PDÉPHILA MIRABILIS: *Humbert-Jacq.*

Marianne North

(1840–90)

'I am a very wild bird, and like liberty,'

penned botanical artist Marianne North in her *Being the Autobiography of Marianne North* (edited by her sister and published in 1892, after her death), summing up an extraordinary life rubbing shoulders with the largely male world of botany and quite literally painting her way around the natural world. Most well known for the 832 oil paintings patch-worked across the walls of the Marianne North Gallery, opened in 1882 in the Royal Botanic Gardens at Kew, and for her prolific illustrative depictions of the plant kingdom, often made while traversing arduous terrain, a closer look at North's work also reveals numerous species of wildlife including small mammals, insects and birds. Thanks to these vividly coloured, richly backgrounded illustrations – showing a bird's habitat as well as its markings and habits – 'Parokeets of Madagascar' nestle within the long-leafed foliage of the 'Ordeal Plant or Tanghin' (*Cerbera manghas*), 'Sugar Birds' feed upon and nest near the 'Fruit of Cythere' (*Spondias dulcis*) in the Seychelles, 'Humming Birds' (*Selasphorus rufus*) congregate on the petals of a 'California Dogwood' (*Cornus Nuttalli)* and 'Honeyflowers' (*Protea mellifera*) attract 'Honeysuckers' in South Africa. At a time when many women spent much of their life indoors, this hyper-real snapshot of life on Earth provided breathtaking escapism not yet afforded by the wonders of colour photography or today's social media scroll.

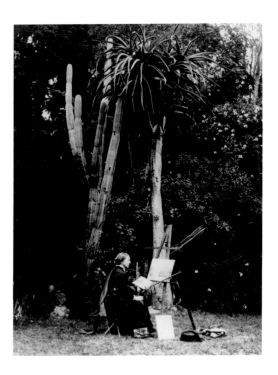

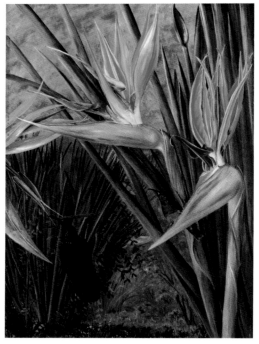

Top Marianne North painting the flora and fauna of South Africa c. 1883
Bottom Avian life beside bird of paradise blooms in Marianne North's *Streitzia and Sugar Birds*

Roger Tory Peterson

(1908–96)

*'Woods! Birds! Flowers! Here are the
makings of a great naturalist.'*

So read the description of American naturalist,
ornithologist, illustrator, educator – and one of the
founding inspirations of the twentieth-century
environmental movement – Roger Tory Peterson in
his Class of 1925 yearbook. Although often teased for
his intense passion for nature, he found an ally in his
seventh-grade teacher who signed up the whole class
to the Junior Audubon club and often taught her
students outside. As a budding art student Peterson
then used the subject of birds to practise art and
photography with submissions to ornithological art
competitions, published articles in *Bird-lore* magazine
and membership of America's oldest ornithological
organization, the Nuttal Club in Boston, winning him
acclaim and contacts. One such meeting with Francis
H. Allen, an editor at Houghton Miffin Company, led
to the publication of the seminal *A Field Guide to Birds*
(1934; sixth edition 2008), inspiring a brand new
species of layman-friendly guidebook using the
Peterson Identification System for the shape, pattern
and field marks of birds – in this case a wide range of
hand-drawn and painted birds of North America – as
opposed to a phylogenetic one, with clear notes on
bird sounds and the most likely habitat and season
in which to spot them. A truly ground-breaking
invention, Peterson Field Guides are now available for
spotting insects, plants and other natural phenomena
as well as birds of the world.

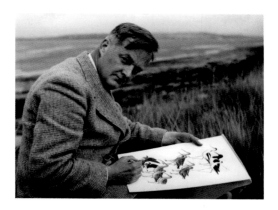

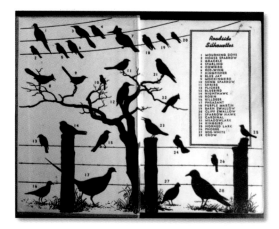

Top Dr Roger Tory Peterson in the field on Hilbre Island, 1952 **Bottom**
End pages of Peterson's *A Field Guide to Birds Western Birds* (1947)

David Allen Sibley

(1961–present)

'Birds make any place a chance for discovery, they make a garden seem wild, they are a little bit of wilderness coming into a city park, and for a birdwatcher every walk is filled with anticipation,'

wrote American ornithologist and largely self-taught illustrator David Allen Sibley for an article on 'Why Do Birds Matter' for Audubon.com in 2013. The son of a Yale ornithologist, Sibley's fascinated appreciation of birds was set at an early age. Childhood birding trips in Connecticut inspired the drawing of birds, which were soon accompanied by notes on the natural history of each species. The seed for the wildly successful *The Sibley Guide to Birds* (Alfred A. Knopf, 2000) was born. Its publication defined a new era in identification of birds in the field. Taking over six years to complete, Sibley set himself the challenge of representing hundreds (810 in total) of native and visiting North American bird species – not just as one image each, but with additional illustrations and layout and text options for every significant plumage variation, flight from above and below and the complete range of vocalizations for each species and all significant subspecies variations. A second edition, published in spring 2014 included 600 completely new images, 111 additional species and more than 3,000 revisions – each bird painstakingly hand drawn and coloured in gouache, from life.

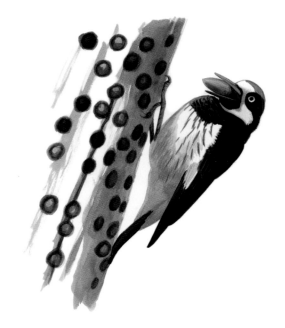

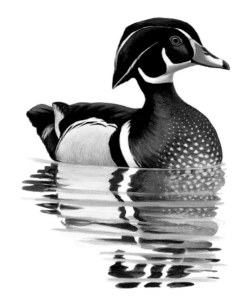

Top *Acorn Woodpecker* and **Bottom** *Wood Duck* from David Allen Sibley's *What It's Like To Be A Bird* (Alfred A. Knopf, 2020)

Matt Sewell

(1976–present)

Every generation has their bird-spotting or inspirational bird book. For British birders finding a love of ornithology somewhere around the 2010s, that accolade quite possibly belongs to Matt Sewell's *Our Garden Birds* (Ebury Press, 2012). Featuring stylized watercolours of fifty-two of Britain's best-loved birds – one for each week of the year – alongside innovative and witty descriptions inspired by Sewell's 'Bird of the Week' blog posts for arts-nature-culture collective Caught by the River, the book quickly became a cult hit. Sewell's parallel passion for birds and street art, plus a stint at art school and as a commercial illustrator, shines through via his bright, quirky watercolour renderings. Sketched as quickly as possible to help capture the over-riding character traits of each feathered friend, the science is still there – in directly observed and researched markings and via scientific species names allowing those wanting to know more to cross-reference with more traditional guides. For those sticking with Sewell's charming foray along the flight paths of the British Isles, further publications include *Our Songbirds* (Ebury Press, 2013), *Our Woodland Birds* (Ebury Press, 2014), *A Charm of Goldfinches & Other Collective Nouns* (Ebury Press, 2016) and the perfectly pocket-sized *Spotting and Jotting Guide* (Ebury Press, 2015), in addition to worldwide art exhibitions and commissions for the RSPB, the National Trust and the Victoria and Albert Museum.

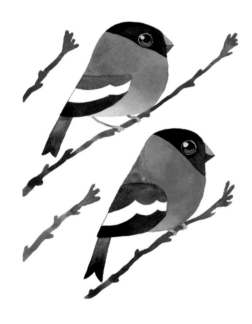

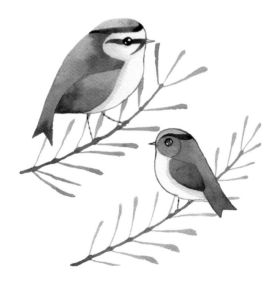

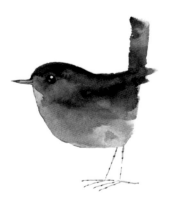

Top Bullfinch couple **Bottom left** Wren **Bottom right** Goldcrest and Firecrest, all from *Our Garden Birds* (Ebury Press, 2012) © Matt Sewell

Jane Kim

(1981–present)

'One Planet, 243 Families, 375 Million Years,'

reads the strapline of *The Wall of Birds* (Jane Kim with Thayer Walker, Harper Design, 2018), a sumptuously produced book, celebrating artist Jane Kim's remarkable mural of the same name, produced for The Cornell Lab of Ornithology in Ithaca, New York. Commissioned by the lab's director John W. Fitzpatrick who happened across some of Kim's mural work in *National Geographic* magazine, the mural stretches 24 metres (78 feet) by 11 metres (35 feet) and depicts 270 life-sized and scientifically accurate bird species and their relatives, simultaneously telling the story of their evolution and diversity.

A graduate of the Rhode Island School of Design, Kim then received a master's certificate in scientific illustration and won an internship at Cornell's prestigious ornithology department in Ithaca, New York. Having walked past the mural space numerous times – then a long stretch of wall painted a drab olive green above a flight of stairs – and already won acclaim for her large-scale work such as *Migrating Mural* (2012) along a 193-kilometre (120-mile) stretch of California's Highway 395, the commission was a dream come true, spawning further nature-inspired murals under the guise of InkDwell studio.

A breathtaking example of science meeting art, Kim had to submit every sketch of her selected birds to a team of experts for an accuracy review before charcoal drawings were then used to create to-scale renderings. Colours were then applied directly with help from a specially created Avian Pantone Chart featuring such particulars as Finch Feet (a peachy mauve), Albatross Light (a light greyish blue) and the ubiquitous Cassowary Neck (a soft ocean blue). Extinct species including relatives such as dinosaurs were painted in a ghostly greyscale.

All in all, the evolutionary mural took two and a half years to complete, and depicts species from every modern bird family and across every continent, from the tiny spatuletail hummingbird to the 9-metre-long (30-foot-long) *Yutyrannus* (ancestor of the first feathered dinosaur), with the National Audubon Society dubbing Kim the Michelangelo of the avian Vatican: soaring praise indeed.

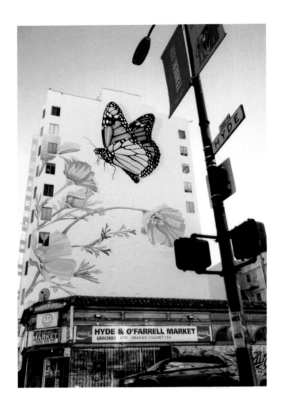

Top San Francisco's section of the *Migrating Mural* by Jane Kim, Ink Dwell Studio pays homage to the Monarch butterfly **Opposite page top** Artist Jane Kim at work on her *The Wall of Birds* mural at the Cornell Lab of Ornithology, Ithaca, New York **Opposite page bottom** Detail of *The Wall of Birds* mural by Jane Kim, Ink Dwell Studio featuring a White-necked Rockfowl, a Yellow-billed Oxpecker, an African Finfoot, a Green Woodhoopoe, a Pin-tailed Wydah and the foot of a Secretary-bird

Find out more about Jane Kim at www.inkdwell.com.
To explore *The Wall of Birds* online visit:
https://academy.allaboutbirds.org/features/wallofbirds/

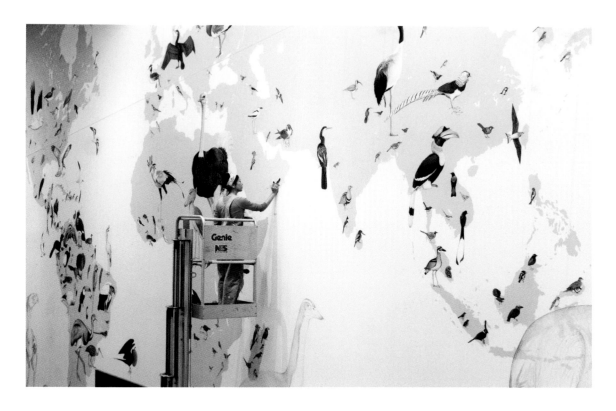

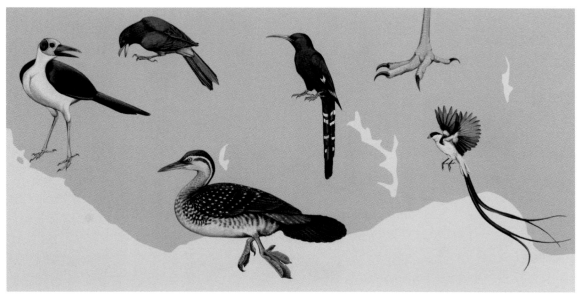

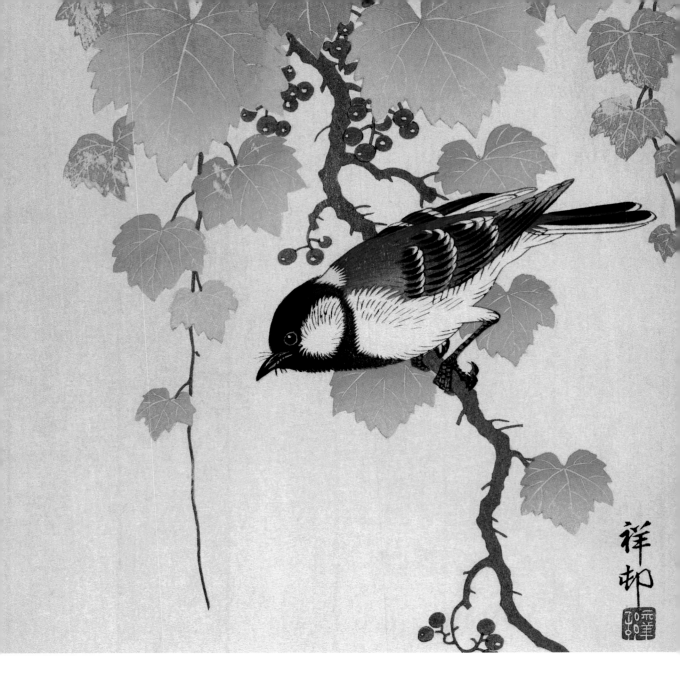

PAINTING AND SCULPTURE

The human relationship with birds and their breadth of species can also be traced through various depictions of avian life in painting and sculpture, from early Australian cave paintings dating back an estimated 40,000 years and spiritual homages to birds and flowers from the Far East, to the twentieth-century works of art history giants such as Pablo Picasso, Georges Braques and Constantin Brancusi, and the more recent explorations of Mark Dion and Tracey Emin. Such works remind us of the symbolism, expressive energy and survival instincts of birds, as well as their beautiful feathers, fascinating form and enviable power of flight.

Kacho-e

(bird-and-flower print, 16th–20th century)

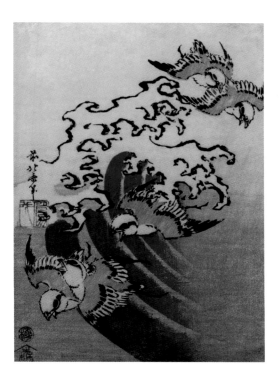

A great tit sits on a plum branch (*Great-tit on a Plum Branch,* Utagawa Hiroshige, *c.*1830s), barn swallows chat chatter in a cherry tree (*Barn Swallows on Weeping Cherry,* Ohara Koson, 1910), a blue bird perches with pride within the burnished foliage of an autumnal acer (*Blue Bird in Autumn,* Ito Sozan, *c.*1910s), a finch prepares to take flight from the stem of a hibiscus flower (*Finch and Hibiscus,* Utagawa Hokusai, *c.*1830) and pairings of birds burst into poetic song (from Kitagawa Utamaro's *Myriad Birds,* 1790). Centuries of artistic and spiritual Chinese and Japanese tradition pervade these beautiful, fleeting moments in the life of flora and fauna – specifically the depiction of 'birds and flowers' – captured by some of the most iconic Asian artists of their time.

Although scenes of nature are centuries old in both Chinese and Japanese art, the specific tradition of *kacho-e,* focusing specifically on bird and flower motifs, elevated the avian world to soaring new heights. A subgenre of the *ukiyo-e* style of Japanese woodblock print and painting popularized in the Edo period (1603–1868), such scenes presented an alternative to the usual play and entertainment-themed 'Pictures of the Floating World' of female beauties, kabuki actors, sumo wrestlers, historic folk tales, travel scenes and erotica. Living in the moment, *kacho-e* style allowed the viewer to be transported into a world beyond everyday fracas, a world of blossom-strewn, gently warbling peace and tranquillity. Look once and see a bird on a flower, look again and become part of that scene.

The eighteenth and nineteenth centuries are considered by many to be the 'golden age' of *kacho-e.* One such master of the woodblock print Kitagawa Utamaro, already well known for his images of beautiful women and courtesans, produced several nature-inspired collections of prints paired with romantic poetry including his *Myriad Birds* (1790). Kitao Masayoshi was commissioned to interpret a pre-existing set of Chinese bird-and-flower hand-scroll paintings, and produced his softly coloured

Opposite page Detail of *Great Tit on Paulownia Branch* (c.1925–36) by Ohara Koson (1877–1945) **Right** Detail of *Waves and Birds* (c.1825) by Katsushika Hokusai (1760–1849)

Compendium of Birds Imported from Overseas (1762). Utagawa Hiroshige, most famous for his collection *One Hundred Famous Views of Edo* (1856–9), added to his portrayal of landscapes, temples, shrines and teahouses with deftly painted and coloured, vertical-format depictions of finches, long-tailed tits, songbirds, kingfishers, sparrows, parrots, pheasants and waterfowl among wild roses, creeping vines, blossoms and grasses. While Katsushika Hokusai (1760–1849), best known for his *Thirty-six Views of Mount Fuji* (*c.*1830–2), including the internationally iconic colour-print masterpiece *The Great Wave off Kanagawa,* also produced stylized prints of birds at rest and in flight.

Moving into the twentieth century and the Shin Hanga (new print) era, Ohara Koson (1877–1945) – also signing under the names Shoson and Hoson – is the undisputed master of *kacho-e,* proliferating what was by this time a ready market with literally hundreds of bird and flower prints. Working for renowned publishers such as Watanabe Shozaburo alongside other *kacho-e* artists of note, including Imao Keinen (1845–1924) and Ito Sozan (1884–*c.*1926), his work was often exported to the United States and Europe where the highly decorative, characterful and tranquil nature of the works held much appeal.

Georges Braque

(1882–1963)

Renowned alongside Picasso as the co-founder of Cubism, the great French painter, collagist and sculptor Georges Braque first began to experiment with the motif of birds in the 1930s as a way to illustrate the Cubist philosophical investigation into differences between reality and representation. In Braque's *Quatre Oiseaux* (1950), for example, are the ghostly birds floating by real or a depiction of a pre-painted bird on a canvas against a studio wall? And in later works such as the mesmerizing pink-and-black lithograph *L'Oiseau Noir et L'Oiseau Blanc* (1960), how much is this work an image of birds and how much a representation of the artist's personal artistic quest? It's also notable that Braque made many of his bird works towards the end of his life and certainly with a more simplified, childlike style than earlier heavily Cubist creations. This was a turnaround in focus to themes of flight and transcendence that marry perfectly with his perpetually enquiring refusal to rest on the wing but also his nearing departure from this world. Famously commissioned to paint a ceiling fresco at the Louvre Museum in 1952, the Salle Henri II is now adorned with his soaring *Deux Oiseaux* against a bright blue sky, a bold rejection of the oppressive order, rigour and symmetry of the pre-war world as well as a brilliant, colour-injecting celebration of nature. As quoted in Alex Danchev's biography *Georges Braques, A Life* (New York, 2005),

> *'The bird is a summing up of all my art ... It is more than painting ... It's as if one heard the fluttering of wings.'*

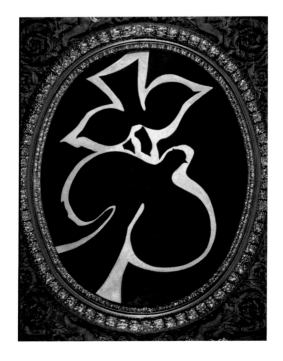

Top Georges Braque's soaring oil on canvas *Deux Oiseaux* (1953), painted on the ceiling of the Louvre Museum in Paris **Opposite page** The beautiful lithograph *L'Oiseau Noir et L'Oiseau Blanc* (1960) appeared as the frontispiece of *The Order of Birds* (1962), a book printed to commemorate Braque's 80th birthday

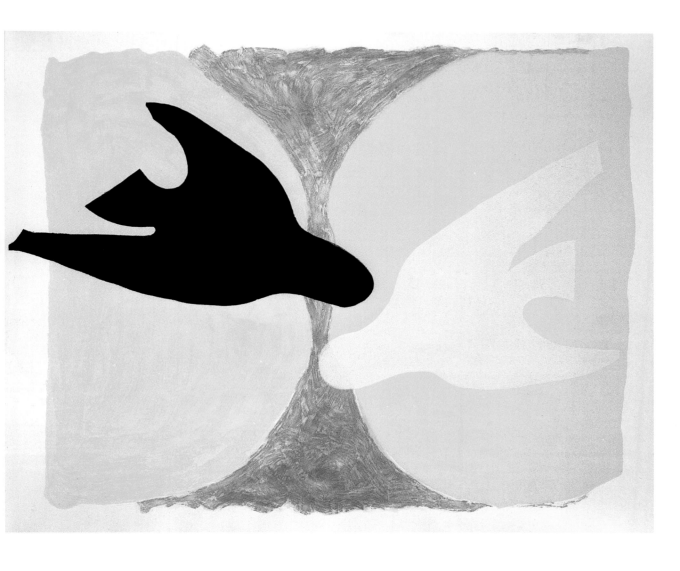

Pablo Picasso
(1881–1973)

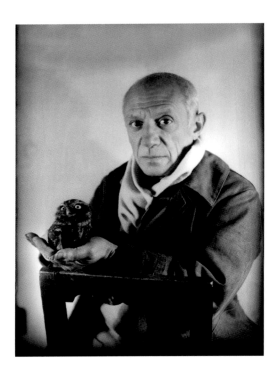

According to French painter and long-time partner of Picasso, Francoise Gilot, 'Pablo loved to surround himself with birds and animals. In general they were exempt from the suspicion with which he regarded his other friends.' Studio companions thus included a dachshund called Lump, an injured owl from Antibes, canaries, pigeons and doves – a particular love of birds inherited from his artist father José Ruiz y Blasco, who specialized in the painting of them.

Picasso's earliest bird-inspired work is an oil painting entitled *Child Holding a Dove* (1901) created when he was just nineteen years of age. One of his last is the monumental sculpture known as the *Chicago Picasso* (1967), speculatively thought to be an abstract portrayal of beast, bird or possibly female muse, or a chimera of all three. The most well known is *La Colombe* (The Dove) selected by the poet, surrealist, and Communist Louis Aragon to illustrate the poster of the first World Congress of Partisans for Peace held in Paris in 1949. A simple yet striking composition of a white dove on a black background, masterfully rendered in black in wash, it symbolizes peace and resilience in response to the fascist-led atrocities of the Spanish Civil War and the Second World War. In this case, Picasso's dove is a portrait of a snow-white Milanese pigeon gifted by fellow artist, friend, and lifelong rival, Henri Matisse (1869–1954). Paying a final homage to the master of the paper-cut, *The Studio (Pigeons)*, in 1957, is a wistful scene of an open window looking out upon the Mediterranean, surrounded by doves. Picasso's *Dove of Peace* series, meanwhile, includes two of his most recognizable works, one being a simple graphic line drawing of a bird with a twig (1949), the other a similarly abstract version with colourful flowers made the same year and used as the emblem of the World Peace Council to this day.

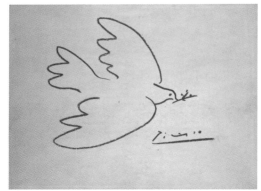

Top The Spanish artist Pablo Picasso in his workshop in Antibes (1946) with his pet Little Owl, Ubu **Bottom** *Dove* (pastel on paper, 1949), one of several iconic images produced by Picasso of this symbolic bird **Opposite page** *Picasso's Child Holding A Dove* (oil on canvas, 1901), now residing in the National Gallery in London and produced when Picasso was just 19 years old, illustrates a love of birds from a young age

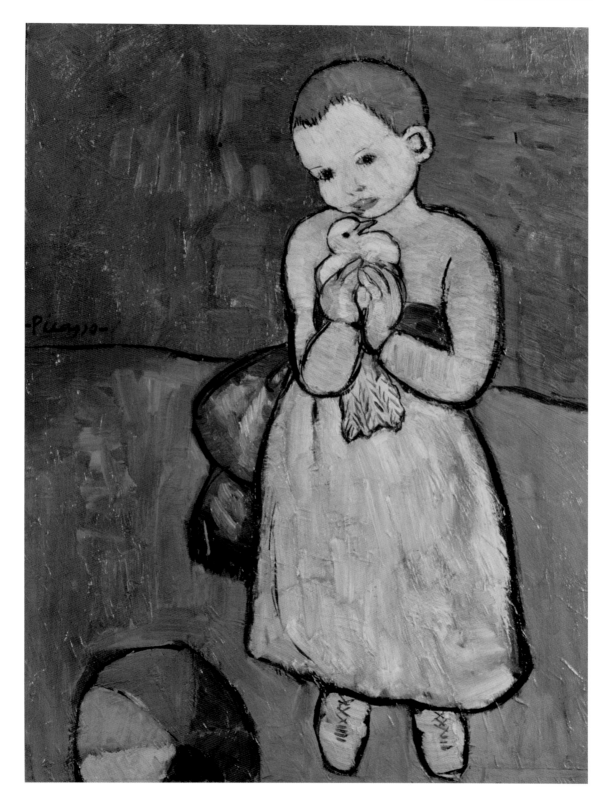

Constantin Brancusi

(1876–1957)

Many artists have become preoccupied with the theme of a bird in flight. For France-based Romanian sculptor Constantin Brancusi, his pared back representations of soaring birds – a series of sixteen versions of an initial *Bird in Space* (1923) – not only paid homage to the wonders of the avian world, they questioned the very nature and meaning of art. Seeking to convey the essential nature of a bird elegantly soaring upward in flight, he intuitively eliminated wings, feathers or an obvious beak in favour of an unfettered thrusting column of bronze or marble, balanced on a slender conical footing, swollen at its centre and sliced cleanly off at the top in a slanted oval plan. Movement rather than physical attribute being the driving force, the title of the work serves to enlighten the viewer should they query the inspiration behind the piece.

To question the artistic merit of such a beautiful and much-heralded piece of sculpture today seems unthinkable, but Brancusi's Bird in Space series was once the subject of a court dispute on exactly that. Arriving in New York from France in 1926 on board the steamship *Paris*, final destination the Brummer Gallery as part of an exhibition of works curated by Brancusi's friend and advocate Marcel Duchamp, a 1926 bronze version of *Bird in Space* (now in the collection of the Seattle Art Museum) was stopped at customs as not fitting the tax-exempt description of sculptural art. That is, 'reproductions by carving of casting, imitations of natural objects, chiefly the human form'. Refusing to let it into the country without a forty per cent 'manufactured metal objects' taxation charge, it was eventually released on bond under the category of 'Kitchen Utensils and Hospital Supplies'. Customs continued to contest its validity as art and the issue went to court, with artists and art experts testifying both for and against the defence.

As director of the Brooklyn Museum at the time, William Henry Fox, affirmed, 'It [*Birds in Space*] has the suggestion of flight, it suggests grace, aspiration, vigour, coupled with speed in the spirit of strength, potency, beauty, just as a bird does'. Brancusi's sixteen birds now thankfully reside in many of the leading galleries of North America and the world.

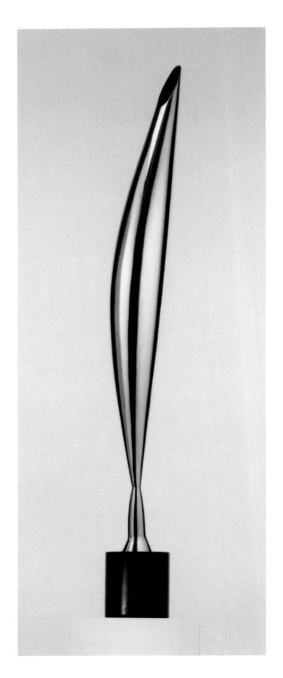

Above *Bird in Space* (polished bronze, 1924), one of sixteen versions of this game-changing series of artworks by Romanian sculptor Constantin Brancusi. Now residing in the Philadelphia Museum of Art, the soaring sculpture epitomises a bird in flight

Barbara Hepworth

(1903–1975)

In 1961, Yorkshire-born sculptor Barbara Hepworth, was invited by the iconic British department store John Lewis to design a sculpture for the façade of their newly restored flagship branch on Oxford Street, London, on the premise that the work should 'have some content that expresses the idea of common ownership and common interests in a partnership of thousands of workers'. Hepworth originally submitted a piece called *Three Forms in Echelon* but John Lewis wanted something more 'Hepworth'. The accepted proposal, a 5.8-metre (19 foot) aluminium cast *Winged Figure*, created in 1961–2 and based on an earlier work from 1957, *Winged Figure I*, and pen and ink drawings now found in The Hepworth Wakefield Gallery, is now one of her most iconic pieces of art as well as a much-loved twentieth-century London landmark. 'I think one of our universal dreams is to move in air and water without the resistance of our human legs,' she explained. 'I wanted to evoke this sense of freedom. If the Winged Figure in Oxford Street gives people a sense of being air-borne in rain and sunlight and nightlight I will be very happy.' Indeed flight and birds were a life-long pre-occupation for Hepworth, be it 'the weight, poise and curvature of the ovoid as a basic form' in works such as *Bird Form* (1963/8/9) or the anatomical and metaphysical properties of wings in *Stringed Figure (Curlew), Version I* (1956) or *Version II* (1959).

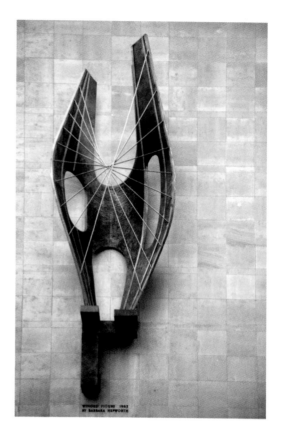

Above *Winged Figure* (1961–2) by the British artist Barbara Hepworth exists as both iconic artwork and landmark upon the flagship John Lewis store in London

Frida Kahlo

(1907–54)

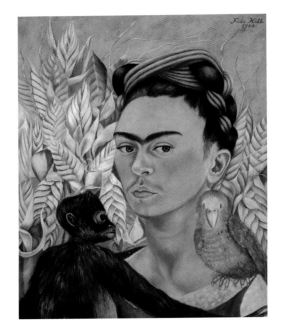

Like Pablo Picasso (see page 336), Mexican artist Frida Kahlo shared her studio with a menagerie of pets including parakeets, macaws, hens, sparrows, an eagle not so eloquently referred to as Gertrudis Caca Blanca (Gertrude White Shit), a fawn called Granizo, a hairless Mexican *Xoloitzcuintle* (a breed of dog with an ancestry traceable back to the Aztecs) by the name of Mr Xoloti, a parrot called Bonito (who would perform tricks at the table for pats of butter) and a couple of spider monkeys known as Fulang Chang and Caimito de Guayabal. Following a case of polio as an infant, a life-changing bus accident as a teenager and subsequent health and reproductive problems throughout her adult life – not to mention a tumultuous marriage with fellow artist Diego Rivera – these treasured animals kept her company at her main residence of Casa Azul (the Blue House), brought her fleeting moments of joy and appeared in countless paintings, many of them self-portraits. Parrots are particularly present in her work – especially in the period following the death of her father and at the onset of intense physical pain – including *Self Portrait with Bonito* (1941), *Me and My Parrots* (also 1941) and *Self Portrait with Monkey and Parrot* (1942). Rather than detract from Kahlo, the parrots add weight to the strength of gaze, provide rich colour and texture and contribute to the folkloric symbolism, intimacy and self-analysis that pervade Kahlo's work. Birds of a feather as it were.

Above Mexican artist Frida Kahlo shared her studio with numerous pets, inspiring several paintings including *Self Portrait with Monkey and Parrot* (oil on masonite, 1942) as now found in the Museo de Arte Latinoamericano de Buenos Aires, Argentina

Karl Martens

(1956–present)

Swedish-American artist Karl Martens's exquisitely rendered watercolour paintings of birds of prey and waterfowl stem from many years of dedicated observation of the avian world. Having drawn and painted birds from childhood and previously created extremely detailed ornithological works, his winning approach no longer includes painting directly from life. Taking influence from both Eastern and Western philosophies, especially Zen Buddhist meditation, he now prefers to paint entirely from memory, applying watercolour from above onto handmade paper positioned on the floor of his studio. Using a selection of traditional Japanese and Chinese paintbrushes he then brings his birds and their typical habits and characters to life via sweeping washes and calligraphic brushstrokes until wings, breasts, tail feathers, beaks and colourful markings come together to make a whole. 'The best result is achieved when no thought is given to it; when the mind rests in emptiness and intuition takes over,' explains Martens, seeking out the emotional essence and intrinsic movement of each subject, from battling pigeons, inquisitive yet tentative wrens and proudly plumed kingfishers to soaring eagles, predatory kites and running mallards. By confronting the unexpected, the unexpected takes flight, delighting bird and art lovers around the world.

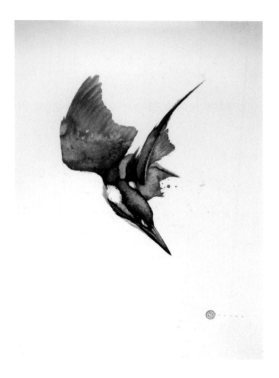

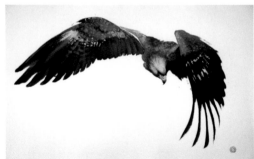

Top Swedish American artist Karl Martens uses sweeping washes and calligraphic brushstrokes to bring birds to life, such as *Kingfisher*, 2020 (52.07cm/20.5in × 36.8cm/14.5in, Watercolour on Arches Paper) and **Bottom** *Golden Eagle*, 2016 (74.9cm/39.5in × 149.8cm/59in, Watercolour on Arches paper)

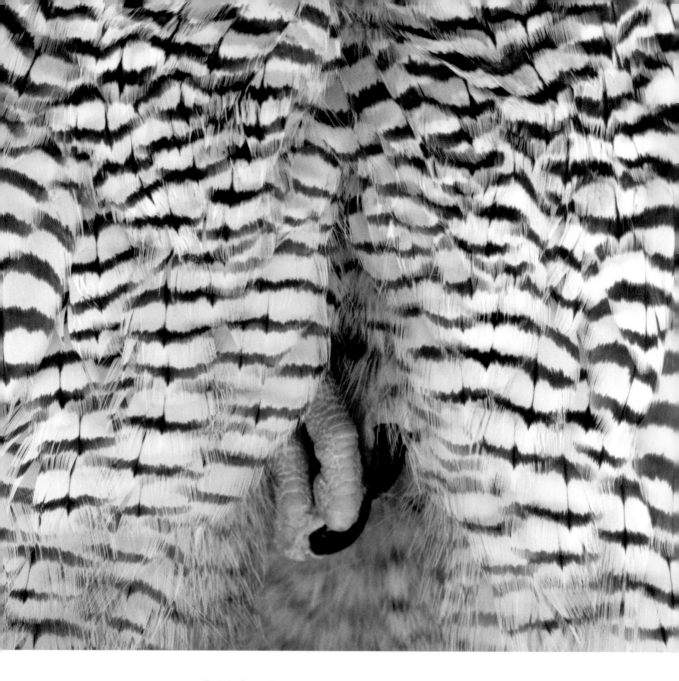

PHOTOGRAPHY AND FILM

The birth of practical photography in 1839, followed by motion picture cameras in the 1890s, provided huge potential for the documentation and expressive illustration of birds, although it would be some decades before technology allowed for the subtle approaches, shutter speed and zoom required for getting a good shot. From the first inspiring and impressively captured black-and-white images of Eric Hosking to the magnificence of full-colour, high-resolution digital artworks by award-winning bird photographers such as Bence Máté or Leila Jeffreys, the medium of film continues to stunningly capture the majesty of birds.

Bird Photographer of the Year

(BPOTY; 2014–present)

A Dalmatian pelican on Lake Kerkini in Greece runs towards the hopeful lens of award-winning photographer Caron Steele in *Dancing on Ice* (2019). Yellow reptilian-like feet peek out from the zoomed-in black-and-white belly feathers of a mature Northern Goshawk courtesy of Pål Hermansen's watchful eye and long lens. While an endangered black skimmer swoops low over water in Ocean City, New Jersey, in the hope of snapping up some tiny fish for its newborn chicks in an image taken from the perspective of a crouching and very patient Nikunj Patel. Each image is a snapshot into the fascinating world of birds, into the power and potential of modern technology and proof of the old adage that good things come to those who wait. Together, they mark five years of the Bird Photographer of the Year Award (BPOTY) in all its avian glory and photographic prowess.

Founded in 2014 by internationally renowned wildlife author and photographer Paul Sterry, nature image expert, author and photographer Rob Read and natural historian and conservationist Andrew Cleave MBE, BPOTY is now a popular highlight of wildlife and cultural calendars, featuring images from a global collective of amateur and professional photographers and birders, across a selection of inspiring categories: Attention to Detail, Best Portrait, Bird Behaviour, Birds in Flight, Birds in the Environment, Black and White, Creative Imagery, Garden and Urban Birds, Inspirational Encounters, Best Portfolio and Conservation Documentary. Judged by an evolving panel of naturalists, bird experts, passionate conservationists, top wildlife photographers and creatives, the call out culminates in a touring exhibition of the most captivating shots. Plus there's a collectable compendium of winners, runners-up and commended entries in the annual William Collins-produced *Bird Photographer of the Year* book.

By entering the competition, photographers not only gain recognition, a potential prize and show their passion for birds, part of the money raised via submission fees goes towards supporting vital work in bird conservation by organizations such as the British Trust for Ornithology, Wildlife Worldwide, Birdfair, the World Land Trust, the National Biodiversity Network and Hookpod. As such, the BPOTY team launched a new Conservation Documentary award for 2020, aimed at highlighting a bird-related conservation or environmental issue via a series of three to six photojournalistic images with extended captions to help the story unfold. Judged by legendary conservationist Mark Carwardine and environmental campaigner Mark Avery, entries for the category's launch included a tale about the loss of nesting habitat of swifts through modern building methods – a situation that could be addressed by factoring nesting sites into new builds – and the danger of major roads to low-flying barn owls scouring grass verges for food.

Indeed, the judges of BPOTY are testament to the quality of the entries, with past and present luminaries including English naturalist, nature photographer, presenter and author Chris Packham CBE, and award-winning wildlife photographers Brian E. Small and David Tipling. In Packham's own words, '[Birds] fly off, don't listen to a word you say and are a much-favoured subject in the wildlife photography genre – hence there is massive competition, making it hard to "say something new" with an image. But the winning image [of the Bird Photographer of the Year] exemplifies this art perfectly – a much photographed, familiar and accessible subject is represented in an entirely new and fabulously imaginative way.' With a Young Bird Photographer of the Year (YBPOTY) also open to young people of all ages up to eighteen, hopefully a new generation of birders and photographers can help celebrate and conserve birds well into the future.

Opposite page Detail of a stunning close up of a Northern Goshawk (*Accipter gentilis*) by Norwegian photographer Pål Hermansen, which won the 'Attention to Detail' category of the Bird Photographer of the Year (BPOTY) 2019

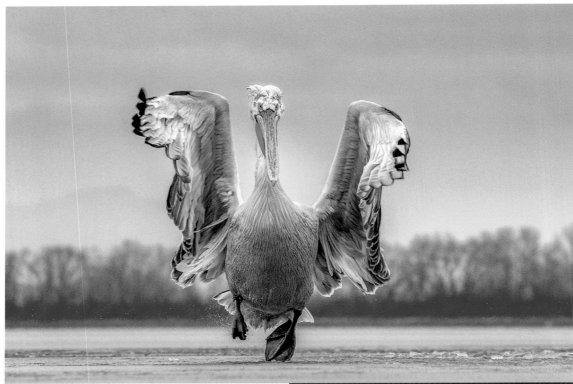

Top BPOTY's winning image 2019, *Dancing on Ice* (2019) by British photographer Caron Steele, captures a Dalmatian Pelican on a frozen Lake Kerkini in Greece **Bottom** BPOTY's 'Birds in Flight' winner 2019, a *Black Skimmer* taken in Ocean City, by American photographer Nikunj Patel

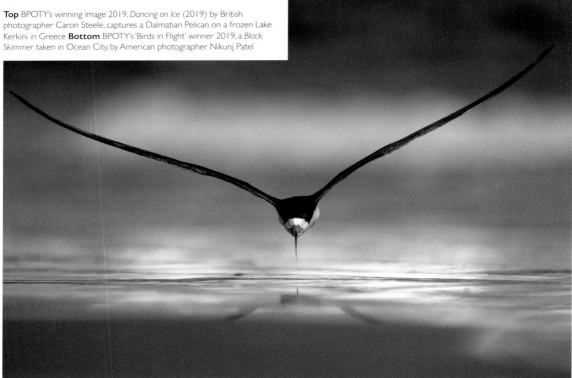

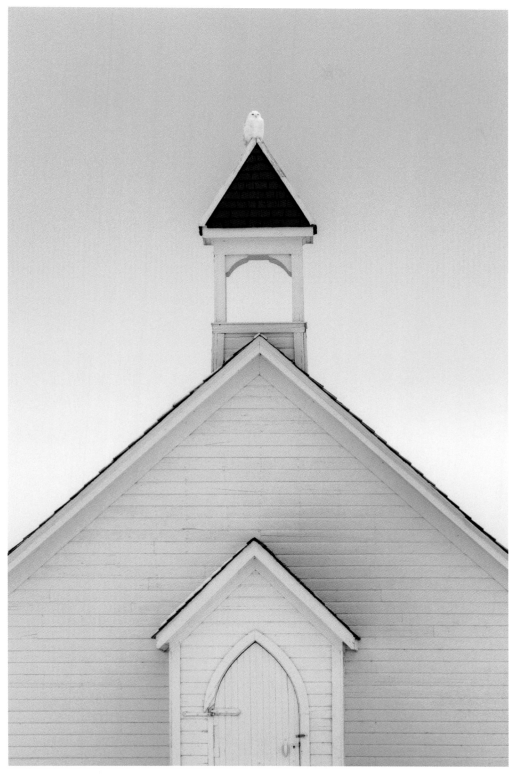

Snowy Owl perching on a rooftop by Canadian photographer Chad Larsen,
winner of BPOTY's 'Garden and Urban Birds' category 2019

Eric Hosking

(1909–91)

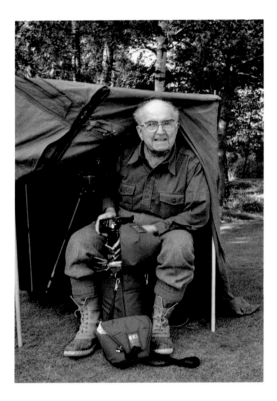

Imagine taking photographs of birds, not with today's perfectly portable digital devices or the aid of other numerous technological advances but with an early Kodak Box Brownie (a very basic, pioneering film camera) or a cumbersome Sanderson field plate camera. For a young Eric Hosking, the arduous task of lugging such equipment around on bird-watching trips, waiting for that winning single shot or working in black and white were not enough to put him off. In fact, such technical obstacles appear to have only spurred the legendary English wildlife photographer and ornithologist on, not only to produce a remarkable body of work but also to help develop new ways of observing and capturing the world on film.

As Eric Hosking's best-selling birdwatching biography *An Eye for a Bird* (1970) illustrates, bird watching and photography was once the pastime of the eccentric few, certainly not something to earn a living from. Having caught the bird photography

bug at the tender age of eight with a picture of a song thrush in its nest, followed by his first commercial sale – of an image of a child at London Zoo next to a baby elephant seal, – Hosking was determined that this was the career for him.

Despite then losing the sight in his left eye after being struck in the face by a tawny owl, he followed his dream, honing his photographic skills, building an extensive library of avian images and taking the first ever flash photograph – ironically, of an owl with its prey. By the mid-1970s he had photographed virtually every species of bird in Britain, was invited by the big names in ornithology to join them on major expeditions around the world and had invented a bird-operated electronic triggering mechanism for ultra-high-speed photography of birds in flight. As British natural scientist and author Miriam Rothschild wrote in her foreword for Eric Hosking's *Classic Birds: 60 Years of Bird Photography* (Jim Flegg and David Hosking, HarperCollins, 1993), a pictorial tribute to Hosking's work,

'Eric Hosking brought birds into all our lives. He opened our eyes to the beauty of their world, their grace and fascination. He probably achieved more for avian conservation than any other naturalist of our day.'

Top Trailblazing British photographer Eric Hosking in the field **Opposite page top** Hosking's *Barn Owl* (*Tyto alba*) in flight with prey (1948) **Opposite page below left** A Sanderson Field Plate camera image of a *Tawny Owl* (*Strix aluco*), the owl that took Eric Hosking's eye, 19 April 1938 **Below right** Hosking's image of *Mantagu's Harrier* (*Cicus pygargus*) in flight, May 1938, also inspired the crest of the RAF's 193 Squadron

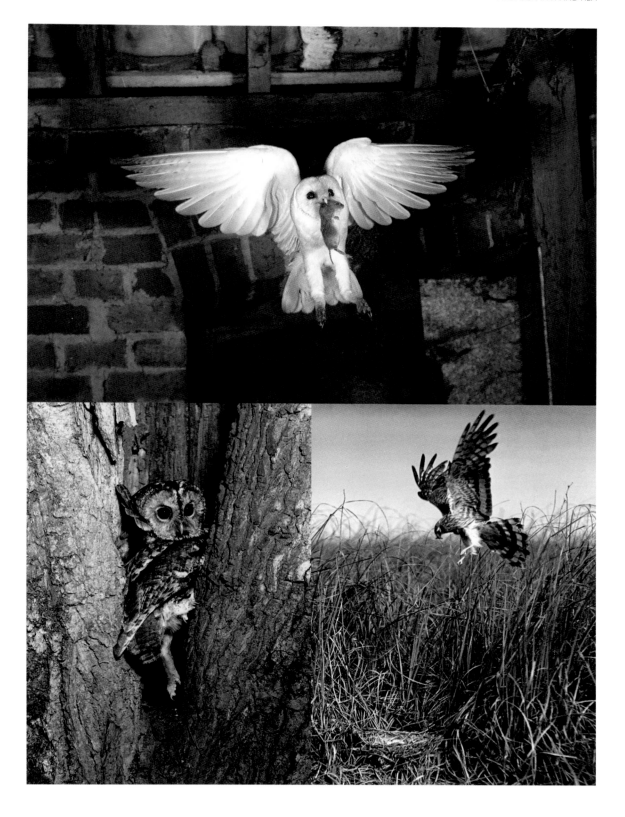

David Attenborough

(1926 –present)

With the far-reaching documentaries of David Attenborough we have now been gifted even greater insights into the as yet mysterious avian world. Part of British naturalist and presenter David Attenborough's 'Life' series of documentaries, *The Life of Birds* (1998) brought the extensive wonder of the avian world into homes around the globe including, but also far beyond, the backyard species of the everyday. Expanding on an episode entitled 'Lords of the Air' from Attenborough's ground-breaking natural history series (1979), *The Life of Birds* took two and a half years to film with a huge amount of dedication to cinematography – including the use of imprinting where human 'mothers' developed a relationship with birds from birth to get closer to them – but also to sound, with bird calling and song recorded simultaneously rather than dubbed onto the film post-production. How birds fly, their peculiar appetites, exquisite plumage, types of communication, ways of courtship and mating, commitment to parenthood and quest for survival are wonderfully narrated by the inimitable Attenborough, alongside the spectacular filming of over 300 bird species such as the kiwi, buff-breasted sandpiper, whooping crane, birds of paradise, ostrich, albatross, Nepalese honeyguide and the show-stealing lyre bird, by some of the world's best wildlife photographers: Barrie Britton, Andrew Anderson, Mike Potts and Justine Evans to name a few. The life of birds – of the rainforest, the desert, the ocean, wilderness, our towns and gardens – at their charismatic best.

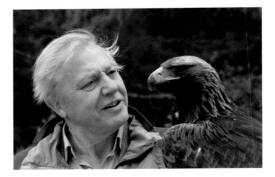

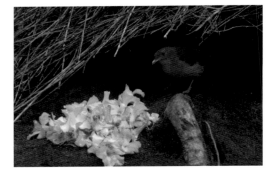

Top British naturalist and TV presenter Sir David Attenborough, face to face with a Golden Eagle (*Aquila chrysaetos*) in 1998 **Bottom** A male Vogelkop Bowerbird (*Amblyornis inornata*) inspects his blooming bower hoard, shot in West Papua, Indonesia for Attenborough's *Life* (2009)
Opposite page Camerawoman Justine Evans getting a bird's eye view of Venezeualan avian life and Sir David Attenborough for *Life of Birds* (1998)

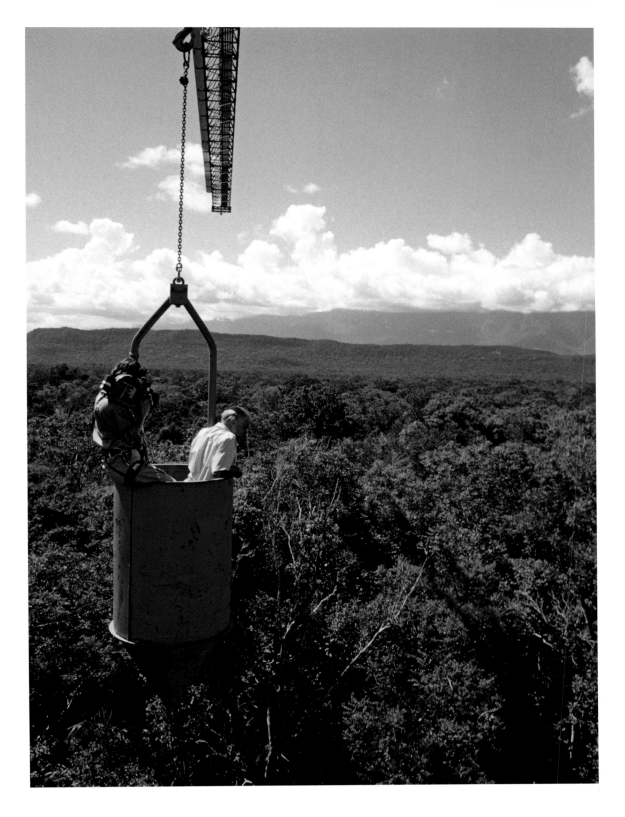

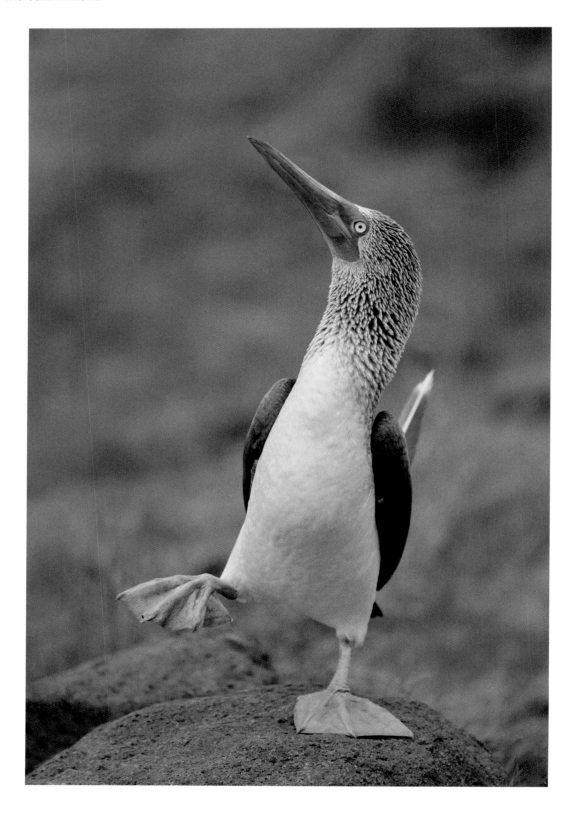

Arthur Morris

(1946–present)

One of Canon's original alumni of their Explorers of Light programme and author of the best-selling and still much pored over pre-digital bird photography handbook *The Art of Bird Photography: The Complete Guide to Professional Field Techniques* (Amphoto Books, 1998), New York teacher turned Florida-based internationally renowned professional photographer Arthur Morris has inspired generations of bird photographers around the world. Segueing from twenty-three years as an inner city schoolteacher to self-taught award-winning nature photographer specializing in avian subjects, thousands of his images – noted for both their artistic design and their technical excellence – have since graced the pages of magazines and galleries from birding publications to *National Geographic* to the Museum of American Bird Art at Mass Audubon. Sticking to a consistently clean, tight and graphic style, whether shooting on film or embracing new technology, Morris's celebratory images are also packed with character and educational insight, from crisply shot perching puffins to incredibly focused soaring owls to perfectly composed feeding wildfowl. Always on hand to offer guidance, through lectures, books or in his online Birds as Art (birdsasart.com) forum, one piece of compositional advice stands out: the background is just as important as the subject. Morris's equally stunning images of both backyard and rare birds, set against deep azure or sunset skies, verdant vegetation or still blue water are certainly testament to that.

Opposite page *Blue-footed Booby Dancing With Raised Foot* in North Seymour, Galapagos Islands and **Below** *Northern Gannets in Love* on Bonaventure Island, Quebec, both by American photographer Arthur Morris, www.birdsasart-blog.com

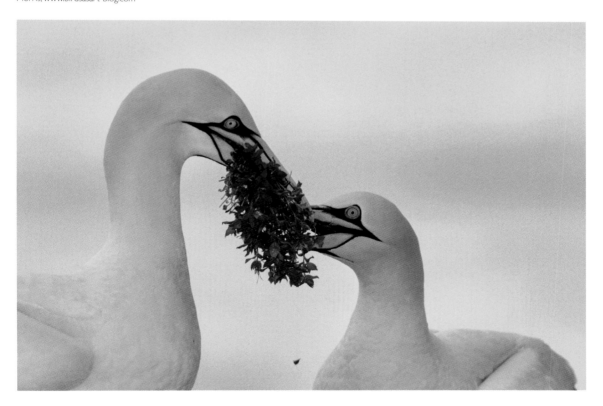

Dudley Edmondson
(1962–present)

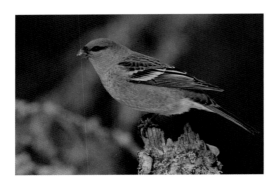

Trek up to Minnesota's Hawk Ridge on the western-most tip of Lake Superior in the United States from mid August to December and you will bear witness to one of nature's most remarkable spectacles – hundreds of migrating raptors heading south for the winter, among them American kestrels, sharp-shinned hawks, northern goshawks, peregrine falcons and eagles. Move to the nearby lakeside city of Duluth, as avid birder and wildlife photographer Dudley Edmondson did in 1989, and you're only a short trip away from the abundant rewards of this nationally renowned bird observatory and surrounding nature reserve all year round.

Having already found respite in the outdoors as a child, looking at bugs and birds in the backyard or out on a family picnic or hike, Edmondson was inspired into more serious birdwatching by a teacher at his senior high school in Columbus, Ohio. Invited on a field trip to watch the birds of the Rio Grande Valley, raptors and birds of prey quickly became something of a highlight with photography providing a way to capture the magnificence of these soaring birds. Moving near Hawk Ridge not only brought Edmondson closer to some of his favourite birds and some of America's most spectacular natural scenery, it also allowed him to cement his career as a professional observer of wildlife. His work has since appeared in numerous birding journals and books, plus visual campaigns for clients such as The Nature Conservancy and the National Parks Service.

Several decades of birding, photography, video reportage, public speaking and nature advocacy has taught Edmondson much about the animals, plants and areas of wilderness that he now engages with everyday, but also the people that he meets along the way. In an endeavour to encourage more African Americans like himself into the pursuit of nature he produced a photographically illustrated anthology of similar experiences in his 2006 book *Black and Brown Faces in America's Wild Places* (Adventure Publications), including thoughts from park rangers, world class mountain climbers, government administrators and fellow artists and ornithologists. He has since been on a mission to inspire more people of colour and minority backgrounds to benefit from America's green spaces, whether that's in their local park or by getting out and exploring surrounding landscapes.

'Nature has been a constant in my life. Through birds, I learned about conservation and so much more in the natural world. Nature's mental and physical health benefits are much needed. As people find themselves sheltering at home, birds and gardens provide an escape from the stress and uncertainty in the world today.'

Above A *Pine Grosbeak* (*Pinicola enucleator*) perches on a branch **Opposite page top** A *Female Northern Cardinal* (*Cardijnalis cardinalis*) foraging for food **Opposite page bottom** A watchful *Great Grey Owl* (*Strix nebulosa*) in the snow, all by American wildlife photographer and author of *Black and Brown Faces in America's Wild Places* (Adventure Publications, 2006), Dudley Edmondson

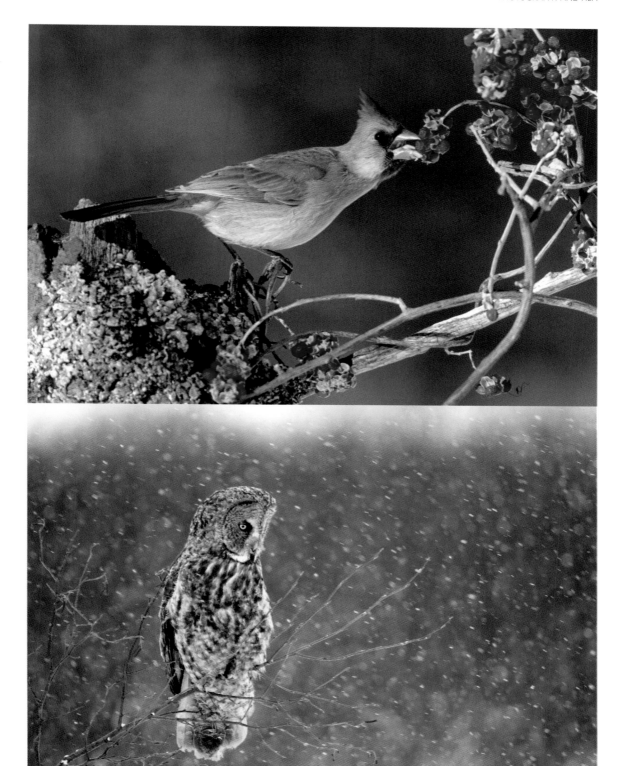

Leila Jeffreys

(1972–present)

Photographing birds up close is difficult; getting them to pose for photographic portraits is near on impossible. Yet Australian photographic and video artist Leila Jeffreys has done just that, working alongside conservationists, ornithologists and bird sanctuaries – and birds such as Jimmy the budgerigar, Seisa the palm cockatoo and Pepper the southern boobook – to produce a remarkably intimate body of avian-inspired work, at once beautiful and questioning. What does it mean to be a bird? How, as humans, should we interact with them? What can we do to help wild birds through issues such as habitat loss and climate change? Jeffrey's first foray into bird documentation culminated in the much-lauded *Portrait of a Budgerigar* (2010) followed by *Bioela Wild Cockatoos* (2012), *Prey* (2014), *Ornithurae* (2017), featuring cockatoos, doves and pigeons alongside birds in trees, and back to budgies with *High Society* (2019). Global exhibitions and books such as *Interview with a Cockatoo (or Two)* (2012) and *Bird Love* (Hatchette/ Abrams 2015) have also compounded Jeffreys' dedication to protecting birds as well as artistically portraying them, leading to an expedition to the Arctic Circle in 2019 on the invitation of British historian and explorer Dr Huw Lewis-Jones – a love and compassion for our feathered friends evident throughout.

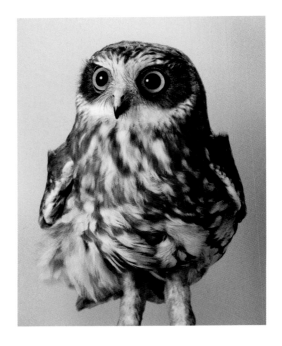

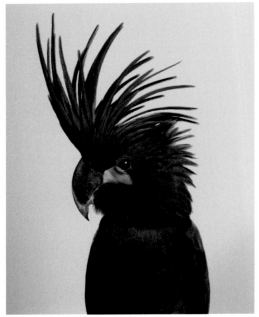

Top Bird portraits of *Pepper Southern Boobook* and **Bottom** *Seisa the Palm Cockatoo*, both by Australian photographer Leila Jeffreys, www.leilajeffreys.com

Thomas Lohr

(1980–present)

In 2015, this German fashion, portrait and still life photographer turned his usually human-focused lens onto the avian world with the publication of his limited edition art book *Birds* (Studio Baer). The initial idea behind the project was to produce a study on textures and colours by zooming in on feathers and plumage 'to show the beauty of birds while approaching it from a different point of view'. Lohr wanted to show a variety of species and an array of plumage so shot a range of birds, travelling to bird parks and menageries across Europe to establish a stunning, masterfully lit portfolio.

'Birds are inspiring creatures, but with this project I wanted to abstract things and look closer at something kind of surreal that I see when looking at birds' feathers in real detail,' reflects Lohr; in most cases, the pictures only give 'an idea of whether the strong, dark feathers belong to the tail or wings of a bird, or whether the pinkish fluff is found on the chest or neck of the animal'.

Each abstract photo of wings, bellies and other bird parts in the book is also beautifully juxtaposed with its scientific name, a contemplative invitation to go deeper behind the scenes of each species – the supremely tactile contrasting feather types of *Grus Monacha* (a hooded crane), the royal blue coat of *Anodorhynchus Hyacinthinus* (a hyacinth macaw), the elegant capes of *Geronticus Eremita* (a northern bald ibis) or *Pelecanus Crispus* (a Dalmatian pelican), the wispy white feathers of *Psophia Crepitans* (a grey-winged trumpeter) or the soft candy-floss pink plumes of *Phoenicopterus Roseus* (a greater flamingo) – and examine our potentially surface-level relationship with the bird world at the same time.

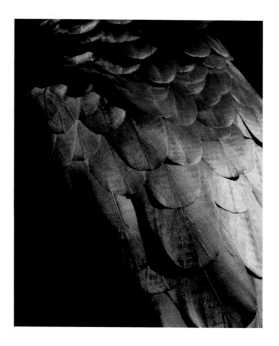

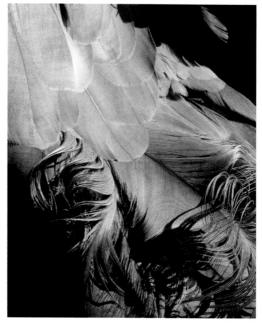

Top *Geronticus Eremita*, showing feather detail of a Northern Bald Ibis and **Bottom** *Grus Monacha*, detailing the contrasting plumage of a Hooded Crane, both by German photographer Thomas Lohr © Thomas Lohr

Bence Máté

(1985–present)

Known as the 'Invisible Wildlife Photographer', Bence Máté's love of photographing animals began in his early childhood growing up by the wetlands of the Hungarian village of Pusztaszer. At fifteen he won Hungary's Young Wildlife Photographer of the Year competition, scooped the grand title of Wildlife Photographer of the Year in 2010 for a *Marvel of Ants* and won the Birds category in 2014 with *Herons in Time and Space*. Indeed, many of his most striking pictures are of birds: an emerald hummingbird in a standoff with a bright green snake; a gulp of great cormorants at feeding time; the time-lapse flight of a hoopoe – each composition so other-worldly, it's hard to imagine that it hasn't been set up or retouched. The magic, however, is all through Máté's phenomenal eye for composition, immense patience and a burning desire to get that winning shot: to the extent of inventing new forms of technology to get closer to nature, including timing and exposure devices and one-way glass photography hides. Although makeshift hide photography has been popular since Eric Hosking's time, the permanence and invisibility factor of Máté's revolutionary design allows unprecedented proximity to the remarkable behaviour of species such as eagles, vultures, owls, bustards, kestrels, waterfowl and plains-dwelling birds. A truly intimate bird's-eye view.

Below The otherworldly *Herons in Time and Space* **Opposite page top** *Airscrew* and **Opposite page bottom** *Hunger,* all by ground-breaking Hungarian photographer Bence Máté © Bence Máté

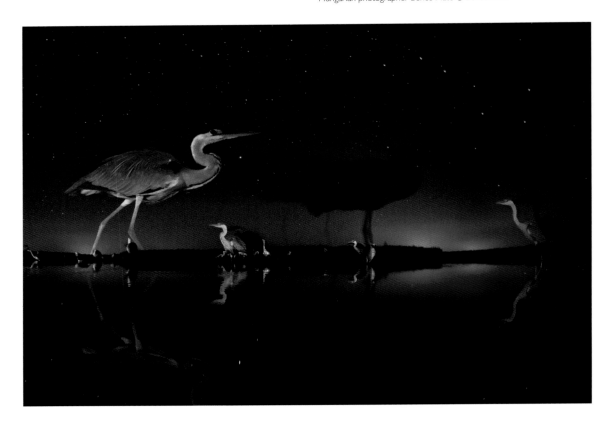

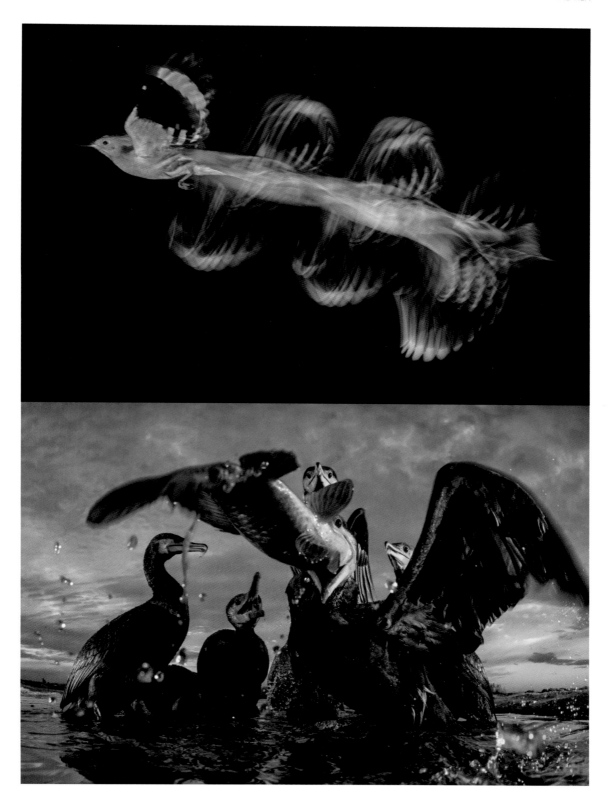

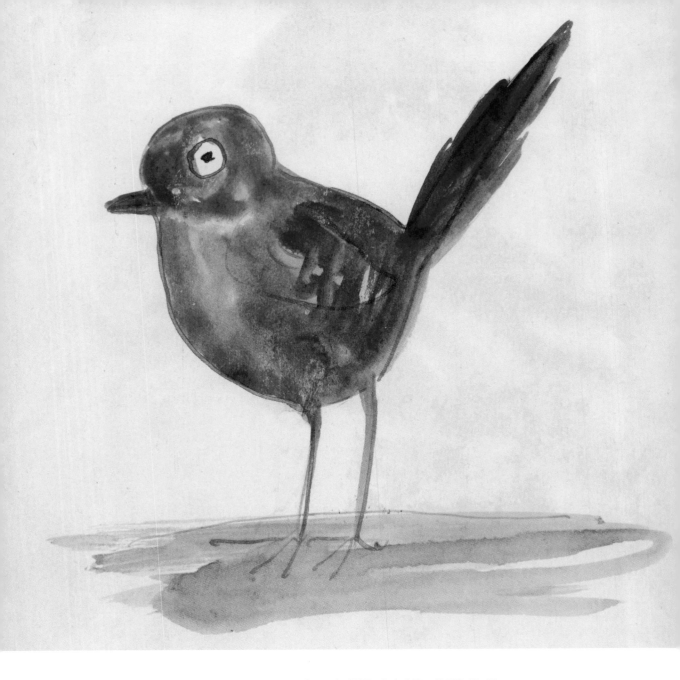

DESIGN, CRAFT AND STYLE

Some of the most memorable and charming images of birds have been rendered through the medium of print from the woodcuts of William Morris and C.F.A. Voysey to the instantly recognizable linocuts of Robert Gillmor or highly stylized silkscreens of Charley Harper. What many of these artists share is the ability to portray the likeness or spirit of a bird in just a few simple lines or shapes, facilitated by a lifetime of observing birds at rest, in flight and in their natural habitats. In their footsteps follow numerous designers and craftspeople, using metal, paper, ceramics, feathers and fabric to share their celebratory visions of some of the most inspiring creatures on Earth.

Edward Lear

(1812–88)

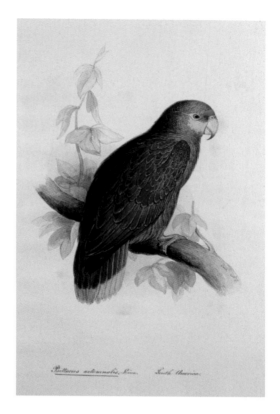

Best known for his nonsense poems and limericks, Edward Lear also took a turn as an ornithological illustrator. Professing to be the twentieth child of a brood of twenty-one, he was raised and taught to draw by his oldest sister Ann, with whom he spent hours copying out flowers, birds and other natural forms from books and catalogues. When his family fell on hard times, a fifteen-year-old Lear advertised his artistic talents professionally, undertaking commercial commissions for 'bread and cheese'. In between commissions he undertook a personal project to create a set of prints entirely devoted to parrots – mainly drawn from life and including species from Australia, Africa and America bred by leading ornithologists – culminating in the richly lithographed, uniquely taxonomic and highly charismatic *Illustrations of the Family of Psittacidae, or Parrots* (1832).

Impressed by this work, the London Zoological Society eagerly commissioned him in 1832 to draw illustrations of birds for the society's taxidermist John Gould (see page 324). He was also appointed by the naturalist Lord Edward Smith-Stanley, 13th Earl of Derby, to catalogue the vast menagerie at Knowsley Hall. Lear ended up staying on the Earl's estate until 1836, working on his bird paintings, establishing a network of high-browed patrons and entertaining the children with the curious characters and verbally inventive rhymes that would later make his name – among them, the childhood favourite, 'The Owl and the Pussycat' from *Nonsense Songs, Stories, Botany, and Alphabets* (1871).

Writing in his diary in 1860, 'Verily I am an odd bird', the then itinerant wanderer and landscape painter – for which he was most known during his lifetime – continued his portrayal of his feathered friends with several sets of imaginary 'coloured birds' and a zoomorphic series of 'nonsense birds', the character-defining colour of *The Dark Blue Bird* and the strange behaviour of the *The Obsequious Ornamental Ostrich, who wore Boots to keep his feet quite dry,* inspiring global audiences, past and present, to engage even more fondly with the sometimes overlooked wonders of the avian world.

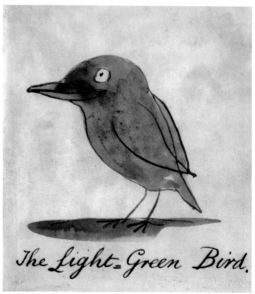

Opposite page *The Dark Blue Bird* from a set of 16 drawings of 'Comic Birds' (1880) by poet, artist and ornithological illustrator Edward Lear **Top** *Psittacus autumnalis*, a Red-Lored Amazon Parrot, of the bird family Psittacidae (1832) **Bottom** *The Light Green Bird* (1880) also from Lear's series of 'Comic Birds'

C.F.A. Voysey

(1857–1941)

Designer of wallpapers, fabrics and furnishings and architect of several country houses, Charles Francis Annesley Voysey was concerned with form and function rather than ornamental complexities, opting for 'simplicity in decoration' and a limited colour palette, 'emphasizing outline, eliminating shading, and minimizing detail'. The animal and plant kingdoms were a constant source of inspiration, juxtaposing birds and other wildlife with flowers, foliage and fruit in designs such as *Apothecary's Garden*; the particularly pared back *Birds and Fruit*, *Blue Birds* and *Seagulls*; also *Rook and Holly*, *Purple Birds*, *Birds and Berries*, *The Owls* and *Birds of Many Climes*. Drawing inspiration from the Arts and Crafts Movement and its founder William Morris (1834–96) – who had begun to focus on writing, activism and the production of designs such as his bird-inspired classics *Birds and Strawberry Thief* by the time the younger artist entered the scene – Voysey's elegant, quietly expressive yet often curvaceously graphic work also helped lay the foundations for the work of Czech painter Alphonse Mucha and the development of Art Nouveau. Both Voysey's and Morris's designs are now particularly celebrated by the Victoria and Albert Museum (V&A), who hold a significant collection of their work, and continue to produce textiles, prints and *objects d'art* inspired by their vintage and time-honoured designs.

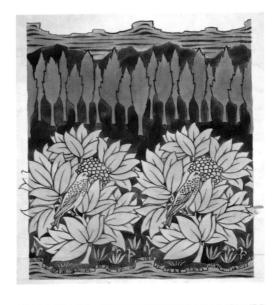

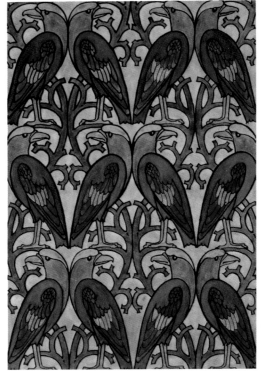

Top *Birds with Fir Tree* **Bottom** *Parrot design*, and **Opposite page** *Owls* All by British designer and architect C.F.A. Voysey

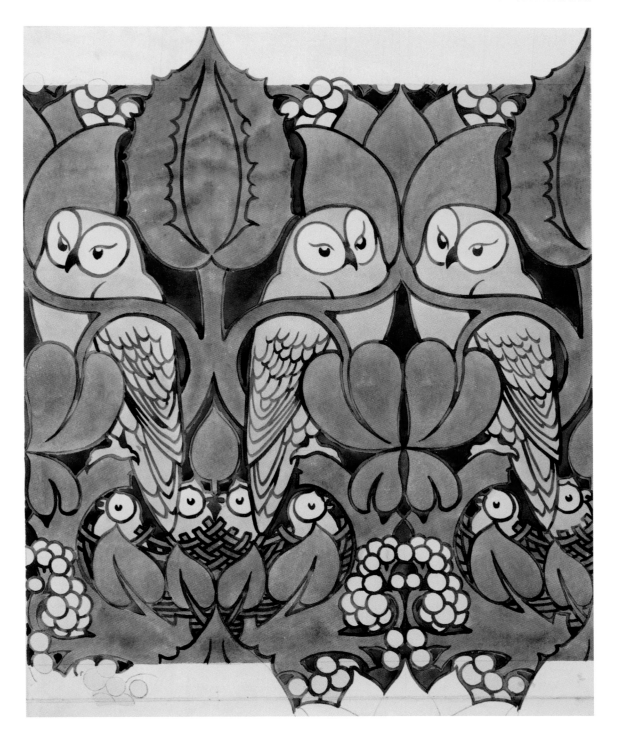

Charley Harper

(1922–2007)

'When I look at wildlife or a nature subject, I don't see the feathers in the wings, I just count the wings.'

American modernist artist Charley Harper mused famously about his uniquely stylized portfolio of birds and other animals. 'I see exciting shapes, colour combinations, patterns, textures, fascinating behaviour, and endless possibilities for making interesting pictures. I regard the picture as an ecosystem in which all the elements are interrelated, interdependent, perfectly balanced, without trimming or unutilized parts.'

Now perching on everything from cups to jigsaws to children's books, Harper's bird portrayals first took flight as a series of illustrations commissioned to accompany an article about feeding station birds in *Ford Times* magazine – a monthly publication produced by the Ford Motor Company, whose art director was Arthur Lougee, and to which Harper would contribute hundreds of images. This first flutter into avian territory comprised eight depictions of birdlife including *Feeding Station* (1954) and *Blue Jay Breakfast* (1954), hand painted in gouache on paper shapes glued to board. Accompanying the article was the invitation to purchase serigraph (silkscreen print) editions of any illustration, hand cut and printed by Charley Harper with colours mixed by his wife Edie. Although the take up wasn't huge, the prints were sufficiently inspiring for the artist to continue producing editions of his work in this way, the perfect medium for his bold colours, clean lines and graphic shapes.

Harper met fellow art student Edie at the Art Academy of Cincinnati, the couple swiftly marrying in 1947 after graduation and spending their honeymoon touring the American West thanks to the benevolence of the Stephen H. Wilder Traveling Scholarship. Having grown up on a farm in West Virginia and spent a great deal of his childhood roaming the Appalachian foothills in order to avoid his chores, this officially funded sojourn was a four-month idyll where both art and nature could become one. Feeling fettered by the constraints of realism and turning back to the swift observation style and on-the-spot paintings developed during time serving with the Intelligence and Reconnaissance Platoon of the 414th Regiment in Germany during World War II, he then began 'trying to simplify the great natural forms and symbolize the design underlying the surface clutter'.

Birds and fish lent themselves particularly well to this new graphic style, with their 'built in functional beauty imposed by their habitats' and requiring 'only a little distortion of what's there already, a thinning of lines and a simpler statement of shape'. Harper's bird-inspired commissions for *Ford Times* became an annual affair leading to such charismatic delights as *Black and White Warbler* (1955), *Everglade Kite* (1957), *Eskimo Curlew* (1957), *Passenger Pigeon* (1957), *Snowy Egret* (1958) and *Painted Bunting* (1958), later accompanied by Harper's equally charming words.

Other notable works include illustrations for the now-coveted *The Giant Golden Book of Biology: An Introduction to the Science of Life* by Gerald Ames and Rose Wyler (Golden Press, 1961) – a 99-page, full-colour, middle school-level introduction to biology covering everything from cells and evolution to physiology and ecosystems; he also received commissions from zoos, wildlife sanctuaries, nature centres and national parks. Indeed, it was once said that if Harper hadn't been an artist, he probably would have been a conservationist. 'Remember that I didn't start out to paint a bird – the bird already existed,' advised Harper to the appreciators of his art. 'I started out to paint a picture of a bird, a picture which didn't exist before I came along, a picture which gives me a chance to share with you my thoughts about the bird.'

Opposite page top American modernist artist Charley Harper is known for his stylized yet carefully observed and wonderfully evocative illustrations of birds. Hand-pulled serigraphs include *Downy Woodpeckers* (18.5cm × 13cm, 1954) and **Bottom** *Red-eyed Vireos* (18.5cm × 13cm, 1959) Both © Charley Harper Art Studio

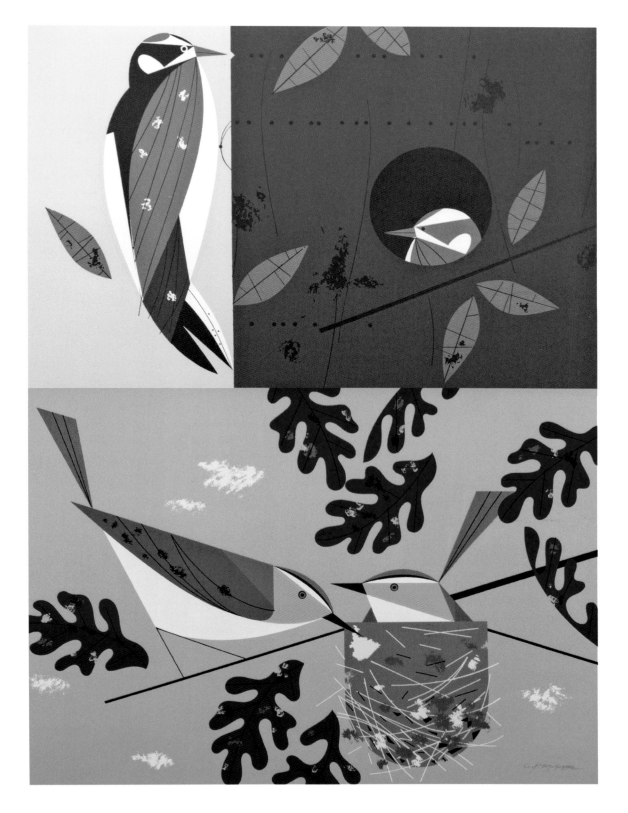

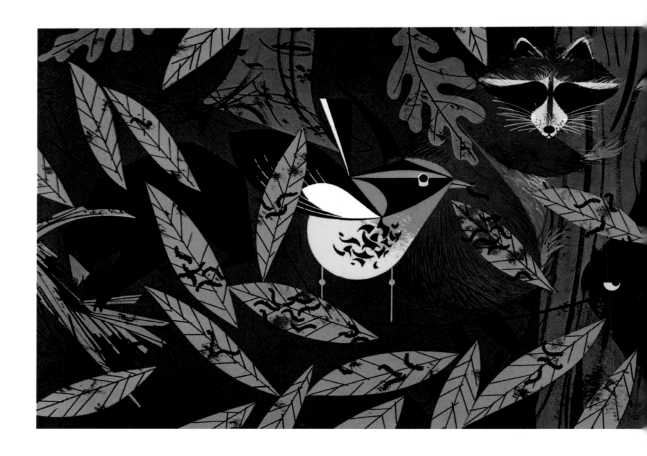

Above *Forest Friends* (1961) one of several illustrations of
ecosystems for artist and author Charley Harper's *The Giant Golden
Book of Biology: An Introduction to the Science of Life* (1961), now
available as a limited edition Giclée print (30cm x 9.75cm, 2011)
Image © Charley Harper Art Studio

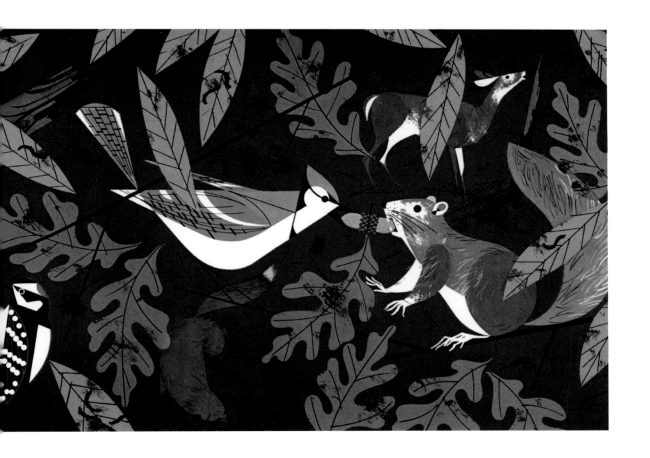

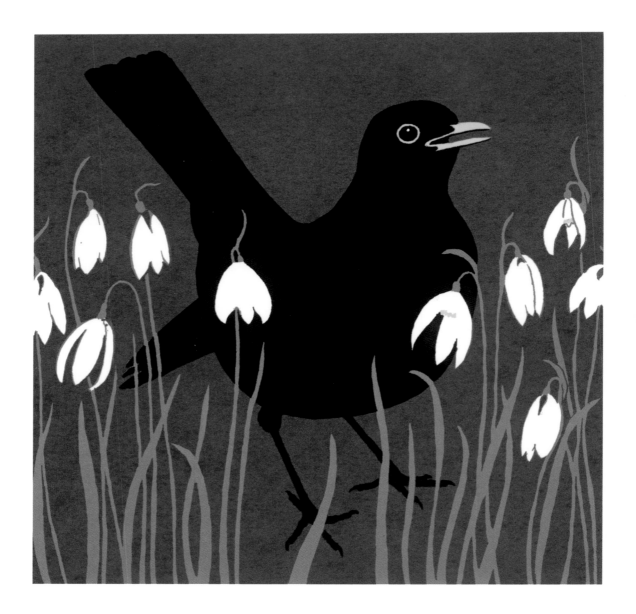

Above *Blackbird and Snowdrops,* a four-colour silk-screen print from the *Blackbird Collection* (2019) © Robert Gillmor MBE

Robert Gillmor MBE

(1936–present)

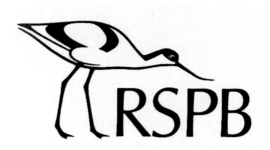

Much inspired by his grandfather Allen Seaby, an ornithological painter and printmaker, and Professor of Fine Art at Reading University, a young Robert Gillmor spent a great deal of time watching the older man working on his colour woodcuts, as well as bird-watching around the flooded gravel pits of Reading where he grew up.

An active member of Reading Ornithological Club, Gillmor's work was first published in the longstanding *British Birds* magazine when he was sixteen, followed by illustrations for *A Study of Blackbirds* by David W. Snow (George Allen & Unwin, 1958), occasional line drawings for the RSPB (Royal Society for the Protection of Birds) and covers for their film programmes. In 1965, his success was sufficient for him to embark on a full-time career as a freelance wildlife artist, receiving such laudable commissions as the original drawing of an avocet for the distinctive RSPB logo, posters for the British Birdfair, covers for the HarperCollins *New Naturalist* series from 1985 onwards and linocut designs for several series of feature stamps for Royal Mail's Post and Go machines – the latter flying Gillmor's birds to destinations both near and far across the globe.

Moving from Reading to Cley next the Sea in Norfolk in 1998 when his children fledged the nest meant Gillmor could be nearer to the inspiring lines of long-legged waders such as oystercatchers, herons, egrets and those iconic avocets. Having been driven to near national extinction by Victorian hunters and egg collectors in the nineteenth century, these emblematic, piebald birds are now a common sight on the coastal wetlands of East Anglia, their long, thin upcurved bills having become a wonderful symbol of both Gillmor's huge contribution to bird conservation and his work to produce some of the most charming and collectable bird-inspired art.

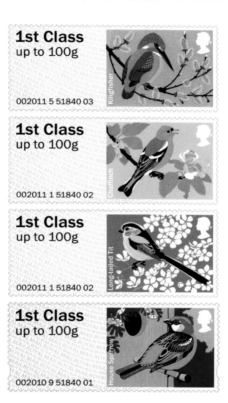

Top Robert Gillmor's original Pied Avocet (*Recurvirostra avosetta*) line drawing design for the RSPB. Reproduced by permission of RSPB, © 2020 All rights reserved. Source: RSPB **Bottom** Gillmor's beautiful linocut depictions of birds have also flown around the world via several series of Royal Mail feature stamps © Royal Mail Group Limited

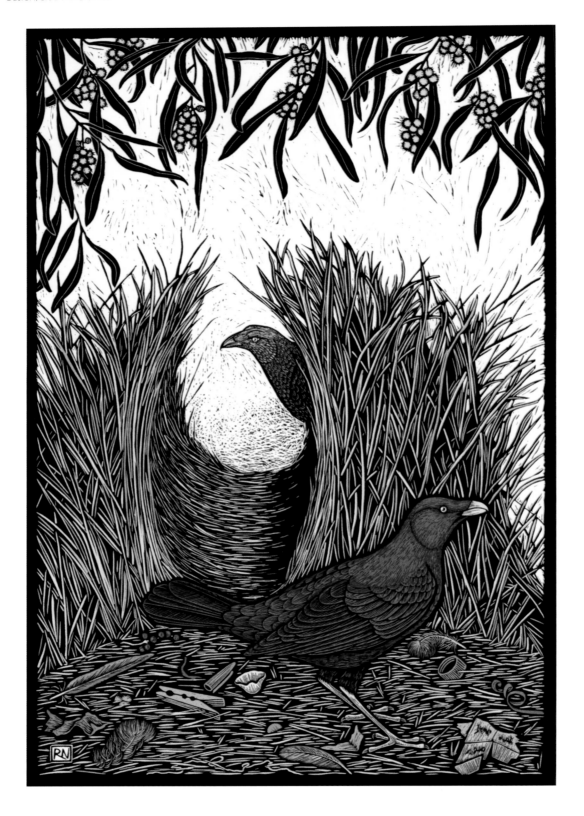

Rachel Newling
(1956–present)

As many artists through the ages have found, birds are particularly good subjects for printmaking due to their distinctive silhouettes, often graphic and colourful markings, quirky behaviour and variation of habitat. If, like British-born printmaker Rachel Newling, you live in Australia, you're also extremely well placed to observe a huge variety of birds, with one in ten of the world's around 11,000 unique bird species tracing their lineages to the 'Land of the Birds' including vast numbers of parrots, pigeons and songbirds, many of which act as vital 'ecosystem engineers' of the landscape-defining rainforests, bush and suburbs, and the flora and fauna within. An apt celebration of all this amazing diversity, Newling's hand-coloured, painterly linocuts juxtapose fan-headed Major Mitchell and red-tailed black cocktaoos with a living, breathing background of beautiful red waratah blooms; male and female regent bowerbirds with yellow-flowered rainforest orchids; and little blue wrens with waterfalls of wisteria blossom. Birds also make an appearance in Newling's Birdland series of pastel drawings, as 'head and shoulder' portraits, including *Osprey*, *Blue Faced Honeyeater*, *Blue Winged Kookaburra* and *Rose Crowned Fruit Dove*. Although many of her limited edition works now live in homes around the world, Newling also keeps a digital version of each, as a growing record and legacy of the Australian birds that abound.

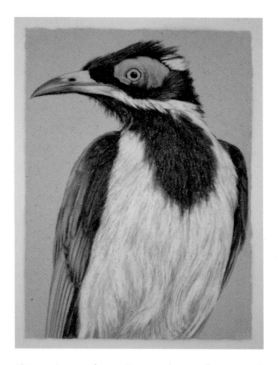

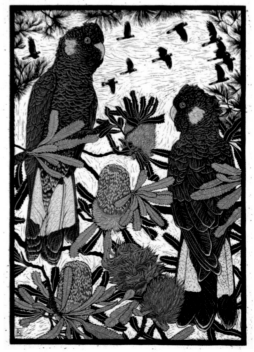

Opposite page *Satin Bowerbird*, a hand-coloured linocut by British-born printmaker Rachel Newling (74cm x 50cm) **Top** Newlings avian oeuvre also includes pastel and paper artworks such as her *Blue-faced Honeyeater* (30cm x 21cm) **Bottom** A linocut celebration of flora and fauna in *Yellow-tailed Black Cockatoo and Banksia* (75cm x 50cm), all © Rachel Newling

Angela Harding
(1960–present)

Bitish backyard birds define the work of artist and printmaker Angela Harding, whose much-loved linocuts, etchings and woodcuts have adorned numerous magazine editorials, book covers, gallery walls and merchandise such as advent calendars and greetings cards, spanning a thirty-year career. Born in Stoke-on-Trent but now living in the aptly named village of Wing, across the ridge from the wildlife-packed Rutland Water Nature Reserve, Harding initiates her artworks through sketches and scribbles of the birds she sees in her garden, on walks through the countryside, or along the coasts of Norfolk, Suffolk or Cornwall. Often, she will have an idea in mind for the composition of a piece from something she has read, observed, imagined or the brief for a commissioned illustration. Her songbirds, wildfowl and birds of prey are often positioned in an atmospheric location, habitat or time of day or night to bring their character even further to life: *Blackbirds and Berries*, *Curlew at Whitby*, pastoral *Common* featuring birds in the foreground and in flight, or the monochrome *Alphabet Birds*. Inspired by 1930s, 40s and 50s artists such as printmaker and landscape artist Eric Ravilious (1903–42) and Impressionistic colourist Winifred Nicholson (1893–1981), her distinctive black prints with a naturalistic colour palette of deep greens, blues and browns, and accents of deep red and sunshine yellow have a similarly traditional feel, paying a timeless homage to our most familiar birds.

For a wonderful overview of her work for bird lovers of all ages, see the fully illustrated *RSPB Birds* (Bloomsbury, 2020) in collaboration with RSPB president Miranda Krestovnikoff.

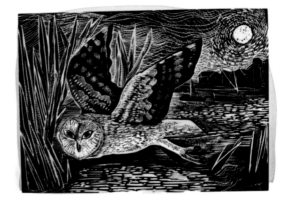

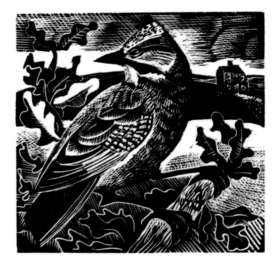

Top *Marsh Owl* (43cm x 37cm), a lino and silkscreen print inspired by watching a Barn Owl fly over the reedbeds at Snape Maltings in evening light **Bottom** *J for Jay* (8cm x 8cm), a wood engraving from the *Alphabet Birds* series **Opposite page** A charming lino and silkscreen depiction of a *Blackbird Stealing Redcurrant* (30cm x 32cm), all by renowned British printmaker Angela Harding. www.angelaharding.co.uk

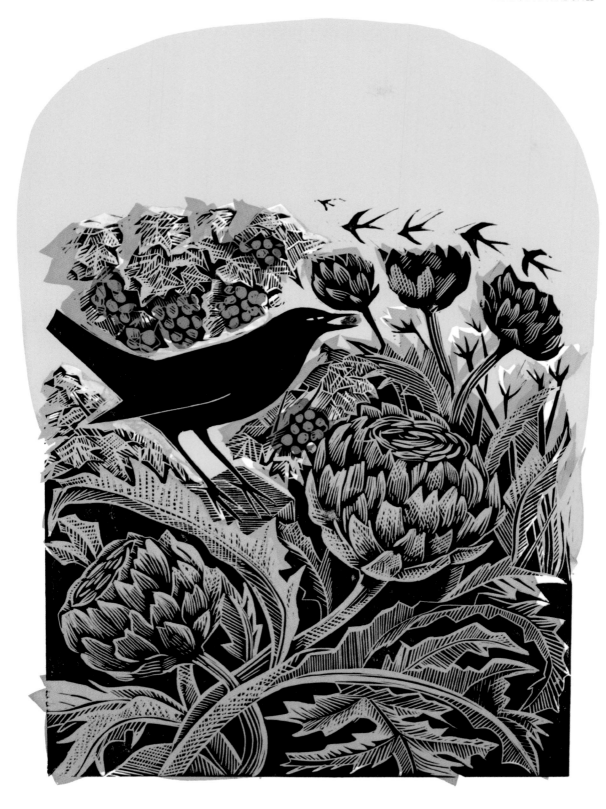

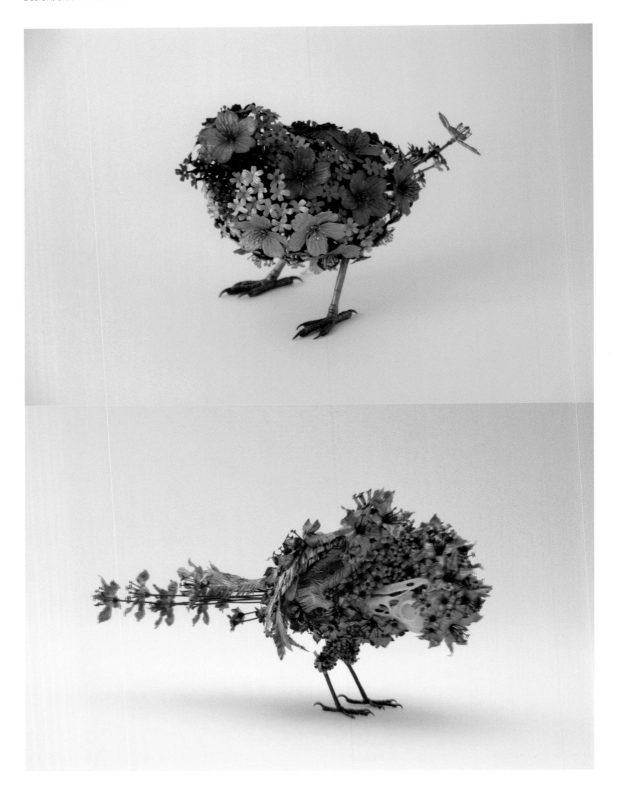

Taiichiro Yoshida

(1989–present)

The animal and plant kingdoms are fused together in Tokyo-based artist Taiichiro Yoshida's dainty bird sculptures (among other wildlife) where wings, tails, feathers and beaks are composed of delicate metal blooms. Created using an ancient hot metalworking technique developed in Japan around the second and third centuries BC, each individual component is heated, carefully beaten and then formed into petals or flowers before being coloured to a white, pink, pinkish brown or copper patina – by heating and cooling the metals at specific temperatures – and conjoined. The result is beautiful but also sometimes unsettling where bird skulls or bones peek out from within *ikebana*-style arrangements of naturally occurring metals such as silver, bronze and copper as in *Fire Bird* (2014). For Yoshida this alludes to the continuation of life after death and the idea of nature reclaiming the body for renewal and regeneration. The use of certain flowers is also symbolic, such as the Japanese ornamental cherry blossom known as *Sakura* (typically *Prunus serrulata*), which is associated with the transient nature of life, and the *Kiku* or chrysanthemum (*Chrysanthemum*), representing longevity and rejuvenation. Such flowers are also often paired with birds in traditional Japanese art (see page 331), from Utagawa Hiroshige's *Bird and Chrysanthemums* (*c.*1830s) to Katsushika Hokusai's *Bullfinch and Weeping Cherry Blossoms* (1834), and Yoshida's sculptural interpretation of this intrinsic relationship between birds and flowers creates a direct flight path between present and past.

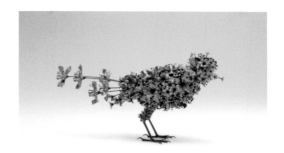

see page 331

Opposite page top Japanese artist Taiichiro Yoshida fuses together delicate metal blooms and delicate bird bones to create tiny avian-inspired sculptures including *Hanasuzume* (110mm × 70mm × 150mm, copper)
Opposite page bottom *Fire Bird* (120mm × 230mm × 100mm, copper, brass, phosphor bronze and bone of the bird) and **Top** *Fire Bird* (110 × 200mm × 60mm, copper, brass, phosphor bronze and bone of the bird)

Swan Song for the Birds

The art history of birds is rife with long-lost species of birds, pushed to extinction by ice ages, evolutionary changes or human intervention, most recently in the form of climate change. As the Coronavirus pandemic has forced us to consider our own humanity, could this be the moment we pull collectively together for the planet, too? Not least the 11,000-plus species of birds that still inhabit our forests, grasslands and shores and the often-taken-for-granted birdsong that provides a natural, hopeful soundtrack to our lives.

In 2010, film director and producer Ceri Levy – best known for his work with British pop bands Blur and Gorrillaz – put out a plea to living, bird-loving creatives, such as Sir Peter Blake, Matt Sewell (see page 329) and Gonzo artist Ralph Steadman to contribute to an exhibition about the plight of endangered birds. 'Ghosts of Gone Birds' subsequently opened in late 2011 in an old East London schoolhouse. The skulking *The Extinct Guadeloupe Caracara* by Steadman and *Choiseul Crested Pigeon* by Rebecca Jewell, plus a powerful handwritten elegy to all those birds that have gone before and those currently in danger by Blake throwing the spotlight on species such as the dodo and species which have joined or are in danger of joining the dodo, the poster bird for extinction.

Over in New York, photographer Denis Defibaugh focused on critically endangered and vanished birds, insects and mammals in his exhibition *Afterlifes of Natural History* (2015), training his lens onto rare specimens of Labrador ducks, great Auks and passenger pigeons found in the natural history museum of Zion National Park, Chicago's Field Museum, The Cornell Lab of Ornithology and the Smithsonian National Museum of Natural History. Using similarly endangered Polaroid Type 55 film, the darkened images are a sobering introduction to the need to conserve our current bird life.

Art relating to 'gone birds' is not only associated with the twenty-first century, however. The red-ochre Aboriginal bird art of a narrow rock shelter in Australia's Arnhem Land, for example, is thought to be a depiction of a large, flightless emu-like megafauna known to scientists as *Genyornis newtoni*, thought to have gone extinct an estimated 40,000 years ago.

Experts think this heavily built, tiny-winged 'thunder bird' co-existed with humans for a considerable amount of time, possibly 15,000 years, and that the art was made by someone who knew the bird well, rather than through oral storytelling. While paintings of dodos by artists such as Roelant Savery (*c*.1626) are glimpses of this long-lost bird – killed to extinction by 1690 by hunting and the introduction of non-native species.

It's not all bad news, however. In January 2020, BirdLife International (www.birdlife.org) released a new study that showed that conservation action has reduced bird extinction rates by 40 per cent, although numbers also show that during the next 500 years, 471 bird species may yet go extinct, expedited by issues such as climate change. Moving forward we need to prevent low-risk species with healthy populations from becoming threatened in the first place as well as preventing Critically Endangered ones from being wiped out. To this effect, a new raft of conservation-aware art and books is also helping to raise awareness about the loss of avian species such as *The Book of Birds: A Field Guide to Wonder and Loss* (Hamish Hamilton, 2022) by acclaimed British nature author Robert Macfarlane and artist and writer Jackie Morris.

Written in the strange age of COVID-19, citizens of the Earth are now in an unprecedented position to collectively take stock. The freedom to go about our daily lives, to be healthy, access nature, flock together and simply exist have all been thrown under the spotlight for generations of humans like never before – well worth remembering as we think about how we treat our planet, our fellow wildlife and the vital, glorious creatures we know as birds.

Opposite page top Detail of *Edwards' Dodo* (c. 1626) by Dutch artist Roelant Savery (1576–1639), also thought to portray a similarly extinct Red Rail (*Aphanapteryx bonasia*) and the hypothetically extinct Lesser Antillean Macaw (*Ara guadeloupensis*) and Martinique Macaw (*Ara martinicus*) **Below left** American photographer Denis Defibaugh's haunting images of a *Passenger Pigeon*, RMSC. **Below right** *Labrador Duck*, Smithsonian, from Defibaugh's *Afterlifes of Natural History* (2015) series pay further homage to forever lost species of birds—and the vital need to conserve our avian world, and indeed all life on Earth. Both © Denis Defibaugh

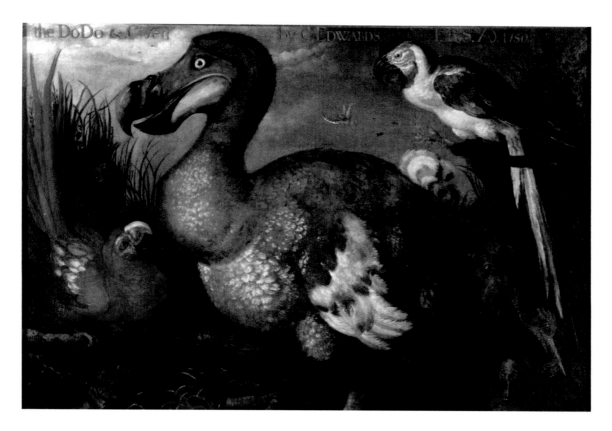

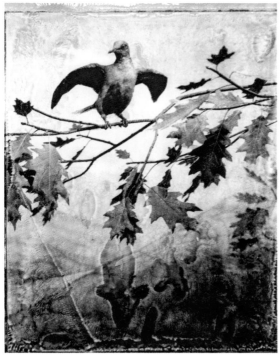

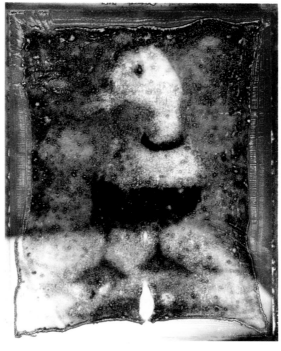

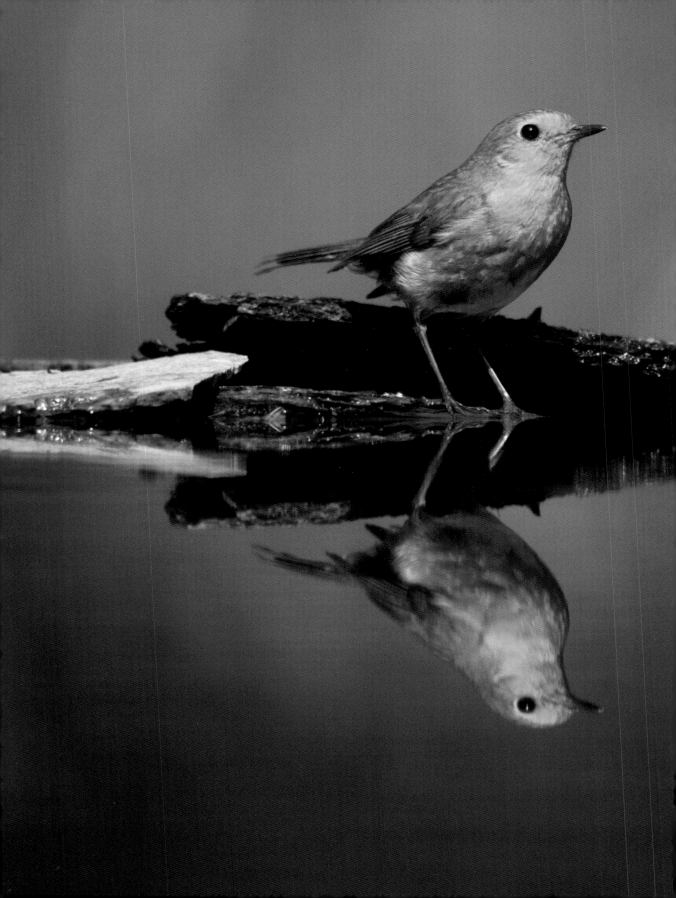

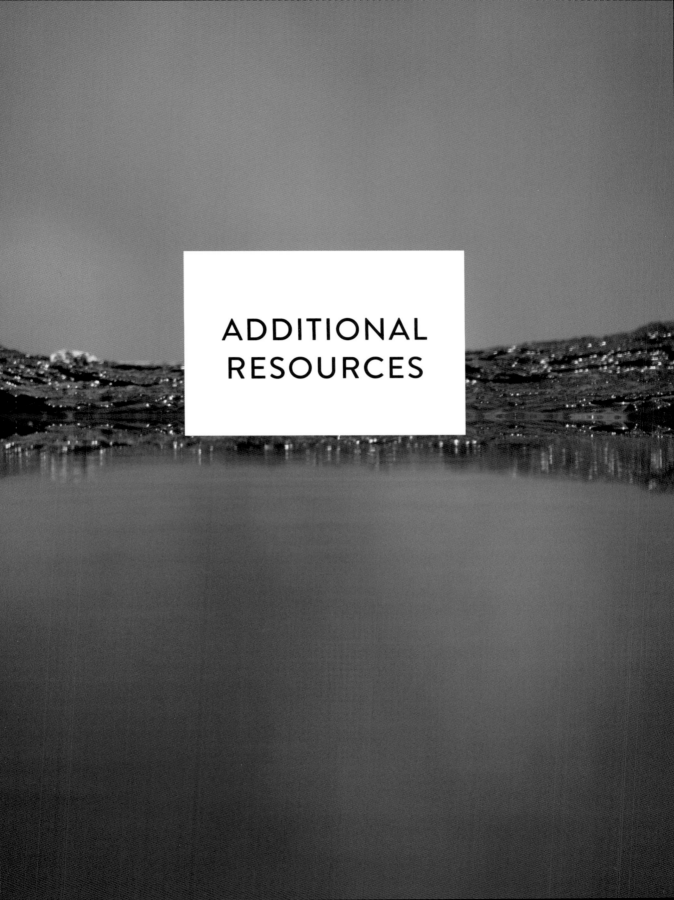

ADDITIONAL
RESOURCES

Dedicated to all the birds around the world who have provided glimpses of beauty and peace during a difficult time for humans.

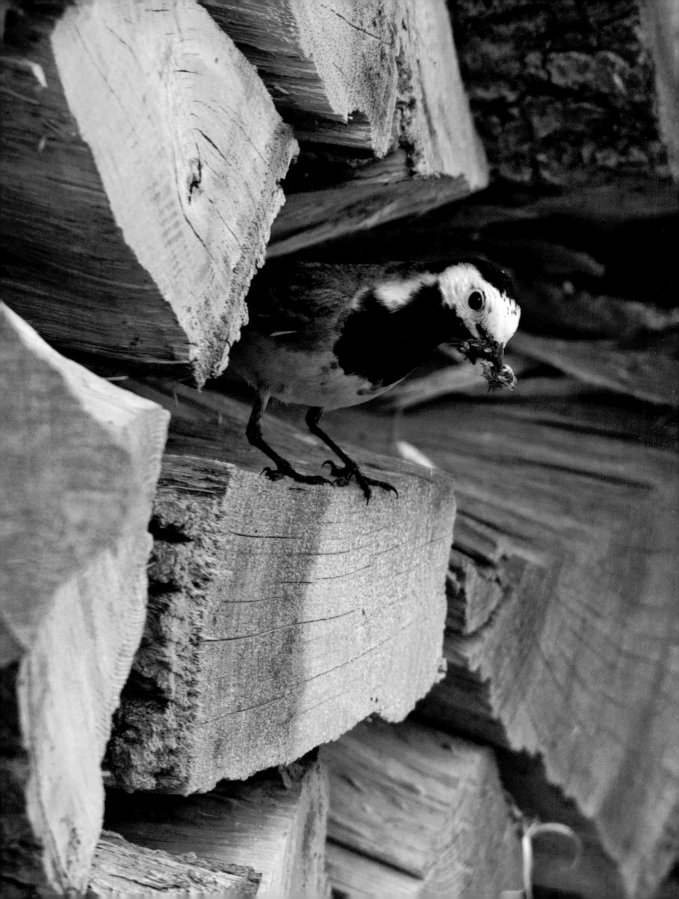

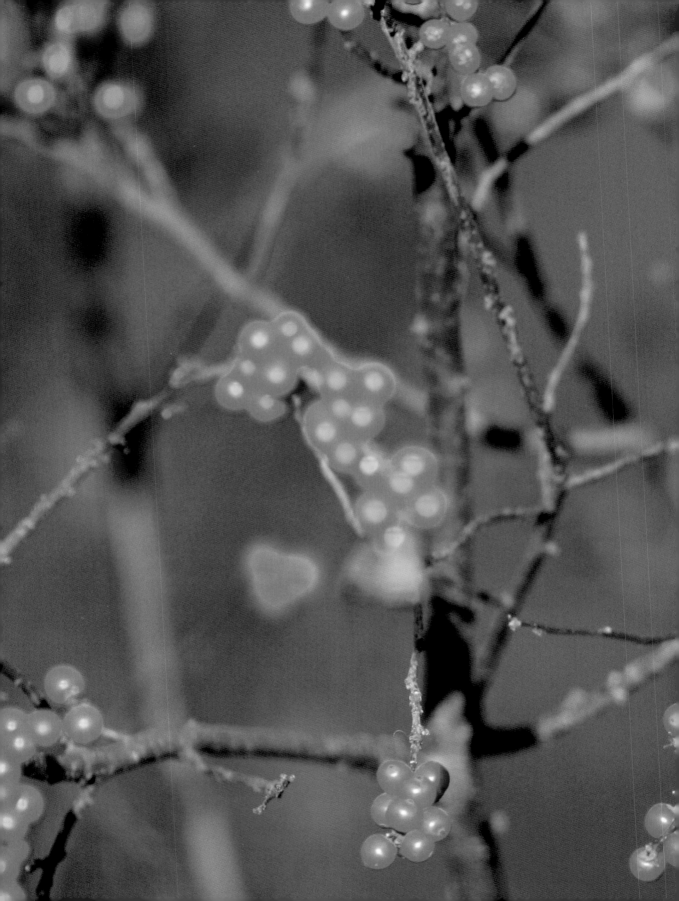

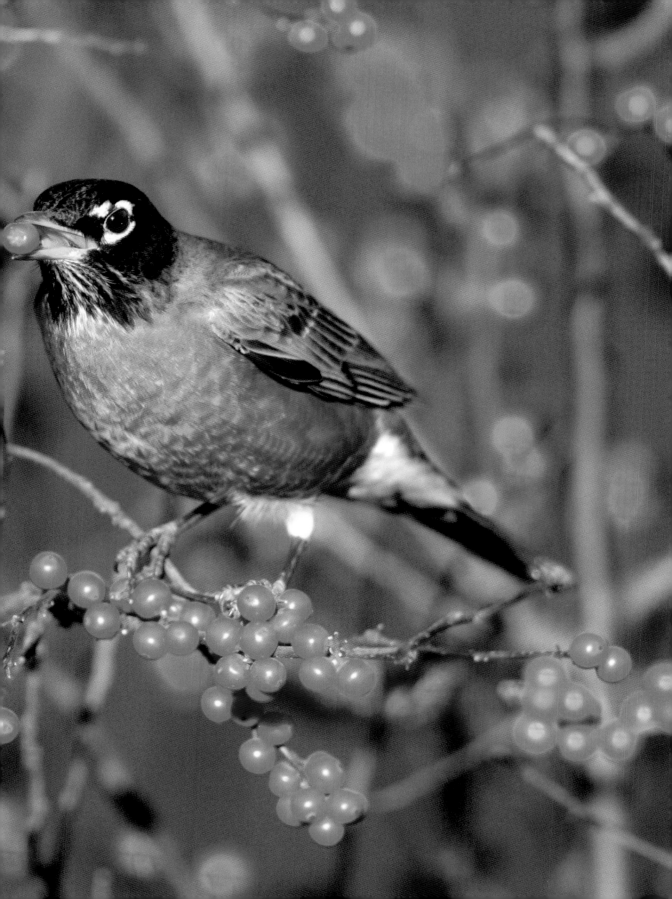

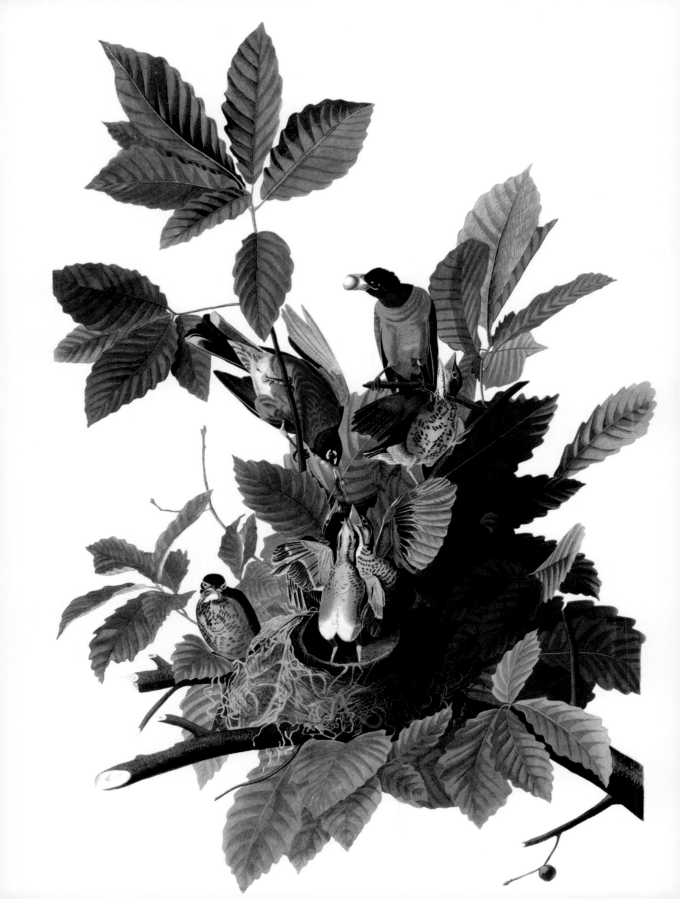

ACKNOWLEDGEMENTS

The contributors wish to thank...

Sonya Patel Ellis thanks the brilliant resources provided by ornithological and bird conservation organisations around the world, to my husband Tom Ellis for helping to turn our front garden into a bird-friendly paradise complete with bird-attracting plants and a wildlife pond, to my children Sylvester and Iggy for turning most of their lockdown home-schooling into an avian-themed world, to Caitlin Doyle for ongoing encouragement and support and to the birds themselves for keeping me going through the coronavirus era with their beautiful antics and birdsong. Long may they continue.

Dominic Couzens extends thanks to Caitlin Doyle for the opportunity to contribute to this book.

Paul Sterry would like to thank his friends and colleagues, Andrew Cleave and Rob Read. If you want to help protect birds, please check out Birds on the Brink, the grant-awarding charity that supports bird-related conservation projects. Visit the website www.birdsonthebrink.co.uk for more information.

The publisher wishes to thank Michael Sand at Abrams for his continued, enthusiastic collaboration on such a beautiful series; Ruth Redford for her incredible hard work on co-managing our behemoth book; Ellie Ridsdale for her beautiful design and calm; Jo Carlill for her excellent picture research and patience; Lynn Hatzius for her gorgeous illustrations; Frances Cooper, Helena Caldon and Abi Waters for their excellent editorial work; Geraldine Beare for the thorough index; Jacqui Caulton and Gareth Butterworth for their additional assistance, and Myles Archibald and Hazel Eriksson for their support. Heartfelt gratitude to Christopher Perrins, Sonya Patel Ellis, Dominic Couzens, and Paul Sterry for their wise and eloquent words. A big thank you to the families of Team Bird for your patience and understanding during this frenetic time, including Rosie, Ava, and Archie; Alba, Beth and Saoirse. You've all been a pleasure to work with, especially in this time of global uncertainty, and thank you to each and every contributor to this wonderful collection. And finally, a skyward thank you to the bright-green ring-necked parakeets of Southwest London, ensuring that I keep an eye ever upward.

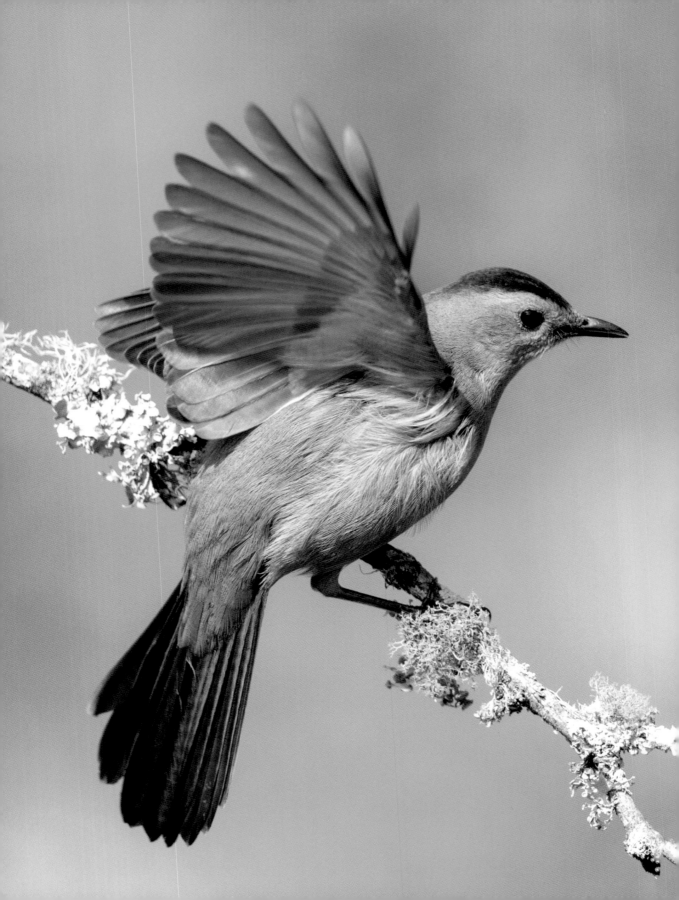

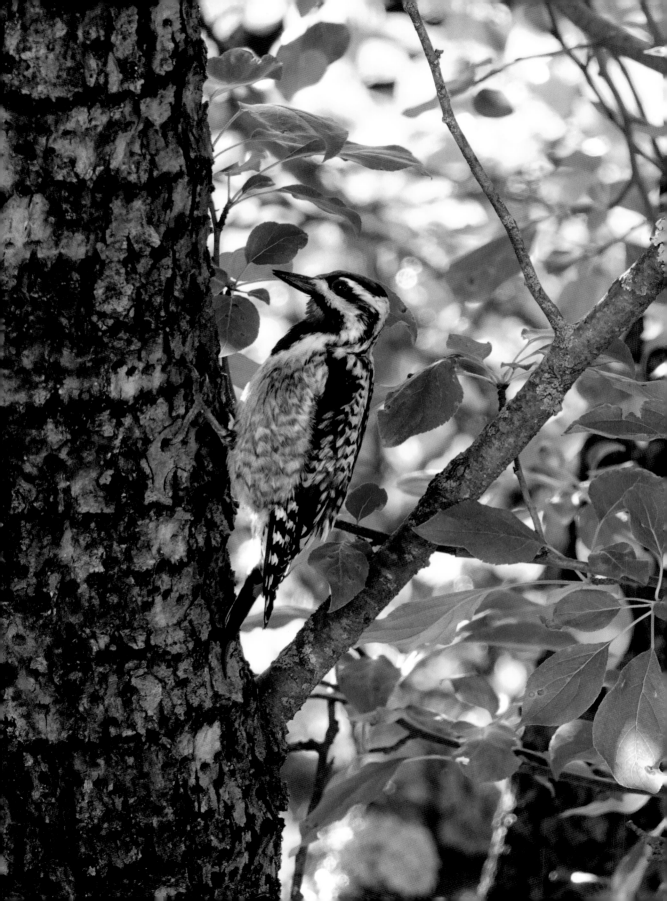

FURTHER
READING AND
RESOURCES

Selected books, magazines, journals and websites to help you become a better birdwatcher or birder and explore the beauty of the avian world.

Books

The Avian World

Ackerman, Jennifer, *The Genius of Birds* (Corsair, 2016).

Attenborough, David, *The Life of Birds* (BBC Books, 1998).

Avery, Mark, *Remarkable Birds* (Thames & Hudson, 2016).

Birkhead, Tim, *Bird Sense* (Bloomsbury Publishing, 2013).

Birkhead, Tim, Jo Wimpenny, and Bob Montgomerie *Ten Thousand Birds: Ornithology since Darwin* (Princeton University Press, 2014).

Birds in Art

Audubon, John James, *The Birds of America* (The Natural History Museum, 2013) [US].

Elphick, Jonathan, *Birds: The Art of Ornithology* (Natural History Museum, 2014) [UK natural history museum].

Harper, Charley and Oldham, Todd, *Charley Harper: An Illustrated Life* (AMMO Books, 2007)

Harper, Charley, *Beguiled by the Wild – the Art of Charley Harper* (Pomegranate Communications Inc, 2011).

Hyland, Angus and Kendra Wilson, *The Book of Birds in Art* (Laurence King, 2016).

Jeffreys, Leila and Michael Graydon, *Bird Love* (Abrams, 2015).

Kim, Jane and Thayer Walker, *The Wall of Birds: One Planet, 243 Families, 375 Million Years* (Harper Design, 2018).

Lederer, Roger J., *The Art of the Bird: The History of Ornithological Art Through Forty Artists* (University of Chicago Press, 2019).

Olson, Roberta and Marjorie Shelley, *Audubon's Aviary: The Original Watercolors for The Birds of America* (Skira Rizzoli, 2012).

Solinas, Francesco, *Edward Lear: The Parrots* (Taschen, 2018).

Attracting Birds

Cromack, David, *Nest Boxes: Your Complete Guide to Fauna* (British Trust for Ornithology, 2018).

Golley, Mark, Stephen Moss and Dave Daly, *The Complete Garden Bird Book: How to Identify and Attract Birds to Your Garden* (The Wildlife Trusts; Bloomsbury Wildlife, 2018).

Green, Jen, *A Practical Illustrated Guide to Attracting & Feeding Garden Birds* (Southwater, 2016).

Moss, Stephen and David Cotteridge, *Attracting Birds to Your Garden* (New Holland, 2011).

Moss, Stephen and Gill Tomblin (Illustrator), *Gardening for Birds: How to Help Birds Make the Most of Your Garden* (Collins, 2000).

Taylor, Marianne, *RSPB Garden Birds* (RSPB; Bloomsbury Wildlife, 2019).

Toms, Mike, *Garden Birds* (Collins New Naturalist Library, Book 140; William Collins, 2019).

Birdwatching and Birding

Couzens, Dominic, *RSPB The Secret Lives of Garden Birds* (A&C Black, 2004).

Couzens, Dominic, *Birds: ID Insights* (Bloomsbury, 2014).

Hulme, Rob, *RSPB Birds of Britain and Europe* (DK, 2018).

i-Spy Garden Birds: What Can You Spot? (Collins, 2018).

Perrins, Christopher, *Birds of Britain and Europe* (New Generation Guides; Collins, 1987).

Sewell, Matt, *Our Garden Birds* (Ebury Press, 2012).

Sterry, Paul, *British Birds: A Photographic Guide to Every Common Species* (Collins Complete Guide; Collins, 2008).

Sterry, Paul and Rob Read, *Collins Life-Size Birds: The Only Guide to Show British Birds at Their Actual Size* (William Collins, 2016).

Sterry, Paul and Paul Stancliffe, *Collins BTO Guide to British Birds* (William Collins, 2015).

Svensson, Lars, Killian Mullarney and Dan Zetterström, *Collins Bird Guide*, 2nd Edition (Collins, 2010).

Children/Poetry

Lear, Edward, *Edward Lear's Nonsense Birds* (The Bodleian Library, 2013).

Krestovnikoff, Miranda and Harding, Angela, *RSPB Birds: Explore Their Extraordinary World* (Bloomsbury, 2020)

Macfarlane, Robert and Jackie Morris, *The Lost Words* (Hamish Hamilton, 2017).

Macfarlane, Robert and Jackie Morris, *A Book of Birds: A Field Guide to Wonder and Loss* (Hamish Hamilton, to be published in 2022).

Websites, Magazines and Journals

Avibase – The World Bird Database
https://avibase.bsc-eoc.org/avibase.jsp?lang=EN

BirdLife International/*BirdLife The Magazine*
www.birdlife.org

Bird Photographer of the Year
www.birdpoty.co.uk

IOC World Bird List
www.worldbirdnames.org

Birdfair
www.birdfair.org.uk

Birdwatch magazine
www.birdguides.com

Bird Watching magazine
www.birdwatching.co.uk

British Birds magazine/British Birds Rarities Committee
www.britishbirds.co.uk

British Trust for Ornithology (BTO)
www.bto.org

RSPB/*Nature's Home* magazine
www.rspb.org.uk

Apps

Audubon Bird Guide
https://apps.apple.com/us/app/
audubon-bird-guide-north-america/
id333227386

https://play.google.com/store/apps/
details?id=com.audubon.mobile.android

BirdTrack
https://apps.apple.com/gb/app/
birdtrack/id596839218

https://play.google.com/store/apps/
details?id=org.bto.btapp&hl=en_GB

Collins Bird Guide
https://apps.apple.com/gb/app/
collins-bird-guide/id868827305

https://play.google.com/store/apps/
details?id=com.natureguides.
birdguide&hl=en_GB

Ebird from the Cornell Lab of Ornithology
https://apps.apple.com/us/app/ebird-by-
cornell-lab-of-ornithology/
id988799279?ign-mpt=uo%3D8

https://play.google.com/store/apps/
details?id=edu.cornell.birds.ebird&hl=en

ibird pro
https://apps.apple.com/gb/app/
ibird-uk-pro-guide-to-birds/
id424729739

https://play.google.com/store/apps/
details?id=com.whatbird.ukpro&hl=en_
GB

Merlin Bird ID from the Cornell Lab of Ornithology
https://apps.apple.com/app/apple-store/
id773457673

https://play.google.com/store/apps/
details?id=com.labs.merlinbirdid.app

Organizations to Support

American Bird Conservancy
https://abcbirds.org/

Bird Life International
http://www.birdlife.org/

British Trust for Ornithology
https://www.bto.org/

Cornell Lab of Ornithology
https://www.birds.cornell.edu/

National Audubon Society
https://www.audubon.org/

RSPB – The Royal Society for the Protection of Birds
https://www.rspb.org.uk

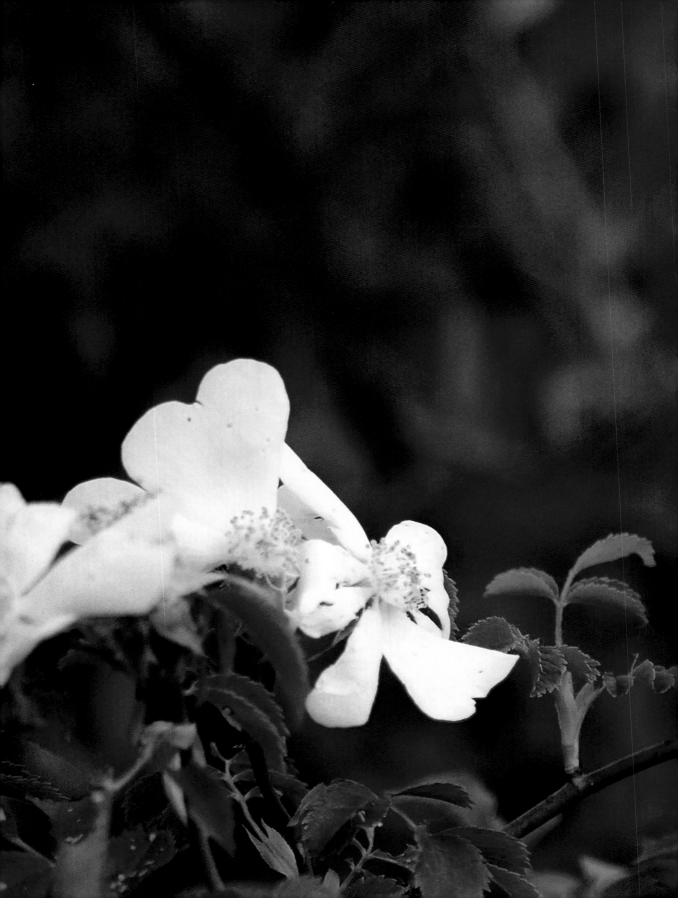

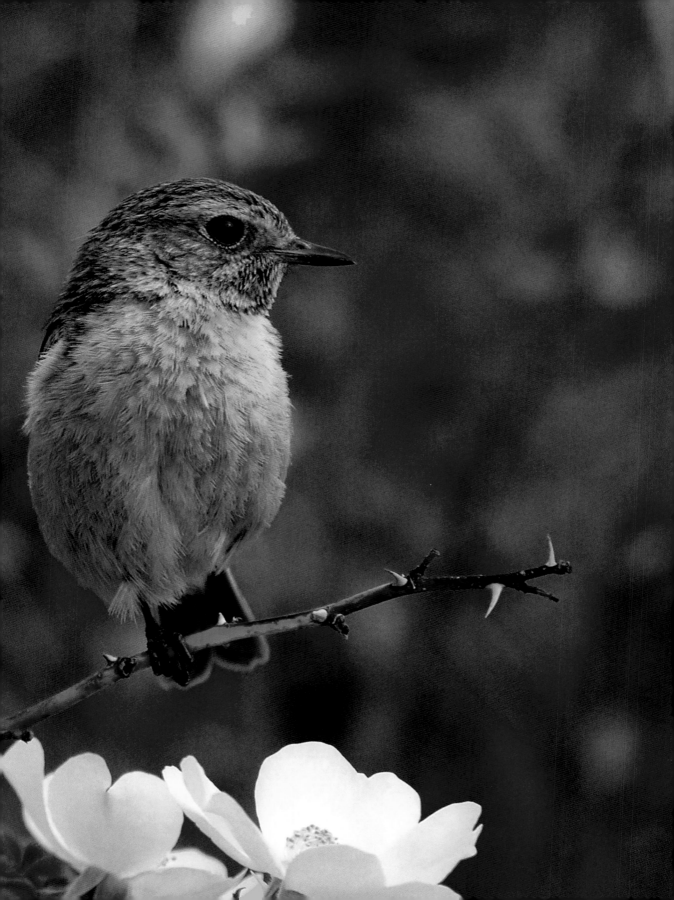

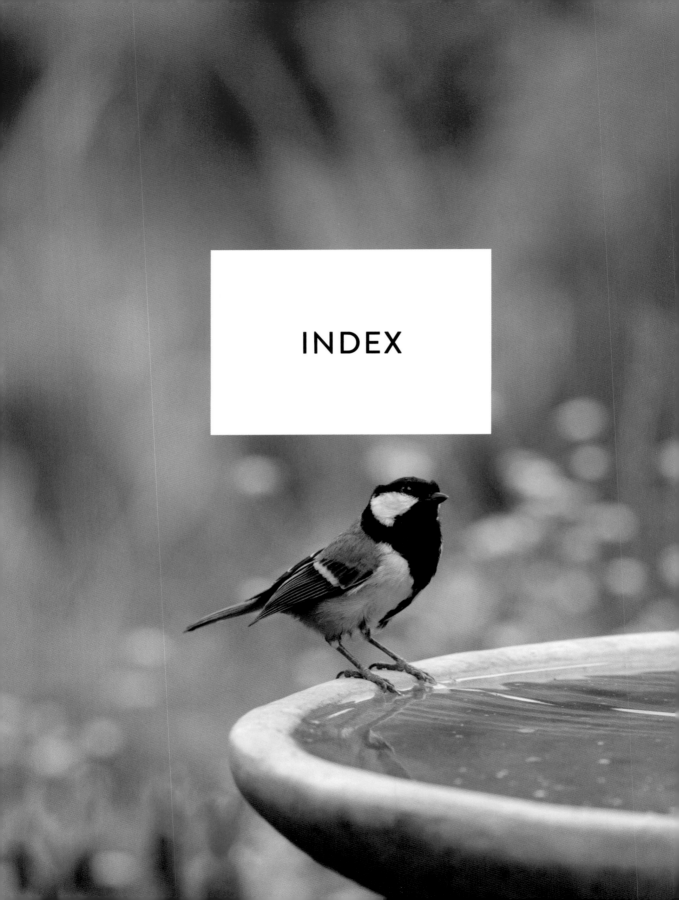

INDEX

A

B

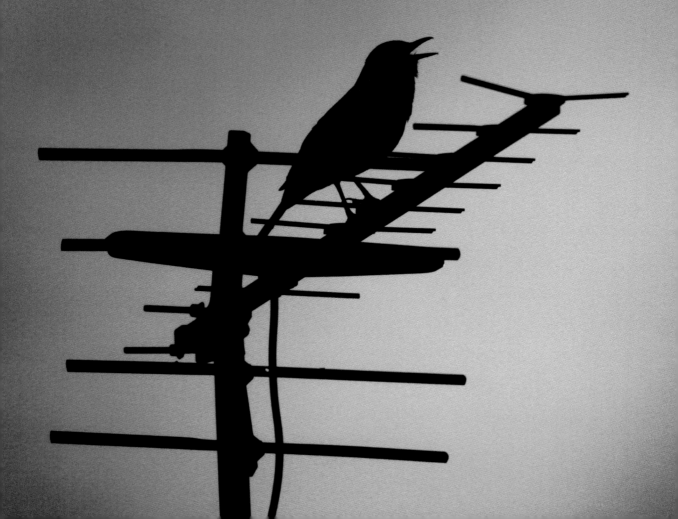

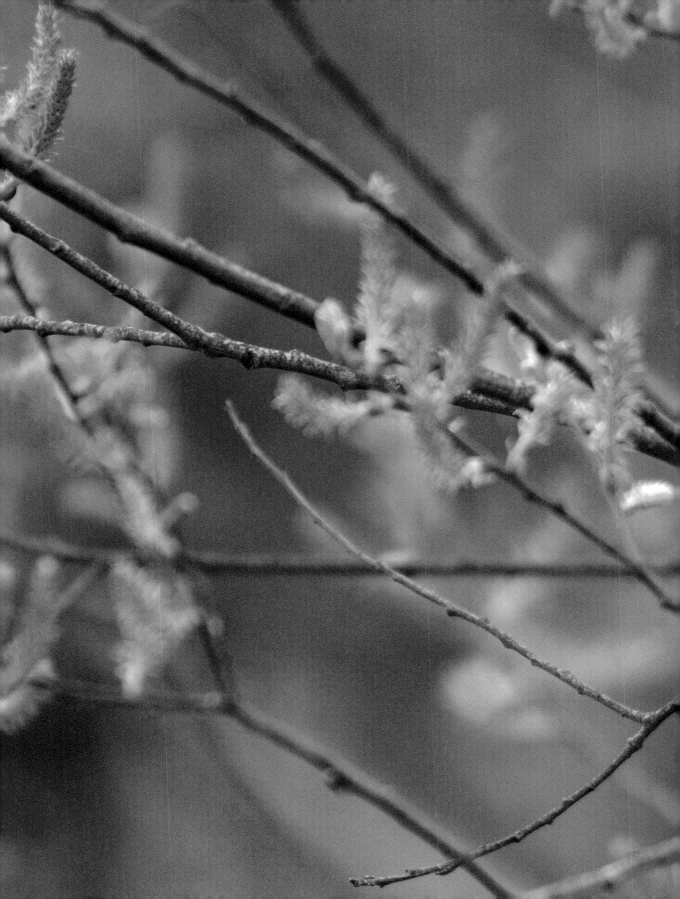

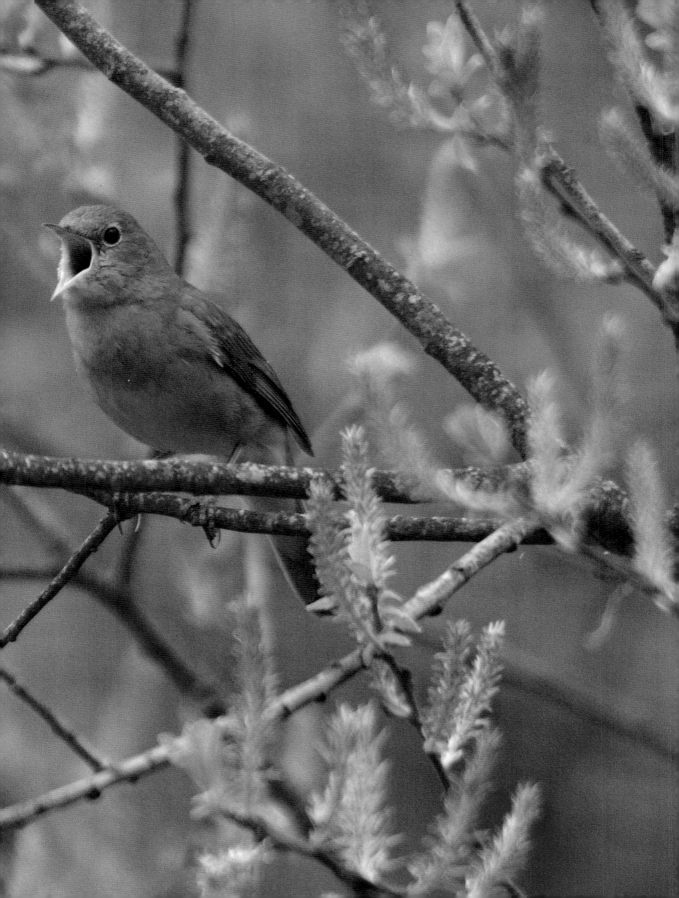

PICTURE CREDITS

All reasonable efforts have been made by the author and publishers to trace the copyright owners of the material quoted in this book and of any images reproduced in this book. In the event that the author or publishers are notified of any mistakes or omissions by copyright owners after publication, the author

For thumbnail photographs on p.34-35, please refer to the main bird identification pages.

Key: t: top, b: below, m: middle, l: left, r: right

Alamy: 18, 21t, 27, 29, 47, 57, 69tr, 70, 81b, 82, 87tl, 92, 105, 109, 117, 123, 127tl, 129, 147, 154b, 156, 169, 176-177, 181, 185b, 186t, 186b, 189t, 189b, 190, 193t, 193bl, 193br, 196, 202mbl, 205, 209, 211t, 211b, 212, 214-215, 226, 227, 229, 232tl, 234-235, 237, 238, 240, 243t, 243bl, 243br, 247t, 247b, 248-249, 250, 251, 252, 254-255, 257, 258bl, 258br, 261, 262-263, 264-265, 267, 270, 273tl, 273b, 275, 276tl, 276tr, 280-281, 282, 283tr, 283b, 286, 287, 288, 290, 292, 297tr, 297b, 298b, 300, 304, 307, 316tl, 321, 324t, 324b, 325, 339, 379, 384, 386, 390-391, 392, 404-405, 412;

© Máté Bence, www.matebence. hu and www.bencemateshides.com: 356, 357t, 357b;

Biodiversity Heritage Library: / Smithsonian Libraries, Elliott Coues, *Key to North American birds*, 1872, p.16 239l, p.80 239r; /National Library Board, Singapore/George Edwards (1694-1773), *A Natural History of Uncommon Birds* Title page 312bl, p.32 312br; /American Museum of Natural History Library, Starling (Winter plumage), Plate 14 from Thomas Alfred Coward, *The birds of the British Isles and their eggs*. First series, 1919 316tr;

Bird Photographer of the Year: / © Pal Hermansen 342, / © Caron Steele 344t, / © Nikunj Patel 344b, / © Chad Larsen 345;

Bridgeman Images: Passer domesticus, house sparrow, Plate 160 from William MacGillivray's *Watercolour drawings of British Animals* (1831-1841) 4; Black And Yellow Warbler, Magnolia Warbler (Dendroica Magnolia) plate CXXIII from '*The Birds of America*' (aquatint & engraving with hand-colouring) / Christie's Images 9; An Owl and two Eastern Bullfinches, from an album '*Birds compared in Humorous Songs, Contest of Poetry of the 100 and 1000 birds*', 1791 (colour woodblock print), Utamaro, Kitagawa (1753-1806) / Private Collection of Claude Monet 16; Bullfinch and weeping cherry-tree, pub. c.1834 (colour woodblock print), Hokusai, Katsushika (1760-1849) 17; A bird's concert. Painting by Frans Snyders (1579-1657). Oil on canvas. Prado Museum, Madrid, Spain 308-309; Pal Lat 1071 Frederick II: Two horsemen with falcons, from '*De Arte Venandi cum Avibus*' (vellum), Italian School, (13th century) / Vatican Library 311t; Scene of the Well: a man with a bird head and seems to fall or being pushed by a bison, Prehistoric / Caves of Lascaux, Dordogne, France 311br; Birds (pen & ink & wash on paper) (b/w photo), Rembrandt Harmensz van Rijn (1606-69) / Musee Bonnat, Bayonne, France 312tl; Accipiter striatus, sharp-shinned hawk, Plate 374 from John James Audubon's *Birds of America* (hand-coloured aquatint), Audubon, John James (1785-1851) / Natural History Museum 315; The Pigeon (gouache on linen), Crawhall, Joseph (1861-1913) / Art Gallery and Museum, Kelvingrove, Glasgow 316b; Five birds. Colour Illustration by Audubon; Yellow billed Magpie, Stellers Jay, Ultramarine Jay and Clark's Crow. /

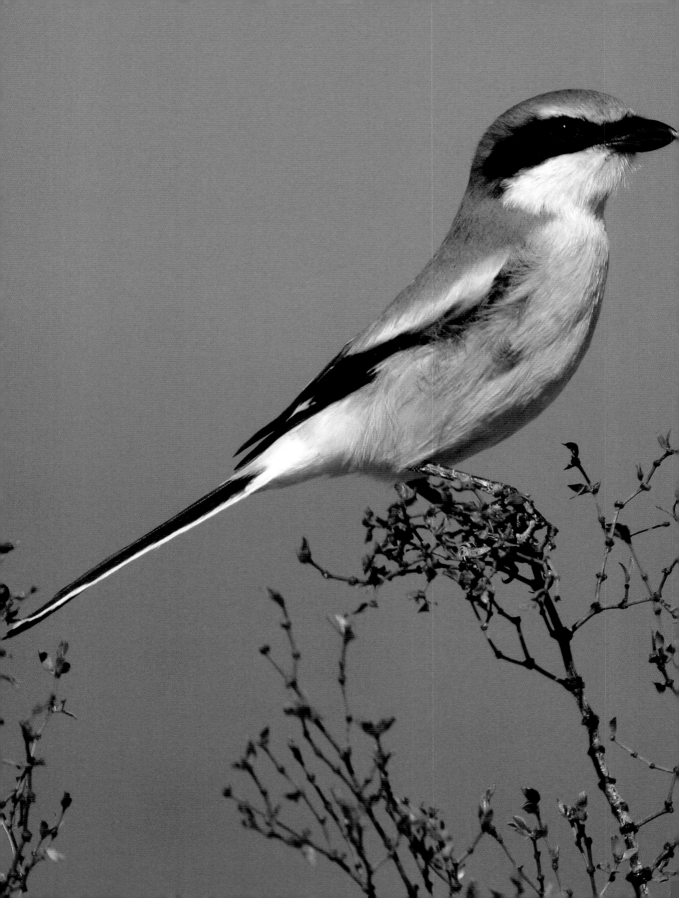

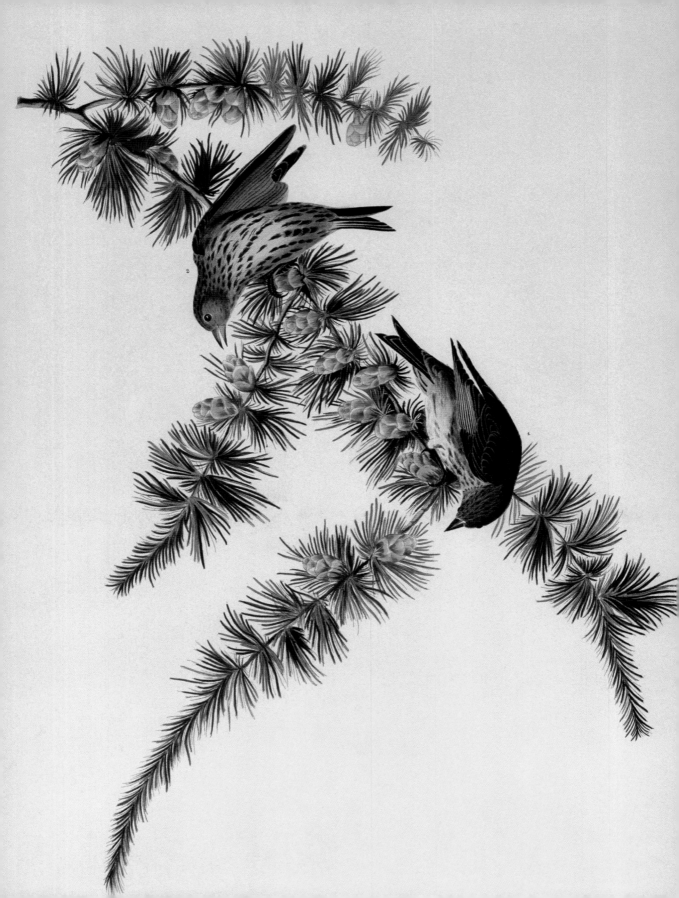

CONTRIBUTOR BIOGRAPHIES

Listed in alphabetical order

Dominic Couzens is an expert bird guide and author. He has published numerous books and articles on natural history, including for *BBC Wildlife* and *Bird Watching*, specializing in birds and mammals. His books include *Extreme Birds, Atlas of Rare Birds, The Secret Lives of Puffins*, and *Top 100 Birding Sites of the World*. He travels widely for writing and speaking, and his website is www.birdwords.co.uk.

Sonya Patel Ellis is a writer, editor and artist exploring the botanical world and the interconnectedness of nature and culture. Authored works include *The Botanical Bible*, *The Heritage Herbal*, and *Nature Tales: Encounters with Britain's Wildlife*. See www.abotanicalworld.com.

Christopher Perrins is an Emeritus Fellow of the Edward Grey Institute of Field Ornithology at the University of Oxford, and Her Majesty's Swan Warden since 1993. He has won a number of awards for his lifelong service to ornithology, including the Royal Society for the Protection of Birds Medal and the British Ornithologists' Union Medal, and is an Honorary Life Fellow of the American Ornithologists' Union. Christopher is the author of several books, including *Collins New Generation Guide to Birds* and *The Illustrated Encyclopedia of Birds*.

Paul Sterry is the author and photographer of more than 50 natural history books, including *Warblers and Other Song Birds of North America, Life-size Birds,* and *The Complete Guide to British Birds*. Having trained as a zoologist, Paul has been a wildlife photographer, rewilding expert, and passionate conservationist for over 30 years. He is also the founding Director and coordinator of the Bird Photographer of the Year (BPOTY) Conservation Fund and co-runs Nature Photographers Photo Library with Rob Read.

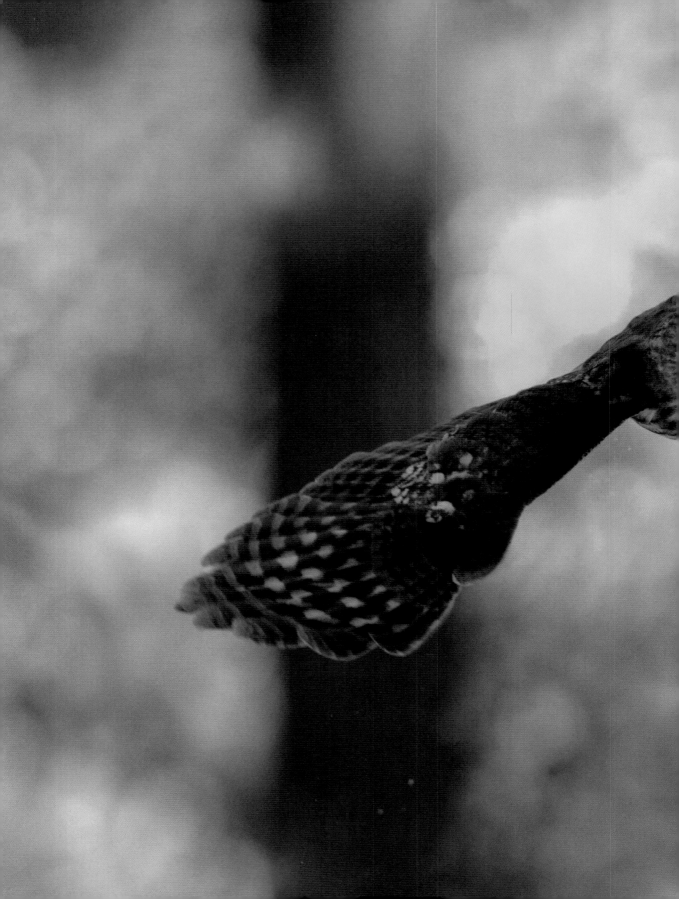

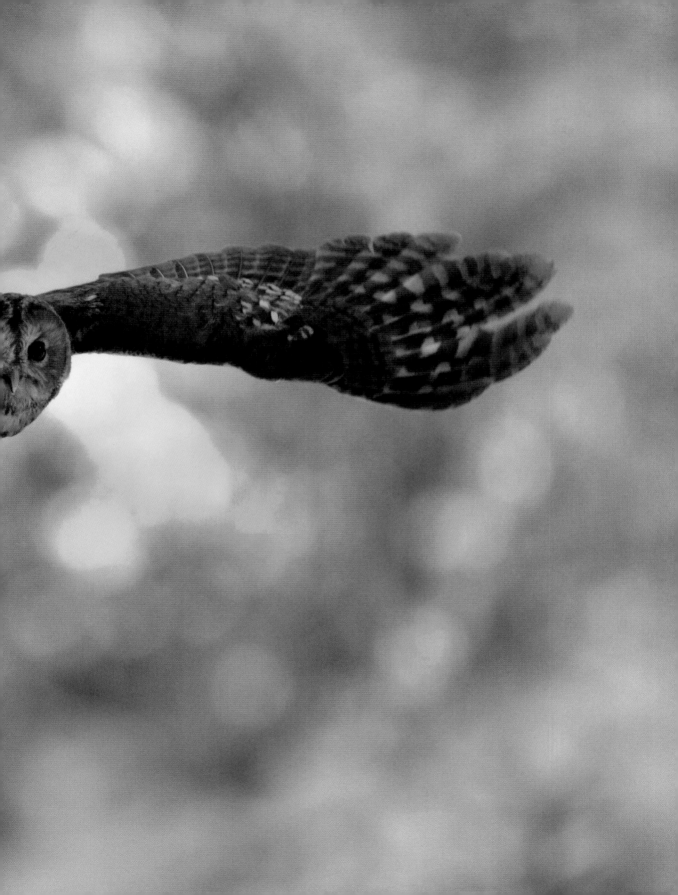

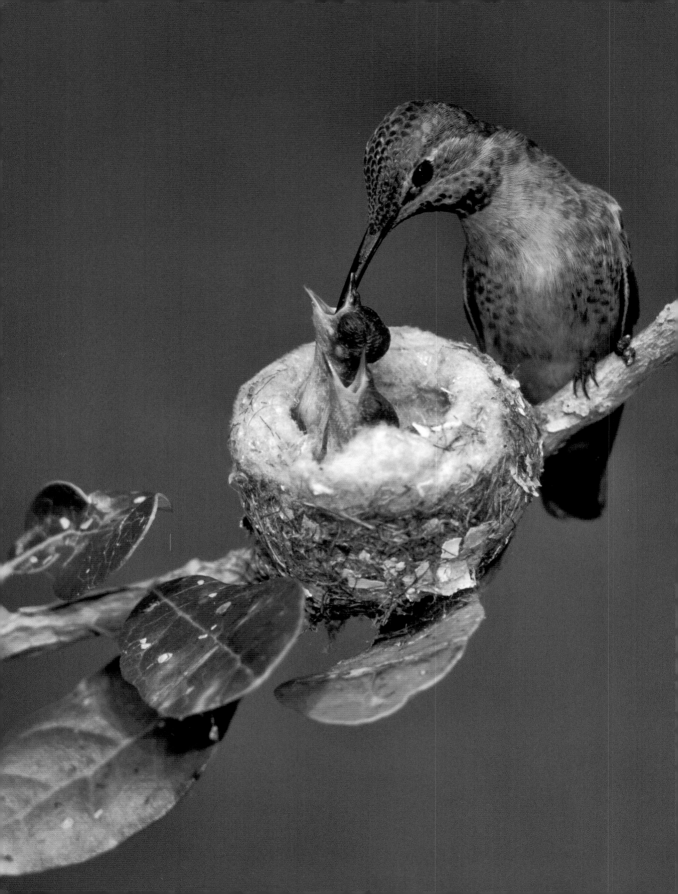